Communications in Computer and Information Science 1118

More information about this series at http://www.springer.com/series/7899

Mohammad S. Obaidat (Ed.)

E-Business and Telecommunications

15th International Joint Conference, ICETE 2018
Porto, Portugal, July 26–28, 2018
Revised Selected Papers

Springer

Editor
Mohammad S. Obaidat
University of Jordan
Amman, Jordan

Nazarbayev University
Astana, Kazakhstan

ISSN 1865-0929 ISSN 1865-0937 (electronic)
Communications in Computer and Information Science
ISBN 978-3-030-34865-6 ISBN 978-3-030-34866-3 (eBook)
https://doi.org/10.1007/978-3-030-34866-3

This Springer imprint is published by the registered company Springer Nature Switzerland AG
The registered company address is: Gewerbestrasse 11, 6330 Cham, Switzerland

Preface

The present book includes extended and revised versions of a set of selected papers from the 15th International Joint Conference on e-Business and Telecommunications (ICETE 2018), held in Porto, Portugal, during July 26–28, 2018.

ICETE 2018 received 214 paper submissions from 51 countries, of which 5% were included in this book. The papers were selected by the event chairs and their selection is based on a number of criteria that includes the reviews and suggested comments provided by the Program Committee members, the session chairs' assessments, and also the program chairs' global view of all papers included in the technical program. The authors of selected papers were then invited to submit revised and extended versions of their papers having at least 30% new material.

ICETE 2018 is a joint conference aimed at bringing together researchers, engineers, and practitioners interested in information and communication technologies, including data communication networking, e-business, optical communication systems, security and cryptography, signal processing and multimedia applications, and wireless networks and mobile systems. These are the main knowledge areas that define the six component conferences, namely: DCNET, ICE-B, OPTICS, SECRYPT, SIGMAP, and WINSYS, which together form the ICETE joint international conference.

The papers selected to be included in this book contribute to the understanding of relevant trends of current research in image and video processing, wireless networks, optoelectronic systems, anonymity in complex transactions for e-Business, decentralized deep neural networks, steganogaphic scheme for MAC-independent opportunistic routing and encoding, predicting CEO misbehavior from observables, compile-time security certification of imperative programming languages, verification of e-commerce protocols for complex transactions, cloudless friend-to-friend middleware for smartphone systems, and mixed traffic sharing and resource allocation for V2X communication systems.

We would like to thank all the authors for their contributions and also the reviewers who helped ensure the high quality of this publication.

July 2018 Mohammad Obaidat

Organization

Conference Chair

Mohammad Obaidat	University of Jordan, Jordan and Nazarbayev University, Kazakhstan

Program Co-chairs

DCNET

Christian Callegari	RaSS National Laboratory, CNIT, Italy

ICE-B

Marten van Sinderen	University of Twente, The Netherlands
Paulo Novais	Universidade do Minho, Portugal

OPTICS

Panagiotis Sarigiannidis	University of Western Macedonia, Greece

SECRYPT

Pierangela Samarati	Università degli Studi di Milano, Italy

SIGMAP

Sebastiano Battiato	University of Catania, Italy
Ángel Serrano Sánchez de León	Universidad Rey Juan Carlos, Spain

WINSYS

Pascal Lorenz	University of Upper Alsace, France

DCNET Program Committee

Baber Aslam	National University of Sciences and Technology, Pakistan
Alejandro Linares Barranco	University of Seville, Spain
Ilija Basicevic	University of Novi Sad, Serbia
Marco Beccuti	University of Turin, Italy
Pablo Belzarena	UdelaR, Uruguay
Christian Callegari	RaSS National Laboratory, CNIT, Italy
Roberto Canonico	Università degli Studi di Napoli Federico II, Italy
Valentín Carela-Español	Auvik Networks Inc., Spain

Paskorn Champrasert	Chiang Mai University, Thailand
Kang Chen	Southern Illinois University, USA
Zesheng Chen	Purdue University Fort Wayne, USA
Luca Deri	Ntop, Italy
A. Dudin	Belarusian State University, Belarus
Enver Ever	Middle East Technical University, Cyprus
Mahmood Fathi	Iranian University of Science and Technology, Iran
Zongming Fei	University of Kentucky, USA
Hiroaki Fukuda	Shibaura Institute of Technology, Japan
François Gagnon	Cégep de Sainte-Foy, Canada
Luis Javier García Villalba	Universidad Complutense de Madrid, Spain
Katja Gilly	Miguel Hernandez University, Spain
Fabrizio Granelli	University of Trento, Italy
Francesco Gringoli	University of Brescia, Italy
Carlos Guerrero	Universitat de les Illes Balears, Spain
Antonio Izquierdo-Manzanares	National Institute of Standards and Technology, USA
Dimitris Kanellopoulos	University of Patras, Greece
Peng-Yong Kong	Khalifa University of Science, Technology and Research, UAE
Michael Kounavis	Intel Corporation, USA
Isaac Lera	Universitat de les Illes Balears, Spain
Pascal Lorenz	University of Upper Alsace, France
Stéphane Maag	TELECOM SudParis, France
Olaf Maennel	Tallinn University of Technology, Estonia
S. Makki	Lamar University, USA
Eliane Martins	Universidade Estadual de Campinas, Brazil
Pascale Minet	Institut National de Recherche en Informatique et en Automatique, France
Liam Murphy	University College Dublin, Ireland
Ibrahim Onyuksel	Northern Illinois University, USA
Philippe Owezarski	LAAS-CNRS, France
Maurizio Patrignani	Roma Tre University, Italy
José Pelegri-Sebastia	Universidad Politécnica de Valencia, Spain
Adrian Popescu	Blekinge Institute of Technology, Sweden
Nasser-Eddine Rikli	King Saud University, Saudi Arabia
Matteo Sereno	University of Turin, Italy
Giovanni Stea	University of Pisa, Italy
Tatsuya Suda	University Netgroup Inc., USA
Fabien Tarissan	CNRS, France
Vicente Traver	ITACA, Universidad Politécnica de Valencia, Spain
Adriano Valenzano	Consiglio Nazionale delle Ricerche, Italy
Bernd Wolfinger	University of Hamburg, Germany
Józef Wozniak	Gdansk University of Technology, Poland
Christos Xenakis	University of Piraeus, Greece

Jianbin Xiong	Guangdong University of Petrochemical Technology, China
Cliff Zou	University of Central Florida, USA

DCNET Additional Reviewer

Waleed Shahid	Military College of Signals, National University of Sciences and Technology, Pakistan

ICE-B Program Committee

Andreas Ahrens	Hochschule Wismar, University of Technology, Business and Design, Germany
Dimitris Apostolou	University of Piraeus, Greece
Ana Azevedo	CEOS.PP-ISCAP/IPP, Portugal
Elarbi Badidi	United Arab Emirates University, UAE
Ilia Bider	DSV, Stockholm University, Sweden
Efthimios Bothos	Institute of Communication and Computer Systems, Greece
Rebecca Bulander	Pforzheim University of Applied Science, Germany
Christoph Bussler	Google, Inc., USA
Wojciech Cellary	Poznan University of Economics, Poland
Chun-Liang Chen	National Taiwan University of Arts, Taiwan
Dickson Chiu	The University of Hong Kong, Hong Kong, China
Soon Chun	CUNY-CSI, USA
Rafael Corchuelo	University of Sevilla, Spain
Peter Dolog	Aalborg University, Denmark
Yanqing Duan	University of Bedfordshire, UK
Hurevren Kilic	Dogus University, Turkey
Abderrahmane Leshob	University of Quebec at Montreal, Canada
Yung-Ming Li	National Chiao Tung University, Taiwan
Rungtai Lin	National Taiwan University of Arts, Taiwan
Peter Loos	German Research Center for Artificial Intelligence, Germany
Babis Magoutas	Information Management Unit, National Technical University of Athens, Greece
Gianluca Carlo Misuraca	European Commission, Joint Research Centre, Spain
Wai Mok	The University of Alabama in Huntsville, USA
Maurice Mulvenna	Ulster University, UK
Wilma Penzo	University of Bologna, Italy
Ruben Pereira	ISCTE, Portugal
Krassie Petrova	Auckland University of Technology, New Zealand
Charmaine Plessis	University of South Africa, South Africa
Pak-Lok Poon	CQUniversity, Australia
Ela Pustulka-Hunt	FHNW Olten, Switzerland
Arkalgud Ramaprasad	University of Illinois at Chicago, USA

Wolfgang Reinhardt	University of the Bundeswehr, Germany
Manuel Resinas	Universidad de Sevilla, Spain
Fernando Romero	University of Minho, Portugal
Gustavo Rossi	Lifia, Argentina
Jarogniew Rykowski	The Poznan University of Economics, Poland
Hassan Sleiman	Renault Group, France
Riccardo Spinelli	Università degli Studi di Genova, Italy
Athena Stassopoulou	University of Nicosia, Cyprus
Zhaohao Sun	PNG University of Technology, Federation University Australia, Papua New Guinea
James Thong	Hong Kong University of Science and Technology, Hong Kong, China
Ben van Lier	Centric, The Netherlands
Alfredo Vellido	Universitat Politècnica de Catalunya, Spain
Wlodek Zadrozny	University of North Carolina at Charlotte, USA
Edzus Zeiris	ZZ Dats Ltd., Latvia

ICE-B Additional Reviewer

Patrick Lübbecke	German Research Center for Artificial Intelligence, Germany

OPTICS Program Committee

Siti Barirah Ahmad Anas	Universiti Putra Malaysia, Malaysia
Hamada Al Shaer	University of Edinburgh, Li-Fi Research and Development Centre, UK
Nicola Andriolli	Scuola Superiore Sant'Anna, Italy
Gaetano Assanto	Università degli Studi Roma Tre, Italy
Ahmad Atieh	University of Jordan, Jordan
Hercules Avramopoulos	National Technical University of Athens, Greece
Luis Cancela	ISCTE-IUL, Portugal
Adolfo Cartaxo	Instituto de Telecomunicações, ISCTE, Instituto Universitário de Lisboa, Portugal
C. Chow	National Chiao Tung University, Taiwan
Ernesto Ciaramella	Scuola Superiore Sant'Anna, Italy
Giampiero Contestabile	Scuola Superiore Sant'Anna, Italy
Bernard Cousin	University of Rennes 1, France
Fred Daneshgaran	California State University, Los Angeles, USA
Marija Furdek	KTH Royal Institute of Technology, Sweden
Marco Genovese	INRIM, Italy
Habib Hamam	Université de Moncton, Canada
Nicholas Ioannides	London Metropolitan University, UK
Miroslaw Klinkowski	National Institute of Telecommunications, Poland
Tsuyoshi Konishi	Osaka University, Japan

Barbara Martini	Consorzio Nazionale Interuniversitario per le Telecomunicazioni, Italy
Rainer Martini	Stevens Institute of Technology, USA
Tetsuya Miyazaki	National Institute of Information and Communications, Japan
Maria Morant	Universitat Politècnica de València, Spain
Masayuki Murata	Osaka University, Japan
Yasutake Ohishi	Research Center for Advanced Photon Technology, Japan
Ibrahim Ozdur	Abdullah Gul University, Turkey
Albert Pagès	Universitat Politècnica de Catalunya, Spain
Anirban Pathak	Jaypee Institute of Information Technology, India
Jordi Perelló	Universitat Politècnica de Catalunya, Spain
Josep Prat	Universitat Politècnica de Catalunya, Spain
João Rebola	Instituto de Telecomunicações, ISCTE-IUL, Portugal
Enrique Rodriguez-Colina	Universidad Autónoma Metropolitana, Mexico
Nicola Sambo	Scuola Superiore Sant'Anna, Italy
Mehdi Shadaram	University of Texas at San Antonio, USA
Georgios Siviloglou	University of Amsterdam, The Netherlands
Salvatore Spadaro	Universitat Politecnica de Catalunya, Spain
Dimitri Staessens	University of Ghent, iMinds, Belgium
Arne Striegler	University of Applied Science Munich, Germany
Michela Svaluto Moreolo	Centre Tecnologic de Telecomunicacions de Catalunya, Spain
Takuo Tanaka	RIKEN, Japan
Bal Virdee	London Metropolitan University, UK
Peter Winzer	Nokia Bell Labs, USA
Hui Yang	Beijing University of Posts and Telecommunications, China
Yi Zhu	Hawaii Pacific University, USA
Kyriakos Zoiros	Democritus University of Thrace, Greece

OPTICS Additional Reviewers

Scott Newman	Optiwave, Canada
Konstantinos Paschaloudis	Democritus University of Thrace, Greece

SECRYPT Program Committee

Ehab Al-Shaer	University of North Carolina at Charlotte, USA
Alessandro Armando	FBK, Italy
Francesco Buccafurri	University of Reggio Calabria, Italy
Ning Cao	WalmartLabs, USA
Dario Catalano	Università di Catania, Italy
Frederic Cuppens	TELECOM Bretagne, France

Nuno Santos	INESC, Portugal
Andreas Schaad	University of Applied Sciences Offenburg, Germany
Cristina Serban	AT&T, USA
Daniele Sgandurra	University of London, UK
Basit Shafiq	Lahore University of Management Sciences, Pakistan
Vicenc Torra	University of Skövde, Sweden
Jaideep Vaidya	Rutgers Business School, USA
Corrado Visaggio	Università degli Studi del Sannio, Italy
Cong Wang	City University of Hong Kong, Hong Kong, China
Haining Wang	University of Delaware, USA
Lingyu Wang	Concordia University, Canada
Xinyuan Wang	George Mason University, USA
Edgar Weippl	SBA and FHSTP, Austria
Zheng Yan	Xidian University, China
Meng Yu	University of Texas at San Antonio, USA
Jiawei Yuan	Embry-Riddle Aeronautical University, USA
Lei Zhang	Refinitiv, USA
Yongjun Zhao	The Chinese University of Hong Kong, Hong Kong, China
Yajin Zhou	Zhejiang University, China

SECRYPT Additional Reviewers

Giada Sciarretta	Fondazione Bruno Kessler, Italy
Bruhadeshwar Bezawada	Colorado State University, USA
Nicole Bussola	Fondazione Bruno Kessler, Italy
Luca Caviglione	National Research Council of Italy, Italy
Sherman Chow	Chinese University of Hong Kong, Hong Kong, China
Gabriele Costa	University of Genoa, Italy
Prokopios Drogkaris	University of the Aegean, Greece
Kazuhide Fukushima	KDDI Research, Japan
Giacomo Giorgi	CNR-IIT, Italy
Elisavet Konstantinou	University of the Aegean, Greece
Francesco Mercaldo	Institute of Informatics and Telematics of Pisa, CNR, Italy
Partha Sarathi Roy	KDDI Research, Japan
Andrea Saracino	Consiglio Nazionale delle Ricerche, Istituto di Informatica e Telematica, Italy
Yifan Tian	Embry-Riddle Aeronautical University, USA
Alessandro Tomasi	Fondazione Bruno Kessler, Italy
Zisis Tsiatsikas	University of the Aegean, Greece

SIGMAP Program Committee

Emmanuel Ifeachor	Plymouth University, UK
Harry Agius	Brunel University London, UK

João Ascenso	Instituto Superior Técnico, Portugal
Ramazan Aygun	The University of Alabama in Huntsville, USA
Arvind Bansal	Kent State University, USA
Jianwen Chen	University of Electronic Science and Technology of China, China
Massimo De Santo	Università degli Studi di Salerno, Italy
Carl Debono	University of Malta, Malta
Giovanni Maria Farinella	Università di Catania, Italy
Zongming Fei	University of Kentucky, USA
Jakub Galka	University of Science and Technology, Poland
Carlos Garre	Universidad Rey Juan Carlos, Spain
Jerry Gibson	University of California, Santa Barbara, USA
Seiichi Gohshi	Kogakuin University, Japan
William Grosky	University of Michigan, Dearborn, USA
Malka Halgamuge	The University of Melbourne, Australia
Razib Iqbal	Missouri State University, USA
Li-Wei Kang	National Yunlin University of Science and Technology, Taiwan
Constantine Kotropoulos	Aristotle University of Thessaloniki, Greece
Choong-Soo Lee	St. Lawrence University, USA
Hyowon Lee	Singapore University of Technology and Design, Singapore
Jing Li	Nanchang University, China
Zhu Liu	AT&T, USA
Martin Lopez-Nores	University of Vigo, Spain
Manuel Marin-Jimenez	University of Cordoba, Spain
Daniela Moctezuma	Conacyt (CentroGEO), Mexico
Luis Morales Rosales	Conacyt, Universidad Michoacana de San Nicolás de Hidalgo, Mexico
Chamin Morikawa	Morpho, Inc., Japan
Alejandro Murua	University of Montreal, Canada
Binh Nguyen	Victoria University of Wellington, New Zealand
Ioannis Paliokas	Centre for Research and Technology, Hellas, Greece
Ioannis Pratikakis	Democritus University of Thrace, Greece
Peter Quax	Hasselt University, Belgium
Paula Queluz	Instituto Superior Técnico, Instituto de Telecomunicações, Portugal
Simone Santini	Universidad Autónoma de Madrid, Spain
Ángel Serrano Sánchez de León	Universidad Rey Juan Carlos, Spain
Pieter Simoens	Ghent University, Belgium
Oscar Siordia	CentroGeo, Mexico
Li Song	Institute of Image Communication and Network Engineering, Shanghai Jiao Tong University, China
Aristeidis Tsitiridis	University Rey Juan Carlos, Spain
Sudanthi Wijewickrama	The University of Melbourne, Australia

Yongxin Zhang	Qualcomm R&D, USA
Bartosz Ziolko	AGH University of Science and Technology, Poland

SIGMAP Additional Reviewers

Nathan Henderson	University of Alabama in Huntsville, USA
Truong Tran	Data Media Lab, USA

WINSYS Program Committee

Andreas Ahrens	Hochschule Wismar, University of Technology, Business and Design, Germany
Aydin Akan	Istanbul University, Turkey
Vicente Alarcon-Aquino	Universidad de las Americas Puebla, Mexico
Fulvio Babich	Università degli Studi di Trieste, Italy
Jose Barcelo-Ordinas	Universitat Politècnica de Catalunya, Spain
Bert-Jan van Beijnum	University of Twente, The Netherlands
Marko Beko	Universidade Lusófona de Humanidades e Tecnologias, Portugal
Luis Bernardo	Universidade Nova de Lisboa, Portugal
Dajana Cassioli	Universität L'Aquila, Italy
Llorenç Cerdà-Alabern	Universitat Politècnica de Catalunya, Spain
Gerard Chalhoub	Universté Clermont Auvergne, France
Chi Cheung	The Hong Kong Polytechnic University, China
Sungrae Cho	Chung-Ang University, South Korea
Roberto Corvaja	University of Padova, Italy
Carl Debono	University of Malta, Malta
Bryan Dixon	California State University, USA
Magda El Zarki	University of California, Irvine, USA
Panagiotis Fouliras	University of Macedonia, Greece
Damianos Gavalas	University of the Aegean, Greece
Janusz Gozdecki	AGH University of Science and Technology, Poland
Fabrizio Granelli	Università degli Studi di Trento, Italy
Aaron Gulliver	University of Victoria, Canada
David Haccoun	École Polytechnique de Montréal, Canada
A. R. Hurson	Missouri S&T, USA
Josep Jornet	University at Buffalo, USA
Georgios Kambourakis	University of the Aegean, Greece
Constantinos Kolias	George Mason University, USA
Charalampos Konstantopoulos	University of Piraeus, Greece
Gurhan Kucuk	Yeditepe University, Turkey
Wookwon Lee	Gannon University, USA
David Lin	National Chiao Tung University, Taiwan
Ju Liu	Shandong University, China
Pascal Lorenz	University of Upper Alsace, France

Elsa Macias López	University of Las Palmas de G.C., Spain
S. Makki	Lamar University, USA
Reza Malekian	Malmö University, Sweden
Pietro Manzoni	Universidad Politecnica de Valencia, Spain
Nidal Nasser	Alfaisal University, Saudi Arabia
Marek Natkaniec	AGH University of Science and Technology, Poland
Amiya Nayak	University of Ottawa, Canada
Cristiano Panazio	Escola Politécnica of São Paulo University, Brazil
Grammati Pantziou	Technological Educational Institution of Athens, Greece
Jordi Pérez-Romero	Universitat Politècnica de Catalunya, Spain
Jorge Portilla	Universidad Politécnica de Madrid, Spain
Jörg Roth	University of Applied Sciences Nuremberg, Germany
Angelos Rouskas	University of Piraeus, Greece
Farag Sallabi	United Arab Emirates University, UAE
Manuel García Sánchez	Universidade de Vigo, Spain
Altair Santin	Pontifical Catholic University of Paraná, Brazil
Nicola Santoro	Carleton University, Canada
Christian Schindelhauer	University of Freiburg, Germany
Winston Seah	Victoria University of Wellington, New Zealand
Kuei-Ping Shih	Tamkang University, Taiwan
Christopher Silva	The Aerospace Corporation, USA
Alvaro Suárez-Sarmiento	University of Las Palmas de Gran Canaria, Spain
Claude Tadonki	Mines ParisTech, Centre de Recherche en Informatique, France
Bishal Thapa	Raytheon BBN Technology, USA
Vasos Vassiliou	University of Cyprus, Cyprus
Sheng-Shih Wang	Minghsin University of Science and Technology, Taiwan
Shibing Zhang	Nantong University, China

WINSYS Additional Reviewer

Vlasios Kasapakis	University of the Aegean, Greece

Invited Speakers

Zeno Geradts	Netherlands Forensic Institute, The Netherlands
Jan Mendling	Vienna University of Economics and Business, Austria
Ismael Ripoll	Universitat Politècnica de València, Spain
Tobias Hoellwarth	EuroCloud Europe, Austria
Miguel P. Correia	Universidade de Lisboa, Portugal

Contents

Optimal VNF Placement: Addressing Multiple Min-Cost Solutions

Zahra Jahedi and Thomas Kunz(✉)

Carleton University, Ottawa, Canada
{zahrajahedi,kunz}@sce.carleton.ca

Abstract. Network Function Virtualization (NFV) can lower the CAPEX and/or OPEX for service providers and allows to deploy services quickly. Randomly placing Network Functions (NF) in the network can cause excessive use of resources such as bandwidth (BW). Consequently, many researchers proposed optimal placement strategies, which place NFs with minimum cost while providing a requested Quality of Service (QoS) level. The cost is typically based on the usage of resources in the network such as BW, memory, etc.

In this paper, we use an Integer Linear Programming (ILP) model designed for the Virtual Network Function Embedding Problem (VNFEP) in wired and wireless networks and solve it with different solvers. We then solve the optimization problem for a sequence of arriving requests and measure acceptance ratio and placement costs. The results gathered from different solvers show different acceptance ratios while all the elements of the models such as the network topology, its available resources, and requested resources are the same. The underlying cause is that each of the solvers uses (potentially) a different optimal solution, as the optimization problem frequently has more than a single min-cost solution. Depending on the selected min-cost solution, the placement of future requests is impacted differently. Two approaches are discussed in this paper to deal with this issue. Firstly, we identify important factors in choosing between multiple min-cost solutions and design a heuristic which smartly selects among all available min-cost placement options. The results show that our heuristic provides a higher acceptance ratio compared to randomly choosing one of the min-cost solutions. Secondly, we provide a joint optimization model which provides an optimal placement of both previous and current requests at once. In this joint optimization model, a new request and previously placed requests will be placed in the network optimally. This may potentially cause a change in the placement of previously placed NFs. The results show that each approach has its advantages and disadvantages. We show in our results that both methods increase the acceptance ratio in comparison to any optimization method that uses the first optimal placement it finds.

Keywords: Network function embedding problem · Network function · Network function virtualization · Integer linear programming · Linear programming solver

M. S. Obaidat (Ed.): ICETE 2018, CCIS 1118, pp. 1–23, 2019.
https://doi.org/10.1007/978-3-030-34866-3_1

1 Introduction

The use of Network Function Virtualization (NFV) and Software Defined Networking (SDN) provides opportunities to offer services with lower CAPEX and/or OPEX for service providers and deploy new services quickly. However, it will introduce new challenges. One of the main challenges is the optimized placement of the virtualized functions based on the characteristics and available resources of the network. Placement of Network Functions (NFs) can affect the path traffic flows take and consequently bandwidth usage in the network [7].

A Service Chain (SC) is a chain of high-level services, where each service is composed of Network Functions (NFs). A chain of NFs with predefined parameters is referred to as a Service Graph (SG). The placement of all NFs of an SG is a Network Function Embedding Problem (NFEP): mapping the Virtual Network Functions (VNF) and the links between them to the physical network. NFEP can be modelled as a mathematical optimization problem which can be solved using different Linear Programming (LP) solvers/tools. LP is a method to achieve the best outcome (such as maximum profit or lowest cost) in where requirements or constraints can be represented by linear relationships.

In this paper, we use the model proposed in [7] for wireless networks. [7] used the existed optimization methods for wired networks and extended it to wireless networks by considering the effect of interference on Bandwidth (BW) usage. [7] formulated the NFEP as an Integer Linear Programming (ILP) optimization model. The objective of the proposed model is to minimize the mapping cost based on the requirements of the NFs and available resources in the network. The mapping cost is based on the consumed resources by the NFs in the physical network which includes: (i) The total units of CPU, memory, and storage used by NFs in physical nodes. (ii) The total units of bandwidth used by virtual links directly by using the link or indirectly due to interference in the physical network.

It is assumed that the SGs arrive over time and are placed optimally by the optimization model which provides a placement with minimum cost. The NFs are then placed, and the available resources are updated for the placement of the next SG. Each SG also has an associated lifetime, upon expiration of that lifetime, the resources occupied by the SG are released and can be used to place future requests. In case the optimization problem becomes infeasible, the current SG cannot be embedded into the network, due to a lack of resources and the request is rejected, resulting in a lower acceptance rate.

We implement the model using different solvers available for solving an LP. All the solvers are provided with the same problem: the topology of the physical network, its available resource, sequence and timing of the arrival of SGs, and the associated requested resources were the same. However, the results gathered from different solvers were different in terms of the acceptance ratio. We observe that the same problem can (potentially) have multiple min-cost solutions and choosing a specific solution will impact resource availability for future requests, resulting in lower or higher acceptance ratios in the long run.

The existence of potentially multiple min-cost solutions can be used in order to increase the number of requests that can be placed in the network. We provide two approaches which use the potential of having more than one min-cost solution to increase the acceptance ratio, i.e., satisfying more requests over time. The first one is to carefully select a specific min-cost solution. We identified one factor that is important in the selection of a min-cost solution to increase the ratio of accepted requests going forward. Based on this factor, we provide a heuristic to smartly choose between (potentially many) min-cost solutions to increase the overall acceptance rate. The second approach not only considers the current SG but also considers the already placed SGs. In the joint optimal placement, we place the new SG jointly with the already placed SGs, potentially resulting in re-configuring the already placed SGs. The joint optimization placement gives us an optimal solution but has two additional costs: higher solution times, and possible reconfiguration of already placed NFs.

The remainder of this paper is organized as follows: Sect. 2 discusses related work on NFEP and the characteristics of the optimization models introduced in the related papers. Section 3 introduces the optimization model, its constraints, variables, and objective function. Section 4 describes the problem at the core of the paper: different solvers provide different solutions when faced with a sequence of SGs. In Sect. 5, we explore whether heuristically choosing one of the (potentially many) min-cost solution can improve the overall performance. In Sect. 6, we avoid the problem: we do not place SGs individually, rather, we place a new SG jointly with all already established SGs. Section 7 describes the modeling environment following the collected results and finally, Sect. 8 concludes the work.

2 Related Work

As our aim is to place/accomodate as many service requests (expressed by the arrival of SGs over time), resulting in high acceptance rates, we explored optimization models provided for NFEP in both wired and wireless networks. The exact solution in most of the proposed approaches formulates NFEP using Linear Programming and can be differentiated based on the constraints and the objective function. The proposed models place the NFs with minimum cost based on the defined parameters. However, none of them consider that there can be more than one optimal solution available for each placement and any choice among them can affect the future placements.

In [4], the authors used Integer Linear Programming (ILP) in order to find an optimum solution for placing Deep Packet Inspection (DPI) as a VNF in the network. In the proposed method, the objective function is to minimize the activation and maintenance cost of the virtual DPI (vDPI) and the considered constraint is the network's available bandwidth.

In [13] the authors used Mixed Integer Linear Programming (MILP) to find an optimum solution. The proposed optimization is based on maximizing the number of services that can be supported in a switch. In this solution, the constraints are based on the number of free cores, the tolerable delay of flows, and links' bandwidth. The objectives of [13] are minimizing maximum link utilization and maximum core utilization, which leads to the distribution of load between available resources.

[3] is another proposed method based on an ILP which aims at minimizing the resource consumption and energy saving by turning off unused resources. [16] is considering the available resources of the nodes, the available bandwidth of the links and the requested QoS as constraints and minimizes the resources usage. In [2], the objective is to minimize the cost of VNF placement. VNF placement cost includes the cost of deploying VNF instances, the cost of using servers and the cost of communication between servers. The constraints are defined based on the available resources of the physical nodes and also a delay threshold. The considered delay is the delay in delivering a service which consists of two components, the network communication delay and the VNF processing delay on the servers.

[6] divided time into slots, where the placement can be changed or modified in each slot. The static version of the proposed method generalizes to the NP-Hard Location Routing Problem (LRP) [6]. The objective is to reduce the cost of requested services at each time slot. The costs include the cost of VNF installation, BW usage, the penalty if the location of already placed requests changed from one time slot to another, as well as the cost of migrating a set of VNF instances from one time slot to another. The constraints are defined based on the processing capacity of the physical nodes. Although [6] considers the replacement and reassignment of NFs, it simply compares the acceptance ratio achieved by replacing the NFs with a solution that randomly places the NFs in the network. It does not, however, consider a comparison among optimal (multiple min-cost) solutions. The objective function of the model proposed by Luizelli et al. [10] aims at minimizing the number of virtual network function instances mapped on the infrastructure in order to minimize the network's provider cost. The constraints are the processing capacity of the physical nodes and delay, which consists of an end to end delay and packet processing delay.

[12] uses Mixed Integer Non-Linear Programming (MINLP), where some of the constraints and the objective function are non-linear. [12] considers the effect of each NF in changing the traffic. As a result of processing a stream of packets, VNFs may change the bandwidth. Example NFs that would do this, mentioned in the paper, are: The Citrix CloudBridge WAN optimizer may compress traffic by 80%, a Stateless Transport Tunneling (STT) proxy adds 76 bytes to each processed packet due to the encapsulation overhead, and a firewall will keep the traffic rates of allowed flows unchanged and will reduce the rates of denied flows to zero.

The topic of NFV in wireless networks has received significant attention in the literature, where most of the focus is on wireless network virtualization. NFV introduces new possibilities to the wireless networks such as the decoupling of functionality in a networking environment by separating the role of the traditional Internet Service Providers (ISPs) into two: infrastructure providers (InPs), who manage the physical infrastructure, and service providers (SPs), who create virtual networks by aggregating resources from multiple infrastructure providers and offer end-to-end network services [5].

[15] introduces virtual WiFi where kernel–based virtual machines are used as a virtual wireless LAN device. The authors of [15] provide an integer linear programming model for placing the VNFs in a hybrid wireless network where there are forwarding nodes, some with processing capacity, and some are access points. The authors assumed that Orthogonal Frequency Division Multiple Access (OFDMA) is being used in order to handle the problem of interference.

[11] considers the embedding of virtual wireless mesh gateways and the virtual links between them. The problem of interference between the wireless links has been solved by considering multi-radio multi-channel networks. Its authors assign orthogonal channels to the neighboring links. The same method has been used in [14] where the interference is being handled separately. Unlike the other models proposed for wireless networks, [7] considers interference in its model and formulates the interference as one of its constraints.

To our knowledge, none of the papers mentioned earlier consider that more than one min-cost solution in NFEP in both wired and wireless networks may exist. As a result, when dealing with a sequence of placement/embedding requests, solvers would select one of them arbitrarily, which may lead to low overall acceptance rates over time. In this paper, we first demonstrate the problem and then propose two distinct approaches that address this issue, aiming to increase the long-term acceptance rate of requests.

3 Optimal NF Placement: Wired and Wireless Networks

As the service requests arrive over time, the embedding algorithm decides where to place the NFs in the physical network subject to various constraints. Each request has an associated duration. If the request is accepted, the required resources will be assigned and when the request expires the used resources will be released.

We are using Integer Linear Programming (ILP) as the optimization method [7]. ILP consists of two parts, an Objective function which calculates the cost of each mapping and chooses the one with the lowest cost, and the constraints, which apply the limitations we have with regard to the resources in the physical network. ILP will choose the mapping that satisfies all of the constraints and minimizes the objective function. In this section, we will recall the variables, constraints and the objective function of the Integer Linear optimization model from [7].

3.1 Input Parameters

- Sets
  - N_p, set of physical nodes where u is representing node $u \in N_p$.

- L_p, set of physical links where $E_{uv} \in L_p$ is representing the physical link connecting node u to v.
- F, set of flows where f is representing flow $f \in F$. Each flow f consists of a set of requested NFs with required resources, SG_f.
- N_f, set of NFs where $i \in N_f$ represents NF_i in flow f.
- L_f, set of virtual links between NFs of flow f, where $e_{f,ij} \in L_f$ represents the virtual link which connects NF i to j.
- $intset_{E_{uv}}$, set of all the links that are connected to the nodes in the transmission range of the sender u or receiver v.

– Constants
  - C_u, available processing units in physical node u.
  - $c_{f,i}$, requested processing units for NF i of flow f.
  - M_u, available memory units in physical node u.
  - $m_{f,i}$, requested memory units for NF i of flow f.
  - S_u, available storage units in physical node u.
  - $s_{f,i}$, requested storage units for NF i of flow f.
  - $BW_{E_{uv}}$, available BW over the physical link between node u and v.
  - $bw_{f,e_{ij}}$, requested BW for the link that is connecting NF, i to j in flow f.

– Decision Variables
  - $x_{f,i,u}$, a binary variable where one means that function i from flow f is placed in physical node u.
  - $F_{f,e_{ij},E_{uv}}$, a binary variable which is equal to one when the virtual link between NFs i and j is mapped to one or more physical links and physical link E_{uv} is one of them. In the case of mapping a virtual link to multiple physical links all the related variables must be set to one.

3.2 Objective Function

The optimization model considers the protocol model [8] in order to include the interference in its optimization. In order to define the objective function, we first define an interference set $intset_{E_{uv}}$ for each physical link based on the definition provided in [7]. It is been assumed, in the case of a single wireless channel, d_{uv} expresses the distance between nodes u and v, and all nodes have the same identical transmission range R. With these assumptions, based on the protocol model the transmission from u to v is successful if the following two conditions are satisfied:

– $d_{uv} \leq R$
– Any node k, such that $d_{ku}, d_{kv} \leq R$, is not transmitting.

These two conditions imply that transmission on the link between nodes u and v will affect the BW usage of all the links whose transmitter is within transmission range of the sender or the receiver. To formulate this as one of the constraints in the optimization, an interference set is defined for each link. It consists of all the links that are connected to the nodes in the transmission range of the sender or receiver.

$$\forall E_{uv} \in L_p : intset_{E_{uv}} = \{E_{u'v'} | d_{u'u} \vee d_{v'v} \vee d_{v'u} \vee d_{u'v} \leq R\}$$

Our objective is to minimize the placement cost. The cost consists of resources that are used in the physical network which include nodes' resources (processing, memory, and storage) and links' BW. The BW usage is defined with the use of interference set which mentioned earlier. Term 1 shows the objective function where the first part considers the nodes' resources and the second part the BW usage. Term 2 is a more detailed version of term 1, expressing the same objective function in terms of the notation introduced earlier. In case of a wired network, the second part of term 2 can be omitted.

$$\sum_{u \in N_p} \sum_{i \in N_f} cost(i,u) + \sum_{E_{uv} \in L_p} cost(f, E_{uv}) \tag{1}$$

$$\sum_{u \in N_p} \sum_{i \in N_f} (c_{f,i} + s_{f,i} + m_{f,i}) * x_{f,i,u} + \\ \sum_{E_{uv} \in L_p} \sum_{e_{ij} \in L_f} (bw_{f,e_{ij}} + \sum_{E_{u'v'} \in intset_{E_{uv}}} bw_{f,e_{ij}}) * F_{f,e_{ij},E_{uv}} \tag{2}$$

3.3 Constraints

Constraints are sets of equalities and inequalities which are defined based on the conditions the optimization model must satisfy. Over-assignment of the physical resources will be prevented by the constraints. The first three constraints ensure that the summation of processing, memory and storage units of the placed NFs do not exceed each node's resources.

$$\sum_{i \in N_f} c_{f,i} x_{f,i,u} \leq C_u, \forall u \in N_p \tag{3}$$

$$\sum_{i \in N_f} m_{f,i} x_{f,i,u} \leq M_u, \forall u \in N_p \tag{4}$$

$$\sum_{i \in N_f} s_{f,i} x_{f,i,u} \leq S_u, \forall u \in N_p \tag{5}$$

Inequality 6 prevents over-assignment of bandwidth in each physical link and considers the effect of interference in wireless networks. The second term in Eq. 6 can be omitted in case of a wired network.

$$\sum_{e_{ij} \in L_f} bw_{f,e_{ij}} F_{f,e_{ij},E_{uv}} + \\ \sum_{e_{ij} \in L_f} \sum_{E_{u'v'} \in intset_{E_{uv}}} bw_{f,e_{ij}} F_{f,e_{ij},E_{u'v'}} \leq BW_{E_{uv}} \tag{6}$$

Each virtual link between the NFs can be mapped to one or more than one of the physical links. In case a set of physical links connected to each other are chosen to connect two NFs, Eq. 7 ensures that all related physical links are chosen.

$$\sum_{E_{uv} \in L_p, u = src} F_{f,e_{ij},E_{uv}} - \sum_{E_{uv} \in L_p, u = dst} F_{f,e_{ij},E_{uv}} = x_{f,i,u} - x_{f,j,u} \quad \forall e_{ij} \in L_f, \forall u \in N_p \tag{7}$$

Last but not least. Each NF should be placed in the physical network once.

$$\sum_{u \in N_p} x_{f,i,u} = 1, \forall i \in N_f \tag{8}$$

4 Impact of Different Solvers

The optimization problem defined in the previous section can have multiple min-cost solutions. Most solvers will find and return one of these and NFs could be placed based on the specific solution returned. To the extent that different solvers implement different algorithms, the first optimal solutions returned by each solver may be different. As we will show in this section, different placements can potentially cause an increase or decrease in the number of future SGs that can be placed in the network. We show the differences in the results that we collect from different solvers and provide in detail example to identify the potential cause of differences between their results.

We use different platforms available for solving LPs such as MATLAB and AMPL. MATLAB has its built-in function which can solve different forms of LP. AMPL is a modeling language designed to be used as a modeling platform for optimization problems such as LPs [1]. We use different solvers with AMPL such as BARON and CPLEX. In order to compare the results, we use the scenario in [7] and solve it both with AMPL and MATLAB. We assume that we have a network of 20 nodes randomly placed and defined nodal resources for each node and BW capacity for the links. As described in Table 1, processing, memory, and storage capacity of the nodes and bandwidth of the links are uniformly distributed between 100 and 150. Requests to accommodate new flows arrive over time following a Poisson process with an average rate of four flows per 100 time units. Each flow has a lifetime, exponentially distributed with an average of $\mu = 1000$ time units and is accompanied by a Service Graph, defining the required NFs and their interconnection to handle this flow. The number of NFs for each request is 6. The computation, memory and storage unit demands of each NF follows a uniform distribution between 1 and 20, see Table 2. The bandwidth requirement of each flow (mapped to each virtual link) falls between 1 and 50 units, uniformly distributed.

Table 1. SGs properties.

Topology	CPU	Memory	Storage	BW
Randomly placed	[100, 150]	[100, 150]	[100, 150]	[100, 150]

Table 2. Physical network properties.

Num of NFs	CPU	Memory	Storage	BW
6	[1, 20]	[1, 20]	[1, 20]	[1, 50]

SGs arrive over time and each request is being placed if possible for the duration of its life time, consuming nodal resources and link BW. We solve this example with both AMPL and MATLAB and assuming that the network is either a wired network or a wireless network (i.e., including the effects of interference in the optimization model). We used the following metrics in order to compare the results and observe the overall performance of the placement model.

- Average cost: average of the units of computation, memory, and storage used for the deployed service requests that are not expired.
- Acceptance ratio: The total number of accepted requests divided by the total number of requests.

We were expecting to achieve the same results in terms of overall acceptance ratio and average placement costs for the same network at the same conditions. Interestingly, we noticed that there are considerable differences between the results collected from AMPL and MATLAB which can be seen in Figs. 1 and 2. Figure 1 shows the acceptance ratio recorded from AMPL when using the CPLEX solver and MATLAB. We can see a visible difference between the acceptance ratios recorded. Figure 2 shows the acceptance ratio of MATLAB and AMPL when using BARON as a solver. In Fig. 1 we assume that the network is wireless and therefore consider the effect of interference in the optimization model.

As we can see in Figs. 1 and 2 there is a noticeable difference between the acceptance ratio recorded from AMPL and MATLAB. Although the network's topology, its nodal resources, and the requests (both their order of arrival as well as the resource required by each SG) are exactly the same, the acceptance ratios differ. The following example shows that choosing between potential min-cost placements can affect the acceptance and placement of future requests.

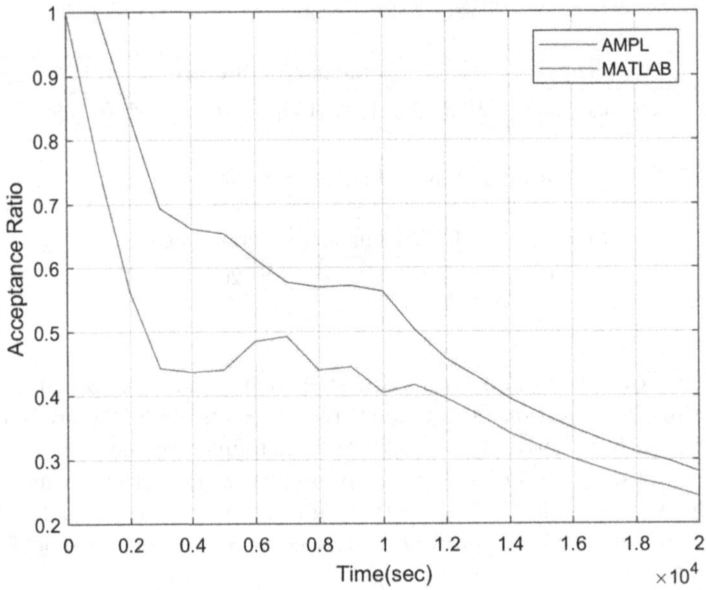

Fig. 1. Acceptance ratio recorded from CPLEX and MATLAB (wireless network of 20 nodes with random topology).

In this example, we assume a wired network. Nodal resources are characterize by a single parameter only, and each request has multiple Network Functions (NFs) which are connected to each other via virtual links. Assume that we have a network of three nodes $N_p = \{n_1, n_2, n_3\}$ and each node has the following resource units $R_p = \{18, 26, 15\}$. As it is shown in Fig. 3, the network has 2 links which connect n_1 to n_2 and n_2 to n_3, $L_p = \{l_{12}, l_{23}\}$. Each of the links has 20 units of available BW.

Assume that we have two requests. The first request has 2 NFs, $NF_1 = \{f_{11}, f_{12}\}$. The required resources for each of the NFs are as follows $Rf_1 = \{18, 10\}$, and the BW requirement for each link is 5 units. The second request includes two NFs, $NF_2 = \{f_{21}, f_{22}\}$ and the required resources are $Rf_2 = \{14, 11\}$. The BW request for each virtual link connecting the NFs is 5 units.

In this scenario, there are two different min-cost placements with the same cost for the first request. The first one will place f_{11} in node 1 and f_{12} in node 2. The second placement places f_{11} in node 2 and the other NF in node 3. We show the remaining nodal resources after both placements in Table 3. Both placements have the same cost, however, by choosing the second placement we cannot place the second request. We believe that this is the main reason behind the difference in the acceptance ratios when using either one of the AMPL solvers or MATLAB.

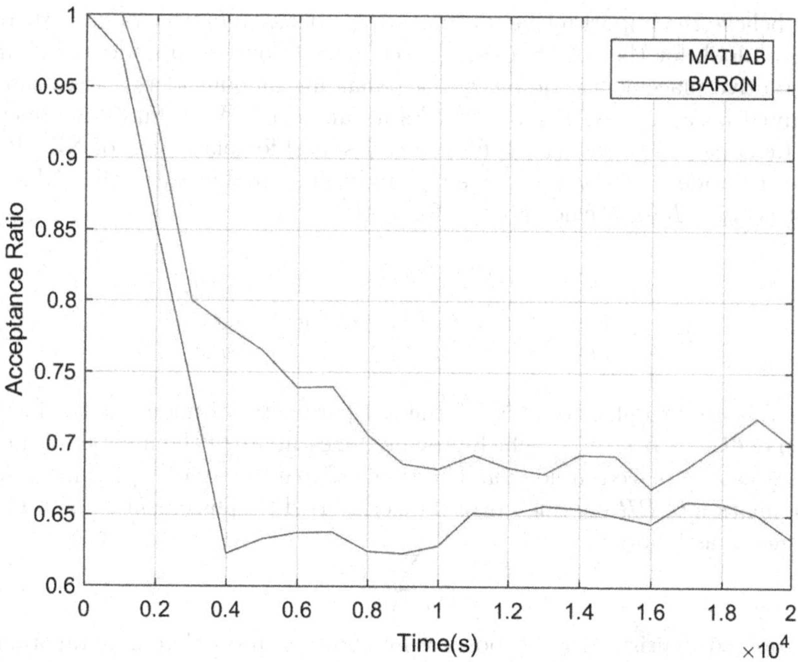

Fig. 2. Acceptance ratio recorded from BARON and MATLAB (wired network of 20 nodes with random topology).

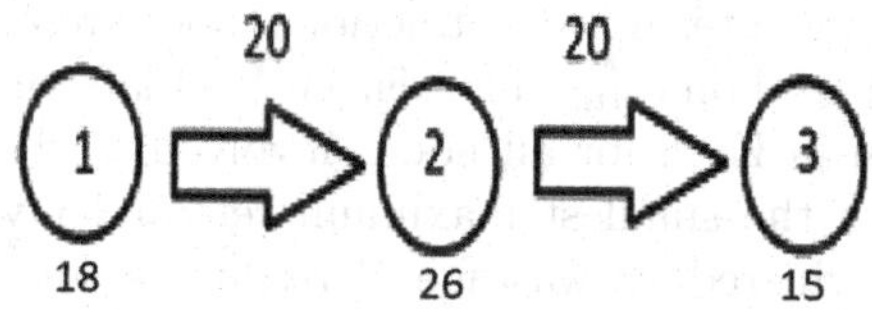

Fig. 3. Network topology.

Table 3. Different placements of the first request.

n_1	Remainder of n_1	n_2	Remainder of n_2	n_3	Remainder of n_3	Cost
f_{11}	0	f_{12}	16	-	15	33
-	18	f_{11}	8	f_{12}	5	33

5 Smart Selection of Min-Cost Solution

Given the possibility of having more than one min-cost solution, the challenge is to choose smartly between them. In this section we identify a parameter that is important in selecting a min-cost solution and provide a heuristic which uses the identified parameter to smartly choose between min-cost solutions. We provide an example and show that considering our heuristic can increase the number of accepted requests.

We believe the important factor in making a decision between min-cost solutions is to look for the solution that leaves more resources in nodes, compared to alternative placements. However, the remaining amount of resources should be counted based on the number of NFs it can cover. We define a parameter, called Remained Resource (RR), for the nodes used for placement of NFs. If we assume the node u has one resource C_u, and the minimum value that NFs can request is c_{min}, RR_u is calculated as follows:

$$\forall u \in N_p$$

$$RR_u = \begin{cases} \lfloor (C_u - \sum_{i \in N_f} x_{f,i,u} c_i)/c_{min} \rfloor & x_{f,i,u} = 1 \\ 0 & else \end{cases} \tag{9}$$

If node u is used to place only NF i, the RR parameter of node u is the integer division of $C_u - c_i$ over c_{min}, which provides an estimate of the number of future NFs that can be placed in node u. The total RR parameter of a placement RR_t is a summation of RR parameters of the nodes used for placement of NFs which is calculated as follows:

$$RR_t = \sum_{u \in N_P} RR_u \tag{10}$$

The proposed heuristic then chooses a min-cost solution that maintains more capacity in the nodes to place future NFs, i.e., the solution with higher RR value. In case of having min-cost placements with the same maximum RR value, the one that has nodes with 0 remaining nodal resources will be chosen. If there is no sauch placement, we determine the fractional nodal resources that remain if we placed future NFs based on c_{min}. That is, we calculate the integer remainder for the integer division in Eq. 9 for all nodes involved in the placement. In the next step, the SG with the smallest maximum remainder will be chosen. The idea here is that this will reduce wastage of resources when placing NFs that require at least c_{min} nodal resources.

The smart heuristic is explained in more detail in the following example. Consider a wired network of 4 nodes as shown in Fig. 4. In this example, each node has one resource and the nodal resources are uniformly distributed between 15 to 25 units. Furthermore, assume that all the links have a BW of 10 units. We have 4 SGs, each composed of three NFs, to place optimally in the network. Table 4

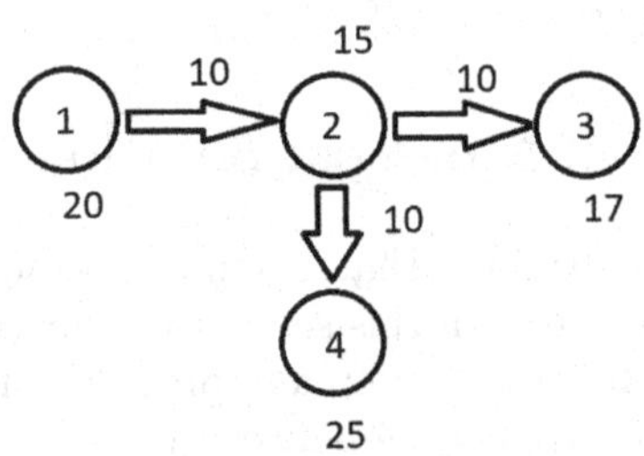

Fig. 4. Network topology.

Table 4. SG requests.

SG	f_1	f_2	f_3	bw
SG_1	5	5	7	4
SG_2	6	6	7	4
SG_3	7	8	5	4
SG_4	5	7	6	4

shows the list of SGs and their requested resources. The requested resources of NFs range from 5 to 10.

To place the first SG, we have three choices. The 3 NFs of SG_1 can be placed all in node 1 or all in node 3 or all in node 4. Table 5 shows all three min-cost solutions for the first SG, the remaining resources in each node, and the resulting RR parameter. Based on our heuristic, the third placement has a higher RR than the other min-cost placements and it will be chosen accordingly. The only min-cost solution for the second SG is to place all of the NFs in n_1 and the associated nodal resources will be 1, 15, 17, and 8. Placement of the third SG has 4 min-cost solutions which are shown in Table 6.

Table 5. First SG min-cost solutions.

Placements	n_1	n_2	n_3	n_4	RR
1, 1, 1	**3**	15	17	25	$\lfloor 3/5 \rfloor = 0$
3, 3, 3	20	15	**0**	25	$\lfloor 0/5 \rfloor = 0$
4, 4, 4	20	15	17	**8**	$\lfloor 8/5 \rfloor = 1$

In this case, as two of the min-cost solutions have the same RR value, the smart selection heuristic chooses the min-cost solution in which the resources of one or more of the physical nodes is completely consumed (i.e., the first placement in the table). Finally, for the 4th SG, we have only one min-cost solution which puts the first two NFs in node 3 and the third one in node 4. During this procedure, if we had used any other min-cost solutions, only 3 of the SGs could have been placed.

Table 6. Third SG min-cost solutions.

Placements	n_1	n_2	n_3	n_4	RR Ratio
2, 2, 3	1	**0**	**12**	8	$\lfloor 0/5 \rfloor + \lfloor 12/5 \rfloor = 2$
2, 2, 4	1	**0**	17	**3**	$\lfloor 0/5 \rfloor + \lfloor 3/5 \rfloor = 0$
3, 3, 4	1	15	**2**	**3**	$\lfloor 2/5 \rfloor + \lfloor 3/5 \rfloor = 0$
3, 3, 2	1	**10**	2	**4**	$\lfloor 10/5 \rfloor + \lfloor 4/5 \rfloor = 2$

6 Joint Optimization

Joint optimization is another avenue to increase the performance of the optimal placement of NFs. The joint placement optimization considers not only the current SG but also already placed SGs in the network. In this model, each time a new SG arrives, we add the new SG to the SGs currently deployed in the network (i.e., SGs that were previously admitted and have not yet expired) and solve this joint placement problem to arrive at a min-cost solution. The new solution may lead to a reconfiguration of already placed NFs. The joint optimization placement uses the same ILP as Sect. 3 with some alterations.

6.1 Joint ILP Model

The joint ILP model considers the current and the previously placed and existing SGs. It provides an optimal placement for all SGs at once. In order to have more than one input for the optimization problem, we provide a model which combines all the SGs and forms a new request each time a SG arrives.

Assume flow f' is the joint flow which represents all previously placed SGs that are not yet expired. When flow f arrives, it will be combined with f' and form a new input for the optimization problem. The new input is the new SG, which is the current flow f connected to f' by a virtual link that has 0 BW request. Figure 5 shows the combination of the SGs where the arrow is the added virtual link that connects two SG to form a new one. The constraints and objective functions are similar to the ones described in Sect. 3 with a small change to consider the requests jointly. The changes are explained in the next section and the other part are the same as the model described earlier.

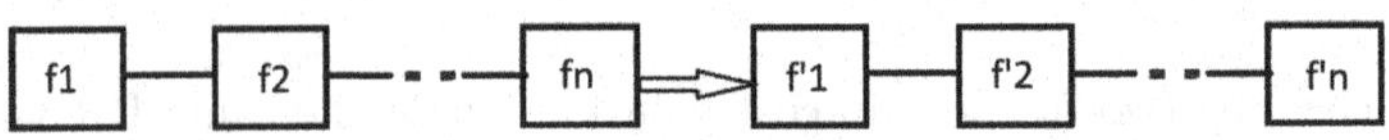

Fig. 5. Combination of two SGs.

6.2 Input Parameters

- Sets
  - N_f, set of NFs where $i \in N_f$ represents NF_i in flow f which is the current flow.
  - $N_{f'}$, set of NFs where $i \in N_{f'}$ represents NF_i in flow f' which includes all previously placed flows.
  - L_f, set of virtual links between NFs of flow f, where $e_{f,ij} \in L_f$ represents the virtual link which connects NF i to j.
  - $L_{f'}$, set of virtual links between NFs of flow f', where $e_{f',ij} \in L_{f'}$ represents the virtual link which connects NF i to j from flow f'.

- Constants
    - $c_{f,i}$, requested processing units for NF i of the current flow f.
    - $c_{f',i}$, requested processing units for NF i of previously placed flows f'.
    - $m_{f,i}$, requested memory units for NF i of the current flow f.
    - $m_{f',i}$, requested memory units for NF i of the previous flows f'.
    - $s_{f,i}$, requested storage units for NF i of the current flow f.
    - $s_{f',i}$, requested storage units for NF i of the previous flows f'.
    - $bw_{f,e_{ij}}$, requested BW for the link that is connecting NF, i to j in flow f.
    - $bw_{f',e_{ij}}$, requested BW for the link that is connecting NF, i to j in flow f'.
- Decision Variables
    - $x_{f,i,u}$, a binary variable where one means that function i from the current flow f is placed in physical node u.
    - $x_{f',i,u}$, a binary variable where one means that function i from the previous flows f' is placed in physical node u.
    - $F_{f,e_{ij},E_{uv}}$, a binary variable which is equal to one when the virtual link between NFs i and j from the current flow f is mapped to one or more physical links and physical link E_{uv} is one of them. In the case of mapping a virtual link to multiple physical links all the related variables must be set to one.
    - $F_{f',e_{ij},E_{uv}}$, a binary variable which is equal to one when the virtual link between NFs i and j of the previous flow f' is mapped to one or more physical links and physical link E_{uv} is one of them. In the case of mapping a virtual link to multiple physical links all the related variables must be set to one.
    - $F_{f'f,e_{i'j'},E_{uv}}$, a binary variable which is equal to one when the virtual link between NFs i' which is the last NF of previous flow f' and j' is the NF from the current flow f is mapped to one or more physical links and physical link E_{uv} is one of them. In the case of mapping a virtual link to multiple physical links all the related variables must be set to one.

6.3 Objective Function

The objective function considers the cost of placement of both current and previous flows. The first two parts of the objective function in (11) represent the cost of placing the current flow f and the next two belong to the previous flows f'. (12) shows (11) in more detail.

$$\sum_{u\in N_p}\sum_{i\in N_f} cost(i,u) + \sum_{E_{uv}\in L_p} cost(f,E_{uv}) + \sum_{u\in N_p}\sum_{i\in N'_f} cost(i,u) + \sum_{E_{uv}\in L_p} cost(f',E_{uv}) \quad (11)$$

$$\sum_{u\in N_p}\sum_{i\in N_f}(c_{f,i}+s_{f,i}+m_{f,i})*x_{f,i,u}+\sum_{u\in N_p}\sum_{i\in N'_f}(c_{f',i}+s_{f',i}+m_{f',i})*x_{f',i,u}+$$
$$\sum_{E_{uv}\in L_p}\sum_{e_{ij}\in L_f}(bw_{f,e_{ij}}+\sum_{E_{u'v'}\in intset_{E_{uv}}}bw_{f,e_{ij}})*F_{f,e_{ij},E_{uv}}+$$
$$\sum_{E_{uv}\in L_p}\sum_{e_{ij}\in L'_f}(bw_{f',e_{ij}}+\sum_{E_{u'v'}\in intset_{E_{uv}}}bw_{f',e_{ij}})*F_{f',e_{ij},E_{uv}} \tag{12}$$

6.4 Constraints

The following constraints will be also updated in order to consider both the current and previous flows.

$$\sum_{i\in N_f}c_{f,i}x_{f,i,u}+\sum_{i\in N_{f'}}c_{f',i}x_{f',i,u}\leq C_u, \forall u\in N_p \tag{13}$$

$$\sum_{i\in N_f}m_{f,i}x_{f,i,u}+\sum_{i\in N_{f'}}m_{f',i}x_{f',i,u}\leq M_u, \forall u\in N_p \tag{14}$$

$$\sum_{i\in N_f}s_{f,i}x_{f,i,u}+\sum_{i\in N_{f'}}s_{f',i}x_{f',i,u}\leq S_u, \forall u\in N_p \tag{15}$$

Inequality 14 is the updated version of inequality 6, which prevents over-assignment of bandwidth for each physical link.

$$\sum_{e_{ij}\in L_f}bw_{f,e_{ij}}F_{f,e_{ij},E_{uv}}+$$
$$\sum_{e_{ij}\in L_f}\sum_{E_{u'v'}\in intset_{E_{uv}}}bw_{f,e_{ij}}F_{f,e_{ij},E_{u'v'}}+$$
$$\sum_{e_{ij}\in L'_f}bw_{f',e_{ij}}F_{f',e_{ij},E_{uv}}+$$
$$\sum_{e_{ij}\in L'_f}\sum_{E_{u'v'}\in intset_{E_{uv}}}bw_{f',e_{ij}}F_{f',e_{ij},E_{u'v'}}\leq BW_{E_{uv}} \tag{16}$$

Eq. 17, which ensures that all the related physical links are chosen, is the updated version of Eq. 7. Equation 18 is an extension of Eq. 16 which is specific to the virtual link connecting the previous flow to the current flow.

$$\sum_{E_{uv}\in L_p,u=src}F_{f,e_{ij},E_{uv}}+\sum_{E_{uv}\in L_p,u=src}F_{f',e_{ij},E_{uv}}-$$
$$\sum_{E_{uv}\in L_p,u=dst}F_{f,e_{ij},E_{uv}}-\sum_{E_{uv}\in L_p,u=dst}F_{f',e_{ij},E_{uv}}=$$
$$x_{f,i,u}+x_{f',i,u}-x_{f,j,u}-x_{f',j,u} \tag{17}$$
$$\forall e_{ij}\in L_f, \forall e_{ij}\in L'_f, \forall u\in N_p$$

If we assume that the last NF from flow f' is i' and the first NF from flow f is j', Eq. 18 ensures that the virtual link between the two flows is mapped to the physical network correctly, although this link does not consume any BW.

$$\sum_{E_{uv}\in L_p, u=src} F_{f'f,e_{i'j'},E_{uv}} - \sum_{E_{uv}\in L_p, u=dst} F_{f'f,e_{i'j'},E_{uv}} = x_{f'f,i,u} - x_{f'f,j,u} \quad (18)$$
$$\forall u \in N_p$$

The next two Equations assures that each NF be placed in the physical network once.

$$\sum_{u\in N_p} x_{f,i,u} = 1, \forall i \in N_f \quad (19)$$

$$\sum_{u\in N_p} x_{f',i,u} = 1, \forall i \in N_{f'} \quad (20)$$

7 Model Results

In this section we first explore the effect of applying the placement model for wired and wireless networks. To that end, we generate a number of multi-hop wireless and wired topologies and place SGs based on the respective models. In order to see the impact of our approach in bigger networks, we increase the number of nodes and observe the results as a function of network size. Next, we show the impact of our suggested approaches in Sects. 5 and 6 on the placement performance for small networks.

7.1 Wired Vs. Wireless Networks

In this section we explore NFEP in wireless networks and the impact of interference in the NF placement. MATLAB is being used for solving our optimization model. The random topologies are generated following the method described in [9], where the nodes are randomly deployed in a square area, based on a uniform distribution. As the number of nodes increases, the area size increases as well, the maintain a constant node density for all network size. The network properties (nodal resources, link bandwidths) are described in Table 1 and the resource requests per SG are summarized in Table 2. The arrival rate and lifetime of flows are the same as the one described earlier as well. The difference in this section is the number of NFs for each of the requests is a number uniformly distributed between 2 and 10.

The program ran for 20000 s in order to reach a steady state where the curves flatten off after initial settling due to the initially unloaded network. Figure 6 shows the average cost for different-sized wired and wireless networks. As expected, the interference model has caused higher bandwidth usage and higher average cost for placing the NFs. Higher BW usage in the wireless network lowers the number of requests that can be placed in the network and reduces

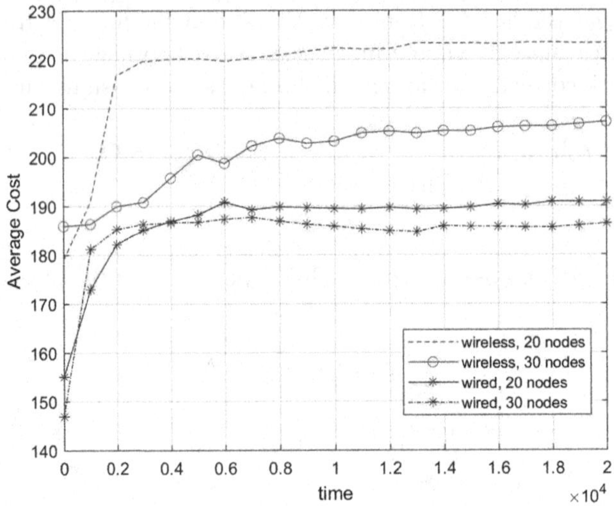

Fig. 6. Average cost in wireless and wired networks with increasing number of nodes [7].

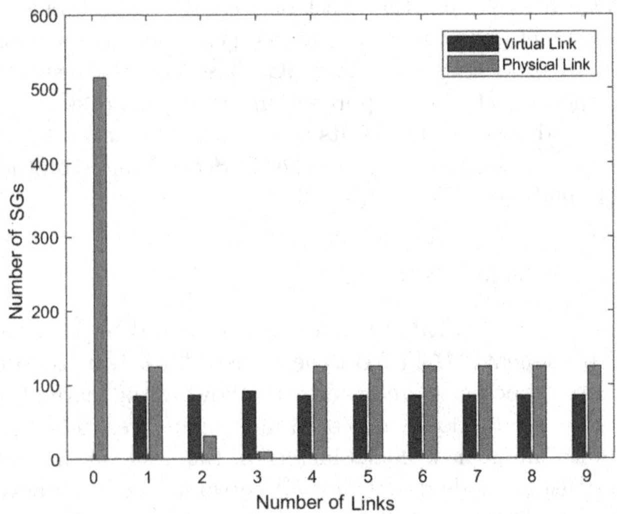

Fig. 7. Number of virtual links in the SG requests (20 Nodes, Random Topology) and number of mapped physical links [7].

the acceptance ratio. Figure 6 also shows that increasing the number of the nodes can decrease the average cost. This is mainly due to the fact that the optimization method minimizes the resource usage for each SG; therefore, it chooses a placement that has fewer physical links involved. Increasing the number of nodes will increase the possibility to use fewer physical links and consequently lower the average cost. Consequently, the cost decrease in the wireless networks, going from 20 to 30 nodes, is higher than in case of wired ones.

We measured the number of assigned links for each accepted SG and also the number of the virtual links that were requested for each SG in the network. Figure 7 shows the results of a 20 node wireless network with random topology. We can see that the majority of SG requests is placed completely in one node, very few placements involve multiple nodes. This is true even though the number of virtual links of the SGs ranges from 1 to 9. Figure 6 and Fig. 7 show that there can be a trade-off between the number of the nodes and BW usage in the network. Increasing the number of nodes increases (overall) resources such as memory, CPU, and storage. While this increases the overall costs for deploying the network, it reduces the average cost of deploying SGs.

Although the placement model places the NFs with the lowest cost possible, it chooses the first min-cost solution the solver finds. As discussed above, this may or may not a good choice for future requests, and we proposed two approaches to address this issue. The next two subsections contain some results when using either approach, demonstrating that both can increase the acceptance ratio in the long run (i.e., over a sequence of requests).

7.2 Smart Selection Heuristic

The ILP in Sect. 3 for wired networks is solved using one of the AMPL solvers named BARON. We used BARON mainly because it solves linear and non-linear optimization problems. We used a small network of 7 nodes where the nodes are randomly placed. The SGs have the same characteristics as previous results in terms of their values and their life time and arrival rate. The number of NFs per SG is 3. To make it easier to analyze the impact of our proposed heuristic, we assumed the network is wired and each node and NF of the SGs has only one resource. Figure 8 shows the acceptance ratio of the ILP and ILP with the use of our proposed smart selection heuristic. It can be seen that our heuristic improves the number of accepted requests (increased acceptance ratio). As the following method has to find all min-cost solutions and choose the one with the highest RR ratio, it can be more time consuming than an optimization method that simply finds a single min-cost solution.

7.3 Joint Optimization

The main difference of the joint model with all previously proposed models is the way it handles SGs. It does not place each SG individually, but combine each newly arrived SG with all the previously placed and not yet expired SGs in order to form a new SG and place the joint SGs optimally. As the requests are accumulated, the complexity of the optimization problem increases. This increases the time required to solve the problem, so we choose a small network and consider only a sequence of 10 SGs. We compare the number of a accepted requests in a small wireless network of 7 nodes randomly placed and connected. The nodal resources and links' BW are chosen uniformly distributed between

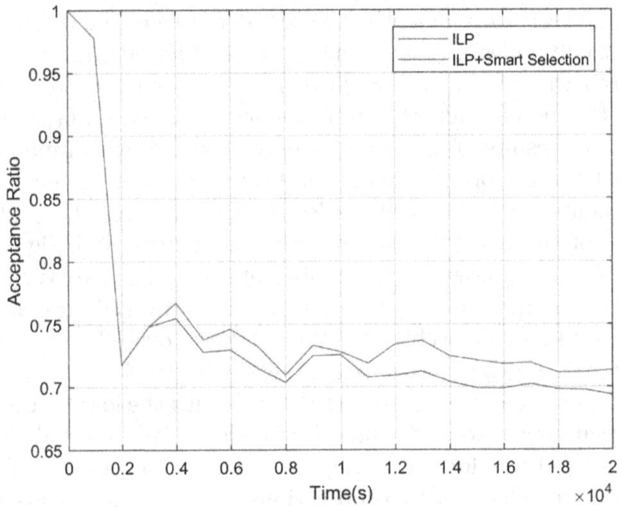

Fig. 8. Acceptance ratio comparison of ILP and ILP with smart heuristic.

100 to 150. The requested resources for SGs are between 20 to 70 units and uniformly distributed. The model is solved by BARON.

We compare the results of the optimization model and the joint optimization in terms of the number of accepted requests and time consumed to provide an optimal solution. Table 7 shows the details of the placement for each SG. It is shown in Table 7 that the ILP uses one node for placing each of the SGs, n_1 for placing the first SG, n_2 for placing the second one and so on. The third column in Table 7 shows the joint ILP placements where the placement for SGs is divided by a comma. For example, for the second SG, it is combined with its previous SG (the first SG) and the NFs of the first one are all being placed in n_1 and the second SG's NFs are being placed in n_5. In another example, the 8th SG is being combined with all the 7 SGs that are previously placed in the network. The first two NFs of the first SG are being placed in n_1 and the third NF of the first SG is placed in n_5.

The number of replaced NFs are calculated based on a comparison between the current placement and the previous one. We count the number of NFs that are replaced. For example, for placing the third SG jointly with previous ones, the first SG is being moved from n_1 to n_4, which means its 3 NFs are being replaced. Similarly, the second SG is being moved from n_5 to n_1, resulting in another 3 replaced NFs. In total, after placing the third SG jointly with previous SGs, 6 NFs are being replaced/moved to a new location.

Table 8 shows the time consumed to place SGs by each method. As we can see from Table 7, the last two SGs are rejected when we consider SGs in isolation, as the approach described in Sect. 3 (and the related work) does. In contrast, the joint ILP can place 9 SGs successfully. It is shown in Table 7 and Table 8 that the higher placement rate of the joint ILP has two additional costs. First, it takes

Table 7. ILP and Joint ILP placements.

SGs	ILP placement	Joint ILP placement	Number of replaced NFs
1	n_1	n_1	0
2	n_4	n_1, n_5	0
3	n_2	n_4, n_1, n_5	6
4	n_3	n_7, n_1, n_5, n_6	3
5	n_5	n_5, n_7, n_4, n_3, n_1	12
6	n_6	$n_6, n_4, n_7, n_1, n_5, n_3$	15
7	n_6	$n_7, n_5, n_1, n_3, n_4, n_6, n_2$	18
8	n_7	$\{n_1, n_5, n_5\}, n_4, n_5, n_7, n_1, n_6, n_2, n_3$	15
9	Rejected	$\{n_1, n_5, n_5\}, n_4, n_5, n_7, n_1, n_6, n_2, n_2, n_3$	3
10	Rejected	Rejected	-

Table 8. Time consumed by ILP and Joint ILP to place SGs.

SGs	ILP Placement timing (sec)	Joint ILP timing (sec)
1	0.02	0.06
2	0.03	0.22
3	0.02	0.22
4	0.02	0.14
5	0.02	0.17
6	0	0.19
7	0.03	0.25
8	0.03	0.27
9	Rejected	14.05
10	Rejected	Rejected

more time to solve the placement model as the size of the optimization problem grows with the number of placed SGs. Second, we may have to reconfigure/move some of the already placed NFs. We can see from Table 7 that by considering more and more SGs the number of replaced NFs grows.

8 Conclusions

Placing NFs in wireless networks can be a challenge due to the scarcity of BW as wireless links interfere with each other, therefore reducing the available BW of links in their vicinity. We first provide a model for placement of NFs in both wired and wireless networks. The optimization model was applied to randomly generated network topologies with multiple sizes to compare the average cost, acceptance ratio and the number of the physical links and virtual links used to deploy SGs. We show that the optimization model tends to place NFs in fewer nodes to reduce the BW usage. When using different solvers on the same model and scenario, we observed different results (in terms of acceptance ratio and placement costs). Using a simple example, we show that often multiple min-cost solutions exist. The long-term performance of embedding SGs in a network depends on which min-cost solution a solver finds. In the related work, the proposed approaches typically use the first min-cost solution found by a solver, which may not be the best choice.

This paper presents two possible options to improve on the state-of-the-art. In our first proposal, we ask the solver to determine all min-cost solutions. We then proposed a heuristic to select a min-cost solution among these candidates, such that the remaining nodal resources can, potentially, accommodate a higher number of future SGs. Our results show that the proposed smart selection heuristic increases the number of accepted requests in a small network of 7 nodes. The second option is to consider each SG jointly with previously placed SGs to place them all optimally. We show that the joint optimization model increases the number of accepted requests. However, it will impose a cost of reconfiguration of already placed SGs and increases the solver runtime.

Extending the experiments already performed in this paper, future work will be devoted to identifying other factors that are important in choosing a min-cost solution. We are working on applying the provided models to larger networks and explore their effects on them. It would be interesting to consider the cost of reconfiguration of the already placed SGs and find a threshold for a number of allowed reconfiguration to take advantage of joint optimization while avoiding unnecessary reconfiguration. Alternatively, the costs of reconfiguration could be included in the optimization model, directing the solver to find a solution for the new problem that is "close to" the currently deployed NFs (i.e., with only a small number of reconfigurations/NF movements).

References

1. AMPL: a modeling language for large-scale optimization. OR/MS Today 36(2), 68 (2009)
2. Ahvar, S., Phyu, H.P., Buddhacharya, S.M., Ahvar, E., Crespi, N., Glitho, R.: CCVP: Cost-efficient centrality-based VNF placement and chaining algorithm for network service provisioning, pp. 1–9. IEEE (2017)
3. Botero, J.F., Hesselbach, X., Duelli, M., Schlosser, D., Fischer, A., de Meer, H.: Energy efficient virtual network embedding. IEEE Commun. Lett. **16**(5), 756–759 (2012)
4. Bouet, M., Leguay, J., Combe, T., Conan, V.: Cost-based placement of vDPI functions in NFV infrastructures. Int. J. Netw. Manage. **25**(6), 490–506 (2015)
5. Chowdhury, N.M.K., Boutaba, R.: A survey of network virtualization. Comput. Netw. **54**(5), 862–876 (2010). https://doi.org/10.1016/j.comnet.2009.10.017. http://www.sciencedirect.com/science/article/pii/S1389128609003387
6. Ghaznavi, M., Khan, A., Shahriar, N., Alsubhi, K., Ahmed, R., Boutaba, R.: Elastic virtual network function placement, pp. 255–260. IEEE (2015)

7. Jahedi, Z., Kunz, T.: Virtual network function embedding in multi-hop wireless networks. In: Proceedings of the 15th International Joint Conference on e-Business and Telecommunications, ICETE 2018, - Volume 1: DCNET, ICE-B, OPTICS, SIGMAP and WINSYS, Porto, Portugal, 26–28 July 2018, pp. 199–207 (2018). https://doi.org/10.5220/0006887401990207
8. Jain, K., Padhye, J., Padmanabhan, V.N., Qiu, L.: Impact of interference on multi-hop wireless network performance. Wireless Netw. **11**(4), 471–487 (2005)
9. Kunz, T., Mahmood, K., Li, L.: Broadcasting in multihop wireless networks: the case for multi-source network coding. In: IEEE International Conference on Communications (ICC), pp. 5157–5162. IEEE (2012)
10. Luizelli, M.C., Bays, L.R., Buriol, L.S., Barcellos, M.P., Gaspary, L.P.: Piecing together the NFV provisioning puzzle: efficient placement and chaining of virtual network functions, pp. 98–106. IEEE (2015)
11. Lv, P., Wang, X., Xu, M.: Virtual access network embedding in wireless mesh networks. Ad Hoc Netw. **10**(7), 1362–1378 (2012)
12. Ma, W., Beltran, J., Pan, Z., Pan, D., Pissinou, N.: Sdn-based traffic aware placement of NFV middleboxes. IEEE Trans. Netw. Serv. Manage. **14**(3), 528–542 (2017)
13. Mohammadkhan, A., Ghapani, S., Liu, G., Zhang, W., Ramakrishnan, K.K., Wood, T.: Virtual function placement and traffic steering in flexible and dynamic software defined networks. In: The 21st IEEE International Workshop on Local and Metropolitan Area Networks, pp. 1–6. IEEE (2015)
14. Park, K., Kim, C.: A framework for virtual network embedding in wireless networks. In: 4th International Conference on Future Internet Technologies, pp. 5–7. ACM (2009)
15. Riggio, R., Bradai, A., Rasheed, T., Schulz-Zander, J., Kuklinski, S., Ahmed, T.: Virtual network functions orchestration in wireless networks. In: 11th International Conference on Network and Service Management (CNSM), pp. 108–116. IFIP (2015)
16. Sahhaf, S., et al.: Network service chaining with optimized network function embedding supporting service decompositions. The 21st IEEE International Workshop on Local and Metropolitan Area Networks, vol. 93, pp. 492–505 (2015)

Anonymity in Complex Transactions for e-Business

Cătălin V. Bîrjoveanu[1(✉)] and Mirela Bîrjoveanu[2]

[1] Department of Computer Science, "Al. I. Cuza" University of Iaşi, Iaşi, Romania
cbirjoveanu@info.uaic.ro
[2] Continental Automotive, Iaşi, Romania
mbirjoveanu@gmail.com

Abstract. Anonymity of the customer and each merchant is a key property that must be considered in a fair exchange e-commerce protocol. The customer may not want to reveal sensitive data of his identity (as credit card number, information about customer's bank, customer's account number) so that this information can not be used by merchant in commercial purpose to build spending habits of the customer. Also, a merchant may want to remain anonymous. For example, a merchant who has business in many areas may want that his customers can not link transactions where the merchant is involved in all these areas. In our previous work [4], a fair exchange e-commerce protocol for complex transactions in that a customer wants to buy several different physical products from different merchants is proposed. This solution provides customer anonymity, non-repudiation, integrity and confidentiality of data exchanged between the parties. In this paper, we extend the solution from [4] obtaining both anonymity of customer and each merchant, while preserving all properties obtained in [4].

Keywords: B2C/B2B · Anonymity · Complex transactions · Fair exchange · Electronic commerce security

1 Introduction

Anonymity of the customer and each merchant is a key property that must be considered in a fair exchange e-commerce protocol. The customer may not want to reveal sensitive data of his identity (as credit card number, information about customer's bank, customer's account number) so that this information can not be used by merchant in building the commercial profile of the customer.

A merchant may want to remain anonymous: e.g. a merchant who has business in many areas may want that his customers can not link transactions where the merchant is involved in all these areas. If a customer is aware that a merchant has business interests in a certain domain, then because of ethical reasons, the customer does not want to buy products from this merchant in another business domain in which the merchant is involved. Moreover, if a customer knows all

M. S. Obaidat (Ed.): ICETE 2018, CCIS 1118, pp. 24–45, 2019.
https://doi.org/10.1007/978-3-030-34866-3_2

business domains of a merchant, then the customer may request special prices from the merchant: the customer may condition the purchase of some products from merchant only if he gets discounts for other products from another business area where the merchant is involved. We consider a B2B scenario in which the customer and merchant have business interests in many areas, and in one of these areas they are competitors, but in another area the customer wants to buy products from merchant. In this case, if the customer has knowledge about involvement of the merchant in all these business area, then the customer may choose not to buy the products from merchant. In all above scenarios, the merchant is disadvantaged because this identity is known.

In the electronic commerce, there are situations in that a customer wishes to buy a pack of products/services composed of several products (physical or digital)/services from different merchants. In this type of e-commerce transactions, the customer is interested in buying all products from the pack or no product at all, namely *aggregate/atomic transactions*. In *optional transactions*, the customer has the flexibility to buy exactly one product from many merchants, and for this, he specifies in his request more possible products according to his preferences but from these options only one will be committed. The combination in any form of aggregate and optional transactions is a *complex transaction*.

Fair exchange in e-commerce protocols for complex transactions is a challenging topic. For complex transactions, an e-commerce protocol in that a customer wishes to buy many products from different merchants assures fair exchange if:

- for any optional transaction from the complex transaction, the customer obtains exactly one product in order of his specified preferences, and
- for any aggregate transaction from the complex transaction, the customer obtains all products,

and each merchant obtains the payment for the corresponding product, or none of them obtains nothing.

In the literature, there are protocols proposed for physical products delivery that provide fair exchange and consider only one customer and one merchant [1–3,7,9,14] and from all this solutions the one proposed in [3] provides also anonymity for both customer and merchant.

There are known many multi-party mboxfair exchange protocols proposed with applications in e-commerce transactions for buying physical products [4], for buying digital goods [10], digital signature of contracts [8,13], and certified e-mail [13].

The solutions proposed in [8,10,13] exchange digital items. Some multi-party non-repudiation solutions exchange different messages [13] in a one-to-many configuration, without taken in to consideration atomicity. In [10], an aggregate transaction is considered, where a customer wants to buy from different merchants several digital products, but optional transactions and anonymity are not considered. In [4], a fair exchange e-commerce protocol for complex transactions in that a customer wants to buy several different physical products from different merchants is proposed. The solution from [4] provides customer anonymity, non-repudiation, integrity and confidentiality of data exchanged between the parties.

In this paper, we extend the solution from [4] obtaining both anonymity of customer and each merchant, while preserving all properties obtained in [4].

The paper is structured as follows: Sect. 2 gives some details about application of the group blind digital signatures for electronic cash, Sect. 3 gives application examples of our protocol, Sect. 4 informally describes our protocol, Sect. 5 presents the protocol, Sect. 6 provides an analysis of the proposed protocol and Sect. 7 contains the conclusion.

2 Group Blind Digital Signatures for Electronic Cash

Our proposal uses the group blind digital signature scheme from [11]. The group blind digital signature schemes are obtained by combining the blind digital signature schemes [6] and the group digital signature schemes [5]. The group blind digital signature scheme from [11] adds the blindness property to the group digital signature scheme from [5].

In what follows we provide some details about the group blind digital signature scheme from [11] applied to provide an electronic cash payment mechanism in which many banks can provide anonymous electronic cash. The scheme considers a group of banks that issues digital coins, a central bank (the group manager) that monitors all banks from group, and customers.

The group blind digital signature (GBDS) scheme consists of the following phases:

- *Setup.* The group manager generates a secret key for him and the group's public key.
- *Join.* If a bank joins the bank's group, then the bank generates a public/private key pair and proves to the group manager that she knows the private key but without revealing the private key to the group manager. If the bank successfully proves the knowledge of the private key, then the group manager provides the group membership certificate to the bank.
- *Sign.* If a customer wants to withdraw electronic cash from his bank, then he generates a digital coin and sends it to his bank. The customer's bank applies the group blind digital signature on the coin, sends it to customer, and withdraws the corresponding amount from the customer's account.
- *Verify.* The customer sends to a merchant the digital coin and the group blind digital signature of his bank on the coin. The merchant checks if the group blind digital signature is valid using the group's public key. If the signature is valid, then the merchant sends the product to customer, and also sends to his bank the digital coin and the group blind digital signature on the coin for redemption.
- *Open.* For a digital coin and a group blind digital signature on the coin, the group manager can determine the identity of signer using his secret key.

GBDS ensures the following properties:

- The signer bank signs a digital coin without knowing its content.
- The signer bank signs a digital coin on behalf of the group of banks.
- If a bank signs a coin then is easy to verify that the coin is signed by a bank from group, but except the group manager, no one can determine the bank that signed the coin.
- The valid signatures on behalf of the bank's group can only be done by the banks from group.
- Neither the group manager nor any bank from the group of banks can sign on behalf of another bank from group.

The security of GBDS is based on the hardness of the discrete logarithm, double discrete logarithm, and the roots discrete logarithm problems.

3 Motivation

Our protocol has applications in Business to Consumer (B2C) and Business to Business (B2B) scenarios.

For a B2B scenario, the customer is the Electron company that manufactures electronic boards for different purposes, on request from his clients. To plan its business, Electron uses an online catalog from where it can buy several electronic components from different merchants denoted by $M1, M2, M3$, e.t.c. From the online catalog, Electron can select products like: resistors (R), capacitors (C), integrated circuits (IC), cables, connectors, printed circuit boards (PCB) and so on. Electron wants to start the production of a new electronic board and therefore wants to prepare its order in form of an e-commerce complex transaction as follows: (100R of 10 kΩ from $M1$ or 70R of 20 kΩ from $M2$) and (50C of 100mF from $M3$ or 100C of 70mF from $M4$) and 70 connectors $DB35$ type from $M5$ and 30PCB from the $M6$. The complex transaction is composed from an aggregate transaction and two optional transactions. For the first optional transaction if Electron can not acquire 100R of 10 kΩ from $M1$ due to lack of stock or delay in delivery time, then its second option is taken into consideration to acquire 70R of 20 kΩ from $M2$. To start the production, Electron needs all types of components specified in its request, so a partial combination (e.g. 100R of 10 kΩ, 100C of 70mF and 30PCB, but without 70 connectors $DB35$ type) is not useful for him. For an optional transaction, Electron must not acquire more than one product (e.g. for the first optional transaction he must not acquire both 100R of 10 kΩ and 70R of 20 kΩ) because then he will remain with unnecessary products. For example, a pack of products that solves the customer's options is: 100R of 10 kΩ, and 100C of 70mF, and 70 connectors $DB35$ type and 30PCB.

A similar scenario can be used in B2C applications. In this case, the customer is a person that likes electronics and wants to build an electronic hobby kit, and for this he uses the online catalog to order the needed components.

4 Informal Description

The protocol we propose uses an online Trusted Third Party (TTP) that will validate the customer's coins and will provide fair exchange if any party misbehaves or prematurely aborts.

Both customer and each merchant may choose to remain anonymous during the protocol execution. Our protocol uses the electronic cash payment mechanism based on group blind digital signatures on behalf of the banks (GBDS) proposed in [11] to provide anonymity of the customer and each merchant in the payment phase. To ensure anonymity of the customer and each merchant in the physical delivery phase of each ordered product from the pack, our protocol is based on existence of a delivery agent whose role is to take the product from a source cabinet and provide it to a destination cabinet. Both source cabinet and destination cabinet provides access to the physical products by passwords to conceal true identity of the customer and each merchant.

Next, we will informally describe the protocol.

When the customer is browsing on the online catalog and decides the products he wants to buy and the options for each product from the pack, he clicks a "submit" button. The protocol searches a sequence of subtransactions to satisfy the customer's options in order of preferences he supplies. A subtransaction is a sequence of protocol's steps in which the customer buys a certain physical product from a certain merchant.

Our protocol can run in multiple rounds. One protocol round consists of three sub-protocols: *Agreement*, *Delivery* and *Payment*.

In *Agreement*, a sequence of subtransactions is started as a possible solution for customer's choices. For each subtransaction, the customer buys a digital coin of appropriate value from his bank. The customer's bank transfers the coin value from the customer's account to a commit-buffer common to all banks and applies a group blind digital signature on the coin. The customer obtains the signature of his bank on the digital coin and sends to TTP the encrypted coin, the decryption key of the coin and the digital signature of his bank on the coin. TTP uses the group public key to verify that the signature on the coin is generated by any bank of the group, verifies freshness of the received coin, and validates the coin by sending to the customer a digital signature on the encrypted coin and its value. This signature will be used later by customer to confirm to merchant that the encrypted coin has exactly a certain value, without the merchant seeing the coin. The customer sends to merchant the purchase order and the digital signature of TTP on the encrypted coin. The purchase order includes the mailing address of the destination cabinet where the product must be posted and a digest of a password that will be set on the product such that only who knows the password can collect the product. The merchant replies to confirm the agreement on subtransaction's terms. The *Agreement* will be completed either with all subtransactions successfully finished or all aborted.

If all subtransactions successfully finished *Agreement*, then *Delivery* simultaneous realizes the physical delivery of products from these subtransactions. For each subtransaction, the corresponding merchant uses a delivery agent to send his product to customer. Also, the merchant sets two passwords for the product: one to allow only to the delivery agent to collect the product from a source cabinet, and the other (received from the customer) to allow only the customer to collect the product from a destination cabinet. After all products from the subtransactions involved in *Delivery* are posted to the destination cabinet, the customer collects the products and provides to the destination cabinet an evidence of the product's collection.

If *Delivery* is successfully for all subtransactions, then *Payment* simultaneously performs the payment for these subtransactions. In each subtransaction, the customer sends to merchant the coin decryption key and his bank's signature on the coin. The merchant sends the coin together with the signature on the coin to his bank for redemption. The merchant's bank verifies the validity of the signature using the group public key, verifies if the coin was not already spent and, if the verification passes then transfers the coin value from commit-buffer in the merchant's account.

In a protocol round some subtransactions can be aborted without solving the customer's options in that round. If the customer's options are not completely explored, new protocol rounds will be executed to search a sequence of subtransactions that will satisfy his choices. The protocol terminates after a round that solves the customer's options, or after a round where, after *Agreement*, all subtransactions are aborted.

5 The Protocol

Our protocol extends our previous work [4] that proposes an e-commerce protocol for physical products delivery in complex transactions that provides fair exchange and anonymity of the customer. The Table 1 presents the notations used in the description of our protocol.

5.1 Protocol Infrastructure

The following assumptions are made for our protocol:

1. All parties use the same algorithms for encryption, hash, digital signature and the same group blind digital signature protocol mentioned in Table 1.
2. Cryptographic algorithms are strong enough.
3. TTP is the group manager, namely Central Bank, that is known by all parties implied in protocol. TTP does not misbehave or collude with any of parties to provide benefits to another party.
4. There are n merchants $M_1, \ldots, M_n$. C can buy a pack of products from these merchants, and each merchant can provide to C only a certain type of product. C and each M_i, have an account to their bank.
5. There is a pseudonym system like in [12] that C and each M_i are using. So, instead of using their true identity, C and each M_i are using their pseudo identity C', respectively M_i'. In the complex transactions protocol, the pseudo identities does not provide any information that links to the true identities.

Table 1. Notations used in the protocol description.

Symbol	Interpretation
C/C'	True identity/pseudo identity of the customer
M_i/M_i'	True identity/pseudo identity of the merchant i, where $1 \leq i \leq n$
CB/M_iB	The bank of customer/merchant M_i
DA_i, SC_i	Delivery Agent i, Source Cabinet i
DC, TTP	Destination Cabinet, Trusted Third Party
$A \rightarrow B$: m	A sends the message m to B
$DC \Rightarrow C'$: m	DC sends m to DA_i that forwards it to M_i' and M_i' to C'
A_{pub}, A_{prv}	(RSA) Public/private key pair of A
A'_{ipub}, A'_{iprv}	One time (RSA) public/private key pair of A
$\{m\}_K, h(m)$	m encrypted with K, m's digest obtained by a hash function h (SHA-2)
$sig_A(m)$	(RSA) Digital Signature with the A's private key A_{prv} on $h(m)$
$sig_{CB}(c_i)$	CB's group blind digital signature on c_i obtained by *Sign* phase of GBDS

6. All banks from group and group manager share a commit-buffer in that each subtransaction's value is stored until the subtransaction is completed successfully or aborted.
7. All banks from group and group manager maintain a global list of coin's serial already spent, validated but unspent, or canceled, to allow any bank to check a coin for double-spending or double-canceling. Each record contains the unique identifier of the subtransaction, the coin's serial and a *spent* flag. The value of *spent* flag has the following meaning: *spent* $= 0$ the coin is validated by TTP but not yet spent, *spent* $= 1$ the coin has already been spent, *spent* $= 2$ the coin has already been canceled.
8. For each substransaction s_i, we consider a source cabinet SC_i, where the physical product is placed by M_i, and DA_i can take the product from SC_i only by knowing a password that is set by M_i for that product when he puts the product in. SC_i is used to replace the correspondence's address of M_i. So, the true identity each M_i, remains hidden if he wants.
9. For each substransaction s_i, we consider a destination cabinet DC, where the physical products are provided by DA_i, and C can collect the product P_i with the identifier Pid_i from DC only by knowing a password that is set by M_i. DC is used to hide the true identity of C if he wants.
10. DC and each SC_i have the ability to digitally sign messages, verify digital signatures on messages and to check if the password entered by C, respectively DA_i, corresponds to the barcode set on product. DC has a video camera mounted that records when C unwraps each packaged product and checks if the product is the ordered one. DC has a device that allows to C, by pushing a button, to send the encrypted recording to TTP. This feature allows TTP to store in a buffer *PidsAborted* the product's identifiers that are not received according to the agreement conditions.
11. Communication channels set between parties provide anonymity, except the cases in that the parties choose to reveal their true identities.

5.2 Prelude

We assume that before the starting of the protocol, the following system setup steps are executed:

1. TTP provides the digital certificate for his public key TTP_{pub} to C and each M_i, where $1 \leq i \leq n$.
2. When C and each M_i create accounts to their banks, each of them generates a public/private key pair, (C_{pub}, C_{prv}) and (M_{ipub}, M_{iprv}), respectively. C provides C_{pub} to CB and each M_i provides M_{ipub} to M_iB. The banks maintain databases with public keys of their clients associated to their accounts.
3. C and each M_i generates a one time public/private key pair (C'_{ipub}, C'_{iprv}), respectively (M'_{ipub}, M'_{iprv}) that each of them will use it only in one subtransaction.
4. The *Setup* and *Join* phases of GBDS protocol are executed.

5.3 Protocol Description

For an aggregate transaction, we define the *aggregation* operator, denoted by $\wedge$, as follows: $Pid_1 \wedge \ldots \wedge Pid_k$ meaning that C wishes to buy exactly k products with product's identifiers $Pid_1, \ldots, Pid_k$. For an optional transaction, we define the *option* operator, denoted by $\vee$, as follows: $Pid_1 \vee \ldots \vee Pid_k$ meaning that C wishes to buy a product that is exactly one of the products with product's identifiers $Pid_1, \ldots, Pid_k$, where the apparition order of the product's identifiers is the priority given by C. This means that C wishes first of all to buy the product Pid_1, but if this is not possible, his second option is Pid_2, and so on.

We build a tree over the product identifiers that C wants to buy using $\wedge$ and $\vee$ operators. For efficiency, we use the *left-child, right-sibling representation* of the tree in that each internal node corresponds to one of the above operators or to a product identifier, while each leaf node corresponds to a product identifier. Each node of the tree is represented by a structure with the following fields: *info* for storing the useful information (product identifier or one of the operators), *left* for pointing to the leftmost child of node, and *right* for pointing to the sibling of the node immediately to the right. The access to tree is realized trough the root.

An example of tree derived from the complex transaction from Sect. 3, is shown in Fig. 1 [4]. Pid_1 corresponds to R of 10 kΩ, Pid_2 to R of 20 kΩ, Pid_3 to C of 100mF, Pid_4 to C of 70mF, Pid_5 to connectors $DB35$ type and Pid_6 to PCB. The root node has $\wedge$ operator as *info*. The root does not have any right sibling and its children are the two nodes having $\vee$ operator as *info* and the nodes with the *info* Pid_5 and Pid_6. A parent-child link is realized as follows: the parent node points only to its leftmost child, and the rest of its children can be accessed starting with the leftmost child via sibling relationship. The first node having as *info* $\vee$ operator defines the product corresponding to the optional subtransaction $Pid_1 \vee Pid_2$.

Next, we will describe the phases of the protocol.

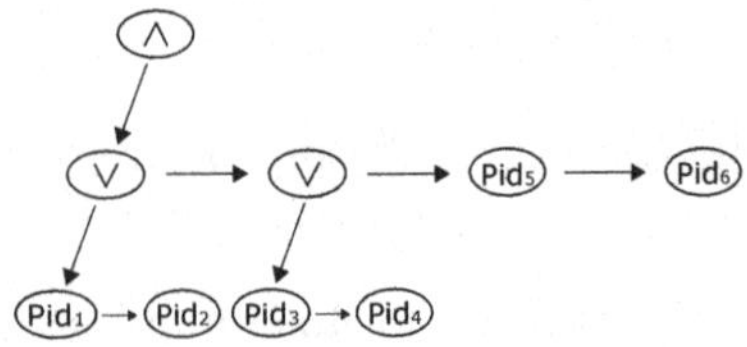

Fig. 1. Tree describing the customer's choices in left-child, right-sibling representation.

5.4 Agreement Sub-protocol

We denote by $s_i = (Sid_i, C', M'_i, Pid_i, fst)$ the subtransaction with the unique identifier Sid_i in which C' buys from M'_i the product with the product's identifier Pid_i. The flag of the subtransaction s_i is denoted by $s_i.fst$ and can have values from the set $\{1, 2, 3, abort\}$. $s_i.fst = 1$ means that s_i successfully completed *Agreement*, $s_i.fst = 2$ means that s_i successfully completed *Delivery*, $s_i.fst = 3$ means that s_i successfully completed *Payment*, and $s_i.fst = abort$ means that s_i has not successfully completed *Agreement* or *Delivery*, or successfully completed *Agreement* but had to be later aborted because s_i belongs to an aggregate transaction for which another subtransaction was already aborted.

In the example from Fig. 1, the first node having as *info* the option operator defines the product corresponding to the optional subtransaction $(Pid_1 \vee Pid_2)$. We define $Ns(p)$ - the state of the node p as a sequence of subtransactions $s_1 \dots s_m$ corresponding to the product defined by p. For a node p, $Ns(p)$ is calculated depending on the $p \rightarrow info$ as follows:

- if $p \rightarrow info = Pid_i$, where $1 \leq i \leq n$, then $Ns(p)$ is returned by $SAgree(C', M'_i, Pid_i)$ sub-protocol. So, if the subtransaction in that C' buys from M'_i the product with the identifier Pid_i successfully finished *Agreement*, then $Ns(p) = (Sid_i, C', M'_i, Pid_i, 1)$, otherwise $Ns(p) = (Sid_i, C', M'_i, Pid_i, abort)$.
  In our example, let be p the node with *info* Pid_1, then $Ns(p) = (Sid_1, C', M'_1, Pid_1, 1)$ if the subtransaction with identifier Sid_1 successfully finished *Agreement*, otherwise $Ns(p) = (Sid_1, C', M'_1, Pid_1, abort)$.
  The *SAgree* sub-protocol will be detailed below in Table 3 [4].
- if $p \rightarrow info = \vee$, then
  $$Ns(p) = \begin{cases} Ns(l), \text{ if } \exists\, l, \text{ the leftmost child of } p \text{ such that } s.fst = 1, \\ \qquad\qquad \text{for all } s \in Ns(l) \\ Ns(r), \text{ otherwise} \end{cases}$$
  where r is the rightmost child of p.
  The node p corresponds to $\vee$ operator w.r.t. the customer's choices and these preferences are prioritized by appearance in the child nodes of p from left to the right. $Ns(p)$ is the node state of the leftmost child of p, denoted $Ns(l)$, for which all subtransactions from $Ns(l)$ have successfully passed *Agreement*. Otherwise, if all subtransactions from node states of all children of p are aborted, then $Ns(p)$ is the node state of the rightmost child of p.

In our example, let be p the first node with $p \rightarrow info = \vee$. $Ns(p) = s_1$, where $s_1 = (Sid_1, C', M'_1, Pid_1, 1)$, if the subtransaction s_1 successfully finished *Agreement*. Otherwise, $Ns(p) = s_2$, where $s_2 = (Sid_2, C', M'_2, Pid_2, fst)$ and $s_2.fst \in \{1, abort\}$.

- if $p \rightarrow info = \wedge$, and $c_1, \ldots, c_k$ are all children of p, then we have two cases:
  1. if $s.fst = 1$, for any s from $Ns(c_j)$, for any $1 \leq j \leq k$, then $Ns(p) = Ns(c_1) \ldots Ns(c_k)$.
  2. otherwise, let c_j be, where $1 \leq j \leq k$, the leftmost child of p with $Ns(c_j) = s_{j1} \ldots s_{jm}$ such that $s_{jl}.fst = abort$, for all $1 \leq l \leq m$. In this case, $Ns(p) = Ns(c_1) \ldots Ns(c_j)$. Even if the subtransactions from $Ns(c_1)$ $, \ldots, Ns(c_{j-1})$ have successfully passed *Agreement*, the aborted subtransactions from $Ns(c_j)$ lead to aborting the entire aggregate transaction corresponding to p. That is why all subtransactions from $Ns(c_1), \ldots,$ $Ns(c_{j-1})$ will be aborted. Thus, will set $s.fst = abort$, for any $s \in Ns(c_r)$, for any $1 \leq r \leq j-1$.

  Because the node p corresponds to $\wedge$ operator, $Ns(p)$ is the sequence of node states of p's children. The sequence of node states of p's children is efficiently calculated until c_j the leftmost child of p for that $Ns(c_j)$ contains only aborted subtransactions.

  In our example, let be p the root node, c_1 the first node (from left) with $c_1 \rightarrow info = \vee$, c_2 the second node with $c_2 \rightarrow info = \vee$, c_3 the node with $c_3 \rightarrow info = Pid_5$ and c_4 the node with $c_4 \rightarrow info = Pid_6$. If $Ns(c_1) = s_1$, $Ns(c_2) = s_4$, $Ns(c_3) = s_5$ and $Ns(c_4) = s_6$, where $s_i = (Sid_i, C', M'_i, Pid_i, 1)$ with $i \in \{1, 4, 5, 6\}$, then $Ns(p) = s_1 s_4 s_5 s_6$. If $Ns(c_1) = s_1$, $Ns(c_2) = s_4$ as above, but $Ns(c_3) = s_5$ with $s_5 = (Sid_5, C', M'_5, Pid_5, abort)$, then $Ns(p) = s_1 s_4 s_5$ and s_1, s_4 will be aborted.

Thus, $Ns(p)$ is a sequence of subtransactions in which either all subtransactions successfully passed *Agreement* or all subtransactions are aborted.

The *Agreement* sub-protocol, described in Table 2 [4], recursively calculates $Ns(t)$ (t is the root of the tree derived from the customer's choices), traversing the tree in a similar manner with depth-first search. For any node p of the tree, we use a *child* array to store the node states of all children of p.

Before the application the *Agreement* sub-protocol in the first round of the protocol, $Ns(p) = \lambda$, for any node p of the tree t (λ is empty string). If the protocol does not terminate after the first round, then for efficiency, in future rounds, the protocol will not apply *Agreement* to those nodes where their state is an aborted subtransaction (as we can see in the lines 1 and 8).

The protocol computes $Ns(p)$ for a node p depending on the node state of the left most child of p at the lines 3–5. In the while loop (lines 7–15) the node state of any child of p except the left most one is computed. The way in which node state is computed is essential to obtain fair exchange and atomicity in a complex transaction (lines 9–14): if an aborted subtransaction/sequence of subtransactions leads to aborting the entire aggregate transaction, but some subtransactions from the aggregate transaction successfully completed *Agreement*, then the ones that are successfully must also be stored in the node state corresponding to

Table 2. Agreement sub-protocol.

```
Agreement(t)
1. if (t→left ≠ NULL and s.fst ≠ abort, for s ∈ Ns(t→left))
2.     child[0] = Agreement(t→left);
3. if ((t→info = ∨ and s.fst = 1, for all s from child[0]) or
4.     (t→info = ∧ and s.fst = abort, for all s from child[0]))
5.         Ns(t) = child[0]; return Ns(t);
6. j = 1; k = t→left→right;
7. while (k ≠ NULL)
8.     if (s.fst ≠ abort, for s from Ns(k)) child[j] = Agreement(k);
9.     if (t→info = ∨ and s.fst = 1, for all s from child[j]) Ns(t)=child[j]; return Ns(t);
10.    if (t→info = ∧ and s.fst = abort, for all s from child[j])
11.        for (c = 0; c ≤ j; c = c + 1) Ns(t) = Ns(t)child[c]; end for
12.        for (all s ∈ Ns(t) such that s.fst ≠ abort)
13.            AggAbort(s); s.fst = abort; end for
14.        return Ns(t);
15.    k = k→right; j = j + 1; end while
16. if (t→info = Pid_i) Ns(t) = SAgree(C', M'_i, Pid_i); return Ns(t);
17. else if (t→info = ∨) k = t →left;
18.                       while (k→right ≠ NULL) k = k→right; end while
19.                       Ns(t) = Ns(k); return Ns(t);
20.      else for (c = 0; c ≤ j - 1; c = c + 1) Ns(t) = Ns(t)child[c]; end for
21.           return Ns(t); end if
22. end if
```

$\wedge$ operator (line 11) and aborted in lines 12–13. For each subtransaction s that successfully completed *Agreement*, the $AggAbort(s)$ procedure will be initiated by TTP to cancel the coin involved in s in the same manner with the messages $1.6'.i$–$1.7'i$ from *Aborting* procedure (Table 3), and the flag of s is set on abort.

For a node with a product identifier as *info* (line 16), the protocol applies the *SAgree* sub-protocol in that the customer establishes the agreement conditions with the merchant for buying the product.

If we have a node corresponding to $\vee$ operator that has all subtransactions from all its children aborted, its node state is computed at the lines 17–19. If we have a node corresponding to $\wedge$ operator that has all subtransactions from all its children successfully completed *Agreement*, its node state is computed at the lines 20–21.

The subtransactions that are initiated in a protocol round can become aborted in different phases of the protocol without solving the customer's options. However, the customer can have many options w.r.t. the products he wants to buy, so new rounds of the protocol must be executed.

Table 3. SAgree sub-protocol.

$SAgree(C', M_i', Pid_i)$

$1.1.i.\ C' \rightarrow TTP : Sid_i,\ \{Sid_i,\ C',\ M_i',\ C'_{ipub},\ K_i\}_{TTP_{pub}},\ \{c_i\}_{K_i},\ sig_{CB}(c_i),$
$\quad sig_{C'}(sig_{CB}(c_i))$

$1.2.i.\ TTP \rightarrow C' : Sid_i,\ T_{iTTP},\ L_i,\ N_{iTTP},\ S_{iTTP}$

where $S_{iTTP} = sig_{TTP}(Sid_i,\ C',\ M_i',\ \{c_i\}_{K_i},\ V_i,\ T_{iTTP},\ L_i,\ N_{iTTP})$

$1.3.i.\ C' \rightarrow M_i' : Po_i,\ sig_{C'}(Po_i),\ \{c_i\}_{K_i},\ V_i,\ T_{iTTP},\ L_i,\ N_{iTTP},\ S_{iTTP}$

where $Po_i = Sid_i,\ C',\ M_i',\ Pid_i,\ Pr_i,\ Q_i,\ V_i,\ DC_{addr},\ h(N_{iC}),\ C'_{ipub}$

if $(M_i\_agreement)$ $1.4.i.\ M_i' \rightarrow C' : Sid_i,\ sig_{M_i'}(sig_{C'}(Po_i)),\ \{M'_{ipub}\}_{C'_{ipub}}$

return $(Sid_i, C', M_i', Pid_i, 1)$

else if $(1.4'.i.\ M_i' \rightarrow C' : Sid_i,\ sig_{M_i'}(Po_i,\ abort))$ $Aborting(s_i)$ **end if**

end if

where the $Aborting(s_i)$ procedure consist of:

$1.5'.i.\ C' \rightarrow TTP : Po_i,\ sig_{C'}(Po_i),\ \{c_i\}_{K_i},\ V_i,\ T_{iTTP},\ L_i,\ N_{iTTP},\ S_{iTTP}$

$1.6'.i.\ TTP \rightarrow C' : Sid_i,\ cancel,\ sig_{TTP}(Sid_i,\ c_i,\ sig_{CB}(c_i),\ cancel)$

$1.7'.i.\ C \rightarrow CB : Sid_i,\ cancel,\ \{c_i,\ sig_{CB}(c_i),\ C,\ C_{acct}\}_{CB_{pub}},$
$\quad sig_{TTP}(Sid_i,\ c_i,\ sig_{CB}(c_i),\ cancel)$

return $(Sid_i, C', M_i', Pid_i, abort)$

Next, we will give details about $SAgree(C',\ M_i',\ Pid_i)$ sub-protocol presented in Table 3. In this sub-protocol C buys a digital coin, validates the coin to TTP, and establishes the agreement with M_i' on the subtransaction's terms.

C and his bank CB run the *Sign* phase of GBDS protocol. C generates a new digital coin that is a number c_i of 256 bits consisting of a unique coin serial number represented on the first 224 bits and the coin value V_i in the last 32 bits. CB transfers the coin value from the C's bank account with CB (C_{acct}) to the commit-buffer and sends to C the signature of CB on c_i on behalf of the bank's group - $sig_{CB}(c_i)$. CB doesn't know the serial number of c_i because his signature on c_i is blind, and only knows the identity of the customer and the value of some digital coin purchased by him.

After C receives $sig_{CB}(c_i)$, he validates at TTP an encrypted version of c_i. C generates a nonce Sid_i as subtransaction identifier, a symmetric key K_i and sends to TTP the message 1.1.i. TTP obtains C'_{ipub}, K_i and c_i, and uses C'_{ipub} to verify the customer's signature on the signed coin. TTP checks if c_i is valid by verifying $sig_{CB}(c_i)$ using the group public key, and checks the status of c_i by verifying the *spent* flag of the c_i's serial in the global list of coin's serial. If all checks out, TTP adds c_i in the list setting the c_i's *spent* flag on 0, and sends to C the message 1.2.i.

The message 1.2.i contains a timestamp T_{iTTP}, a lifetime of encrypted coin's validity L_i, a nonce N_{iTTP} all to avoid replay attacks, and S_{iTTP} - the signature of TTP. On reception, C checks if T_{iTTP} and L_i are recently enough, and then verifies S_{iTTP}.

C initiates the agreement by sending to M_i the message 1.3.i that includes the purchase order Po_i. Po_i contains the product identifier Pid_i, the price Pr_i of the product and the quantity Q_i of ordered products. Also, Po_i includes $h(N_{iC})$ whose goal is to be used as a barcode on product and is set by M_i such that only who knows the password N_{iC} can collect the product from the mailing address DC_{addr} of DC.

On reception, M_i verifies Po_i, if T_{iTTP} and L_i are recently enough, the signature of C on Po_i, and S_{iTTP}. If M_i is satisfied (the true value of the boolean variable M_i*_agreement*), S_{iTTP} assures him that $\{c_i\}_{K_i}$ represents the encryption of a valid coin (signed by a bank from the group, and its lifetime has not expired) of value V_i from Po_i. M_i sends to C the message 1.4.i as an acknowledgment of his agreement. After reaching the agreement, $s_i = (Sid_i, C', M'_i, Pid_i, 1)$ is returned as the state of the node with *info* Pid_i.

If M_i is not satisfied, he sends an abort message 1.4′.i to C who applies *Aborting*(s_i) procedure. In *Aborting*(s_i), C cancels c_i in the messages 1.5′.i–1.7′.i and $s_i = (Sid_i, C', M'_i, Pid_i, abort)$ is returned as the state of the node with *info* Pid_i. To cancel the coin, C uses TTP to obtain in the message 1.6′.i a cancellation request of the coin and C sends it to CB. CB checks if $sig_{CB}(c_i)$ is a valid signature, TTP's signature, and if c_i has not already been spent or canceled by checking the global list of coin's serial. If all checks are satisfied, CB sets the *spent* flag of c_i to 2, transfers the coin value from commit-buffer to C_{acct}, and sends to C a signed acknowledgment of successfully cancellation of c_i.

If after M_i receives 1.3.i, he doesn't continue the sub-protocol, C will apply *Aborting*(s_i).

After *Agreement* is completed, $Ns(t-root)$ is stored in the variable Ps that indicates the protocol state. So, Ps is the sequence of the subtransactions for which all successfully completed *Agreement* or all aborted.

5.5 Delivery Sub-protocol

If all subtransactions from Ps successfully completed *Agreement*, then *Delivery* can be started to physically deliver the products involved in each subtransaction from Ps.

Delivery sub-protocol for an arbitrary subtransaction s_i is described in Table 4. In the message 2.1.i, M_i posts the physical product P_i (with Pid_i

Table 4. Delivery sub-protocol.

$2.1.i : M_i' \rightarrow SC_i : Sid_i,\ P_i$

$2.2.i : SC_i \rightarrow M_i' : Sid_i,\ sig_{SC_i}(Sid_i,\ M_i',\ Pid_i,\ DA_i)$

$2.3.i : M_i' \rightarrow DA_i : Sid_i,\ Pid_i,\ SC_{iaddr},\ DC_{addr}, \{M_i',\ M_{ipub}',\ N_{iM_i}\}_{DA_{ipub}},$
$\quad sig_{M_i'}(Sid_i,\ M_i',\ Pid_i,\ SC_{iaddr},\ DC_{addr},\ N_{iM_i})$

$2.4.i : SC_i \rightarrow DA_i : Sid_i,\ P_i$

$2.5.i : DA_i \rightarrow SC_i : Sid_i,\ sig_{DA_i}(Sid_i,\ M_i',\ Pid_i,\ DA_i,\ SC_{iaddr},\ DC_{addr},\ N_{iM_i})$

$2.6.i : DA_i \rightarrow DC : Sid_i,\ P_i$

$2.7.i : DC \Rightarrow C' : Sid_i, sig_{DC}(Sid_i,\ M_i',\ Pid_i,\ DA_i,\ DC_{addr})$

$2.8.i : DC \rightarrow C' : Sid_i,\ P_i$

$2.9.i : C' \rightarrow DC : Sid_i, sig_{C'}(Sid_i,\ M_i',\ Pid_i,\ DC_{addr},\ C',\ N_{iC})$

identifier) at the emailing address SC_{iaddr} of SC_i, from where P_i is taken by DA_i. P_i has two barcodes set by M_i: $h(N_{iM_i})$ to control the access of DA_i to SC_i, and $h(N_{iC})$ to control the access of C to DC. Upon receiving the product from M_i, SC_i confirms to him by a signed acknowledgment in the message 2.2.i. M_i sends to DA_i a delivery request message 2.3.i. N_{iM_i} has the same goal as N_{iC}, but in this case the password N_{iM_i} is shared only between M_i and DA_i. DA_i obtains M_{ipub}' and N_{iM_i}, and checks the signature of M_i. In the message 2.4.i, DA_i collects the product P_i from SC_i by proving he knows the password N_{iM_i}. To confirm the collection of P_i, DA_i sends to SC_i a signed acknowledgment in the message 2.5.i. In the message 2.6.i, DA_i posts P_i to DC. Upon receiving P_i from DA_i, DC confirms him in the message 2.7.i by a signed acknowledgment which DA_i forwards to M_i, and M_i to C. C collects P_i from DC using the password N_{iC} and checks if the collected product meets the specifications from Po_i. If C is satisfied, he sends to DC a signed acknowledgment in the message 2.9.i.

If all subtransactions from Ps successfully completed *Delivery*, then each subtransaction's flag from Ps is set to 2.

5.6 Payment Sub-protocol

If C collects all products involved in each subtransaction from Ps and is satisfied, then he sends the payment for each product to the suitable merchant. Below, we present the *Payment* sub-protocol for an arbitrary subtransaction s_i from Ps.

$3.1.i.\ C' \rightarrow M_i' : Sid_i,\ \{K_i\}_{M_{ipub}'},\ sig_{C'}(K_i),\ sig_{CB}(c_i)$

M_i obtains the key K_i, verifies $sig_{C'}(K_i)$, and recovers c_i by decrypting with K_i the encrypted coin received in the message 1.3.i. M_i verifies $sig_{CB}(c_i)$ and, if c_i is valid, he sends it to M_iB in the message 3.2.i for redemption.

$3.2.i : M_i \rightarrow M_iB : Sid_i,$
$\quad \{c_i,\ sig_{CB}(c_i),\ sig_{M_i}(c_i,\ sig_{CB}(c_i)),\ M_i,\ M_{iacct}\}_{M_iB_{pub}}$

M_iB checks M_i's signature, checks $sig_{CB}(c_i)$ and check the status of c_i. If all checks are satisfied, M_iB updates the global list of coins by setting the *spent* flag of c_i on 1, transfers the c_i's value from commit-buffer to the M_i's bank account with M_iB (M_{iacct}), and sends to M_i a signed acknowledgment of successfully redemption of c_i; otherwise, M_iB sends to M_i an error message.

3.3.i. $M_iB \rightarrow M_i$: $sig_{M_iB}(ack)$

If all subtransactions from Ps successfully completed *Payment*, then each subtransaction's flag from Ps is set to 3.

If in a subtransaction s_i from Ps, C does not send to M_i the decryption key K_i of the encrypted coin or sends to M_i in 3.1.i a wrong decryption key, then M_i sends to TTP all the messages received/sent from/to C in s_i. TTP checks the messages of s_i and if all checks are successfully, then sends to M_i the corresponding decryption key K_i that TTP knows from *Agreement* sub-protocol:

$TTP \rightarrow M_i'$: $Sid_i, \{K_i\}_{M'_{ipub}}, sig_{TTP}(K_i), sig_{CB}(c_i)$.

M_i decrypts c_i using K_i, checks $sig_{CB}(c_i)$ and continues the sub-protocol with the message 3.2.i.

5.7 The Complex Transaction Protocol

In this section, we present the protocol for complex transactions from Table 5 [4].

t is the root of the tree build from C's buying options. For any node p of the tree t, *Empty*($Ns(t)$) sets $Ns(p) = \lambda$. A **while** iteration corresponds to a protocol round that executes the three phases of the protocol. Ps - the sequence of subtransactions that have run *Agreement* is obtained at line 3. If all subtransactions from Ps successfully completed *Agreement*, then *Delivery* may take place to physically deliver the products involved in each subtransaction from Ps. The sequence of subtransactions that have run *Delivery* is stored in Ps at line 5. Further, if all subtransactions from Ps successfully completed *Delivery*, then *Payment* takes place and the sequence of subtransactions that solves the options of C is returned.

If after *Agreement*, Ps contains only aborted subtransactions, then Ps will be returned at line 12 as an evidence of the protocol's failure.

If after *Agreement* all subtransactions from Ps successfully completed *Agreement*, but some of these subtransactions did not successfully completed *Delivery* (e.g. some merchant doesn't post the product or posts a wrong product), is treated at line 9. In this case, *Aborting*() procedure is applied to abort all the substransactions from Ps that successfully completed *Agreement*. According to assumption 10 from Sect. 5.1, DC has a device that allows C to send to TTP the encrypted recording of the moment when C receives products that are not in conformity with the agreement established. The identifiers of these products are stored in the buffer *PidsAborted* used at line 10 to update the tree with the root t. *Update*(t) updates $Ns(p)$, for any node p of the tree, as follows:

- if $p \rightarrow info = Pid_i$, then we have the following cases:
  - if $Ns(p)$ has the flag on *abort*, then $Ns(p)$ remains unchanged;

Table 5. The complex transaction protocol.

```
Empty(Ns(t));
while (1)
        Ps = Agreement(t);
        if (s.fst = 1, for all s from Ps)
                Ps = Delivery(Ps);
                if (s.fst = 2, for all s from Ps)
                        Ps = Payment(Ps);
                        return Ps;
                else Aborting(s), for all s from Ps;
                        Update(t);
                end if
        else return Ps;
        end if
end while
```

    • if $Pid_i \in PidsAborted$, then $Ns(p) = (Sid_i, C', M_i', Pid_i, abort)$;
    • in all other cases $Ns(p) = \lambda$.
  - if $p \rightarrow info \neq Pid_i$, then $Ns(p) = \lambda$.

By *Update*(t), the states of the nodes corresponding to products from aborted subtransactions in the current protocol's round are mentained in the tree with the root t, so that these products are not taken into consideration in a new protocol's round.

In a new round, the protocol searches a new sequence of subtransactions that will successfully finish all three sub-protocols. The protocol terminates when encounters a round in which the protocol state Ps computed after that round contains a sequence of subtransactions that successfully finish all three sub-protocols, or when encounters a round in that Ps computed after *Agreement* has all subtransactions aborted. In the last case, the protocol can not solve the options of C.

6 Security Analysis

6.1 Fair Exchange

Our protocol assures fair exchange if after the protocol execution, either C gets the sequence of physical products corresponding to his buying options and each M_i gets the payment for the corresponding product, or none do. We remark that from the design of our protocol, after its execution, C can obtain either a sequence of products that solves his options, or nothing. Furthermore, after the protocol execution, C can 't obtain a partial sequence of products.

If C and each M_i behave honestly, the proposed protocol assures fair exchange. In what follows, we will consider all possible scenarios in which any M_i or C behave dishonest or prematurely aborts the protocol.

If C behaves dishonest, then the following scenarios are possible:

1. After *Delivery*, Ps is a sequence of subtransactions that successfully completed *Delivery* sub-protocol. So, C collected all products involved in any subtransaction from Ps and he is satisfied. However, in *Payment* sub-protocol, for a subtransaction s_i from Ps, C does not send to M_i the decryption key of the encrypted coin or sends to M_i a wrong decryption key. This scenario is solved as mentioned in *Payment* sub-protocol, TTP providing to M_i the corresponding decryption key.
2. C sends the same coin to TTP (in 1.1.i) in two different sessions of *Agreement* sub-protocol, to initiate two different subtransactions s_i, s_j with two distinct merchants, in the same round or in different rounds of the protocol. This scenario is solved because all banks and TTP maintain a global list of coin's serial already spent, validated but unspent, or canceled. On reception from C of the first request for coin validation, TTP adds the coin to the list, and any new validation request of the same coin from C is detected by TTP. Thus, TTP detects double spending from C and aborts the second subtransaction s_j by setting $s_j.fst = abort$.
3. In a subtransaction s_i from *Agreement* sub-protocol in some round of the protocol, C sends to M_i in the message 1.3.i, an encrypted coin already spent in a subtransaction from the same round or from a previous round of the protocol. If the coin wasn't used to buy from M_i, then M_i detects this by verifying TTP's signature S_{iTTP} that validated the encrypted coin. Otherwise, if the coin was already used to buy from M_i, then M_i can check this by verifying Sid_i and N_{iTTP}. So, M_i detects double spending from C, and sends to TTP the message 1.3.i he received from C in s_i. TTP checks the message 1.3.i, obtains the coin, checks the coin in the global list of coin's serial, and aborts s_i by setting $s_i.fst = abort$.
4. In a subtransaction s_i from *Agreement* sub-protocol, C sends to M_i in the message 1.3.i, an encrypted coin of insufficient value. In this scenario, M_i checks if the value from Po_i corresponds with the encrypted coin's value validated by TTP. If these values are not equal, then M_i sends to TTP the message 1.3.i he received from C in s_i. TTP checks the message 1.3.i, sends to C a cancellation request of the coin as in the message 1.6$'$.i from Table 3 to allow C to cancel his coin, and aborts s_i by setting $s_i.fst = abort$.
5. In a subtransaction s_i from *Agreement* sub-protocol in some round of the protocol, C sends to M_i in the message 1.3.i, an encrypted coin that has already been canceled in an aborted subtransaction s_j during the procedure *Aborting*(s_j) in the same round or in a previous round of the protocol. C's intention is to buy a product without paying for it. M_i checks if T_{iTTP} and L_i are recently enough. In this scenario, these values are not recently enough,

and M_i detects the dishonest behavior of C. Like in the scenario 3, M_i sends to TTP the message 1.3.i he received from C in s_i. TTP checks the message 1.3.i, obtains the coin, checks the coin in the global list of coin's serial, and aborts s_i by setting $s_i.fst = abort$.

6. In *Agreement* sub-protocol, C sends to CB 1.7$'$.i many times for multiple redemption of the same canceled coin. This scenario is solved because CB checks if the coin received in a cancellation request has already been canceled.

If M_i behaves dishonest, then the following scenarios are possible:

1. In a subtransaction s_i from *Agreement* sub-protocol, M_i receives from C a correct message 1.3.i, but he sends to C an abort message 1.4$'$.i or doesn't continue the sub-protocol. Such behavior brings no benefit to M_i because he is in possession of an encrypted coin with a key that does not know, so he can't get the payment. But C has bought a coin which can not be used by him. In both scenarios, C applies *Aborting*(s_i) to cancel and to redeem the coin, and to abort s_i. If the aborted s_i is a component of an aggregate transaction, then all other subtransactions from the aggregate that successfully completed *Agreement* sub-protocol will be aborted by *AggAbort* procedure and by setting their flags on *abort*.
2. $Ps = s_1 \ldots s_k$ is a sequence of subtransactions that successfully completed *Agreement* sub-protocol. In s_i from Ps, M_i sent 1.4.i to C, but in *Delivery* sub-protocol he doesn't post the product or posts a product that doesn't comply with the specifications from Po_i. M_i does not have any benefit from this behavior, but can prejudice the other honest merchants involved in $s_1 \ldots s_k$. In s_i, C pushes the button of the DC's device that allows sending to TTP the recording of the moment when C unwraps the packed product, proving to TTP that the product is wrong. Because the product from s_i is not complying with the specifications from Po_i, the rest of the products involved in the sequence $s_1 \ldots s_k$ can't solve the customer's options. So, C sends to TTP all the messages received/sent from/to each M_j, where $1 \leq j \leq k$. TTP checks the information received from C, applies *Aborting*(s_j), where $1 \leq j \leq k$ and triggers an off-line procedure sending to M_i the proof of his dishonest behavior. Also, TTP requests from M_i the payment for the transportation services of products provided by the honest merchants to DC and back. After TTP receives the payment, he returns the transportation costs to each honest merchant from $s_1 \ldots s_k$.
3. In *Payment* sub-protocol, M_i sends many times the same 3.2.i for multiple redemption of the same coin. This scenario is solved by M_iB checking if the coin received in 3.2.i has already been spent by checking the value of the *spent* flag of the coin.

Each party involved in protocol must keep a record of every message sent or received including signed acknowledgments of DC, DA_i and SC_i, where $1 \leq i \leq n$. DC, DA_i, SC_i, have no interest not to follow the protocol steps, because their interest is to get profit from fees for such services provided in e-commerce transactions. However, if one of the parties mentioned above behaves dishonest, the other parties send the records to TTP to trigger off-line mechanisms to ensure fairness.

6.2 Anonymity

Our protocol ensures customer's anonymity if no party and no coalition between parties can make a link between the true identity of the customer, C, and the pseudo identity of the customer, C', which he uses in protocol.

In our protocol, we use an electronic cash payment based on group blind digital signatures on behalf of the banks. The only steps from our protocol in that the customer uses his true identity are GBDS protocol's steps and in the message $1.7'.i$ in that the customer cancel his coin, because CB must know C_{acct} to charge it with the coin's value or to redeem the coin's value. In GBDS protocol, CB knows only that C bought a coin with a certain value, but it doesn't know the serial of the coin. Following, CB can't associate C with the coin bought by him, maintaining thus the anonymity of the customer. Also, in the message $1.7'.i$, the customer reveals his true identity only to CB, but this does not destroy the customer's anonymity because the coin will be canceled and not used anymore. Another feature of GBDS protocol is the anonymity of CB: any party can check if $sig_{CB}(c_i)$ is valid, without knowing who is the bank that signed the coin c_i. CB is not known by any other party (except C), so, CB can't participate in no coalition with any other party to destroy the customer's anonymity. To ensure customer's anonymity when C collects the physical products, our protocol doesn't use the customer's correspondence address but uses a destination cabinet where the product is placed.

We show in Table 6, the information that each party from protocol knows after protocol execution. The information have the following meaning. For example, we consider the first row: y under the column C and CB means that C and CB know C - the true identity of the customer; n under the column M_i, M_j with $j \neq i$, M_iB, M_jB with $j \neq i$, DA_i, SC_i and DC means that the true identity of the customer is not known to M_i, M_j with $j \neq i$, M_iB, M_jB with $j \neq i$, DA_i, SC_i and DC. $C\&s_i$ means that C performs the subtransaction s_i. The meaning is extended for $C'\&s_i$, $M_i\&s_i$, $M_i'\&s_i$.

From Table 6, we observe that no party alone has sufficient information to link the true identity of the customer, C, with the pseudo identity C'. Only C can disclose this information if he wants.

We analyze the coalition of the maximum size that can be formed by parties involved in protocol to try to destroy customer's anonymity. The coalition of the maximum size consists of the following parts: $M_1, \ldots, M_n, M_1B, \ldots, M_nB$, $DA_1, \ldots, DA_n, SC_1, \ldots, SC_n$, and DC. For any $1 \leq i \leq n$, DA_i has information only about entities M_i', SC_i and DC, and no information about C. For any $1 \leq i \leq n$, SC_i and M_iB have no information about C. DC has the information $C'\&s_1, \ldots, C'\&s_n$, but no information about C. For any $1 \leq i \leq n$, M_i has the information $C'\&s_i$. So, the only information related to customer obtained by the coalition of the maximum size is $C'\&s_1, \ldots, C'\&s_n$, but no information about the customer's true identity. Thus, customer's anonymity is preserved.

Table 6. Informations that each party knows after protocol execution.

Info	Entity								
	C	M_i	M_j $j \neq i$	CB	M_iB	M_jB $j \neq i$	DA_i	SC_i	DC
C	y	n	n	y	n	n	n	n	n
M_i	n	y	n	n	y	n	n	n	n
$M_j, j \neq i$	n	n	y	n	n	y	n	n	n
CB	y	n	n	y	n	n	n	n	n
M_iB	n	y	n	n	y	n	n	n	n
$M_jB, j \neq i$	n	n	y	n	n	y	n	n	n
DA_i	n	y	n	n	n	n	y	y	y
SC_i	n	y	n	n	n	n	y	y	n
DC	y	y	y	n	n	n	y	y	y
C'	y	y	y	n	n	n	n	n	y
c_i	y	y	n	n	y	n	n	n	n
$c_j, j \neq i$	y	n	y	n	n	y	n	n	n
$C\&\ s_i$	y	n	n	n	n	n	n	n	n
$C'\&\ s_i$	y	y	n	n	n	n	n	n	y
M_i'	y	y	n	n	n	n	y	y	y
$M_j', j \neq i$	y	n	y	n	n	n	n	n	n
$M_i\&s_i$	n	y	n	n	n	n	n	n	n
$M_i'\&s_i$	y	y	n	n	n	n	n	n	y
$M_j\&s_j, j \neq i$	n	n	y	n	n	n	n	n	n

A merchant M_i uses his true identity only in communication with M_iB in the coin redemption from *Payment* sub-protocol. M_iB knows personal information about M_i (such as M_{iacct}), but it doesn' t know information about the pseudo identity M_i'. Moreover, M_iB is not known to any other party (except M_i), and can't participate in coalitions to destroy the anonymity of M_i. Our protocol doesn't use the correspondence address of the merchant M_i, but uses a source cabinet SC_i where the product is placed by M_i. Is easy to see from the Table 6 that no party alone has sufficient information to link the true identity of the merchant, M_i, with the pseudo identity M_i', where $1 \leq i \leq n$.

The coalition of the maximum size that can be formed by parties involved in protocol to try to destroy the anonymity of the merchant M_i consists of the following parts: C, CB, $M_1, \ldots, M_{i-1}, M_{i+1}, \ldots, M_n, M_1B, \ldots, M_{i-1}B$, $M_{i+1}B, \ldots, M_nB, DA_1, \ldots, DA_n, SC_1, \ldots, SC_n$, and DC. C and DC have the information $M_i'\&s_i$, for any $1 \leq i \leq n$, but no information about M_i. CB has no information about any merchant M_i, where $1 \leq i \leq n$. For any $1 \leq i \leq n$, DA_i and SC_i have information only about M_i', and no information about M_i. For any $1 \leq j \leq n$ with $j \neq i$, M_j has the information $M_j\&s_j$, and no information about M_i. For any $1 \leq j \leq n$ with $j \neq i$, M_jB has information only about the entity M_j, and no information about M_i. Thus, the only information related to the merchant M_i obtained by the coalition of the maximum size is $M_i'\&s_i$, and the anonymity of the merchant M_i is preserved.

7 Conclusions

We extend the solution from [4] obtaining both anonymity of customer and each merchant, while preserving all properties obtained in [4].

The customer's and merchant's anonymity in complex transactions for physical products delivery is not easy to obtain. For anonymity, the challenge in our protocol was to guarantee this requirement in agreement, payment and delivery of physical products. We extend the protocol proposed in [4] to provide also the anonymity of each merchant involved. For this, in each subtransaction we introduced a source cabinet where the physical product is placed by merchant. A delivery agent can take the product from the source cabinet only by knowing a password that is set by merchant for that product. The source cabinet is used to replace the correspondence's address of the merchant, so, his true identity remains hidden in delivery phase. In agreement and payment we use a pseudo identity for each merchant to conceal his true identity.

References

1. Alaraj, A.: Fairness in physical products delivery protocol. Int. J. Comput. Netw. Commun. (IJCNC) **4**(6), 99 (2012)
2. Androulaki, E., Bellovin, S.: APOD: anonymous physical object delivery. In: Goldberg, I., Atallah, M.J. (eds.) PETS 2009. LNCS, vol. 5672, pp. 202–215. Springer, Heidelberg (2009). https://doi.org/10.1007/978-3-642-03168-7_12
3. Bîrjoveanu, C.V.: Anonymity and fair-exchange in e-commerce protocol for physical products delivery. In: 12th International Conference on Security and Cryptography, pp. 170–177. SCITEPRESS (2015). https://doi.org/10.5220/0005508801700177
4. Bîrjoveanu, C.V., Bîrjoveanu, M.: Preserving anonymity in fair exchange complex transactions e-commerce protocol for B2C/B2B applications. In: 15th International Joint Conference on e-Business and Telecommunications, ICETE 2018, vol. 1, pp. 99–110. SCITEPRESS (2018). https://doi.org/10.5220/0006850802650276
5. Camenisch, J., Stadler, M.: Efficient group signature schemes for large groups. In: Kaliski, B.S. (ed.) CRYPTO 1997. LNCS, vol. 1294, pp. 410–424. Springer, Heidelberg (1997). https://doi.org/10.1007/BFb0052252
6. Chaum, D., Fiat, A., Naor, M.: Untraceable electronic cash. In: Goldwasser, S. (ed.) CRYPTO 1988. LNCS, vol. 403, pp. 319–327. Springer, New York (1990). https://doi.org/10.1007/0-387-34799-2_25
7. Djuric, Z., Gasevic, D.: FEIPS: a secure fair-exchange payment system for internet transactions. Comput. J. **58**(10), 2537–2556 (2015)
8. Draper-Gil, G., Ferrer-Gomila, J.L., Hinarejos, M.F., Zhou, J.: An asynchronous optimistic protocol for atomic multi-two-party contract signing. Comput. J. **56**(10), 1258–1267 (2013)

9. Li, H., Kou, W., Du, X.: Fair e-commerce protocols without a third party. In: 11th IEEE Symposium on Computers and Communications. IEEE (2006). https://doi.org/10.1109/ISCC.2006.74
10. Liu, Y.: An optimistic fair protocol for aggregate exchange. In: 2nd International Conference on Future Information Technology and Management Engineering. IEEE (2009). https://doi.org/10.1109/FITME.2009.145
11. Lysyanskaya, A., Ramzan, Z.: Group blind digital signatures: a scalable solution to electronic cash. In: Hirchfeld, R. (ed.) FC 1998. LNCS, vol. 1465, pp. 184–197. Springer, Heidelberg (1998). https://doi.org/10.1007/BFb0055483
12. Lysyanskaya, A., Rivest, R.L., Sahai, A., Wolf, S.: Pseudonym systems. In: Heys, H., Adams, C. (eds.) SAC 1999. LNCS, vol. 1758, pp. 184–199. Springer, Heidelberg (2000). https://doi.org/10.1007/3-540-46513-8_14
13. Onieva, J.A., Lopez, J., Zhou, J.: Secure Multi-Party Non-Repudiation Protocols and Applications. Springer, Heidelberg (2009). https://doi.org/10.1007/978-0-387-75630-1
14. Zhang, Q., Markantonakis, K., Mayes, K.: A practical fair exchange e-payment protocol for anonymous purchase and physical delivery. In: 4th ACS/IEEE International Conference on Computer Systems and Applications. IEEE (2006). https://doi.org/10.1109/AICCSA.2006.205188

Generation of High Quality Microwave Signal Using Different Optoelectronic Techniques

Mohamed Mousa[1(✉)], Abdelrahman E. Afifi[2], Mohamed Abouelatta[2], and Kamel M. Hassan[1]

[1] Faculty of Engineering and Technology, Future University, N 90th Street, Cairo, Egypt
Mohamed.Mossa@fue.edu.eg
[2] Faculty of Engineering, Ain Shams University, Cairo, Egypt

Abstract. Generation of a high quality microwave signal based on optical electronic components using oscillation or using filtration have been investigated and implemented experimentally. The experimental results of signal generation using optoelectronic oscillator (OEO) are taken for three different long delay optical fiber lengths. The generated signal has a narrow bandwidth (less than 200 Hz) at carrier frequency of 2.31 GHz with phase noise less than −80 dBc/Hz at 1 kHz offset. Second proposed scheme to improve the quality of an RF signal is presented (optoelectronic Brillouin filter). The 6 dB linewidth of the filter output is reduced to sub hertz and the low frequency noise below 1 kHz is reduced about 10 dB. The scheme consists of a Brillouin-semiconductor optical amplifier (SOA), ring laser fitted with an RF intensity modulator and an APD detector. The optical loop acts as a cavity filter to the RF signal. A jitter in the cavity resonances due to temperature variations is completely eliminated from the output beat signal. There is a 10 dB increase in the phase noise at the FSR frequency and its harmonics. The setup is tested with signals generated by two different microwave sources and at frequencies up to 10 GHz, the limit of the used APD. Sources with RF linewidth less than the optical FSR produces one output mode with sub-hertz line width. For larger line width signals more than one RF frequency is produced, separated by the FSR, each showing the Brillouin linewidth proposed models for both systems are given.

Keywords: High quality microwave signal · Optoelectronic oscillator (OEO) · Microwave photonic signal generation · Brillouin ring laser · Fiber delay line

1 Introduction

A high-quality microwave signal has a lot of applications in our life nowadays. There are different techniques to get it. Some of these techniques are generation or filtration based on optical components and phenomenon

Optoelectronic oscillator (OEO) is one of these techniques; it is a type of oscillators that uses optical signals to benefit from the high performance of optical components and very low loss and weight of optical fiber compared to coaxial cables. It can generate microwave frequencies with the ability of frequency tuning.

M. S. Obaidat (Ed.): ICETE 2018, CCIS 1118, pp. 46–65, 2019.
https://doi.org/10.1007/978-3-030-34866-3_3

The first technique used in this field is based on the use of long fiber delay line to stabilize the microwave oscillator [1], This system suffers from a contradiction between narrow linewidth, which requires long fiber, and selectivity for single mode operation that needs shorter fiber.

Another technique can be used is replacing the long fiber delay line by a short fiber ring resonator (FRR), which provides high quality factor and high stability compared to the generated signal using the first technique. This system suffers from synchronization of the laser source frequency and of the resonance frequency of the ring which is subject to temperature variations and requires strict control on the ring temperature [2–4].

The third technique is based on Brillouin selective side band amplification has been introduced recently. Brillouin oscillator doesn't need narrow band pass microwave filter neither microwave amplifier. On the other hand this oscillator requires a laser source with a very narrow spectral width, high output power as well as it requires long fiber length [5–7].

Each technique has its unique features. The recent researches in this field show a phase noise aslow as −92.69 dBc/Hz at 10 kHz offset frequency from the oscillation frequency (2.26 GHz) carrier using optical delay line of 25.24 km and Q factor of 2.04×10^9 [8], there is other technique generates two tone signals in a range from 4 GHz to 12 GHz with phase noise about −105 dBc/Hz at 10 kHz offset frequency from the oscillation frequency (9.95 GHz and 10.66 GHz) [9].

In this work we get better phase noise −104 dBc/Hz at 10 kHz offset frequency from the oscillation frequency (2.31 GHz) carrier using shorter optical delay line of 6.6 km and a lower Q factor of 0.019×10^9 using generation technique.

Using filteration technique based on Brillouin phenomena, we get higher Q factor up to about $10 \times 10^9$and the phase noise of the output from 10 to 600 Hz offset frequency shows an average improvement of 15 dB for the output over the input. The improvement degrades to 5 dB for frequencies up to 1 kHz. From 1 kHz to 10 kHz offset frequency the improvement degrades. This filteration technique shows almost the same output performance parameters with different input resources at different frequencies up to several GHz.

In this chapter, microwave oscillator based on the first technique and a microwave filter based on Brillouin phenomenahave been analysed and implemented. The rest of this chapter is organized as follows: opto electronioc oscillator (OEO) experimental results is presented in Sect. 2; length effect on (OEO) stability and critical fiber length have been investigated in Sect. 3. Optoelectronic Brillouin filter experimental results is given in Sect. 4; discussion and theoretical considerations of optoelectronic Brillouin filter are given in Sect. 5 and finally, the conclusion is presented in Sect. 6.

2 Optoelectronic Oscillator (OEO) - Experimental Results

The Optoelectronic oscillator (OEO) structure is shown in Fig. 1 [10]. Electrical signal which is driven from the microwave filter is applied to Mech-Zender modulator. At the beginning this signal is coming from noise, the loop gain is changing till the oscillation is sustained; in this case input to the Mech-Zender modulator will be the microwave signal.

The used laser source (Agilent 81940A), the modulator is Mach-Zander modulator (JDSU: 2.5 Gb/s Bias-Free Modulator with Integral Attenuator), the detector is avalanche photodiode (OF3240 N-MS-YT) with gain about 24 dB, the filter is cavity band pass filter (DSC-2310B-10M01) with 3 dB bandwidth 10 MHz and the results are taken using RF spectrum analyser up to 3 GHz (R&S FSP 9 k-3G). Optoelectronic oscillator has been implemented using different fiber delay lengths (2.1 km, 4.2 km and 6.6 km respectively).

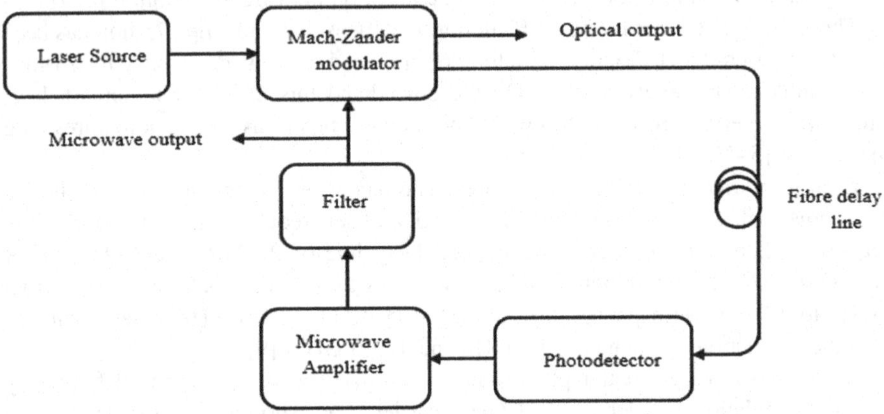

Fig. 1. Optoelectronic oscillator (OEO) structure.

The experimental results agree with the expected ones for the main parameters. First parameter is the frequency spectral range (FSR), (Eq. (1)). Second parameter is the three dB bandwidth (Δf), (Eq. (2)). Third one is the oscillation frequency phase noise (L_{Osc}(fm)), (Eq. (3)) [11–13].

$$FSR = 1/\tau \tag{1}$$

$$\Delta f = \rho_{N}.G_A^2/\left(2\pi\tau^2 p_{Osc}\right) \tag{2}$$

$$L_{Osc}(f_m) = \left(f/\left(2^{1.5}.Q.f_m\right)\right)^2.(\Delta\varnothing_A)^2 \tag{3}$$

Where (τ) is the fiber delay line length, (ρ_N) the equivalent input noise density injected into the oscillator, (G_A) the amplifier gain, (P_{Osc}) the oscillation power, (Q) the quality factor, (f) the oscillation frequency, (f_m) a certain frequency offset and($\Delta\varnothing_A$) the spectral density of the amplifier phase fluctuations.

The output spectrum contains several modes. The number of these modes depends on the free spectral range value (FSR) and the filter bandwidth. Recall that (FSR) is proportional to the inverse of the fiber delay line length (L).

The output microwave signal using 2.1 km fiber delay line with span 300 kHz is shown in Fig. 2, where Fig. 3 shows the oscillation mode with span 20 kHz [10].

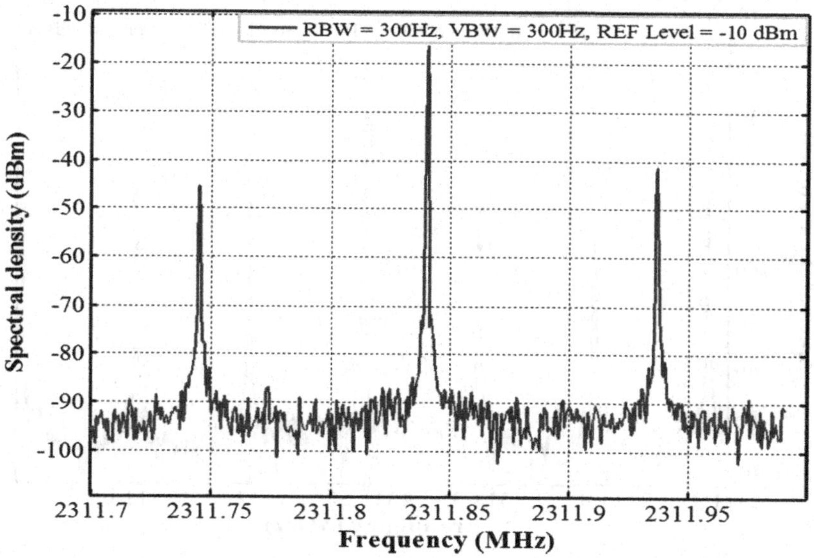

Fig. 2. OEO output signal using 2.1 km fiber delay line (Span 300 kHz).

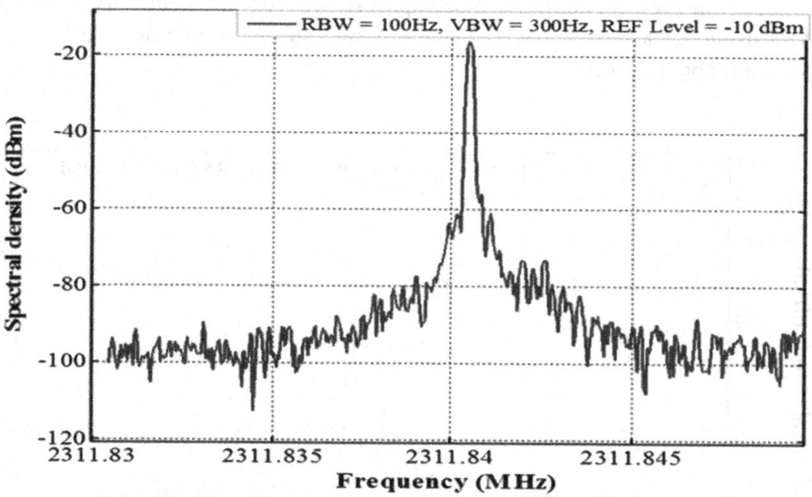

Fig. 3. OEO output oscillation mode using 2.1 km fiber delay line (Span 20 kHz).

Using fiber length of 4.2 km, the output spectrum is shown in Figs. 4 and 5. For optical fiber length of 6.6 km, the output spectrum is illustrated in Fig. 6 [10].

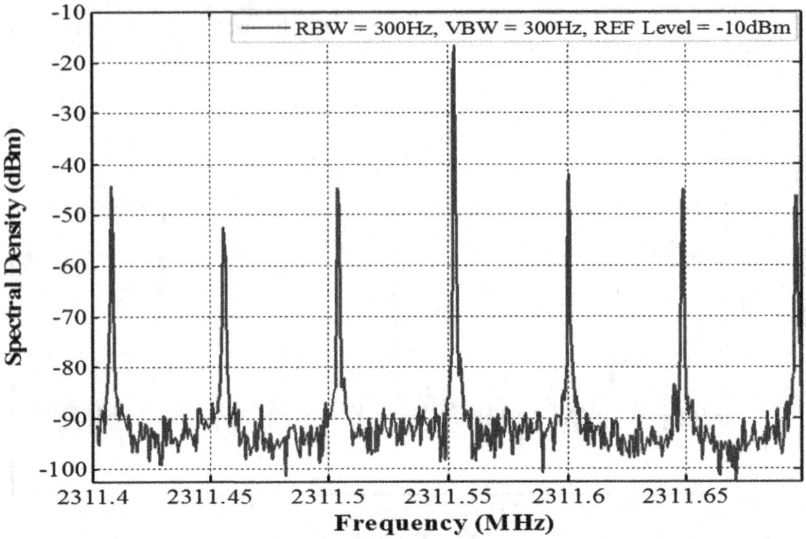

Fig. 4. OEO output signal using 4.2 km fiber delay line (Span 300 kHz).

As shown in Figs. 2 and 4, the mode spacing between the modes decreases from 95.2 kHz using 2.1 km to 47.6 kHz using 4.2 km and the oscillation side band suppression ratio about 25 dB.

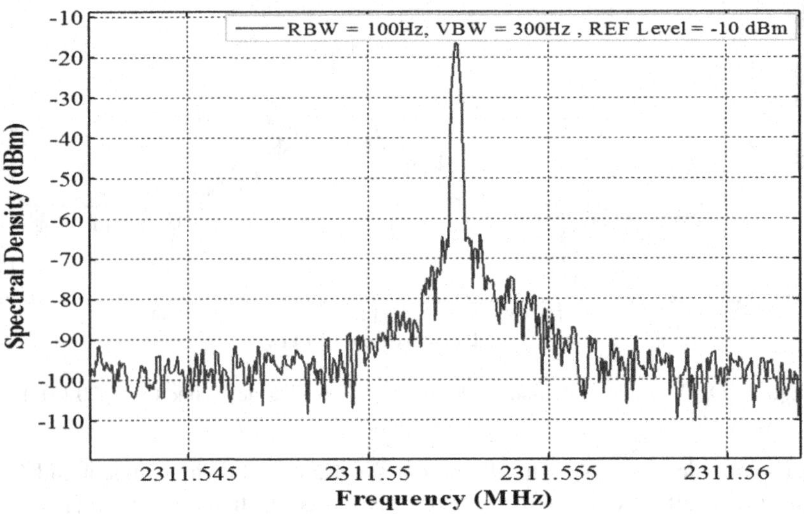

Fig. 5. OEO output oscillation mode using 4.2 km fiber delay line (Span 20 kHz).

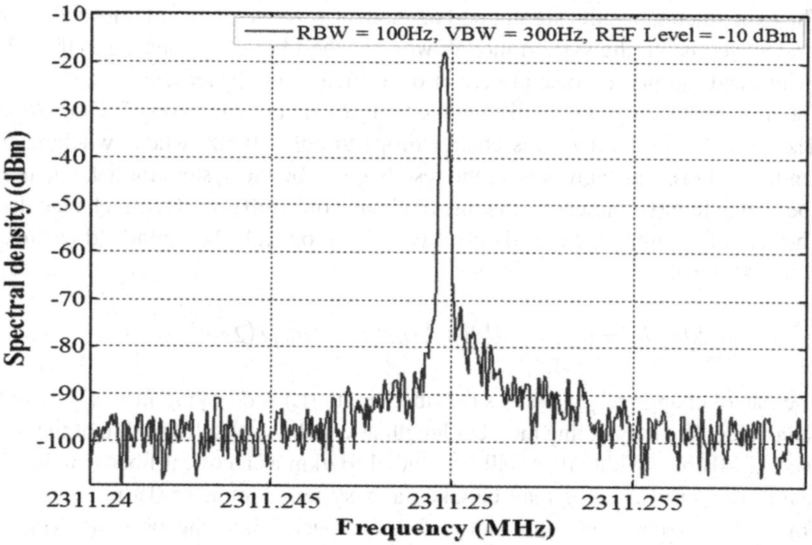

Fig. 6. OEO output oscillation mode using 6.6 km fiber delay line (Span 20 kHz).

The oscillation frequency using different lengths is changed by a small amount as a result of the bandwidth of the used filter and as it must be a multiple of the (FSR).

3 Length Effect on (OEO) Stability and Critical Fiber Length

Tables 1 and 2 show the main parameters and performance parameters, respectively of the optoelectronic oscillators using different optical fiber lengths [10].

Table 1. Oscillator parameters using three different fiber delay lines.

Fiber delay line (km)	Oscillation frequency (MHz)	Output power (dBm)	FSR (KHz)
2.1	2311.8405	−16.4	95.2
4.2	2311.5524	−16.4	47.6
6.6	2311.2498	−17.86	30.3

Table 2. Oscillator performance parameters using three different fiber delay lines.

Fiber delay line (km)	Measured Δf (3 dB) (Hz)	Phasenoise [L_{Osc}(1 kHz)] (dBC/Hz)	Phasenoise [L_{Osc}(10 kHz)] (dBC/Hz)
2.1	150	−80	−100
4.2	130	−82	−101.5
6.6	120	−84	−104

The experimental results are in good agreement with the expected ones which have been calculated using the system model; whereas the fiber length increases the −3 dB bandwidth and the phase noise at certain offset frequency decreases.

The measured change in −3 dB bandwidth is 20 Hz (150 Hz using 2.1 km drops to 130 Hz using 4.2 km) where this change drops to only 10 Hz (when switching from 4.2 km to 6.6 km). This agrees with the results given by the system model, whereas as the fiber delay line (L) increases, the rate of change of −3 dB bandwidth change decay.

The rate of change of the 3-dB bandwidth with optical fiber length (d (Δf)/dL) is given by (4), [10].

$$d(\Delta f)/dL = (G_A)^2.c^2\{[d(\rho_N)/dL]\,L - 2\rho_N\}/\left(2\pi.n^2.p_{Osc}.L^3\right) \tag{4}$$

The rate of change of (Δf) versus the fiber length (L) is decaying fast as (L) exceeds a certain value. We may define the fiber length at which the absolute value of the rate of change of 3-dB bandwidth |d (Δf)/dL| reaches 1 Hz/km as a critical fiber length of this oscillator. This critical value may be taken as a system parameter (L_C).

For a given equivalent input noise density injected into the oscillator (ρ_N), the oscillation power (P_{Osc}), the amplifier gain (G_A) and the refractive index of the used fiber “n”. There will be a specific value for (L_C). The designer of this oscillator will choose the delay fiber line length based on this value where longer length will add costs without considerable gain in reducing the 3-dB bandwidth (Δf).

4 Optoelectronic Brillouin Filter Experimental Results

The Optoelectronic Brillouin filter structure is shown in Fig. 7. A c-band tunable laser source (Agilent 81940A) with variable output power from 4 to 20 mW and linewidth of 100 kHz is used. The output is fiber coupled to a (2 × 2) 50/50 optical fiber directional coupler. The output of the coupler is connected to 6.6 km SM fiber where the Brillouin signal is being generated which propagates back to the coupler.

The output of the backward Brillouin beam from the coupler is fed to a semiconductor optical amplifier (SOA) (AlphionSAC20r) with facet reflectivity 10^{-4}. The output of the SOA feeds a fiber polarization controller (PC) which is connected to the input of the optical intensity modulator (JDSU Hermetic 10 Gb/s with integrated attenuator modulator) with about 9 dB insertion losses.

The modulator output is connected to a (2 × 2) 90/10 optical fiber directional coupler. The10% output either goes to the avalanche photo detector (APD) (AT-10SFA-DC) with 8.5 GHz typical bandwidth and conversion gain 1240 V/W, or goes to an optical spectrum analyzer (OSA) (Agilent 86143B).

The output of the APD is connected to the RF spectrum analyzer (43 GHz Anritsu MS2830A). The 90% output of the directional coupler is fed through 40 dB fiber isolator to the other end of the 6.6 km fiber. The total losses inside the loop is 18.1 dB (9 dB insertion loss of modulator, 1.3 dB fiber loss, 3.8 dB couplers loss, 0.5 dB isolator loss and 3.5 dB connectors loss (10 × 0.35 dB)). The SOA gain at driving current of 180 mA is 15 dB.

The output of the pump laser, set at 1549.93 nm wavelength and 11 mW, is injected into the single mode optical fiber to generate a backward Brillouin beam in the anticlockwise direction.

The additional gain needed for oscillation in the anticlockwise direction over that produced by the SOA occurs in a small Spectral width of about 20 MHz of the Brillouin gain in the fiber. The gain produced by the SOA is just less than the threshold gain for oscillation in the loop, and the addition of the Brillouin gain allows oscillations at the stokes shifted wavelength only.

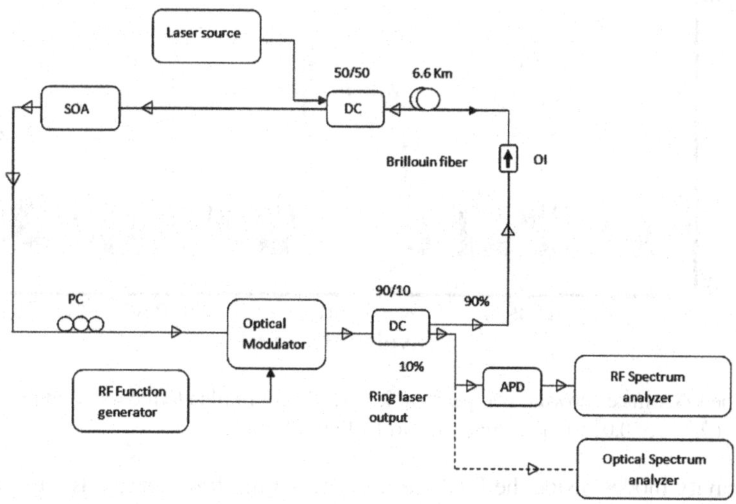

Fig. 7. Experimental setup for producing a high quality RF signal. (SOA: semiconductor optical amplifier; DC: fiber directional coupler; PC: fiber polarization controller; APD: avalanche photo detector, and OI: optical isolator).

The OSA trace of the output is shown in Fig. 8. It shows two peaks. The first peak in the trace is at 1549.93 nm which is identified as the reflected laser signal from the 50/50 coupler. The second peak is at 1550.018 nm with a shift of 0.088 nm corresponding to frequency shift of 10.87 GHz typical of Brillouin shift in the fiber [14]. Hence this peak is identified as the Brillouin beam. The Brillouin beam is seen to be 8 dB higher than that of the reflected laser signal.

The output of the RF spectrum analyzer with the RF signal generator switched off is shown in Fig. 9. The peak of the signal is at 10.87 GHz which is the result of the beating the Brillouin with reflected laser source signals.

The smearing of the trace seen in the figure is a result of the narrow cavity resonances, which jitters due to temperature variations. When the resolution bandwidth (RBW) of the spectrum analyzer is increased to 1 MHz the envelope of this trace is produced and its linewidth is measured to be 18.14 MHz indicating the linewidth of the Brillouin beam.

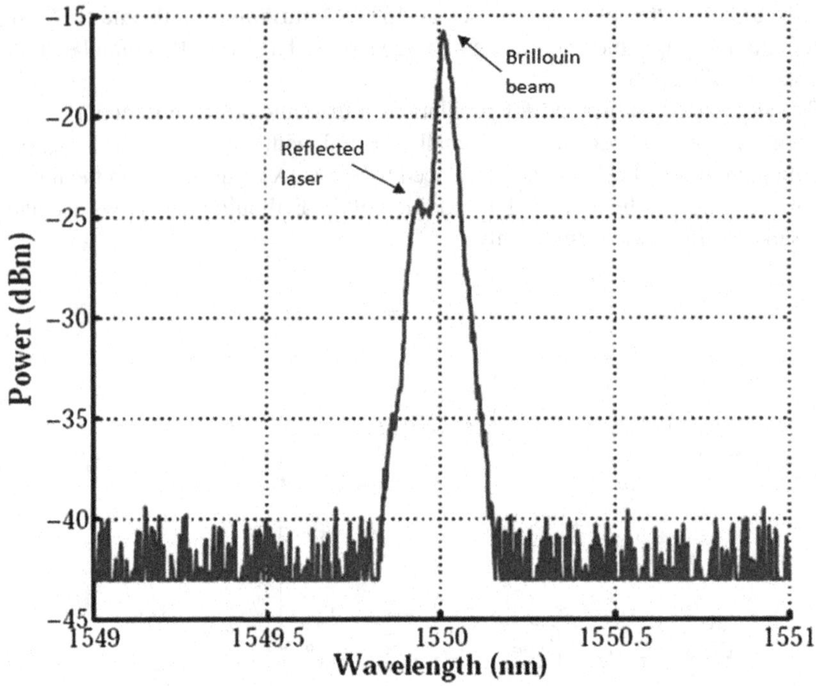

Fig. 8. The OSA trace showing two peaks at λ = 1549.93 nm (due to the reflected pump laser) and peak at λ = 1550.018 nm (corresponds to Brillouin beam).

The cavity modes inside the Brillouin beam can't be shown easily as a result of its instability with temperature variations, but their beating with each other is stable at the cavity free spectral range (FSR) and its harmonics. Figure 10 shows the beating between the cavity modes separated by 30.57 kHz, which defines the FSR of the setup loop.

The span of the RF spectrum analyzer trace showing output detected modes is reduced to 300 Hz enlarging the signal of the tens beat of the cavity modes at 305.588 kHz is shown in Fig. 11. The scanning parameters are such that RBW is reduced to 1 Hz and the video bandwidth (VBW) is set also at 1 Hz. The 6 dB linewidth is measured to be 780 MHz. The 3 dB and 10 dB linewidths are also measured giving 570 MHz and 990 MHz, respectively.

The previous result shows how the generated cavity modes are very narrow. This is used to filter a microwave signal as we shall see in the following. When the micro-wave generator is switched on the RF signal modulates the propagating Brillouin beam. It generates side modes separated from Brillouin beam by the modulation frequency.

Since the RF frequency is greater than Brillouin gain linewidth the modulation side modes will propagate but not oscillate inside the loop. It experiences the SOA gain only, which is less than the threshold gain.

The generated modulation side modes will be with the same line width of the generated Brillouin beam. They contain many cavity modes; these cavity modes beat at the detector to produce the RF signal. Figure 12 shows the spectrum analyzer trace when the RF generator is switched on and adjusted to 1 GHz.

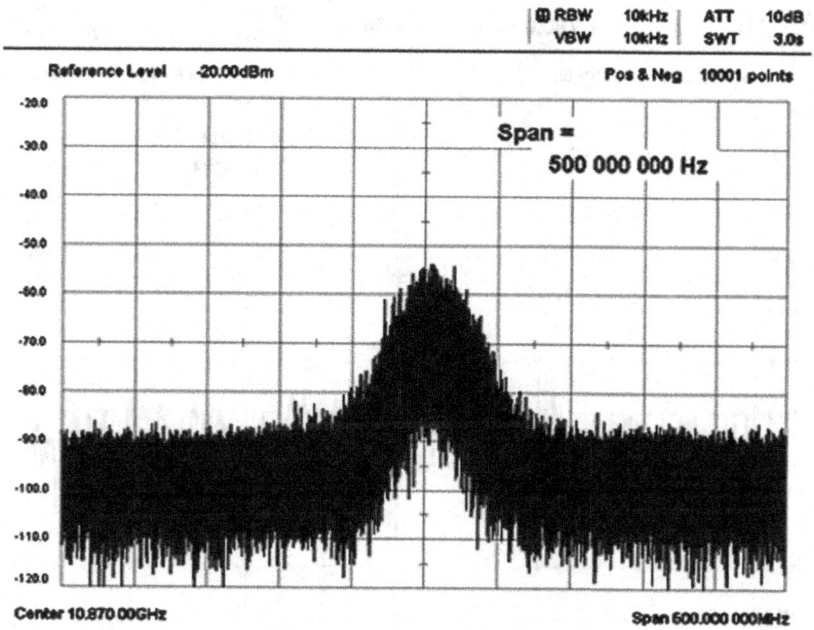

Fig. 9. The RF spectrum analyzer trace showing beating between the reflected pump laser and generated Brillouin beam with RF signal generator switched off.

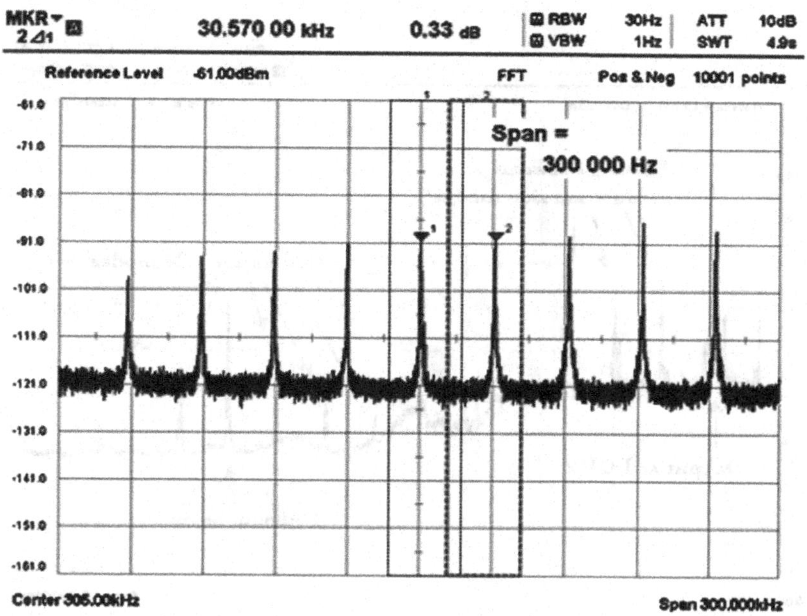

Fig. 10. The RF spectrum analyzer trace showing output detected modes at the harmonics of FSR of setup loop.

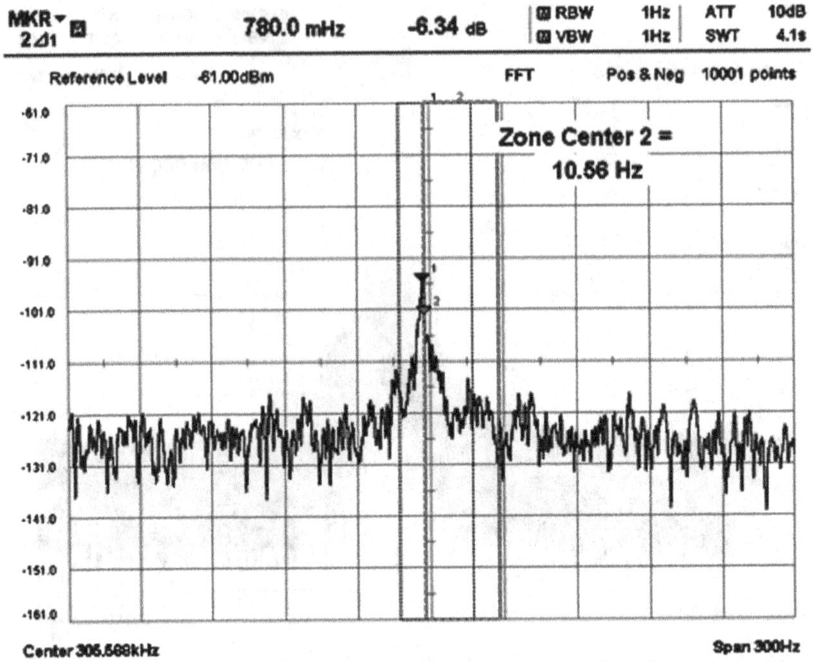

Fig. 11. The RF spectrum analyzer trace showing the tens beat of the cavity mode at 305.588 kHz and its 6 dB linewidth.

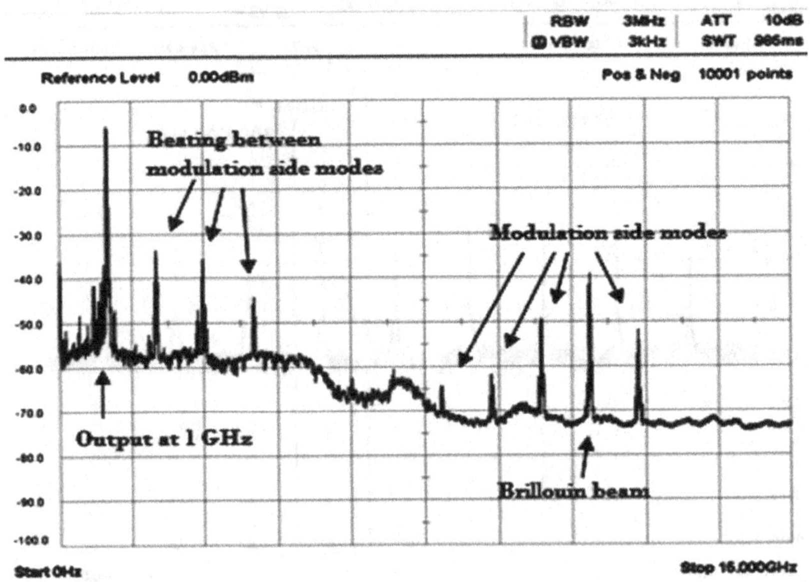

Fig. 12. The RF spectrum analyzer trace showing output signal with span15 GHz.

The output signal doesn't show the right hand side of the Brillouin modulation side modes as a result of the limited detector bandwidth (8.5 GHz). Focusing on the low frequency part of the spectrum, Fig. 13 shows the output at center frequency 1 GHz and span 500 KH.

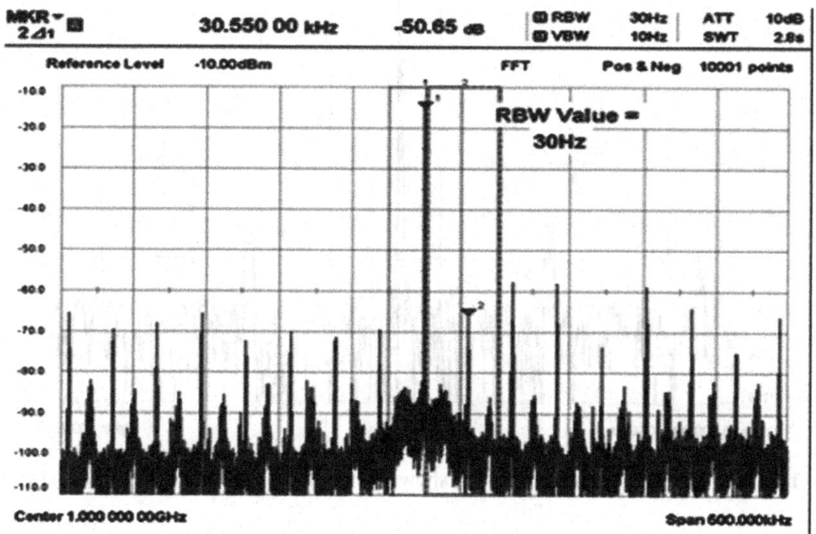

Fig. 13. The RF spectrum analyzer trace showing output at 1 GHz surrounded by cavity modes.

It shows a signal at the input RF frequency with small side modes separated by the FSR of the cavity. The difference between the intensity of the output modulation frequency and that of the surrounding cavity modes are more than 45 dB.

An expansion of Fig. 13 around the signal frequency is shown in Fig. 14. The 6 dB linewidth is shown to be 660 MHz while that at 3 dB, 10 dB and 20 dB are measured to be 480 MHz, 840 MHz and 1.17 Hz, respectively.

Figure 15 shows the spectrum of the input RF signal with a half 6 dB linewidth of 720 MHz. The half BW at 3 dB, 10 dB and 20 dB have been measured giving 510 MHz, 900 MHz and 1.26 Hz, respectively.

The phase noise of the input and output at 1 GHz are shown in Figs. 16 and 17, respectively. The phase noise from 10 to 600 Hz shows an average improvement of 15 dB for the output over the input. The improvement degrades to 5 dB for frequencies up to 1 kHz. From 1 kHz to 10 kHz the improvement degrades. However the phase noise shows an increase at exactly the FSR and its harmonics which is logic due to the environmental change of FSR.

The frequency of the generator has been changed from 1 GHz to 3 then to 7 with basic results obtained with the 1 GHz given above. Table 3 shows the measured linewidths for different input and output frequencies and Table 4 shows the Phase noise at different input and output frequencies (at different offsets).

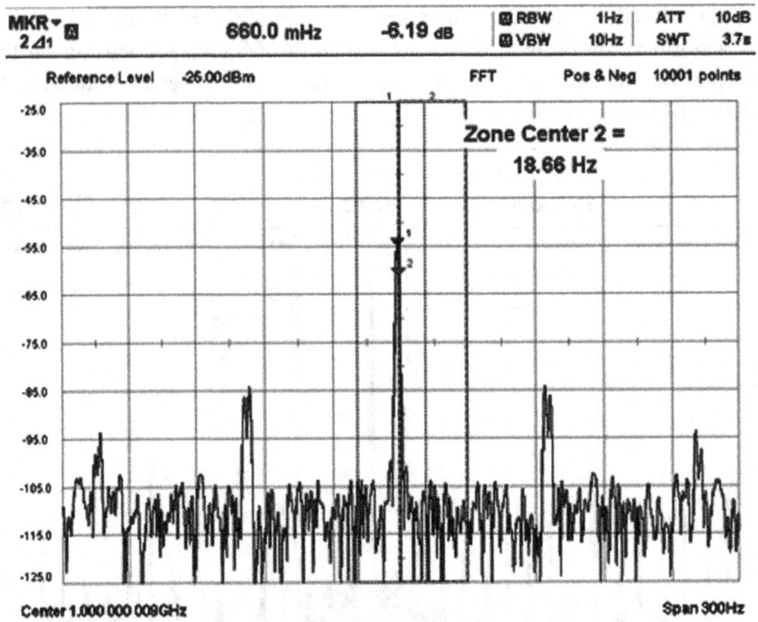

Fig. 14. The RF spectrum analyzer trace showing output at 1 GHz and its 6 dB linewidth.

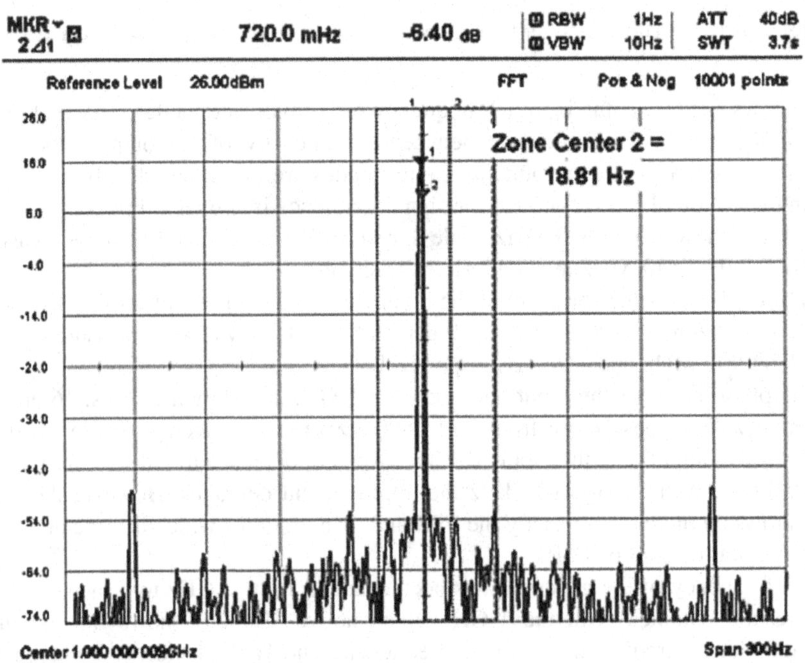

Fig. 15. The RF spectrum analyzer trace showing input at 1 GHz and its 6 dB line-width.

Carrier Freq. 1 000 000 000 Hz Reference Level 0.00 dBm
ATT 10 dB

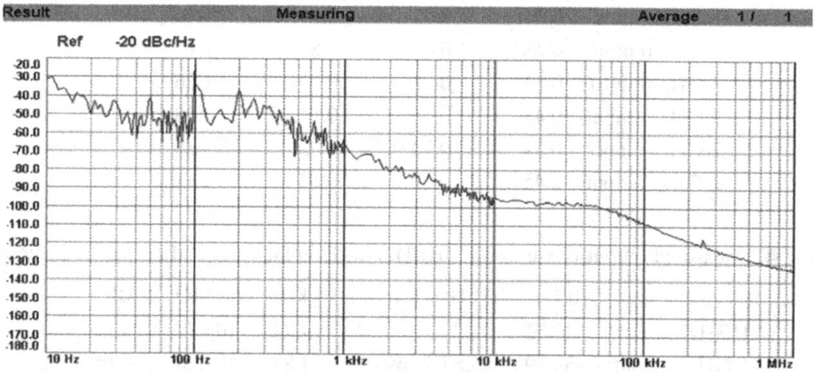

Carrier Level -5.90 dBm Frequency Error -282.56 Hz

Marker List

MKR	Frequency	Level	MKR	Frequency	Level
1	10 Hz	-30.52 dBc/Hz	5	100 kHz	-108.77 dBc/Hz
2	100 Hz	-34.20 dBc/Hz	6	1 MHz	-133.50 dBc/Hz
3	1 kHz	-66.02 dBc/Hz	7	10 MHz	**.** dBc/Hz
4	10 kHz	-94.74 dBc/Hz			

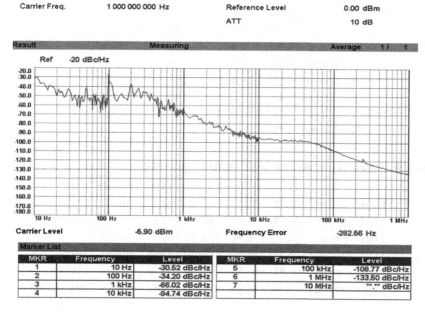

Fig. 16. The RF spectrum analyzer trace showing Phase noise of the input at 1 GHz.

Carrier Freq. 1 000 000 000 Hz **Reference Value =** 0.00 dBm
ATT **-20 dBc/Hz** dB

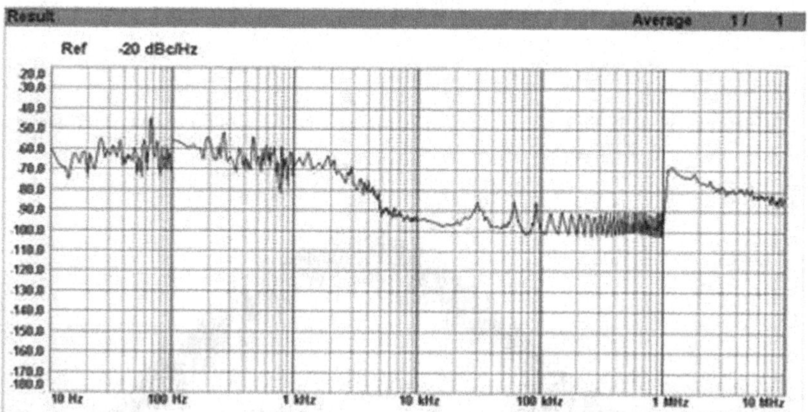

Carrier Level -8.39 dBm Frequency Error -84 466.57 Hz

Marker List

MKR	Frequency	Level	MKR	Frequency	Level
1	10 Hz	-59.59 dBc/Hz	5	100 kHz	-100.06 dBc/Hz
2	100 Hz	-55.87 dBc/Hz	6	1 MHz	-98.65 dBc/Hz
3	1 kHz	-69.05 dBc/Hz	7	10 MHz	-83.93 dBc/Hz
4	10 kHz	-94.83 dBc/Hz			

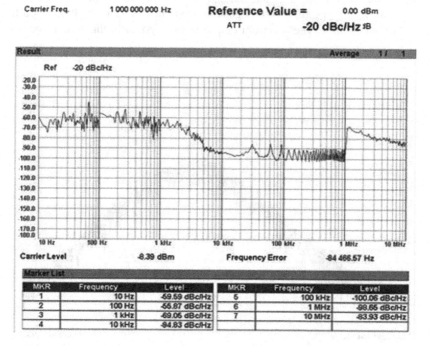

Fig. 17. The RF spectrum analyzer trace showing Phase noise of the output at 1 GHz.

Table 3. Measured linewidths for different input and output frequencies.

	3 dB (Hz)	6 dB (Hz)	10 dB (Hz)	20 dB (Hz)
1 GHz (input)	0.51	0.72	0.9	1.26
1 GHz (output)	0.48	0.66	0.84	1.17
3 GHz (input)	0.51	0.72	0.9	1.26
3 GHz (output)	0.48	0.66	0.81	1.08
7 GHz (input)	0.51	0.72	0.93	1.32
7 GHz (output)	0.45	0.63	0.81	1.11

Table 4. Measured output phase noise (dBc/Hz) at different input and output frequencies.

	10 Hz	100 Hz	1 kHz	10 kHz	100 kHz	1 MHz
1 GHz (input)	−30.52	−34.2	−66.02	−94.74	−108.77	−133.5
1 GHz (output)	−59.59	−55.87	−69.05	−94.83	−100.06	−98.65
3 GHz (input)	−41.03	−80.41	−90.18	−99.51	−107.88	−130
3 GHz (output)	−65.5	−67.68	−88.63	−93.89	−104.68	−99.51
7 GHz (input)	−49.41	−61.33	−69.68	−88.95	−103.86	−117.64
7 GHz (output)	−64.36	−60.03	−90.85	−96.12	−101.92	−99.02

To check the filter performance on wider linewidth input signal, the function generator (Anritsu MS2830A) is then replaced by the function generator (hp 8350B). Figure 18 shows the spectrum of this generator output at 9.22 GHz. It shows a linewidth of about 20 kHz. The spectrum output of our system in this case is shown in Fig. 19.

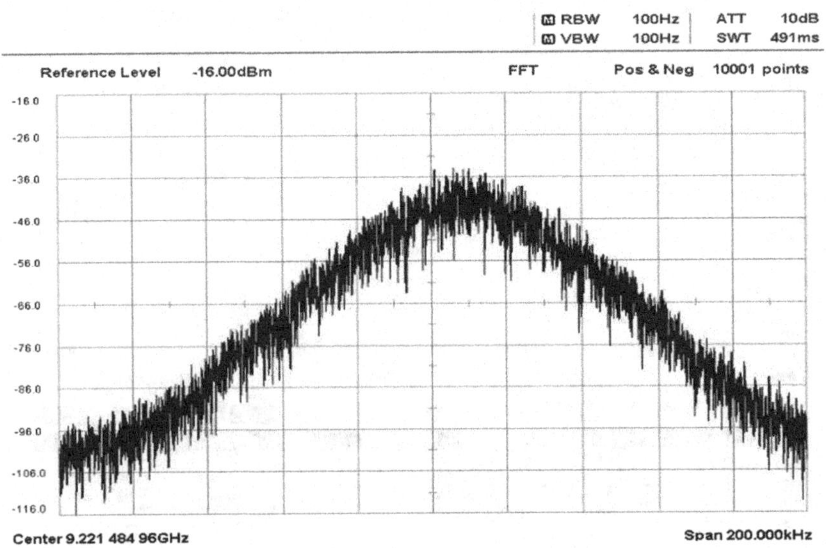

Fig. 18. The RF spectrum analyzer trace of input signal at 9.22 GHz using the function generator hp 8350B.

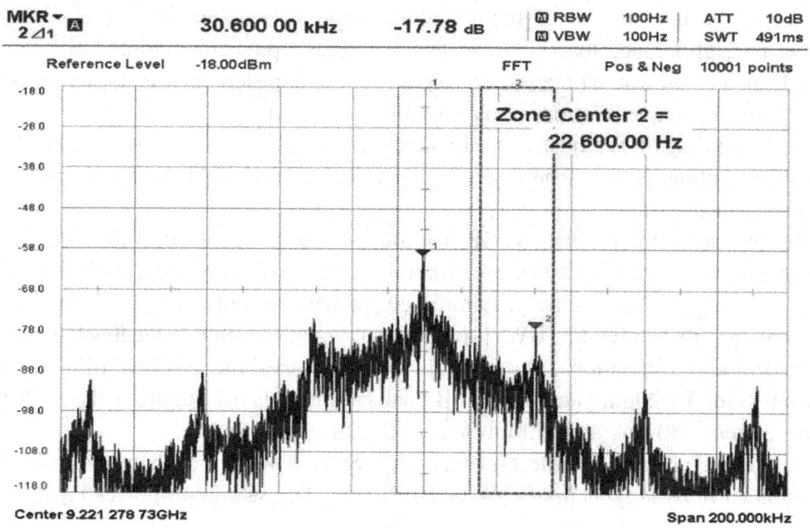

Fig. 19. The RF spectrum analyzer trace showing the output signal at 9.22 GHz.

The filter action of the Brillouin laser loop is clear producing outputs separated by the FSR, each as before with a very narrow bandwidth. The ratio of the central mode to the nearest largest side mode is 17.78 dB.

5 Discussion and Theoretical Considerations of Optoelectronic Brillouin Filter

The optoelectronic Brillouin filter constitutes fiber Brillouin SOA ring resonator with intensity modulator. We first analyze the setup with no RF input to the intensity modulator switched off. The fiber ring laser oscillator of the proposed setup can be modeled by the block diagram of Fig. 20.

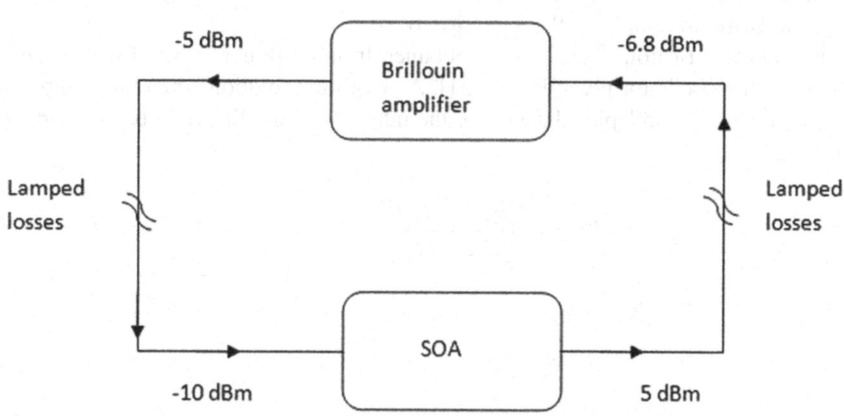

Fig. 20. The power levels of the oscillating optical wave.

The inputs and outputs of the Brillouin amplifier and the SOA are connected together through lamped losses. Power levels at their inputs and outputs are measured and indicated as shown. The SOA driving current is adjusted such that its gain is just below threshold for oscillations. It is found to be 180 mA.

The Brillouin gain is adjusted just to start oscillations. This is found to be at 11 mW pump laser output power. The overall gain is above threshold only over the small Brillouin gain linewidth.

The ring cavity modes have a FSR determined mainly by the Brillouin fiber length. With this setup three objectives are accomplished, achieving better stability of the lasing wavelength [15]; increase the amplified spontaneous emission (ASE) in the SOA which enlarges its bandwidth (BW) [16], and making the amplitude feedback parameter in the Brillouin oscillations closer to 1 which reduces the FWHM of the stokes spectrum in the Brillouin gain [17]. 1 dB gain saturation is measured for the SOA with driving current 180 mA at 1550 nm and −10 dBm input power.

The effective carrier lifetime τ_{eff} of a typical SOA is 40 P_s. The saturation energy of index guided SOA is typically E_{sat} = 5–10 PJ [18]. The saturation power P_{sat} is given by

$$P_{sat} = E_{sat}/\tau_{eff} \tag{5}$$

Hence, the P_{sat} is about 125 mW. The saturated gain is given by [19]

$$G = G_o.e^{\left[P_o\frac{(G-1)}{GP_{sat}}\right]} \tag{6}$$

G_o is the unsaturated gain and P_o is the output power. Working out the algebra at P_o = 5 dBm and G_o = 16 dB we find that G is 15 dB which is measured experimentally. This shows that the given values for τ_{eff} seems to be correct. The importance of τ_{eff} is that it sets a limit for the modulation frequency of a modulated input for amplification without distortion in the SOA.

In our case this seems to be 25 GHz. The effective carrier lifetime τ_{eff} can be decreased to 10 P_s if the driving current increase to 0.5 A. However, in this case the lamped loses should also increase to keep the balance between the gains of the SOA and of the Brillouin amplifier the same as above.

The saturated Brillouin gain can be obtained from a full treatment of the dynamics of the Brillouin oscillator given in [20, 21]. A simplified solution when the pump laser power is considered undepleted gives for the intensity of the Brillouin beam inside the fiber as [22].

$$I_s(z) = \left[\frac{b_o(1 - b_o)}{G(z) - b_o}\right] I_P(0)exp^{-\alpha z} \tag{7}$$

Where

$$G(z) = e^{\left[(1-b_o)\left(\frac{g_o}{\alpha}\right)(1-e^{-\alpha z})\right]} \tag{8}$$

$I_p(0)$ is the input pump power intensity, $b_o = I_S(0)/I_P(0)$, $g_o = g_B I_P(0)$, $g_B = 5*10^{-11}$ m/W for typical silica fiber and the zero in parenthesis is indicates at the input end of the Brillouin fiber from the pump side. The unsaturated gain (G_A) and the saturated gain (G_s) values are given as [22]

$$G_s = I_s(0)/\left[I_P(L).exp^{-\alpha L}\right] \tag{9}$$

$$G_A = e^{\left(g_o L_{eff}\right)} \tag{10}$$

Where $L_{eff} = (1 - e^{-\alpha L})/\alpha$

L is the length of the Brillouin fiber and α its intrinsic attenuation coefficient. The setup of our experiment here uses three sections of fiber attached by connectors. This adds losses in the fiber transmission. An equivalent distributed loss for the α parameter is found to be 0.35 dB/km. At pump power of 5 mW G_A is found to be 110 dB. The calculated value for G_s is found to be 3.6 dB.

This is higher than the measured overall gain of the Brillouin fiber shown in Fig. 20 which is 1.8 dB. This is probably due to the unsaturated pump considered for the calculation above. This result, however, shows how heavily the Brillouin gain is saturated. The linewidth $\Delta\upsilon_s$ of the Brillouin oscillator can be calculated using the results given in [17] as

$$\Delta\upsilon_s = \Delta\upsilon_P/k^2 \tag{11}$$

Where $\Delta\upsilon_P$ is the pump laser linewidth and; $k = 1 + \gamma_A/\Gamma_c; \gamma_A = \pi\Delta\upsilon_B; \Gamma_c = -c\ln(R)/(nL)$, $\Delta\upsilon_B$ is the FWHM of the Brillouin gain which is found here to be 18.14 MHz; R is the amplitude feedback parameter which is the inverse of the Brillouin gain, found here to be 0.66; and n is fiber mode refractive index which is 1.4565 at 1550 nm.

This gives, $\Gamma_c = 1.3\times10^4$ and, hence $k = 4.3\times10^3$. This indicates a mode reduction in $\Delta\upsilon_s$ of seven orders of magnitudes relative to $\Delta\upsilon_P$. Since, the pump laser used in our setup has a linewidth of 100 kHz, the above calculations predicts a linewidth of order 10 MHz.

However, the experimental data, Fig. 11 shows a linewidth of 570 MHz. the difference between this result and that of the theoretical calculations is probably due, on one hand, to the limitations of the RF spectrum analyzer used and, on the other hand, to the inaccuracy of the theoretical model used here. This can be explained as follows.

The derivation of Eq. (6) has not taken into account the fiber attenuation since the fiber length considered for this model is few meters only. The fiber used here is 6.6 km with increased equivalent distributed attenuation.

When the RF input to the optical modulator is switched on the input to the fiber is modulated having a central mode separated by the RF frequency from two side modes.

Only the central mode enjoys gain due to the narrow BW of the Brillouin gain. More side modes occur but with successively reduced power. This is shown in Fig. 10. The beating of these modes at the detector produces back the RF signal but after being passed throw the Brillouin cavity filtering effect. It is clear from the results of Figs. 14, 15 that the linewidth of the output ($\Delta \upsilon_o$) is reduced from that of the input ($\Delta \upsilon_i$), (As long as $\Delta \upsilon_i$ is less the FSR of the Brillouin cavity) according to;

$$(\Delta \upsilon_o)^{-1} = \left[(\Delta \upsilon_i)^{-2} + (\Delta \upsilon_S)^{-2}\right]^{0.5} \tag{12}$$

For larger $\Delta \upsilon_i$ than the FSR more than one mode is produced at the output separated by the FSR each with linewidth $\Delta \upsilon_B$, this is shown in Fig. 19. To increase the FSR of the cavity a shorter fiber should be used. But then the Pump Laser Power should be increased to keep the balance between the SOA and the Brillouin gains the same.

6 Conclusion

Generation of microwave signals of high performance based on optical techniques has been investigated and tested experimentally.

The main features and limitations of the used techniques have been discussed. A new design term, we call it the critical fiber length (L_C) has been introduced. This will simplify the design approach.

A developed setup based on using very narrow Brillouin beams has been introduced. This technique produced microwave signal of very narrow linewidth (less than 1 Hz).

This technique is not sensitive to temperature variations or to vibrations.

For the continuity of the work presented in the research we believe that there are mainly two points of interest: the first is the replacing the SMF by PM fiber. We believe that this may greatly enhance the system performance. The second direction is related to investigate the techniques that may be used to reduce the SOA effective time (τ_{eff}) to increase the bandwidth of SOA used.

Acknowledgements. The experimental work has been done in the laboratory of laser and optical communication at Faculty of Engineering, Ain Shams University. Egypt. The authors would like to appreciate the help given by prof. Mahmoud Ahmed and his team.

References

1. Yao, X.S., Maleki, L.: Opto-electronic oscillator. J. Opt. Soc. Am. B **13**(8), 1725–1735 (1996)
2. Yariv, A.: Universal relations for coupling of optical power between microresonators and dielectric waveguides. Electron. Lett. **36**(4), 321–322 (2000)
3. Yariv, A.: Critical coupling and its control in optical waveguide-ring resonator systems. Photonics Technol. Lett. **14**(4), 483–485 (2002)

4. Merrer, P.H., Brahimi, H., Llopis, O.: Optical techniques for microwave frequency stabilization: Resonant versus delay line approaches and related modelling problems. In: 2008 IEEE Topical Meeting on MicrowavePhotonics, pp. 146–149 (2008)
5. Yao, X.S.: High-quality microwave signal generation by use of Brillouin scattering in optical fibers. Opt. Lett. **22**(17), 1329–1331 (1997)
6. Li, J., Lee, H., Vahala, K.J.: Microwave synthesizer using an on-chip Brillouin oscillator. Nat. Commun. **4**, 2097 (2013)
7. He, G.S., Kuzmin, A., Prasad, P.N.: Pump spectral linewidth influence on stimulated Brillouin scattering (SBS) and stimulated Raman scattering (SRS) and self-termination behavior of SRS in liquids. Ann. Phys. **528**(11–12), 852–864 (2016)
8. Correa-Mena, A.G., et al.: Performance evaluation of an optoelectronic oscillator based on a band-pass microwave photonic filter architecture. Radioengineering **26**(3), 642–646 (2017)
9. Gao, B., et al.: A frequency-tunable two-tone RF signal generator by polarization multiplexed optoelectronic oscillator. IEEE Microw. Wirel. Compon. Lett. **27**(2), 192–194 (2017)
10. Mousa, M., Afifi, A.E., Abouelatta, M., Hassan, K.M.: Generation of high stability microwave signal using optoelectronic oscillator based on long fiber delay line. In: International Conference on Optical Communication Systems (OPTICS/ICETE), Porto, Portugal, (2018)
11. Leeson, D.B.: A simple model of feedback oscillator noise spectrum. Proc. of the IEEE **54** (2), 329–330 (1966)
12. Chang, W.S.C. (ed.): RF Photonic Technology in Optical Fiber Links. Cambridge University Press, Cambridge (2002)
13. Leeson, D.B.: Oscillator phase noise: a 50-year review. IEEE Trans. Ultrason. Ferroelectr. Freq. Control **63**(8), 1208–1225 (2016)
14. Shen, Y., Zhang, X., Chen, K.: All-optical generation of microwave and millimeter wave using a two frequency Bragg grating-based Brillouin fiber laser. J. Light. Technol. **23**(5), 1860 (2005)
15. Stepanov, D.Y., Cowle, G.J.: Properties of Brillouin/Erbium fiber lasers. IEEE J. Sel. Top. Quantum Electron. **3**(4), 1049–1057 (1997)
16. Baveja, P.P., Kaplan, A.M., Maywar, D.N., Agrawal, G.P.: Pulse amplification in semiconductor optical amplifiers with ultrafast gain-recovery times. In: OPTO. International Society for Optics and Photonics (2010)
17. Yariv, A.: Quantum Electronics (1989)
18. Wiesenfeld, J.M., et al.: Distortionless picosecond pulse amplification and gain compression in a traveling wave InGaAsP optical amplifier. Appl. Phys. Lett. **53**(14), 1239–1241 (1988)
19. Agrawal, G.P.: Fiber-Optic Communication System. Wiley, Hoboken (2002)
20. Tang, C.L.: Saturation and spectral characteristics of the Stokes emission in the stimulated Brillouin process. J. Appl. Phys. **37**(8), 2945–2955 (1966)
21. Inns, R.H., Batra, I.P.: Saturation and depletion in stimulated light scattering. Phys. Lett. A **28**(8), 591–592 (1969)
22. Agrawal, G.P.: Nonlinear Fiber Optics, Chap. 9. Academic, San Diego (1989)

Steganogaphy Using Mac-Independent Opportunistic Routing and Encoding (MORE) Protocol Based Communications

Mohamed Amine Belhamra and El Mamoun Souidi(✉)

Laboratory of Mathematics, Computer Science,
Applications and Information Security, Faculty of Sciences,
Mohammed V University in Rabat, BP 1014 RP, 10000 Rabat, Morocco
mabelhamra@gmail.com, emsouidi@gmail.com

Abstract. In this paper, we first propose an enhanced version of the proposed steganoraphic scheme using MORE protocol, increasing its security and performances. To do so, we use matrix permutation keys for the embedding (*resp.* extraction) process, and we give optimized embedding and retrieval algorithms leading to a 50% reduced time/computation complexity. Furthermore, we analyse the proposed schemes and discuss their vulnerability to steganalysis attacks, then we propose an enhancement against these attacks.

Keywords: Information hiding · Network steganography · Random network coding · Opportunistic routing · Steganalysis · Kolmogorov-Smirnov (KS) attack · Chi square (χ^2) attack

1 Introduction

The term *Steganography* originates from the ancient Greek words *stegano* and *graphein*, where the former word means covered (concealed), while the latter means writing. That is, the purpose of steganography is to hide secret information within an ordinary message (cover-medium) such as texts, images, audio files *etc.*, in such way that no one realizes its existence apart from the sender(s) and the intended receiver(s). Hence, steganography is the art and science of imperceptible communications. A particular property over which steganographic methods are classified is the type of the used cover-medium in the process. In the following, we constrain ourselves to a specific class which is mainly based on protocol-related functions associated with the Open System Interconnect-Reference Model (OSI-RM) layers, referred to as Network Steganography (NS). The cover-mediums are in this case established using the control data and timing properties of the transmission or the user data.

Many NS schemes have been studied in the literature, hereafter we cite some well known proposals.

NS techniques that embeds secret bits into user data (presentation layer) such as voice samples, images, *etc.* have been heavily studied. In [1] for example,

M. S. Obaidat (Ed.): ICETE 2018, CCIS 1118, pp. 66–86, 2019.
https://doi.org/10.1007/978-3-030-34866-3_4

the famous method that modifies the least significant bits (LSB) of the digital signals have been developed while in paper [18], distortion-less schemes exploiting redundancy in Redundant Residue Number System (RRNS) codes are introduced. Furthermore, a scheme that exploits the application layer by inserting secret bits into the HTTP's headers and tags is given in [4]. NS methods can also exploit the adjustment of the messages to the type of network or means of transport. The Retransmission Steganography (RSTEG) [11] technique for protocols with retransmission schemes is based on the successful acknowledgement of received TCP segments to intentionally invoke retransmission, then the retransmitted segment carries secret data in the payload field. Two additional approaches were proposed in [10], where one idea consists in hiding secret messages in reserved parts of the packet's headers, taking into consideration that protocols in general do not impose specific values for the unused/reserved parts. In particular, the authors proposed the use of the IP header's Don't Fragment (DF) flag when the transmitted packets are smaller than the path's Maximum Transfer Unit (MTU). Another proposed solution exploiting the unused fields of the Session Initiation Protocol (SIP) to hide information is given in [12].

Furthermore, schemes exploiting the physical and data link layers of the OSI model were given in [7,8]. The physical layer based method called WiPad (Wireless Padding) [7] is intended for IEEE 802.11 Orthogonal Frequency Division Multiplexing (OFDM) networks, and the secret data is inserted into the padding of transmitted symbols. The data link layer based scheme for Wireless Local Area Networks (WLANs), called Hidden Communication System for Corrupted Networks (HICCUPS) [8], consists in using transmission frames with intentionally wrong checksums. That is, only terminals that are aware of the scheme read such frames and extract hidden data from payload field. A method proposed in [9] embeds data within the cyclic prefix, its embedding capacity varies according to the used modulation (see Table 3) respectively, in Binary and Quadrature Phase Shifting Keying (BPSK and QPSK), and in 16-Quadrature Amplitude Modulation (QAM) and 64-QAM.

Moreover, the authors in [13] were first to develop a scheme where more than one protocol is exploited, known as Padding Steganography (PadSteg). Such class of schemes is called inter-protocol steganography. Table 1 summarizes the techniques discussed above, for further reading, a good classification of NS methods based on patterns is given in [6].

Researchers in the field always aim to propose new/modified steganographic protocols exhibiting enhanced properties (*i.e.,* higher embedding capacity, more robustness against adversary attacks). Especially for new communication technologies emerging with the evolution of communicating mediums and terminals such as smart-phones [5].

In this paper we propose an enhanced version of the steganoraphic scheme proposed for the MORE Protocol [3]. In order to increase the security and complexity performances, we use secure matrix permutation keys for the extraction process, and we optimize the embedding and retrieval algorithms in time/computation complexity. Finally, we give a deep steganalysis of the scheme and discuss its vulnerability to statistical attacks, then we propose a new steganographic scheme against these attacks.

Table 1. Summary of some NS based protocols and associated OSI-RM layers.

<table>
<tr><th>OSI-RM layers</th><th colspan="2">Example of applications</th></tr>
<tr><td>Application</td><td colspan="2">HTTP Header manipulation (Van Horenbeeck [4])</td></tr>
<tr><td>Presentation</td><td colspan="2">LSB of voice samples modification for VoIP (Bender et al. [1])</td></tr>
<tr><td>Session</td><td colspan="2">SIP header manipulation (Szczypiorski and Mazurczyk [12])</td></tr>
<tr><td>Transport</td><td>Intentional TCP segments retransmissions (Mazurczyk et al. [11])</td><td rowspan="3">Ethernet frame's padding for different upper layers protocols (Jankowski et al. [13])</td></tr>
<tr><td>Network</td><td>Packets sorting and IP header manipulation (Kundur and Ahsan [10])</td></tr>
<tr><td rowspan="2">Data Link</td><td>Intentionally corrupted frames (Szczypiorski [8])</td></tr>
<tr><td colspan="2">IEEE 802.11 MAC sublayer, MORE's transfer matrix [3]</td></tr>
<tr><td>Physical</td><td colspan="2">Padding of OFDM symbols for WLANs (Szczypiorski and Mazurczyk [7]) Embedding within the cyclic prefix using PSK based modulations [9]</td></tr>
</table>

This paper is organized as follows: In Sect. 2, we recall some facts about Network Steganography and the proposed steganographic scheme for MORE Protocol [3]. In Sect. 3, we first discuss the proposed enhancement to the protocol and give the steganalysis perspective, then we propose the new scheme against statistical attacks before concluding the paper in Sect. 4.

2 Definitions and Background

In this section, we first recall relevant properties of Network Steganography, then we discuss the proposed steganographic scheme for the MORE protocol.

2.1 Network Seganography

Network Steganography (NS) are steganographic schemes based on functions of communication protocols in contemporary networks.

The features constituting the base of NS are formulated as follows:

- Some functions of the protocols are modified. The modifications may be:
  - Functions of the protocols introduced to correct the imperfectness of communication channels (errors, delays, *etc.*).
  - Functions of the protocols introduced to define the communication type (*e.g.* query/response, file transfer, *etc.*) and/or to adapt the form of messages to the transmission medium (*e.g.* fragmentation, segmentation, *etc.*).

- The effects of these modifications are difficult to discover (*e.g.*, to seem resulting from the imperfectness of the communication network and/or protocols).

NS schemes are classified into storage, timing and hybrid methods based on how the secret messages are encoded into the carrier. Storage methods hide data by modifying packet's fields, while timing methods hide information in the timing of protocol packets. Hybrid techniques combines both the timing and storage methods.

The reliability and effectiveness of a steganographic scheme are evaluated with three main properties [2]. The first one is the *embedding capacity*, which is the percentage of the secret message bits to the total cover bits. Second one is the *embedding average distortion*, the ratio of the changed bits in the cover to the total cover bits. When the embedding rate is low, it becomes more difficult to reliably detect the message. The third parameter is the *embedding efficiency*, the average number of embedded bits per unit distortion.

2.2 Related Work

Hereafter, we first recall the MORE Protocol, then remind the steganographic scheme. For further understanding see [3].

Source. The source breaks up the file into batches of γ uncoded (native) packets. When the 802.11 MAC is ready, the source creates a random linear combination of these packets (current batch) and broadcasts the coded packet $p'_i = \sum \beta_{ij} p_j$, where the β_{ij} are random coefficients picked by the node, and the p_j's are the native packets from the same batch.

The sender attaches a header to each data packet, in which it reports packet's information such as the code vector, the batch ID, *etc.* The sender keeps the transmission until the batch is acknowledged by the destination, at which time the sender proceeds to the next batch.

Forwarders. In a nutshell, when a forwarder node hears a packet while listening to the transmissions, it checks whether it is innovative (*i.e.* linearly independent from the packets previously received from this batch) in which case the forwarder keeps it. The arrival of this new packet triggers the node to broadcast a coded packet (a random linear combination of the coded packets it has heard from the same batch) and broadcasts it. If the received packet is of the form $p'_i = \sum_j \beta_{ij} p_j$, then the resulting coded packet expressed in terms of the native packets:

$$p'' = \sum_i (r_i \sum_j \beta_{ij} p_j) = \sum_j (\sum_i r_i \beta_{ij}) p_j \quad (1)$$

where r_i's are randomly picked numbers.

Destination. When a destination receives a packet, it checks whether it is innovative (linearly independent from previously received packets) and keeps it in this case. Once the destination receives γ innovative packets, it decodes the whole batch using the inversion of the transfer matrix:

$$\begin{pmatrix} p_1 \\ p_2 \\ \vdots \\ p_\gamma \end{pmatrix} = \begin{pmatrix} \beta_{11} & \cdots & \beta_{1\gamma} \\ \vdots & \ddots & \vdots \\ \beta_{\gamma 1} & \cdots & \beta_{\gamma\gamma} \end{pmatrix}^{-1} \begin{pmatrix} p'_1 \\ p'_2 \\ \vdots \\ p'_\gamma \end{pmatrix} \tag{2}$$

As soon as the destination decodes the batch, it sends an acknowledgement to the source to allow it to move to the next batch.

The Steganographic Protocol. The media cover is the triangular matrices, *i.e.*, the LU factorization of M_t which is the transfer matrix of MORE's scheme (For more details see [3]). The protocol for the whole process is the pair of maps defined as:

$$\begin{aligned} \mathcal{E} : \mathbb{F}_{2^n}^{\gamma^2} &\rightarrow \qquad \mathcal{M}_\gamma(\mathbb{F}_{2^n}), \\ S_{\gamma^2} &\mapsto \mathcal{E}_l(S_f) \times \mathcal{E}_u(S_l). \end{aligned} \tag{3}$$

and

$$\begin{aligned} \mathcal{R} : \mathcal{M}_\gamma(\mathbb{F}_{2^n}) &\rightarrow \qquad \mathbb{F}_{2^n}^{\gamma^2}, \\ M_t = LU &\mapsto (\mathcal{R}_l(L)||\mathcal{R}_u(U)). \end{aligned} \tag{4}$$

The matrices L and U are respectively the lower and upper matrices resulting from the LU decomposition of the transfer matrix M_t, the $||$ function is defined as the concatenation of the first and last parts of S (*i.e.* $S_{\gamma^2} = (S_f||S_l)$).

The description of the algorithms is as given below (see [3]):

The map $\mathcal{E}_l$: Transforms an array input of $\frac{\gamma(\gamma-1)}{2}$ symbols to its associated lower triangular square matrix, and returns it as an output.
The map $\mathcal{E}_u$: Transforms an array input of $\frac{\gamma(\gamma+1)}{2}$ symbols to its associated upper triangular square matrix, and returns it as an output.
The map $\mathcal{R}_l$: Transforms a lower triangular square matrix input of size γ to its associated array of symbols and returns it as an output.
Finally, the map $\mathcal{R}_u$ transforms an upper triangular square matrix input of size γ to its associated array of symbols and returns it as an output.

Example 1. [3] We consider a batch of 3 packets $P = \{p_1, p_2, p_3\}$, that a source A needs to transmit to one or a set of receivers B and J, over a wireless network using the MORE protocol. We model A's, B's and J's transmission ranges, respectively, as source's C_1, forwarder's C_2, and destination's C_3 ranges (see Fig. 1).

In a typical MORE setting over a field of size $q = 2^8$, node A can hide a secret binary sequence M of size $|M| \leq 72$ bits in one batch, for a node B in the next-hop to recover it as shown in Fig. 1. *i.e.*, in A's transmission range.

Recall that in our scheme, node B could be a receiver as well as a forwarder. To do so, node A first cuts M into $\lceil \frac{|M|}{8} \rceil = 9$ blocks:

$\{<M_1>_{2^8}, <M_2>_{2^8}, ..., <M_9>_{2^8}\}$ each in $\mathbb{F}_{2^8}$, and gathers them in a 3 and 6 dimensional arrays, respectively S_f and S_l. We denote here by $< \cdot >_q$ for a positive integer q, the corresponding binary representation in $\mathbb{F}_q$.

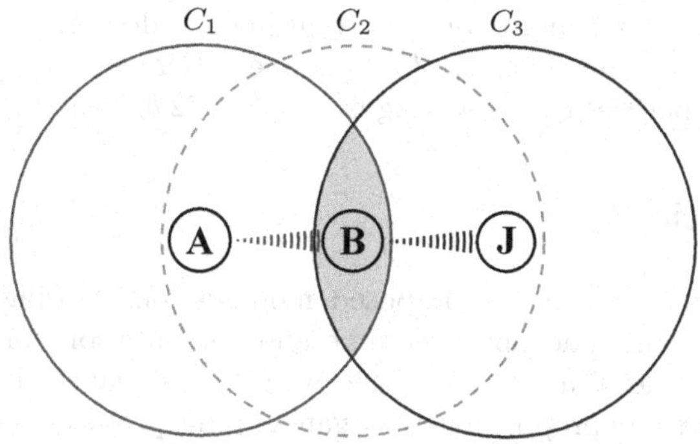

Fig. 1. A's, B's and J's transmission ranges.

- Node A constructs the transfer matrix $M_t \in \mathcal{M}_\gamma(\mathbb{F}_{2^8})$ such that

$$M_t = \mathcal{E}_l(S_f) \times \mathcal{E}_u(S_l).$$

as stated before.
- Node A sends the linear combinations of the batch, *i.e.* $p_i = \sum_{j=1}^{3} \beta_{ij} p_j$ for $i = 1, 2, 3$, where β_{ij} are M_t's elements and p_i *'s* (*resp.* $p'_j s$) are the coded packets (*resp.* original packets) of our settings. Then A attaches the encoding vector in the header as MORE ensures.

Set $\mathfrak{m}_i = <M_i>_{2^8}$ for $i = 1, 2, ..., 9$. So:

$$L = \begin{pmatrix} 1 & 0 & 0 \\ \mathfrak{m}_1 & 1 & 0 \\ \mathfrak{m}_2 & \mathfrak{m}_3 & 1 \end{pmatrix}, \tag{5}$$

$$U = \begin{pmatrix} \mathfrak{m}_4 & \mathfrak{m}_5 & \mathfrak{m}_6 \\ 0 & \mathfrak{m}_7 & \mathfrak{m}_8 \\ 0 & 0 & \mathfrak{m}_9 \end{pmatrix} \tag{6}$$

Then the constructed transfer matrix $M_t = LU$ becomes as in (7), where all arithmetic operations are performed over $\mathbb{F}_{2^8}$.

$$M_t = \begin{pmatrix} \mathfrak{m}_4 & \mathfrak{m}_5 & \mathfrak{m}_6 \\ \mathfrak{m}_1.\mathfrak{m}_4 & \mathfrak{m}_1.\mathfrak{m}_5 + \mathfrak{m}_7 & \mathfrak{m}_1.\mathfrak{m}_6 + \mathfrak{m}_8 \\ \mathfrak{m}_2.\mathfrak{m}_4 & \mathfrak{m}_2.\mathfrak{m}_5 + \mathfrak{m}_3.\mathfrak{m}_7 & \mathfrak{m}_2.\mathfrak{m}_6 + \mathfrak{m}_3.\mathfrak{m}_8 + \mathfrak{m}_9 \end{pmatrix} \tag{7}$$

The node B as stated previously, must be in A's transmission range for the decoding process:

- The node B as a next-hop forwarder or/and receiver, waits until it receives the whole 3 innovative combinations, then reassembles the transfer matrix M_t.
- The node B decomposes M_t as LU, then retrieves the array of secret blocks $S = (\mathcal{R}_l(L)||\mathcal{R}_u(U))$.

Where again, matrices L and U are the resulting LU decomposition.

A hides in this scheme 9 blocks of bits in one batch transmission process, *i.e.* the embedding capacities in this setting is 3^2 *spb* $= 72$ *bpb* and 0.1 *spo* $= 0.8$ *bpo*.

3 Contribution

In this section, we explain the proposed modifications leading to secure the steganographic scheme and optimize time and computation complexity of the embedding and retrieval algorithm. Then we give a steganalysis perspective of the former schemes and propose a new steganographic protocol against statistical attacks.

3.1 Optimizing the Protocol

Securing the Scheme. The steganographic scheme is based on forming the upper and lower triangular matrices, in such way that from their resulting product, one can recover them without ambiguity. This characteristic makes the protocol insecure for an adversary who knows the existence of the cover communication, and particularly if he knows the embedding map. Hence, to avoid such possibilities, the use of an embedding/retrieval key is of great interest.

In linear algebra, it is a well known fact that for any square matrix $A \in \mathcal{M}_n(\mathbb{F})$ where n is a positive integer, there exist a lower-uni-triangular matrix $L \in \mathcal{M}_n(\mathbb{F})$ and an invertible upper-triangular matrix $U \in \mathcal{M}_n(\mathbb{F})$ such that $A = LU$ if and only if all its leading principal minors are non-zero *i.e.*, for all integers $k \in [1, n]$, $det(A[k]) \neq 0$, where we denote by $A[k]$ the square block matrix $A(i, j)$ for $i, j = 1, 2, ..., k$.

The *LU-factorization with partial pivoting (LUP)* refers often to LU factorization with only row permutations $PA = LU$, where L and U are again lower and upper triangular matrices, and P is a permutation matrix, which, when left-multiplied to A, reorders the rows of A. It turns out that all square matrices can be factorized in this form ([14], Corollary 3). *i.e.*, for all invertible matrices $A \in \mathcal{M}_n(\mathbb{F})$, there exist a permutation matrix $P \in \mathcal{M}_n(\mathbb{F})$, a lower uni-triangular matrix $L \in \mathcal{M}_n(\mathbb{F})$, and an upper triangular invertible matrix $U \in \mathcal{M}_n(\mathbb{F})$ with $P^T A = LU$ (or equivalently $A = PLU$).

If A satisfy $det(A[k]) \neq 0$, then taking the permutation matrix P as the identity matrix is one solution.

In our case, since we construct matrices L and U, we propose to use in addition a key permutation matrix rather than only the LU product. *i.e.*,

$$M_t = PLU, \tag{8}$$

Hence, the key P is the only permutation assuring to correctly recover hidden information.

Complexity Optimization. For complexity optimization task, we propose a variant of the algorithms, where the embedding (*resp.* retrieval) scheme is performed in (*resp.* from) the triangular matrices in parallel rather than separately. Which obviously divide the time and computation complexity by two.

Hereafter we give the algorithms where Algorithms 1 and 2, are respectively the embedding and retrieval algorithms of the scheme.

Algorithm 1. $\mathcal{E}_S$ Transforming an array of γ^2 symbols to its associated transfer matrix.

Input: Key permutation P, size of the finite field q, and the array of symbols $S = [s_1, s_2, ..., s_{\gamma^2}]$, where $s_i \in \mathbb{F}_{2^n}$ for $i = 1, 2, ..., \gamma^2$.
Output: Transfer matrix $M_t = PLU$

```
int[][]L = I_γ; (I_γ : identity matrix)
int[][] U;
int k = 1, l = 1;
int i = 1, j;
while i ≤ γ do
   for j = 0; j ≤ i; j++ do
      U[j][i] = S[k++];
      L[i][j] = S[k++];
   end for
   U[j][i] = S[k++];
   i++;
end while
return PLU
```

Note 1. The triangular matrices obtained via LU-decomposition are kept to simplify Gaussian elimination in order to obtain the inverse of M_t for MORE's related decoding process. Hence, the complexity of the LU-decomposition does not figure out in the embedding capacity just as stated in [3].

That is, after creating the lower and upper triangular matrices using a given array $s = \{s_1, s_2, \cdots, s_{\gamma^2}\}$ of secret symbols $s_i \in \mathbb{F}_q$:

$$L = \begin{pmatrix} 1 & & & \\ s_1 & 1 & & \text{\Large 0} \\ s_2 & s_\gamma & 1 & \\ \vdots & \vdots & \vdots & \ddots \\ s_{\gamma-1} & s_{2\gamma-3} & \cdots & s_{\frac{\gamma(\gamma-1)}{2}} \; 1 \end{pmatrix} \tag{9}$$

and

$$U = \begin{pmatrix} s_{\frac{\gamma(\gamma-1)}{2}+1} & s_{\frac{\gamma(\gamma-1)}{2}+2} & s_{\frac{\gamma(\gamma-1)}{2}+3} & \cdots & s_{\frac{\gamma(\gamma+1)}{2}} \\ & s_{\frac{\gamma(\gamma+1)}{2}+1} & s_{\frac{\gamma(\gamma+1)}{2}+2} & \cdots & s_{\frac{\gamma(\gamma+3)}{2}-1} \\ & & s_{\frac{\gamma(\gamma+3)}{2}} & \cdots & \vdots \\ & \text{\Large 0} & & \ddots & \vdots \\ & & & & s_{\gamma^2} \end{pmatrix} \tag{10}$$

Algorithm 2. $\mathcal{R}_S$ Retrieval algorithm of the array of symbols S.

Input: Square transfer matrix M_t of size γ, identity matrix I_γ, and the secret key (permutation matrix P).
Output: Array of symbols S.

```
int k, i, , j, l = 0;
int[][] U, L;
U ← P^T M_t;
L ← I_γ;

for k = 1, k ≤ γ; k + + do
  p ← U[k][k];
  for i = k + 1, i ≤ γ; i + + do
    q ← U[i][k]; U[i][k] ← 0; L[i][k] ← q/p;
    S[l] ← L[i][k]
    for j = k + 1, j ≤ γ; j + + do
      U[i][j] ← U[i][j] − U[k][j].q/p;
      S[γ(γ−1)/2 + l] ← U[i][j], l + +;
    end for
  end for
end for
return S;
```

Finally, we compute the matrix

$$M_t = PLU, \tag{11}$$

where if we consider σ the corresponding permutation to P, *i.e.*,

$$P_{(i,j)} = \begin{cases} 1 & \text{if } i = \sigma(j) \\ 0 & \text{otherwise} \end{cases} \tag{12}$$

Hence, if we let $A = LU$ we have

$$M_{t(i,j)} = A_{(\sigma^{-1}(j),j)}, \tag{13}$$

and inversely, since the inverse of a permutation matrix is its transpose, to retrieve the array S we need to recover $A = P^T M_t$.

The Protocol. Taking into consideration a scenario of a sender and a receiver in the steganographic scheme using MORE protocol as stated in ([3], Part 3), and we consider the matrix

$$M_t = PLU, \tag{14}$$

where again, P is a key permutation matrix (can be chosen randomly as well), which we will use as the secret key for the retrieving algorithm.

We use M_t as the transfer matrix for the current batch to send. The uniqueness of the factorisation is obtained thanks to the condition $diag(L) = (1, ..., 1)$.

Table 2. Embedding capacity for typical MORE settings.

Field size q	Capacity in *bpb*	Capacity in *bpo*
2^8	$8\gamma^2$	1.6
2^{16}	$16\gamma^2$	2.2
2^{32}	$32\gamma^2$	6.4

Note that we suppose the elements s_i for $i = 1, 2, ..., \gamma^2$, to be non zero, in order to assure the non zero determinant condition of NC. Otherwise, we can code the zero elements as a non used agreed upon character.

Hereafter, we describe the network steganographic protocol, the protocol for the whole process is the pair of maps defined as:

$$\begin{array}{llll} \mathcal{E}_S : \mathbb{F}_q^{\gamma^2} & \rightarrow & \mathcal{M}_\gamma(\mathbb{F}_q), \\ S & \mapsto & PLU. \end{array} \tag{15}$$

and

$$\begin{array}{lll} \mathcal{R}_S : \mathcal{M}_\gamma(\mathbb{F}_q) & \rightarrow & \mathbb{F}_q^{\gamma^2}, \\ M_t & \mapsto & S, \end{array} \tag{16}$$

where $\mathcal{E}_S$ and $\mathcal{R}_S$, are respectively the embedding and retrieval maps as defined in algorithms (1) and (2) respectively.

Embedding Capacity:
The number of symbols per batch embedded remains as given in [3], *i.e.*,

$$C_{e|b} = \gamma^2 spb = log_2(q)\gamma^2 bpb, \tag{17}$$

with *spb* and *bpb* are denoting the pseudo units : symbols per batch and bits per batch, respectively.

While the time complexity of the protocol is narrowed to half, and hence doubling the embedding capacity per operation time:

$$C_{e|o} = \frac{\gamma^2}{\Theta(5\gamma^2)}\ spo = \frac{1}{5}\ spo.$$

i.e,

$$C_{e|o} = \frac{log_2(q)}{5}\ bpo, \tag{18}$$

where *spo* and *bpo*, denoting respectively the pseudo units: symbols per operation time and bits per operation time. Table 2 summarizes the embedding capacity for typical MORE settings.

Efficiency Comparison. Using the proposed modified protocol, the embedding capacity of this scheme is γ times greater than MORE's bandwidth (*i.e.* γ packet per transmission phase).

Table 3. Comparison of embedding capacity with some NS steganographic scheme.

Channel covert	Used carrier	Embedding capacity in *bps*
WLAN/HW	IEEE 802.11 Cyclic prefix [9]	3.25M (BSPK), 6.5M (QPSK), 13M (16-QAM), and 19.5M (64-QAM)
WLAN/HW	IEEE 802.11 FCF [16]	16.8
WLAN/HW	IEEE 802.11 [8]	216K
WLAN/HW	IEEE 802.11 Padding [7]	1.1M for data frames, 0.44M for ACKs
Network/SS	VoIP stream payload [17]	32K
WLAN/HW	IEEE 802.11 MORE's transfer matrix [3]	~640M (800 MHz Celeron)
WLAN/HW	IEEE 802.11 MORE's transfer matrix (Present scheme)	~1.6G (1 GHz Single core) ~1.28G (800 MHz Celeron)

Considering the MORE's batch size is set to $g = 32$ packets, and the packet size is 1500 Bytes. Taking into consideration the whole packet with headers added by other protocols, the embedding capacity is

$$C_{e|b} = 32\ spb = 48000 \times 8\ bpb = 384K\ bpb = 0.384M bpb.$$

and

$$C_{e|o} = 0.2\ spo = 1.6\ bpo.$$

Thus, for a 1 GHz single Core processor the embedding capacity is

$$C_{e|o} = 1.6 10^9 bs^{-1} = 1,6\ Gbs^{-1}.$$

That is, for the machine's characteristics used in [3] for the implementation (*i.e.* 800 MHz Celeron), the embedding capacity in bits per second for a field size $q = 2^8$ is twice the capacity given in [3] (*i.e.*, ~1.28 Gbps). Furthermore, the scheme remains distortion-less. In Table 3, we give some NS protocols, mostly WLANs related, and their associated embedding capacity in *bps*.

3.2 A New Steganographic Protocol Against Statistical Attacks

In this part of the paper we describe the new steganographic scheme. We first analyse and discuss the vulnerability of the former protocol to statistical attacks, then we introduce the proposed one.

Steganalysis Perspective. Steganalysis is the science of detecting the existence of embedded secret information. The specific detection methods target specific steganographic systems, and consists of subjective and statistical methods. The subjective methods make use of human eyes to look for suspicious artefacts, while statistical methods (such as the chi-square (χ^2) test) perform mathematical analysis in order to find statistical differences between the altered and non-altered messages. The general detection methods are applied to all steganographic system and consist in the extraction of a feature vector and the classification which employs some powerful classifiers such as support vector machines or neural networks. As an adversary attacking a steganographic protocol, we have to distinguish between the following scenarios: If the presence of a steganographic protocol and its structure and functionality are known to the adversary, it is easy to detect the covert communication. However, if the adversary have no knowledge of the protocol, and only knows its existence, he can inject random noise, or reverse engineer the protocol. On another hand, if the protocol is known but not detected, a blind attack can be performed, by sending disruptive commands to terminate the communication. Finally, if the adversary has no information at all, then no specific attack on the steganographic scheme is possible.

In contrast to protocols vulnerable to the human eye such as image based information hiding techniques, subjective attacks are not a problem for our schemes since we use plain binary represented algebraic codes. Hence, only statistical attacks are of interest in our case.

Let $S = (s_1, s_2, ..., s_\omega)$ be the array of secret symbols to send using the MORE protocol, where elements s_i for $i = 1, 2, ..., \omega$, are supposed non zero in order to assure the non zero determinant condition of NC ($i, e.$ we can code the zero elements as a non used agreed upon character). We consider the symbols to be drawn uniformly in $\mathbb{F}_q \setminus 0_{\mathbb{F}_q}$.

To model the problem, without loss of generality we consider the field $\mathbb{F}_q = \mathbb{Z}/\mathbb{Z}_q$ where q is prime, and $X = [X_1, X_2, ..., X_\omega]$ to be a series of independent and identically distributed (*iid*) variables with values $x_1, x_2, ..., x_\omega$ drawn uniformly in $\mathbb{F}_q$ elimination the zero element ($i, e.X_i \sim U_{[1,q-1]}$), where we refer by $U_{[1,q-1]}$ to the uniform distribution in the discrete set $[1, q-1]$. Hence,

$$\mathbb{E}(X_i) = \sum_{i=1}^{q-1} x_i \mathbb{P}(x_i) = \frac{q}{2} \tag{19}$$

where we denote by $\mathbb{P}(X_i)$ and $\mathbb{E}(X_i)$ respectively, the probability and the expectation measures of the variable X_i for $1 \leq i \leq \omega$.

Now consider the variables Y_i, Z_i, for $0 \leq i \leq \delta$ where δ is a positive integer, to be uniformly and *iid* in $[1, q-1]$, we have

$$\mathbb{E}(Y_0 + \sum_{j=1}^{\delta} Y_j Z_j) = \mathbb{E}(Y_0) + \sum_{j=1}^{\delta} \mathbb{E}(Y_j Z_j) = \mathbb{E}(Y_0) + \sum_{j=1}^{\delta} \mathbb{E}(Y_j)\mathbb{E}(Z_j)$$

since the condition of independence is satisfied.

Denote by $W_\delta = Y_0 + \sum_{j=1}^{\delta} Y_j Z_j$. Hence,

$$\mathbb{E}(W_\delta) = \frac{q}{2} + \frac{\delta(\delta+1)}{2}\frac{q^2}{4} = \frac{q}{2} + \frac{\delta(\delta+1)q^2}{8}.$$

So for the expectation $\mathbb{E}(W_\delta)$ to be equal to the uniform expectation $\frac{q}{2}$, it must verify

$$\mathbb{E}(W_\delta) = \frac{\delta(\delta+1)q^2}{8} \equiv 0 \; [mod \; q] \tag{20}$$

i.e, there exist an integer $k \in \mathbb{F}_q$ such that:

$$\frac{\delta(\delta+1)q^2}{8} = kq$$

or equivalently, δ and k must verify the equation

$$\delta^2 + \delta - \frac{8k}{q} = 0 \tag{21}$$

where δ refers to the row's (*resp.* column's) index of the lower (*resp.* upper) triangular matrix.

Note 2. Recall that we have considered the secret symbols to be uniformly, independently and identically and distributed (*iid*) in $\mathbb{F}_q$. We can use the same approach when the *iid* secret symbols follow different distributions, since parameter δ plays a major role in the expectation of the variable $W_\delta = Y_0 + \sum_{j=1}^{\delta} Y_j Z_j$. *e.g.*, if we consider the expectation $\mathbb{E}(X) = f(q)$, then the equation to solve becomes

$$f(q) + \frac{\delta(\delta+1)}{2} f^2(q) \equiv \frac{q}{2} \; [mod \; q] \tag{22}$$

rather than (20).

Finally, it is trivial that using a transfer matrix of γ^2 symbols non-uniformly distributed over $\mathbb{F}_q$ is sufficient for an adversary, to sense the existence of a covert communication channel via statistical attacks.

We suppose in the following $X = [X_1, X_2, ..., X_{\gamma^2}]$ to be a series of variables with values $x_1, x_2, ..., x_{\gamma^2}$, and $F_{\gamma^2}(x)$ be the empirical cumulative distribution function of X, *i,e.*:

$$F_{\gamma^2}(x) = \frac{\text{number of } X_i\text{'s} \leq x}{\gamma^2}$$

χ^2 *Attack*: The χ^2 test is a statistical test for detecting randomness, based on the differences between the expected number of some chosen event occurrences and its real values, *i.e.*, the purpose of the test is to evaluate how likely the observations that are made would be, assuming the null hypothesis is true.

For our case we test the hypothesis:

H_0 : "The X_i's are *iid* random variables with distribution function F".

Where the distribution function for variable X is defined as $F(x) = \mathbb{P}(X \leq x)$.

Hence to test the distribution's uniformity of a given sample, we divide the range of $[1, q]$ into k adjacent intervals

$$[a_0, a_1[; [a_1, a_2[; \cdots ; [a_{k-1}, a_k[$$

and we let N_j denote the number of X_i 's in $[a_{j-1}, a_j[$ and let p_j denote the probability of an $X_i \in [a_{j-1}, a_j[$, so $p_j = F(a_j) - F(a_{j-1})$. Then the test statistic is

$$\chi^2 = \sum_{j=1}^{k} \frac{(N_j - np_j)^2}{np_j}$$

If H_0 is true, then np_j is the expected number of the n variables X_i that fall in the j-th interval, and so we expect χ^2 to be small.

Furthermore, when H_0 is true, the distribution of χ^2 converges to a chi-square distribution with $(k-1)$ degrees of freedom as $n \to +\infty$.

The chi-square distribution with $(k-1)$ degrees of freedom is the same as the Γ distribution with parameters $\frac{(k-1)}{2}$ and 2. Hence, we reject H_0 if

$$\chi^2 > {\chi^2}_{k-1,1-\alpha}$$

where ${\chi^2}_{k-1,1-\alpha}$ is the $(1-\alpha)$ quantile of the χ^2 distribution with $(k-1)$ degrees of freedom. Then for our case:

$$\chi^2 = \frac{k}{n} \sum_{j=1}^{k} \left(N_j - \frac{n}{k}\right)^2 \tag{23}$$

Kolmogorov-Smirnov (KS) Attack: Another powerful attack that could break the steganographic scheme is the two-samples *Kolmogorov-Smirnov (KS)* test [15]. KS test verifies the hypothesis that two samples are drawn from the same distribution. A low KS test statistic means that the distributions are similar, whereas a high KS test statistic means the distributions are different.

KS test is applicable to a variety of types of data with different distributions. Hence the statistic defined by:

$$D_{\gamma^2} = sup_x |F_{\gamma^2}(x) - F(x)| \tag{24}$$

has the (KS) distribution, where sup_x is the least upper bound of the set of distances.

Now we reject H_0 if $D_{\gamma^2} > d_{\{\gamma^2, 1-\alpha\}}$, where $d_{\{\gamma^2,1-\alpha\}}$ is the $(1-\alpha)$ quantile of the KS distribution. Here α is the significance level of the test (*i.e.*, probability of rejecting H_0 given that H_0 is true). Hence, an attacker knowing the MORE protocol, or observing different samples of MORE's batch transmission, can test different transfer matrices via KS and probably find a high statistic.

As stated above, the existence of hidden data can be detected, and the system confronted to passive and/or active statistical attacks.

The Proposed Technique. In the rest of this paper, we describe the proposed steganographic scheme for MORE based wireless multicast communications. To do so, we take advantage on a first hand, of the transfer matrix M_t of the protocol, *i.e.* the random process managing the coefficients of the linear combinations. And on a second hand, of the ability of a sender node to change its transmission range at ease, and broadcast packets to all neighbouring nodes.

Thus, we define the new covert channel as the sender's next-hop, where the receiver becomes in the transmission range. Additionally, we denote by $<b>_{2^n}$, the binary $\mathbb{F}_{2^n}$-representation of the integer b on n bits, where $1 \leq b \leq 2^n - 1$.

We consider a wireless RLNC network setting, where the nodes A, B and J are communicating via the MORE protocol, over a finite field $\mathbb{F}_q$ of size q, with γ denoting the number of packets in one batch $P = (p_1, p_2, ..., p_\gamma)$.

Recall that for each batch, the source must creates at least γ random linear combination of the γ native packets and broadcasts the coded packet, for the receiver to be able to decode the sources.

Sender Side. Say we want to hide a secret binary sequence M of length $|M|$ bits. First we cuts it into $m = \lceil \frac{|M|}{\lceil log_2(q) \rceil} \rceil$ non-zero blocks

$$M_q = <M_1>_q, <M_2>_q, ...<M_m>_q,$$

where we denote by $\lceil . \rceil$ the ceiling function.

We divide the range of $[1, q-1]$ into k adjacent intervals

$$[a_0, a_1[; [a_1, a_2[; \cdots ; [a_{k-1}, a_k[$$

Then we create a matrix S of k columns S_i, containing the symbols M_{2^n}, in such way that for all $s \in S_i, 1 \leq i \leq k : a_{i-1} < s \leq a_i$.

We map each secret symbol in M_{2^n} to its corresponding column, and in parallel, we save the associated indices (i, j) as binary 1 in a key matrix $\mathcal{K}_S$ of equal size, that will be used later for the extraction process.

When a given array reaches a size of 5, we complete via Algorithm 4, the matrix S by random values, drawn from the associated interval, until it reaches 5 elements (*i.e.*, to assure an uniform distribution of the secrets). We save once again the associated indices (i, j) in $\mathcal{K}_S$ as 0.

Once the insertion of M^o in S is completed, we complete one last time S and $\mathcal{K}_S$, as stated above, to form adequate square matrices S and $\mathcal{K}_S$ (*i.e.*, of size multiple of γ).

Finally, we embed S in $\lceil \frac{k}{\gamma} \rceil$ batch transmissions, as square blocks of size γ, each one as the transfer matrix for a corresponding batch.

Note 3. Note that the scheme can be applied similarly using a first in first out (FIFO) approach, for the case where the secret symbols are drawn randomly in the sender side.

Remark 1. We denote by $rand_{[a_{i-1}, a_i[}$ the random function returning a value uniformly in $[a_{i-1}, a_i[$.

Algorithm 3. *Arrange(int[] M^o, int l_M, int c)*: Arranges an ordered array M^o as a Matrix S of k columns with corresponding key matrix $\mathcal{K}_S$.

Input: Integers $\{a_0, a_1, \cdots, a_k\}$ referring to the intervals discussed above, ordered array M^o of symbols in $\mathbb{F}_q$, and an integer counter c for the arrangement process.
Output: Matrix S of k columns and the corresponding key $\mathcal{K}_S$.

```
int[][k]S, K_S;
int l_1 = c, l_2 = c, ··· , l_k = c;
intj = 0;
if (c = Null) then
  c = 0;
end if
for (int i = c; i ≤ l_M − 1; i++) do
  while (M^o[i] > a_j) do
    j++;
  end while
  S[l_j][j] = M^o[i];
  K_S[l_j][j] = 1;
  l_j++;
  if (l_j = 5(1 + c) && M^o[i + 1] ≤ a_j then
    RandFill(S, c, j);
  end if
  if (i ≥ l_M)&& (!IsInteger(l_j/γ)||!IsInteger(k/γ)) then
    l = l_j;
    for (int i = l; i < ⌈l/γ⌉; i++) do
      for (int j = k; j < ⌈k/γ⌉; j++) do
        S[i][j] = rand_[a_{i−1}, a_i[;
        K_S[i][j] = 0;
      end for
    end for
    return S, K_S;
  end if
  Arrange(M^o, Null, c++);
end for
```

Algorithms. Algorithm 3 arranges an array M of l_M symbols. Algorithm 4 completes the null values of the array S with random values from the corresponding interval. Algorithm 5 completes the null values of the array S with random values from the associated intervals, and embeds the corresponding square block of dimension γ. Finally, Algorithm 6 retrieves secret symbols in matrix M_t with $\mathcal{K}_{M_t}$ and c being respectively the corresponding key matrix and counter, then saves it in the array S^o.

Remark 2. Note that we used here the value 5 considering that the sample n to be tested by an adversary should be $n \geq 5k$. We can use another value according to a given case as long as the statistical tests performed are negative.

Algorithm 4. *RandFill(int[][] S, int c, int j)* Completes the null values of the array S with random values from the corresponding interval.

Input: The array S to be completed.
Output: Array S with completed values.

```
for (int i = 0; i < k; i++) do
  if (i = j) then
    i++;
  end if
  if (i ≥ k) then
    break
  end if
  while (l_i < 5(c+1)) do
    S[l_i][i] = rand_[a_{i-1}, a_i[;
    K_S[l_i][i] = 0;
    l_i++;
  end while
end for
return S,
```

Algorithm 5. *EmbedBlock(int[][] S, int[][] $\mathcal{K}_S$, int c, int γ)*: Completes the null values of S with random ones, then embeds the corresponding square block of dimension γ.

Input: The array S to be completed and the associated key $\mathcal{K}_S$, a counter c to iterate over S, and γ the dimension of the square transfer matrix M_t.
Output: Zero if the filling is completed.

```
Int[γ][γ] M_t;
if (c = Null) then
  c = 0;
end if
for (int i = c; i < γ(1+c); i++) do
  for (int j = c; i < γ(1+c); i++) do
    M_t[i][j] = S[c+i][c+j];
    K_{M_t}[i][j] = K_S[c+i][c+j];
  end for
end for
Embed(M_t, K_{M_t}); ( Embedding M_t as transfer matrix)
if (S[c+γ−1][c+γ−1] = Null) then
  return 0;
end if
EmbedBlock(S, K_S, c++, γ);
```

Remark 3. We denote by $Embed(M_t, \mathcal{K}_{M_t})$ the process of embedding M_t for the next batch, where $\mathcal{K}_{M_t}$ is the associated key.

Receiver Side. The receiver on the other hand, via Algorithm 6, constructs the secret matrix S^o using the transfer matrices M_t and associated key matrices $\mathcal{K}_{M_t}$ corresponding to each batch, and then concatenates them properly. If for a given batch, the key matrix is not provided, it means that the corresponding transmission do not contain secrets.

Algorithm 6. *Retrieve(int[][] S, int[][] M_t, int[][] $\mathcal{K}_{M_t}$, int c)*: Retrieves secret symbols in matrix M_t using key $\mathcal{K}_{M_t}$ and counter c.

Input: Matrix S for collecting secrets, square matrix M_t, key matrix $\mathcal{K}_{M_t}$ and counter c.

Output: Matrix S filled with the secret symbols when the sender sends a Null $\mathcal{K}_S$.

```
if (K_{M_t} = Null) then
  return S;
end if
if (c = Null) then
  c = 0;
end if
for (int i = c; i < γ(1 + c); i + +) do
  for (int j = c; j < γ(1 + c); j + +) do
    if (K_{M_t}[i][j] = 1) then
      S°[c + i][c + j] = M_t[i][j];
    end if
  end for
end for
```

The Protocol. Let P be a vector in $\mathbb{F}_q^\gamma$ containing the γ packets to be sent in the r'th batch transmission. We describe in the following the embedding and retrieval maps for this case:

$$\begin{array}{rcl} \mathcal{E} : \mathbb{F}_q^{\gamma^2} & \rightarrow & \mathcal{M}_\gamma(\mathbb{F}_q), \\ M_t & \mapsto & M_t.P \end{array} \tag{25}$$

and

$$\begin{array}{rcl} \mathcal{R} : \mathcal{M}_\gamma(\mathbb{F}_q) \times \mathcal{M}_\gamma(\mathbb{F}_2) & \rightarrow & \mathbb{F}_q^{\gamma^2}, \\ (M_t, \mathcal{K}_{M_t}) & \mapsto & Retrieve(S, M_t, \mathcal{K}_{M_t}, r). \end{array} \tag{26}$$

Embedding Capacity: The embedding capacity of the scheme depends naturally on the distribution of the secret symbols. Hence it varies between:

- 5 symbols per $\frac{n}{\gamma^2}$ batch transmissions as a minimum value, which occurs when successive secret symbols are dense in a given interval.
- n symbols per $\frac{n}{\gamma^2}$ batch transmissions which is the maximum value, occurring when the secret symbols are effectively uniformly *iid*.

Note 4. Once again, the value n here is $n = 5k$, which is the minimum size of sample for good steganalysis tests as discussed in Sect. (3.2).

As stated above, the embedding capacity of the protocol depends on how the symbols are distributed in the secret matrix S to hide.

We consider q, γ as stated above, n the number of symbols in a sample and $|S|$, the number of symbols in S, (*i.e.*, $|S| = \frac{l \times k}{\gamma^2}$).

$$\frac{5\gamma^2}{n}\ spb \leq C_{\mathsf{e}|b} \leq \gamma^2\ spb \tag{27}$$

$$\frac{5\gamma^2}{n}.\lceil log_2(q)\rceil bpb\ \leq C_{\mathsf{e}|b} \leq \gamma^2.\lceil log_2(q)\rceil\ bpb \tag{28}$$

where we denote by *spb* and *bpb* respectively, the pseudo units: symbols per batch and bits per batch.

Considering that affectation, comparison and incrementation are elementary operations: For the *RandFill()* Algorithm, we have one loop of order k where the other embedded loop does not exceed 5, thus

$$\Theta\big(RandFill()\big) = \Theta\big(5k\big) \tag{29}$$

where $\Theta(.)$ is the asymptotically tight bound on the running time (Landau notations).

In the *Arrange()* Algorithm, we have two embedded loops with (*i.e.*, $\Theta\big(k.l_M\big)$), with a call to *RandFill()* (*i.e.*, $\Theta\big(5k\big)$), two embedded loops of order $(\Theta\big(\frac{5k}{\gamma^2}\big))$, and one recursive call function:

$$\Theta\big(Arrange()\big) = \Theta\big(k(l_M + \frac{5}{\gamma^2} + 5)\big) \approx \Theta\big(kl_M\big) \tag{30}$$

The *EmbedBlock()* and *Retrieve()* Algorithms on the other hand, each is approximately $\Theta\big(\gamma^2\big)$ (the *Embed()* call is considered as a MORE's task):

$$\Theta\big(EmbedBlock()\big) = \Theta\big(k\big), \tag{31}$$

and

$$\Theta\big(Retrieve()\big) = \Theta\big(\gamma^2\big). \tag{32}$$

Hence the overall complexity of the algorithms is

$$\Theta\big(k(l_M + 5) + 2\gamma^2\big) \approx \Theta\big(kl_M + 2\gamma^2\big), \tag{33}$$

Furthermore, if we consider the secret array message to be sufficiently large comparing to the batch size γ, the overall complexity becomes $\Theta\big(kl_M\big)$.

Finally, for $l_M = 100$ the embedding capacity per operation time is:

$$\frac{1}{k}\ spo \leq C_{\mathsf{e}|o} \leq 1\ spo \tag{34}$$

$$\frac{\lceil log_2(q)\rceil}{k}\ bpo\ \leq C_{\mathsf{e}|o} \leq .\lceil log_2(q)\rceil\ bpo \tag{35}$$

where *spo* and *bpo* respectively, denoting the pseudo units: symbols per operation time and bits per operation time.

Note 5. Since the random generator is part of MORE protocol for constructing the transfer matrix, we consider complexity of maps $rand_{[a_{i-1},a_i[}$ in the embedding capacity. Additionally, intervals $[a_{i-1}, a_i[$ being relatively small comparing to $[1, q[$, using tables may be more efficient than using generator functions.

4 Conclusion

In this work, we proposed an enhanced version of MORE's steganoraphic protocol to increase security and complexity performances, by using simple matrix permutation keys and optimizing the embedding and retrieval algorithms. We gave a deeper steganalysis perspective and discussed the vulnerability of the scheme. Finally, we proposed a new steganographic scheme against statistical attacks.

References

1. Bender, W., Gruhl, D., Morimoto, N., Lu, A.: Techniques for data hiding. IBM Syst. J. **35**(3/4), 313–336 (1996)
2. Bierbrauer, J., Fridrich, J.: Constructing good covering codes for applications in steganography. In: Shi, Y.Q. (ed.) Transactions on Data Hiding and Multimedia Security III. LNCS, vol. 4920, pp. 1–22. Springer, Heidelberg (2008). https://doi.org/10.1007/978-3-540-69019-1_1
3. Belhamra, M.A., Souidi, E.M.: A steganogaphic scheme for mac-independent opportunistic routing and encoding (MORE) protocol. In: Proceedings of the 15th International Joint Conference on e-Business and Telecommunications, ICETE. SECRYPT, Porto, Portugal, 26–28 July, vol. 2, pp. 254–264 (2018)
4. Van Horenbeeck, M.: Deception on the network: thinking differently about covert channels. In: Proceedings of the 7th Australian Info, Warfare and Security Conference (2006). School of Computer and Information Science, Edith Cowan University, Perth, Western Australia
5. Mazurczyk, W., Caviglione, L.: Steganography in modern smartphones and mitigation techniques. IEEE Commun. Surv. Tutor. **17**(1), 334–357 (2015)
6. Wendzel, S., Zander, S., Fechner, B., Herdin, C.: Pattern-based survey and categorization of network covert channel techniques. ACM Comput. Surv. **47**(3), 50, 1–50, 26 (2015)
7. Szczypiorski, K., Mazurczyk, W.: Steganography in IEEE 802.11 OFDM symbols. Secur. Commun. Netw. **9**(2), 118–129 (2016)
8. Szczypiorski, K.: Steganography in TCP/IP networks. In: State of the Art and a Proposal of a New System-HICCUPS, Institute of Telecommunications' seminar, Warsaw University of Technology, Poland (2003)
9. Grabski, S., Szczypiorski, K.: Steganography in OFDM symbols of fast IEEE 802.11n networks. In: 2013 IEEE Symposium on Security and Privacy Workshops, San Francisco, CA, USA, 23–24 May 2013, pp. 158–164 (2013)
10. Kundur, D., Ahsan, K.: Practical internet steganography: data hiding in IP. In: Proceedings Texas Workshop Security of Information Systems (2003)
11. Mazurczyk, W., Smolarczyk, M., Szczypiorski, K.: Retransmission steganography and its detection. Soft. Comput. **15**(3), 505–515 (2011)

12. Mazurczyk, W., Szczypiorski, K.: Covert channels in SIP for VoIP signalling. In: Jahankhani, H., Revett, K., Palmer-Brown, D. (eds.) ICGeS 2008. CCIS, vol. 12, pp. 65–72. Springer, Heidelberg (2008). https://doi.org/10.1007/978-3-540-69403-8_9
13. Jankowski, B., Mazurczyk, W., Szczypiorski, K.: PadSteg: introducing inter-protocol steganography. Telecommun. Syst. **52**(2), 1101–1111 (2013)
14. Gentle, J.E.: Numerical Linear Algebra for Applications in Statistics. Springer, New York (2012)
15. Justel, A., Peña, D., Zamar, R.: A multivariate Kolmogorov-Smirnov test of goodness of fit. Stat. Probab. Lett. **35**(3), 251–259 (1997)
16. Krätzer, C., Dittmann, J., Lang, A., Kühne, T.: WLAN steganography: a first practical review. In: Proceedings of the 8th Workshop on Multimedia & Security, MM&Sec 2006, Geneva, Switzerland, 26–27 September 2006, pp. 17–22 (2006)
17. Mazurczyk, W., Szaga, P., Szczypiorski, K.: Using transcoding for hidden communication in IP telephony. Multimed. Tools Appl. **70**(3), 2139–2165 (2014)
18. Belhamra, M.A., Souidi, E.M.: Introduction to steganography in RRNS based communications. In: Proceedings of the 2nd International Conference on Networking, Information Systems & Security, NISS 2019, Rabat, Morocco, 27–28 March, pp. 21:1–21:7. ACM (2019)

Automated Verification of E-Commerce Protocols for Complex Transactions

Cătălin V. Bîrjoveanu[1(✉)] and Mirela Bîrjoveanu[2]

[1] Department of Computer Science, "Al. I. Cuza" University of Iaşi, Iaşi, Romania
cbirjoveanu@info.uaic.ro

[2] Continental Automotive, Iaşi, Romania
mbirjoveanu@gmail.com

Abstract. In our previous work [8] we defined *complex transactions* as the combination in any form of aggregate and optional transactions. The solution from [8] proposes an e-commerce protocol for complex transactions in that the customer wants to buy several different physical products from different merchants ensuring strong fair exchange, atomicity, effectiveness, timeliness, non-repudiation, integrity and confidentiality. In this paper, we improve the protocol for complex transactions from [8] by providing a more efficient protocol for each subtransaction from complex transaction. Also, we formally verify our improved solution using AVISPA. The verification results obtained using AVISPA demonstrate that our improved solution preserves all security requirements obtained in [8].

Keywords: Electronic commerce security · Complex transactions · Fair exchange · Formal verification

1 Introduction

In [8] we defined *complex transactions* as the combination in any form of aggregate and optional transactions. In electronic commerce, in *aggregate/atomic transactions* a customer wishes to buy a pack of products/services composed of several products (physical or digital)/services from different merchants, and the customer is interested in buying all products from the pack or no product at all. *Optional transactions* add more flexibility for customer. In this type of transactions, the customer wants to buy exactly one product from many merchants, and for this, he specifies in his request more possible products according to his preferences but from this options only one will be committed.

Besides the basic security requirements as confidentiality, authentication and non-repudiation, in e-commerce protocols, *fair exchange* is an essential security requirement. To achieve fair exchange, the proposed protocols are based on a Trusted Third Party (TTP) that can be inline, online or offline. The protocols that are based on inline TTP (that is used in every message) or on online TTP (that is used in every protocol instance) are not efficient because TTP becomes a

M. S. Obaidat (Ed.): ICETE 2018, CCIS 1118, pp. 87–110, 2019.
https://doi.org/10.1007/978-3-030-34866-3_5

bottleneck. Using offline TTP (that is involved in a protocol instance only when an exception appears) removes the disadvantage mentioned above. One goal of our protocol is to obtain the fair exchange requirement in complex transactions using an offline TTP.

In the literature there are proposed protocols for the payment of physical products that provide fair exchange and consider only one customer and one merchant [1,7,11,15,23].

There are known multi-party fair exchange protocols proposed with applications in e-commerce transactions for buying physical products [8], buying digital goods [16], digital signature of contracts [13,18], certified e-mail [24] and non-repudiation [19,22].

The solution proposed in [16] considers an aggregate transaction where a customer wants to buy several digital products from different merchants. This solution does not consider optional transactions and timeliness requirement is not assured. The paper from [13] proposes a multi-two party contract signing protocol where a consumer and many providers want to sign a contract pairwise. The solution from [13] assures only weak fairness requiring that all parties receive the expected items, or all honest parties will have enough evidence to prove that they have behaved correctly in front of an arbiter. In [22], an optimistic multi-party non-repudiation protocol is proposed, which allows the sender to exchange different messages with multiple recipients for non-repudiation evidences, but without taking into consideration atomicity. The solution from [8] proposes an e-commerce protocol for complex transactions in that the customer wants to buy several different physical products from different merchants ensuring strong fair exchange and atomicity for complex transactions, effectiveness, timeliness, non-repudiation, integrity and confidentiality.

In this paper, we improve the protocol for complex transactions from [8] by providing a more efficient protocol for each subtransaction from complex transaction. The improved subtransaction protocol contains only six messages compared to the one from [8] that contains ten messages. Also, we formally verify our improved solution using AVISPA. The verification results obtained using AVISPA demonstrate that our improved solution preserves all security requirements obtained in [8].

Our protocol has use cases in Business to Consumer (B2C) and Business to Business (B2B) scenarios as shown in [8].

The paper is structured as follows: Sect. 2 defines security requirements of complex transaction protocol, Sect. 3 describes the complex transaction protocol. Section 4 presents the formal specification and verification of the subtransaction protocol using AVISPA. Section 5 contains the security analysis of the complex transaction protocol. A comparative analysis is provided in Sect. 6 and Sect. 7 contains the conclusion.

2 Security Requirements

In what follows, we will discuss the security requirements we want to achieve in our optimistic fair exchange protocol for complex transactions: *effectiveness*, *fairness*, *timeliness*, *non-repudiation* and *confidentiality*. These requirements are stated and analyzed in [14,17] for certified electronic mail protocols, [13] for contract signing protocols, and [11] for electronic payment protocols for physical products.

Effectiveness requires that if every party involved in the complex transactions protocol behaves honestly, does not want to prematurely terminate the protocol, and no communication error occurs, then the customer receives his expected digital receipts from merchants, and the merchants receive their payments from the customer, without any intervention of Trusted Third Party (TTP). This is a requirement for *optimistic protocols*, where TTP intervenes only in case of unexpected situations, such as a network communication errors or dishonest behavior of one party.

Fairness for complex transactions requires:

- for any optional transaction from the complex transaction, the customer obtains exactly one digital receipt for the product's payment, and
- for any aggregate transaction from the complex transaction, the customer obtains the digital receipts for the payments of all products,

and each merchant obtains the corresponding payment for the product, or none of them obtains nothing. This requirement corresponds to the *strong fairness* requirement stated in [3].

Timeliness requires that any party involved in the complex transactions protocol can be sure that the protocol execution will be finished at a certain finite point of time, and that after the protocol finish point the level of fairness achieved cannot be degraded.

Non-repudiation in the complex transaction protocol requires that neither the customer nor any of merchants can deny their involvement in the complex transaction.

Confidentiality in the complex transaction protocol requires that the content of messages sent between participating parties is accessible only to authorized parties.

3 The Complex Transactions Protocol

In the complex transactions protocol (*CTP*), we consider that one customer can buy products in complex transactions from many merchants. *CTP* has the following participants: the customer (the payment Web segment), the merchants, the payment gateway and the bank.

Table 1 [8] presents the notations used in the description of *CTP*. We use hybrid encryption with the same meaning as in [8]. Hybrid encryption $\{m\}_{PubKA}$ of the message m with the public key *PubkA* means $\{m\}_K$, $\{K\}_{PubKA}$: the message m is encrypted with an AES session symmetric key K, which is in turn encrypted using *PubKA*. If two parties use the session symmetric key K in a hybrid encryption, then they will use K to hybrid encryption of all the messages that will be transmitted between them for the remainder of session.

We make some considerations about the communication channels we will use in *CTP*. In [14] are considered three types of communication channels: *operational*, *resilient* and *unreliable*. Operational communication channels (messages are correctly received in a finite amount of time) impose a not realistic assumption for the current networks. In *CTP*, we consider resilient communication channels (messages can be delayed but not lost) between PG and C, respectively between PG and M, that is similarly with assumption from [8]. The other communication channels are unreliable (messages can be lost).

Table 1. Notations used in the protocol description.

Notation	Interpretation
C, PG, Mi	Identity of Customer, Payment Gateway, Merchant i, where $1 \leq i \leq n$
$PubKA$	RSA public key of the party A
$\{m\}_{PubKA}$	Hybrid encryption of the message m with $PubKA$
$h(m)$	Digest of m obtained by applying of a hash function h (SHA-2)
$SigA(m)$	RSA digital signature of A on $h(m)$
$A \rightarrow B{:}m$	A sends the message m to B

3.1 The Preparation Phase

Before *CTP* execution, a preparation phase is needed. The customer is browsing through the online catalog where the products from merchants are posted. After the customer decides the products pack he wants to buy and the options/alternatives for each product from the pack, he clicks a "submit" button on the online catalog and the download of the payment Web segment is started. The payment Web segment has the same role as in the complex transactions protocol from [8], thus we use the term *customer* and *payment web segment* interchangeable, the context indicating which of them we refer to. The payment Web segment is a software digitally signed by payment gateway that runs on the customer's computer. The payment Web segment requires from customer the credit card information and a challenge code that will be used to authenticate and authorize the customer for using the credit card. For each subtransaction involved in the complex transaction (corresponding to the products the customer wishes to buy), the payment Web segment generates a RSA session public/private key pair for customer. We consider that the payment Web segment has the digital certificates for the public keys of each merchant and payment gateway. Also, each merchant/payment gateway has the digital certificate for the payment gateway/each merchant's public key.

For an aggregate transaction, we define the *aggregation* operator, denoted by $\wedge$, as follows: $Pid_1 \wedge \ldots \wedge Pid_k$ meaning that C wishes to buy exactly k products with product's identifiers $Pid_1, \ldots, Pid_k$. For an optional transaction, we define the *option* operator, denoted by $\vee$, as follows: $Pid_1 \vee \ldots \vee Pid_k$ meaning that

C wishes to buy a product that is exactly one of the products with product's identifiers $Pid_1, \ldots, Pid_k$, where the apparition order of the product's identifiers is the priority given by C. This means that C wishes first of all to buy the product Pid_1, but if this is not possible, his second option is Pid_2, and so on.

From C's choices describing the sequence of products he wishes to buy, we build a tree over the product identifiers selected by C using $\wedge$ and $\vee$ operators. To represent the tree, we use the *left-child, right-sibling representation* in that each internal node corresponds to one of the above operators or to an identifier, while each leaf node corresponds to an identifier. Each node of the tree is represented by a structure with the following fields: *info* for storing the useful information (identifier or one of the operators), *left* for pointing to the leftmost child of node, and *right* for pointing to the sibling of the node immediately to the right. The access to tree is realized trough the root.

A possible example of complex transaction is (Pid_1 or Pid_2) and (Pid_3 or Pid_4) and Pid_5 and Pid_6, where Pid_i are product's identifiers that C wishes to buy from different merchants. A tree derived from the above complex transaction is shown in Fig. 1 [8]. The root node has $\wedge$ operator as *info*. The root does not have any right sibling and its children are two nodes having $\vee$ operator as *info* and the nodes with the *info* Pid_5 and Pid_6.

Next, we will describe the subtransaction protocol (*SP*) in which the customer C buys a certain physical product from a certain merchant M.

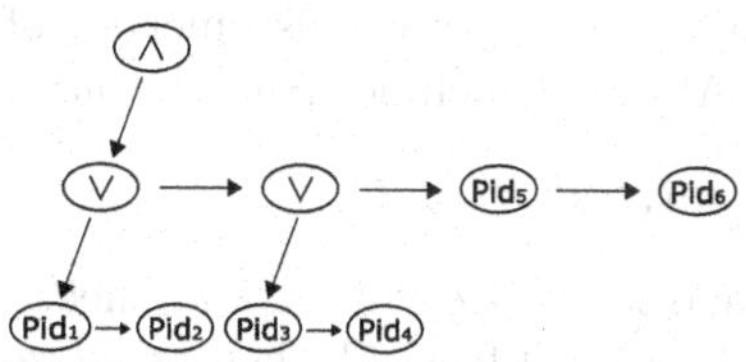

Fig. 1. Tree describing the customer's choices in left-child, right-sibling representation.

3.2 The Subtransaction Protocol

CTP uses *SP*. *SP* is an improved variant of STP protocol from [8]. The major difference between *SP* and STP protocol is that *SP* consists of two sub-protocols: the exchange sub-protocol and the resolution sub-protocol. In *SP*, the subtransaction's identifier is generated by payment Web segment, which allows us that setup and exchange sub-protocols from STP to be combined into only one exchange sub-protocol in *SP*. Also, this improvement allowed us to eliminate one resolution sub-protocol from STP.

Next, we will describe *SP*'s sub-protocols messages that are graphically represented in Fig. 2.

Exchange Sub-protocol. In the first message, the payment Web segment sends to M a payment message PM and a purchase order message PO, both encrypted with $PubKM$. The message is hybrid encrypted with M's public key $PubKM$.

Message 1: $C \rightarrow M$:$\{PM, PO\}_{PubKM}$
$PM = \{PI, SigC(PI)\}_{PubKPG}$

PM is build by payment Web segment by encrypting with PG's public key of the payment information PI and the customer's signature on PI. The encryption of PI with PG's public key assures that PI cannot be found out by M.

$PI = C, CardN, CCode, Sid, Amount, PubKC, M$

PI contains the data provided by user: his identity C, card number $CardN$ and a challenge code $CCode$ issued by bank. The challenge code is provided to user by bank via SMS an it has a minimum length of four characters. The payment Web segment generates a fresh random number Sid that will be used as an unique identifier of the subtransaction and includes it in PI. Also, PI contains the amount $Amount$, $PubKC$, and merchant's identity M.

$PO = OI, SigC(OI)$

PO is build from the order information OI provided by C and the signature of C on OI. OI contains the identity of customer C, of merchant M and the product's identifier Pid. Also, OI includes Sid, $Amount$, and $PubKC$.

$OI = C, M, Pid, Amount, Sid, PubKC$

Upon receiving message 1, M decrypts it and checks the signature of C on OI. If M agrees with PO received from C, then he stores PO as an evidence of C's order and sends message 2 to PG.

Message 2: $M \rightarrow PG$:$\{PM, SigM(Sid, C, M, PubKC, Amount)\}_{PubKPG}$

In message 2, M sends to PG the payment message PM and his signature on the subtransaction identifier, C's public key and amount. Upon receiving message 2, PG decrypts it, checks C's signature on PI and checks if C is authorized to use the card by checking if the combination of $CardN$ and $CCode$ is valid. If these checks are successfully passed, then also C proves as being the owner of the public key $PubKC$. PG checks M's signature, and if checking is successful, then it has the confirmation that both C and M agreed on Sid, $PubKC$ and $Amount$. Also, PG checks the freshness of $PubKC$, and Sid to avoid any replay attack from dishonest merchants. If some check fails, then PG sends to M a response $ABORT$ for aborting the subtransaction. If all checks are successful, PG sends the payment message to the bank. The bank checks C's account balance, and if it is enough, then the bank makes the transfer in M's account providing an response YES ($Resp = YES$) to PG that forwards it to M in message 3.

Otherwise, if checking C's account balance fails, then also the transfer fails and the bank provides an response $ABORT$ ($Resp = ABORT$) to PG that forwards it to M in the message 4. Also, PG stores the messages 2 and 3 in its databases as an evidence of the subtransactions details.

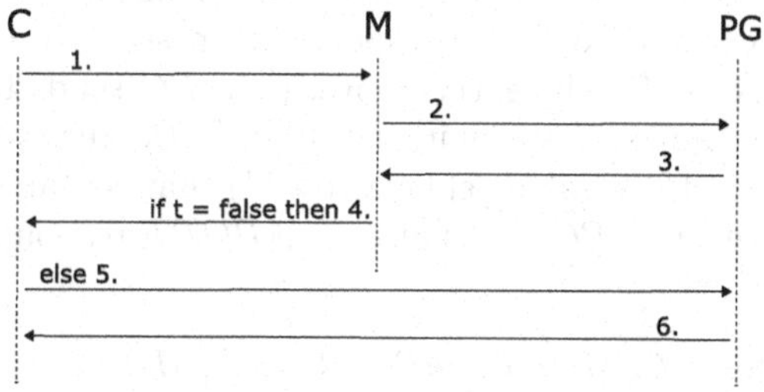

Fig. 2. *SP* message flow.

Message 3:
$PG \rightarrow M$:$\{Resp, C, M, Sid, SigPG(Resp, C, M, Sid, Amount)\}_{PubKM}$

Upon receiving message 3, M decrypts it and sends to C, in the message 4, the response and PG's signature on response both encrypted with $PubKC$.

Message 4:
$M \rightarrow C$:$\{Resp, C, M, Sid, SigPG(Resp, C, M, Sid, Amount)\}_{PubKC}$

C decrypts message 4 and checks PG's signature. If checking is successful, then C has the guarantee of the response's authenticity (it is from PG) and it corresponds to the current subtransaction. The presence in response of Sid, and $Amount$ proves the response's freshness and it is not replayed by a dishonest merchant. A response with $Resp = YES$ means that the subtransaction successfully finished and the content of message 4 ($Resp, C, M, Sid, SigPG(Resp, C, M, Sid, Amount)$) is a digital receipt for the payment of product. A response with $Resp = ABORT$ means that the content of message 4 is a proof of the subtransaction's abort.

Resolution Sub-protocol. If C sends the payment in message 1, but he does not receive message 4, or receives an invalid message from M, then an unfair case appears: C sends the payment and it was processed, but C did not receive any response. In this case, a timeout interval t (e.g. in the order of seconds or minutes) is defined, in which C waits message 4 from M. If t expires and C does not receive message 4 from M or receives an invalid message, then C initiates the resolution sub-protocol with PG (the messages 5 and 6) to receive a response w.r.t. the current subtransaction.

Message 5: $C \rightarrow PG$:$\{Sid, Amount, PubKC,$
$SigC(Sid, Amount, PubKC)\}_{PubKPG}$

Upon receiving message 5, PG decrypts it and checks if a response has been generated for the entry Sid, $Amount$ and $PubKC$. If PG finds in its database a response for the entry above, and checking the signature of C using $PubKC$ is successful, then it sends to C the response in message 6. Otherwise, if PG does not find a response for the entry above, then PG sends to C an $ABORT$ response in message 6 and stores it in its database. If PG receives the payment in message 2 (sent by M afterward or replayed by M) that contains the information from the entry above, then PG sends also an $ABORT$ response to M.

Message 6:
$PG \rightarrow C$:$\{Resp, C, M, Sid, SigPG(Resp, C, M, Sid, Amount)\}_{PubKC}$

3.3 CTP Description

In the complex transaction protocol, a subtransaction s, denoted by $SP(C, M_i, Pid_i)$, is an instance of SP in which C buys the physical product with Pid_i identifier from the merchant M_i. We define $St(s)$ the state of the subtransaction s as being the content of messages 4 (identical with message 6) that C will receive in s. More exactly, $St(s) = (Resp, C, M, Sid, SigPG(Resp, C, M, Sid, Amount))$, where $Resp \in \{YES, ABORT\}$.

For $St(s)$ a state of the subtransaction s, we denote by $St(s).Resp$ the response ($Resp$) in $St(s)$, and by $St(s).Sig$ the signature in $St(s)$.

We define $Ns(p)$ - the state of the node p as a sequence of subtransaction states $St(s_1) \ldots St(s_m)$ corresponding to the product defined by p. For a node p, $Ns(p)$ is calculated depending on the $p \rightarrow info$ as follows:

- if $p \rightarrow info = Pid_i$, where $1 \leq i \leq n$, then $Ns(p) = St(SP(C, M_i, Pid_i))$. For simplicity, we consider that M_i is the merchant that sells the product with Pid_i identifier, where $1 \leq i \leq n$.
- if $p \rightarrow info = \vee$, then

$$Ns(p) = \begin{cases} Ns(l), \text{ if} \exists\, l, \text{ the leftmost child of } p \text{ such that } St(s).Resp = YES, \\ \qquad\qquad \text{for all } St(s) \in Ns(l) \\ Ns(r), \text{ otherwise} \end{cases}$$

  where r is the rightmost child of p.
  The node p corresponds to $\vee$ operator w.r.t. the customer's choices and this preferences are prioritized by appearance in the child nodes of p from left to the right. $Ns(p)$ is the node state of the leftmost child of p, denoted $Ns(l)$, for which all subtransactions from $Ns(l)$ have successfully finished SP. Otherwise, if all subtransactions from node states of all children of p are aborted, then $Ns(p)$ is the node state of the rightmost child of p.
- if $p \rightarrow info = \wedge$, and $c_1, \ldots, c_k$ are all children of p, then we have two cases:

1. if $St(s).Resp = YES$, for any $St(s)$ from $Ns(c_j)$, for any $1 \leq j \leq k$, then $Ns(p) = Ns(c_1) \ldots Ns(c_k)$.
2. otherwise, let be c_j, where $1 \leq j \leq k$, the leftmost child of p with $Ns(c_j) = St(s_{j1}) \ldots St(s_{jm})$ such that $St.(s_{jl}).Resp = ABORT$, for all $1 \leq l \leq m$. In this case, $Ns(p) = Ns(c_1) \ldots Ns(c_j)$. Even if the subtransactions states from $Ns(c_1), \ldots, Ns(c_{j-1})$ are YES (that means that the subtransactions from $Ns(c_1), \ldots, Ns(c_{j-1})$ have successfully finished *SP*), the aborted subtransactions $s_{j1}, \ldots, s_{jm}$ from $Ns(c_j)$ lead to aborting the entire aggregate transaction corresponding to p. That is why all subtransactions states from $Ns(c_1), \ldots, Ns(c_{j-1})$ will be aborted. Thus, will set $St(s).Resp = ABORT$, for any $St(s) \in Ns(c_r)$, for any $1 \leq r \leq j-1$.
   Because the node p corresponds to $\wedge$ operator, $Ns(p)$ is the sequence of node states of p's children. For efficiency, the sequence of node states of p's children is calculated until c_j the leftmost child of p for that $Ns(c_j)$ contains only aborted subtransaction states.

Thus, $Ns(p)$ contains a sequence of subtransaction states in which either all subtransactions successfully finished *SP* or all subtransactions are aborted.

CTP, described in Table 2 [8], recursively calculates $Ns(t)$ (t is the root of the tree derived from the customer's choices), traversing the tree in a similar manner with depth-first search. For any node p of the tree, we use a *child* array to store the node states of all children of p.

At the lines 2–4, the protocol computes $Ns(p)$ for a node p, depending on the node state of the left most child of p. For a node p with a least two children, the while loop (the 6–14 lines) computes the node state of any child of p except the left most one. We remark that way in which node state is computed is essential to obtain the fair exchange and atomicity of a complex transaction (lines 8–12): if an aborted subtransaction/sequence of subtransactions leads to aborting the entire aggregate transaction, but some subtransactions from the aggregate transaction successfully completed *SP*, then the ones that are successful must also be stored in the node state corresponding to $\wedge$ operator (line 11) and afterwards aborted by applying *AggregateAbort* sub-protocol (line 12). We will describe *AggregateAbort* sub-protocol in the Sect. 3.3.

At line 15, the protocol computes $Ns(p)$ for a node p with a product identifier as *info*.

The node state for a node that corresponds to $\vee$ operator, for which all subtransactions states from all its children are aborted, is computed at lines 16–18. The node state for a node that corresponds to $\wedge$ operator for that all subtransactions states from all its children successfully completed *SP*, is computed at lines 19–20.

AggregateAbort Sub-protocol. As we discussed in the previous section, in *CTP*, there may be cases in which an aborted subtransaction/sequence of subtransactions leads to aborting the entire aggregate transaction, but some subtransactions from the aggregate transaction successfully completed

Table 2. Complex transactions protocol.

```
CTP(t)
if (t → left ≠ NULL)  child[0] = CTP(t → left);
if ((t → info = ∨ and St(s).Resp = YES, for all St(s) from child[0]) or
    (t → info = ∧ and St(s).Resp = ABORT, for all St(s) from child[0]))
        Ns(t) = child[0];  return Ns(t);
j = 1;  k = t → left → right;
while (k ≠ NULL)
        child[j] = CTP(k);
        if (t → info = ∨ and St(s).Resp = YES, for all St(s) from child[j])
                Ns(t) = child[j];  return Ns(t);
        if (t → info = ∧ and St(s).Resp = ABORT, for all St(s) from child[j])
                for (c = 0; c ≤ j; c = c + 1)  Ns(t) = Ns(t)child[c]; end for
                AggregateAbort(Ns(t));  return Ns(t);
        k = k → right;  j = j + 1;
end while
if (t → info = Pid_i)  Ns(t) = St(SP(C, M_i, Pid_i));  return Ns(t);
else if (t → info = ∨)  k = t → left;
                while (k → right ≠ NULL)  k = k → right; end while
                Ns(t) = Ns(k);  return Ns(t);
      else  for (c = 0; c ≤ j - 1; c = c + 1)  Ns(t) = Ns(t)child[c]; end for
            return Ns(t);
      end if
end if
```

SP. As a result, an unfair case occurs for C: the entire aggregate transaction is not successful, but C has paid for certain products. For example, for a node p that corresponds to $\wedge$ operator, *CTP* computes the node state $Ns(p) = St(s_1)\dots St(s_k)St(s_{k+1})\dots St(s_m)$, where $St(s_i).Resp = YES$ for any $1 \leq i \leq k$ and $St(s_j).Resp = ABORT$ for any $k+1 \leq j \leq m$. The entire complex transaction corresponding to the node p is not completed successfully because the component subtransactions $s_{k+1}, \dots, s_m$ are aborted, but in the same complex transaction C paid for the products involved in the subtransactions $s_1, \dots, s_k$. So, the fairness will be obtained by applying $AggregateAbort(Ns(p))$ sub-protocol in that entire aggregate transaction will be aborted. Next, we will describe $AggregateAbort(Ns(p))$ sub-protocol.

To solve the unfair case mentioned above, the payment Web segment initiates the $AggregateAbort(Ns(p))$ sub-protocol by sending to PG in the message 7 a customer request to abort $Ns(p)$. The message 7 is build from $Ns(p)$ and the customer's signature on $Ns(p)$, both encrypted with $PubKPG$.

Message 7: $C \rightarrow PG$:$\{Ns(p), SigC(Ns(p))\}_{PubKPG}$

Upon receiving the message 7, PG decrypts it, obtains the sequence of subtransaction states $St(s_1) \ldots St(s_m)$ in $Ns(p)$, and checks the signature of C on $Ns(p)$ to be sure that this request comes from C. Also, PG checks his signature from each subtransaction state $St(s)$ from $Ns(p)$. If all checks are successfully passed, then PG sends to the bank the customer's request. The bank aborts any subtransaction's state $St(s) = (Resp, C, M, Sid, SigPG(Resp, C, M, Sid, Amount)) \in Ns(p)$, such that $St(s).Resp = YES$ by canceling the transfer corresponding to $St(s)$ from customer's account into merchant's account, and updating $St(s)$ by:

1. $OldSt(s) = St(s)$,
2. $St(s).Resp = ABORT$ and
3. $St(s).Sig = SigPG(St(s).Resp, C, M, Sid, Amount, OldSt(s))$.

By updating $St(s)$ as above, $St(s)$ becomes aborted, and PG's signature is updated including the old subtransaction state. In this way, any party (C, M_i, or PG) can check afterward PG's signature from the updated $St(s)$ to ensure that the subtransaction s that successfully completed SP has been authorized aborted. Thus, we remark that no party can have 2 different independent subtransaction states for the same subtransaction.

The bank sends the new $Ns(p)$ computed above (in that any subtransaction state is aborted) to PG that forwards it to C in message 8.

Message 8: $PG \rightarrow C$:$\{Ns(p), SigPG(Ns(p))\}_{PubKC}$

PG stores message 8 in its database for transaction's evidence.

Also, in message 9, PG sends simultaneously the subtransaction state $St(s) \in Ns(p)$ just aborted by the above procedure, to each merchant M involved in the subtransaction s.

Message 9: $PG \rightarrow M$:$\{St(s)\}_{PubKM}$

4 Formal Specification and Verification of SP

4.1 AVISPA Tool

To verify the security requirements of *SP*, we used the AVISPA tool for automated validation of large-scale Internet security protocols [21]. In AVISPA, a protocol has to be specified in the High Level Protocol Specification Language (HLPSL) [4,5,10]. This means to specify the protocol itself, the scenario to analyze, and the security properties to verify. A HLPSL specification is automatically translated, using the hlpsl2if translator, into the Intermediate Format (IF) that is the input for four back-ends that implement different verification techniques. The Avispa tool includes the back-ends: Cl-AtSe (Constraint-Logic-based Attack Searcher) - a model checker that uses constraint solving techniques [20], OFMC (On-the-Fly Model-Checker) - a model checker that uses symbolic techniques [6], SATMC [2] (SAT-based Model-Checker) and TA4SP [9] (Tree Automata for the Analysis of Security Protocols) - a tool using tree automata based on automatic approximations. All these back-ends are considering a Dolev-Yao intruder [12] that controls the communication channels on the network under the perfect cryptography assumption.

HLPSL is a role based language. Each participant is specified by a basic role, and a protocol's session is specified by a composition of the basic roles. The protocol's steps are modeled by transitions in the corresponding basic role.

4.2 Protocol's Roles

Next, we will emphasize the most important aspects of each basic role.

The customer role in HLPSL is described in Fig. 3. The customer role has as parameters the identities of the customer, merchant and payment gateway, the card number *CardN*, the challenge code *CCode*, the product's identifier *Pid*, the amount *Amount*, and the public keys of the merchant and payment gateway. The parameters of *channel* type *Snd* and *Rcv* are considered according to the Dolev-Yao intruder model, in which all messages sent by agents will be received by intruder. The local variables of the customer role are specified using *local* keyword. The customer role has four transitions. Typically, a transition consists of a trigger and an action performed when the trigger occurs. A trigger occurs when the role instance is in a corresponding state and an appropriate message is received on *Rcv* channel. The state of the role instance is defined by *State* variable. An action performed after a trigger is represented by sending a message on *Snd* channel. The first transition corresponds to the message 1 of *SP*. This transition is triggered if the customer receives the *start* signal to begin the protocol's session. In this transition, the customer generates a new subtransaction identifier *Sid*, a new public key *PubKC* and a new symmetric session key *Kcm* to be used in the hybrid encryption. The values for these variables are assigned by *new()* function. A digital signature of a message is specified by encryption of the message hash using the corresponding private key. In this transition, the customer's digital signature of the payment information $PI = C, CardN, CCode, Sid, Amount, PubKC, M$ is represented by encryption using the customer's corresponding private key $inv(PubKC)$ of the hash of PI. The effect of this transition is that message 1 is sent by customer to the merchant on *Snd* channel and a sequence of *secret* and *witness* events corresponding to the security requirements are specified. We will describe the *secret* and *witness* events below in the Sect. 4.5.

The second transition corresponds to the reception by customer of the message 4 of *SP*. The effect of this transition is specification of a sequence of *request* events. Also, the *request* event will be described below in the Sect. 4.5.

The third transition corresponds to the message 5 from *SP*, and this transition is triggered by receiving the timeout *t*.

```
role customer (C, M, PG: agent,
        CardN, CCode, Pid: text,
        Amount: nat,
        PubKM, PubKPG: public_key,
        Hash: hash_func,
        Snd, Rcv: channel(dy))
played_by C def=

 local State: nat,
       Sid: text,
       PubKC: public_key,
       Kcm, Kcpg: symmetric_key,
       PM: {agent.text.text.text.nat.public_key.agent.
            {hash(agent.text.text.text.nat.public_key.agent)}_inv(public_key)}_public_key,
       PO: agent.agent.text.nat.text.public_key.
           {hash(agent.agent.text.nat.text.public_key)}_inv(public_key),
       Resp: nat

 init State := 0

 transition

  1. State  = 0 /\ Rcv(start)  =|>
     State' :=1
     /\ Sid' :=new()
     /\ PubKC' :=new()
     /\ Kcm' :=new()
     /\ PM' :={C.CardN.CCode.Sid'.Amount.PubKC'.M.
              {Hash(C.CardN.CCode.Sid'.Amount.PubKC'.M)}_inv(PubKC')}_PubKPG
     /\ PO' :=C.M.Pid.Amount.Sid'.PubKC'.{Hash(C.M.Pid.Amount.Sid'.PubKC')}_inv(PubKC')
     /\ Snd({PM'.PO'}_Kcm'.{Kcm'}_PubKM)
     /\ secret(CardN,scn,{C,PG})
     /\ secret(Pid,sp,{C,M})
     /\ secret(Amount,sa,{C,M,PG})
     /\ witness(C,PG,pg_c_pi,C.CardN.CCode.Sid'.Amount.PubKC'.M)
     /\ witness(C,M,m_c_oi,C.M.Pid.Amount.Sid'.PubKC')

  2. State  = 1 /\ Rcv({Resp'.C.M.Sid.{Hash(Resp'.C.M.Sid.Amount)}_inv(PubKPG)}_Kcm)  =|>
     State':= 2
     /\ request(C,PG,c_pg_resp,Resp'.C.M)
     /\ request(C,M,c_m_oi,C.M.Pid.Amount.Sid.PubKC)

  3. State  = 2 /\ Rcv(t)  =|>
     State':= 3
     /\ Kcpg' := new()
     /\ Snd({Sid.Amount.PubKC.{Hash(Sid.Amount.PubKC)}_inv(PubKC)}_Kcpg'.{Kcpg'}_PubKPG)

  4. State  = 3 /\ Rcv({Resp'.C.M.Sid.{Hash(Resp'.C.M.Sid.Amount)}_inv(PubKPG)}_Kcpg)  =|>
     State':= 4
     /\ request(C,PG,c_pg_resp,Resp'.C.M)
     /\ request(C,M,c_m_oi,C.M.Pid.Amount.Sid.PubKC)

end role
```

Fig. 3. Customer role in HLPSL.

The fourth transition corresponds to the reception by customer of the message 6 from *SP*. In this transition the same *request* events are specified as in the second transition.

The merchant role is specified in Fig. 4. The first transition of the merchant's role is triggered if the merchant receives the message 1 of *SP* and if the pair formed by product identifier and amount $(Pid, Amount)$ is in the merchant's list of products *PList*. The effect of this transition is sending the message 2 of *SP*. The second and the third transitions correspond to the reception of message 3 from *SP* and the sending of the message 4 from *SP*.

The payment gateway role is specified in Fig. 5. The payment gateway role includes as parameters two lists *CIList* and *RList*. *CIList* is the payment gateway's list of records of payment information for each customer. For example, the record from *CIList* corresponding to the customer C is $C.CardN.CCode$. *RList* is the payment gateway's list of records corresponding to the responses sent by *PG* in message 3 of *SP*. The local variable *Resp* is used to model payment gateway responses from SP.

The payment gateway role has four transitions. The first transition is triggered if the payment gateway receives the message 2 of *SP* and if the payment information of the customer are in *CIList*, meaning that the customer is authorized to use the card. The result of this transition is that the payment gateway generates a positive response, adds the response to *RList*, and sends the message 3 to merchant. In the second transition, if the payment information are not in *CIList*, then a negative response is generated, added to *RList*, and message 3 is sent. The transitions 3 and 4 models the messages of Resolution sub-protocol from *SP*. In the transition 3, if payment gateway receives message 5 from *SP* and has a response in *RList* corresponding to the customer's request, then the response is sent to customer. In the transition 4, if payment gateway receives message 5 from *SP* and does not have a response in *RList* corresponding to the customer's request (the variable *State* is 0), then a negative response is generated, added to *RList*, and sent to customer.

4.3 Protocol's Sessions

A session of *SP* is an instance of *SP* specified by parallel composition (using the $\wedge$ operator) of the basic roles as shown in Fig. 6. This role is parametrized by all variables necessary for one session of the protocol.

4.4 Execution Environment

The environment role shown in Fig. 7 is a top-level role in which the protocol is analyzed. This role specifies the initial knowledge of the intruder and the protocol scenario to be verified. The intruder's initial knowledge includes the identities of customer, merchant and payment gateway, all public keys, his own private key, his payment information, a product identifier *pid*3 and an amount $amount3$, and the hash function. The constant i is used to refer to the intruder. The protocol scenario to be verified is a parallel composition of three protocol's

```
role merchant (C, M, PG: agent,
        PubKM, PubKPG: public_key,
        PList: (text.nat) set,
        Hash: hash_func,
        Snd, Rcv: channel(dy))
played_by M def=

 local State: nat,
       Pid: text,
       Amount: nat,
       Sid: text,
       PubKC: public_key,
       Kcm, Kmpg: symmetric_key,
       X: {agent.text.text.text.nat.public_key.agent.
          {hash(agent.text.text.text.nat.public_key.agent)}_inv(public_key)}_public_key,
       Resp: nat

 init State := 0

 transition

  1. State  = 0 /\
     Rcv({X'.C.M.Pid'.Amount'.Sid'.PubKC'.
          {Hash(C.M.Pid'.Amount'.Sid'.PubKC')}_inv(PubKC')}_Kcm'.{Kcm'}_PubKM)
     /\ in(Pid'.Amount' , PList) =|>
     State' :=1
     /\ Kmpg' :=new()
     /\ Snd({X'.{Hash(Sid'.C.M.PubKC'.Amount')}_inv(PubKM)}_Kmpg'.{Kmpg'}_PubKPG)
     /\ witness(M,C,c_m_oi,C.M.Pid'.Amount'.Sid'.PubKC')
     /\ witness(M,PG,pg_m_a,Amount')

  2. State  = 1 /\ Rcv({1.C.M.Sid.{Hash(1.C.M.Sid.Amount)}_inv(PubKPG)}_Kmpg) =|>
     State':= 2
     /\ Snd({1.C.M.Sid.{Hash(1.C.M.Sid.Amount)}_inv(PubKPG)}_Kcm)
     /\ request(M,PG,m_pg_resp,Resp')
     /\ request(M,C,m_c_oi,C.M.Pid.Amount.Sid.PubKC)

  3. State  = 1 /\ Rcv({0.C.M.Sid.{Hash(0.C.M.Sid.Amount)}_inv(PubKPG)}_Kmpg) =|>
     State':= 2
     /\ Snd({0.C.M.Sid.{Hash(0.C.M.Sid.Amount)}_inv(PubKPG)}_Kcm)
     /\ request(M,PG,m_pg_resp,Resp')

end role
```

Fig. 4. Merchant role in HLPSL.

sessions (protocol's instances), where payment gateway is TTP and the intruder may play the customer and merchant role. In the environment role, the section of local variable initialization (specified by the *init* keyword) specifies the product list *PList* initially known by merchant, the payment gateway's list *CIList* of records of payment information for the customer *c* and the intruder *i*, and an empty list *RList* of responses.

```
role paymentgateway (C, M, PG: agent,
        PubKM, PubKPG: public_key,
        CIList: (agent.text.text) set,
        RList: (agent.agent.nat.text.nat.public_key.{hash(nat.agent.agent.text.nat)}_inv(public_key)) set,
        Hash: hash_func,
        Snd, Rcv: channel(dy))
played_by PG def=

 local State: nat,
       CardN, CCode: text,
       Amount: nat,
       Sid: text,
       PubKC: public_key,
       Kcpg, Kmpg: symmetric_key,
       Resp: nat

 init State := 0 /\ Resp :=0

 transition

  1. State  = 0
    /\ Rcv({{C.CardN'.CCode'.Sid'.Amount'.PubKC'.M.
            {Hash(C.CardN'.CCode'.Sid'.Amount'.PubKC'.M)}_inv(PubKC')}_PubKPG.
            {Hash(Sid'.C.M.PubKC'.Amount')}_inv(PubKM)}_Kmpg'.{Kmpg'}_PubKPG)
    /\ in(C.CardN'.CCode' , CIList)  =|>
    State' :=1
    /\ Resp' :=1
    /\ RList' :=cons(C.M.Resp'.Sid'.Amount'.PubKC'.{Hash(Resp'.C.M.Sid'.Amount')}_inv(PubKPG) , RList)
    /\ Snd({Resp'.C.M.Sid'.{Hash(Resp'.C.M.Sid'.Amount')}_inv(PubKPG)}_Kmpg')
    /\ request(PG,C,pg_c_pi,C.CardN'.CCode'.Sid'.Amount'.PubKC'.M)
    /\ witness(PG,C,c_pg_resp,Resp'.C.M)
    /\ request(PG,M,pg_m_a,Amount')
    /\ witness(PG,M,m_pg_resp,Resp')

  2. State  = 0
    /\ Rcv({{C.CardN'.CCode'.Sid'.Amount'.PubKC'.M.
            {Hash(C.CardN'.CCode'.Sid'.Amount'.PubKC'.M)}_inv(PubKC')}_PubKPG.
            {Hash(Sid'.C.M.PubKC'.Amount')}_inv(PubKM)}_Kmpg'.{Kmpg'}_PubKPG)
    /\ not(in(C.CardN'.CCode' , CIList))  =|>
    State' :=1
    /\ RList' :=cons(C.M.Resp.Sid'.Amount'.PubKC'.{Hash(Resp.C.M.Sid'.Amount')}_inv(PubKPG) , RList)
    /\ Snd({Resp.C.M.Sid'.{Hash(Resp.C.M.Sid'.Amount')}_inv(PubKPG)}_Kmpg')
    /\ witness(PG,C,c_pg_resp, Resp.C.M)
    /\ request(PG,M,pg_m_a,Amount')
    /\ witness(PG,M,m_pg_resp,Resp)

  3. State = 1
    /\ Rcv({Sid.Amount.PubKC.{Hash(Sid.Amount.PubKC)}_inv(PubKC)}_Kcpg'.{Kcpg'}_PubKPG)
    /\ in(C.M.Resp'.Sid.Amount.PubKC.{Hash(Resp'.C.M.Sid.Amount)}_inv(PubKPG) , RList) =|>
    State' :=2
    /\ Snd({Resp'.C.M.Sid.{Hash(Resp'.C.M.Sid.Amount)}_inv(PubKPG)}_Kcpg')
    /\ witness(PG,C,c_pg_resp, Resp'.C.M)

  4. State=0
    /\ Rcv({C.M.Sid'.Amount'.PubKC'.{Hash(Sid'.Amount'.PubKC')}_inv(PubKC')}_Kcpg'.{Kcpg'}_PubKPG)  =|>
    State' :=3
    /\ Resp' :=0
    /\ RList' :=cons(C.M.Resp'.Sid'.Amount'.PubKC'.{Hash(Resp'.C.M.Sid'.Amount')}_inv(PubKPG) , RList)
    /\ Snd({Resp'.C.M.Sid'.{Hash(Resp'.C.M.Sid'.Amount')}_inv(PubKPG)}_Kcpg')
    /\ witness(PG,C,c_pg_resp, Resp'.C.M)

 end role
```

Fig. 5. Payment gateway role in HLPSL.

```
role session(C,M,PG: agent,
        CardN, CCode, Pid: text,
        Amount: nat,
        PubKM, PubKPG: public_key,
        Hash: hash_func,
        PList: (text.nat) set,
        CIList: (agent.text.text) set,
        RList: (agent.agent.nat.text.nat.public_key.{hash(nat.agent.agent.text.nat)}_inv(public_key)) set,
        Snd, Rcv: channel(dy))
def=
 composition
    customer (C,M,PG,CardN,CCode,Pid,Amount,PubKM,PubKPG,Hash,Snd,Rcv)
    /\ merchant (C,M,PG,PubKM,PubKPG,PList,Hash,Snd,Rcv)
    /\ paymentgateway (C,M,PG,PubKM,PubKPG,CIList,RList,Hash,Snd,Rcv)

end role
```

Fig. 6. Session of *SP* in HLPSL.

```
role environment() def=

 local PList: (text.nat) set,
        CIList: (agent.text.text) set,
        RList: (agent.agent.nat.text.nat.public_key.{hash(nat.agent.agent.text.nat)}_inv(public_key)) set,
        Snd, Rcv: channel(dy)

 const c, m, pg, i: agent,
        cn1,cc1,cn2,cc2, pid1,pid2,pid3: text,
        amount1,amount2,amount3: nat,
        pubkm,pubkpg,pubki: public_key,
        h: hash_func,
        scn, sp, sa, pg_c_pi, c_pg_resp, m_c_oi, c_m_oi, pg_m_a, m_pg_resp: protocol_id,
        t: text

 init PList :={pid1.amount1, pid2.amount2, pid3.amount3}
      /\ CIList :={c.cn1.cc1, i.cn2.cc2}
      /\ RList := {}

 intruder_knowledge = {c, m, pg, cn2, cc2, pubkm, pubkpg, pubki, inv(pubki), pid3, amount3, h}

 composition
     session(c,m,pg,cn1,cc1,pid1,amount1,pubkm,pubkpg,h,PList,CIList,RList,Snd,Rcv)
    /\ session(c,i,pg,cn1,cc1,pid2,amount2,pubki,pubkpg,h,PList,CIList,RList,Snd,Rcv)
    /\ session(i,m,pg,cn2,cc2,pid3,amount3,pubkm, pubkpg,h,PList,CIList,RList,Snd,Rcv)

end role
```

Fig. 7. Environment role in HLPSL.

4.5 Security Requirements in HLPSL

The security requirements that are analyzed for our protocol are described in the section goal from Fig. 8. In HLPSL, secrecy and authentication properties

```
goal

 secrecy_of scn
 secrecy_of sp
 secrecy_of sa
 authentication_on pg_c_pi
 authentication_on c_pg_resp
 authentication_on m_c_oi
 authentication_on c_m_oi
 authentication_on pg_m_a
 authentication_on m_pg_resp

end goal
```

Fig. 8. Protocol verification HLPSL.

are the only properties that can be specified directly by *goal facts*. A goal fact is specified in a basic role as an effect of a specific transition.

To model confidentiality of an information *E*, we use the *secret* goal fact in the form *secret(E,identifier,agents_set)* in the basic role where *E* is generated or communicated for the first time. The meaning of this fact is that *E* is a secret shared between the agents from *agents_set*. The second parameter, *identifier*, is a constant of *protocol_id* type declared in the environment role, and used with *secrecy_of* keyword in the goal section. A violation of this goal fact occurs if there is a protocol execution in which the intruder learns *E* and he is not in the set *agents_set*. For example, in our protocol, we require that card number *CardN* to be known only by customer and payment gateway. For this, we introduce in first transition of the customer role the goal fact *secret(CardN,scn,{C,PG})*, and in the goal section we specify *secrecy_of scn*. In a similar manner we specify the confidentiality of *Pid* between customer and merchant, and confidentiality of *Amount* between customer, merchant and payment gateway.

In HLPSL, two forms of authentication can be directly specified: strong authentication and weak authentication. In our protocol we require strong authentication. To model the strong authentication of an agent *A* to an agent *B* with agreement on an information *E*, two authentication goal facts are used: *witness* and *request*. The goal fact *witness(A,B,identifier,E)* is specified in the role of the authenticated agent *A*, meaning that *A* wants to authenticate itself to *B* agreeing on the information *E*. The goal fact *request(B,A,identifier,E)* is specified in the role of the agent *B* that does the authentication, meaning that *B* accepts the authentication of *A* and agrees with *A* on *E*. The *identifier* parameter is a constant of *protocol_id* type declared in the environment role, and used with *authentication_on* keyword in the goal section. So, strong authentication is achieved if for an emitted *request*, a corresponding *witness* was previously emitted for the same information. A violation of strong authentication occurs if there is a protocol execution in which for a *request* the is no previously generated a corresponding *witness*. Weak authentication is specified by the keyword *weak_authentication_on*, followed by a constant identifier, used like for strong authentication in agents roles with the goal facts *witness* and *wrequest*. In weak authentication, a *witness* can be used for several *wrequest* contrarily to strong authentication where it can be used for only one request.

For example, in our protocol, we require that the payment gateway strong authenticates the customer on the payment information. For this, we introduce in first transition of the customer role the goal fact *witness(C,PG,pg_c_pi,C.CardN.CCode.Sid'.Amount.PubKC'.M)*, in first transition of payment gateway role the goal fact *request(PG,C,pg_c_pi,C.CardN'.CCode'.Sid'.Amount'.PubKC'.M)*, and in the goal section we specify *authentication_on pg_c_pi*. In a similar manner we ask that customer strong authenticates payment gateway on response using the *c_pg_resp* identifier. Also, we require strong mutual authentication between customer and merchant on the order information using *m_c_oi* and *c_m_oi* identifiers, payment gateway strong authenticates merchant on amount using *pg_m_a* identifier, and merchant strong authenticates payment gateway on response using *m_pg_resp* identifier.

Fairness is not explicitly modeled in HLPSL. So, AVISPA can not directly verify fairness requirement. *SP* ensures fairness if the customer obtains the digital receipt (response) and the merchant obtains the payment for product. The merchant obtains the payment for product from customer, but the payment is processed by payment gateway. The customer obtains the digital receipt from merchant, but however the digital receipt is generated by payment gateway. In conclusion, we can state that *SP* ensures fairness if payment gateway strong authenticates customer on payment information, and customer strong authenticates payment gateway on digital receipt.

PG strong authenticates *C* on *PI* provides an evidence that *M* received message 1 from *C* containing payment message *PM* and purchase order *PO*, and also *PG* received from *M* message 2 containing *PM* and *M*'s signature. *C* strong authenticates *PG* on the response *Resp* provides an evidence that *M* received *Resp* from *PG* and *M* sent *Resp* to *C*.

Therefore, we model fairness in HLPSL by strong authentication goals *witness* and *request* using the identifiers *pg_c_pi* and *c_pg_resp* as described above.

4.6 SP Verification Results

Verification of SP specification using Cl-AtSe and OFMC did not show any attack. The verification was done using both typed and untyped model. By default, verification is done using typed model in which all variables and constants are typed. The option untyped model considers all variables to be of generic type, and this option is used for detection of type-flaw attacks. The other two back-ends SATMC and TA4SP are not offering support for our analysis.

The confidentiality requirements in *SP* are verified by secret goal facts. The verification results demonstrate the confidentiality of card number *CardN* between *C* and *PG*, of *Pid* between *C* and *M*, and of *Amount* between *C*, *M* and *PG*.

The authentication requirements in *SP* are verified by witness and request goal facts. The verification results demonstrate that *PG* strong authenticates

C on *PI*, *C* strong authenticates *PG* on *Resp*, strong mutual authentication between *C* and *M* on *OI*, *PG* strong authenticates *M* on *Amount*, and *M* strong authenticates *PG* on *Resp*.

Fairness requirement in *SP* is verified by strong authentication requirements. The verification results demonstrate that fairness is achieved because *PG* strong authenticates *C* on *PI* and *C* strong authenticates *PG* on *Resp*.

Non-repudiation requirements in *SP* are implicitly verified by strong authentication requirements. The verification results demonstrate that *C* can not deny its involvement in *SP* because *PG* strong authenticates *C* on *PI*, and *M* can not deny its involvement in *SP* because *PG* strong authenticates *M* on *Amount*.

5 CTP Security Analysis

In this section, we will analyze the security requirements stated in Sect. 2 for our *CTP*.

5.1 Effectiveness

If every party involved in the complex transaction protocol from Table 2 behaves according to the protocol's steps, does not want to prematurely terminate the protocol and there are no network communication delays/errors, then our protocol assures that the customer receives the digital receipts from merchants, and each merchant receives his corresponding payment from the customer without TTP involvement. Therefore, our protocol meets the effectiveness requirement.

5.2 Fairness

In our *CTP*, fairness may not be insured only for *C*. The payment Web segment performs customer's side protocol actions and is a soft digitally signed by *PG* that is a trusted party. So, any corruption of the payment Web segment by user or *M* is impossible.

CTP uses *SP*. To obtain fairness in *CTP*, a necessary but not sufficient condition is to obtain fairness in *SP*. In Sect. 4, the fairness verification results for *SP* obtained in AVISPA showed that there is no attack. So, our *SP* ensures fairness.

Fairness obtained in all subtransactions from a complex transaction does not directly imply that fairness is ensured in entire complex transaction. So, in addition to fairness in *SP*, to obtain fairness in *CTP*, two requirements must be also ensured. First, for any optional transaction from the complex transaction, *C* obtains exactly one digital receipt for the payment of only one product, and corresponding merchant obtains the payment for the product, or none of them obtains nothing. The product is either an individual product, or an aggregate product that corresponds to a $\wedge$ operator. Also, the digital receipt is either an individual receipt corresponding to an individual product, or is a sequence of receipts corresponding to an aggregate product. As we have seen in Table 2,

CTP ensures this requirement. Secondly, for any aggregate transaction from the complex transaction, C obtains the digital receipts for the payments of all products, and each merchant obtains the corresponding payment for product, or none of them obtains nothing. In *CTP*, the node state for a node corresponding to $\wedge$ operator is computed as follows: if all subtransactions from all node states of all children of the node $\wedge$ have successfully finished *SP*, then the node state of $\wedge$ is the sequence of node states of its children. Otherwise, the node state of $\wedge$ is the sequence of node states of its children until to the leftmost child that contains only aborted subtransaction states in its node state. But, in this last case, an unfair case occurs for C: the entire aggregate transaction is not successful, but C has paid for certain products and he received the digital receipt for these. We note that this is the only case in that fairness for C can be violated in *CTP*. In this case, as we have seen in *CTP*, *AggregateAbort* sub-protocol is applied. More exactly, C (payment Web segment) initiates *AggregateAbort* sub-protocol from Sect. 3.3 to abort any subtransaction that successfully finished *SP* and that belongs to the unsuccessful aggregate transaction. Thus, the unfair case for C is solved: the entire aggregate transaction is aborted, meaning that any subtransaction which belongs to the aggregate transaction is aborted.

As a result, fairness exchange of payment for digital receipt in complex transactions and complex transactions atomicity are preserved.

5.3 Timeliness

Any party can be sure that *CTP* execution will be finished at a certain finite point of time. We have introduced a timeout interval t in *SP* when C waits the message 4 from M. If t expires, then C initiates Resolution sub-protocol with *PG*. If in *CTP*, a complex transaction contains subtransactions that successfully finished *SP* and also contains an aborted subtransaction, then *AggregateAbort* sub-protocol is executed between C and *PG*, to abort any subtransaction from the complex transaction. The communication channel between C and *PG* is resilient, and as a result, *CTP* execution will be finished at a certain finite point of time. After *CTP* finish point, the level of fairness achieved cannot be degraded. If after the finish point, C has the digital receipts of payments for products, then each merchant obtains also the corresponding payment for his product. On the other side, if each merchant involved obtains the payment for his product, then, after the protocol finish point, C gets the corresponding digital receipts from the messages 4 or messages 6. Moreover, if after the finish point, C has not received the digital receipts, then also the corresponding merchant does not get the payment; if each merchant involved has not get the payment, then C also does not receive the digital receipts.

5.4 Non-repudiation

In any subtransaction from *CTP* neither the customer nor any of merchants can deny their involvement in the complex transaction. These non-repudiation requirements are obtained as a direct consequence of authentication as we shown in Sect. 4.

5.5 Confidentiality

As a result of verification results obtained in Sect. 4, *CTP* ensures confidentiality requirements for the most relevant information from each subtransaction: *CardN*, *Pid* and *Amount*.

6 Comparative Analysis

Table 3 [8] provides a comparative analysis between the security requirements obtained by our protocol and the security requirements obtained by the most related solutions to our proposal.

Table 3. Multi-party fair exchange e-commerce protocols: a comparative analysis.

Scenario	Our protocol	Liu	Draper-Gil	Yanping
	Payment for physical products in complex transactions	Payment for digital products in aggregate transactions	Contract signing	Non-repudiation
Atomicity	Y	Y	Y	N
Effectiveness	Y	Y	Y	Y
Fairness	S	W	W	S
Timeliness	Y	N	Y	Y
Non-repudiation	Y	Y	Y	Y
Confidentiality	Y	N	Y	Y

Y = YES, N = NO
S = Strong
W = Weak

7 Conclusions

In this paper, we proposed an improved version of the optimistic fair exchange e-commerce protocol for complex transactions from [8]. We significantly reduced the number of messages from subtransaction protocol which is an important part of complex transaction protocol. This leads to a more efficient complex transaction protocol. To prove the correctness of our solution, we formally verify it using AVISPA. The verification results obtained demonstrate that our improved solution preserves all security requirements obtained in [8].

References

1. Alaraj, A.: Fairness in physical products delivery protocol. Int. J. Comput. Netw. Commun. (IJCNC) **4**(6), 99 (2012)
2. Armando, A., Compagna, L.: SATMC: a SAT-based model checker for security protocols. In: Alferes, J.J., Leite, J. (eds.) JELIA 2004. LNCS, vol. 3229, pp. 730–733. Springer, Heidelberg (2004). https://doi.org/10.1007/978-3-540-30227-8_68

3. Asokan, N.: Fairness in electronic commerce. Ph.D. thesis, University of Waterloo, Canada (1998)
4. AVISPA Team: AVISPA v1.1 User Manual. Version: 1.1 (2006). http://www.avispa-project.org/
5. AVISPA Team: HLPSL Tutorial: A Beginner's Guide to Modelling and Analysing Internet Security Protocols. Version: 1.1 (2006). http://www.avispa-project.org/
6. Basin, D., Modersheim, S., Vigano, L.: OFMC: a symbolic model-checker for security protocols. Int. J. Inf. Secur. **4**, 181–208 (2005). https://doi.org/10.1007/s10207-004-0055-7
7. Bîrjoveanu, C.V.: Anonymity and fair-exchange in e-commerce protocol for physical products delivery. In: 12th International Conference on Security and Cryptography, pp. 170–177. SCITEPRESS (2015). https://doi.org/10.5220/0005508801700177
8. Bîrjoveanu, C.V., Bîrjoveanu, M.: An optimistic fair exchange e-commerce protocol for complex transactions. In: 15th International Joint Conference on e-Business and Telecommunications, ICETE 2018, SECRYPT, vol. 2, pp. 277–288. SCITEPRESS (2018). https://doi.org/10.5220/0006853502770288
9. Boichut, Y., Héam, P-C., Kouchnarenko, O.: Automatic verification of security protocols using approximations. Research Report RR-5727, INRIA (2005)
10. Chevalier, Y., et al.: A high level protocol specification language for industrial security-sensitive protocols. In: Workshop on Specification and Automated Processing of Security Requirements, pp. 193–205. Austrian Computer Society (2004)
11. Djuric, Z., Gasevic, D.: FEIPS: a secure fair-exchange payment system for internet transactions. Comput. J. **58**(10), 2537–2556 (2015)
12. Dolev, D., Yao, A.: On the security of public-key protocols. IEEE Trans. Inf. Theory **2**(29), 198–208 (1983)
13. Draper-Gil, G., Ferrer-Gomila, J.L., Hinarejos, M.F., Zhou, J.: An asynchronous optimistic protocol for atomic multi-two-party contract signing. Comput. J. **56**(10), 1258–1267 (2013)
14. Ferrer-Gomila, J.L., Onieva, J.A., Payeras, M., Lopez, J.: Certified electronic mail: properties revisited. Comput. Secur. **29**(2), 167–179 (2010). https://doi.org/10.1016/j.cose.2009.06.009
15. Li, H., Kou, W., Du, X.: Fair e-commerce protocols without a third party. In: 11th IEEE Symposium on Computers and Communications. IEEE (2006). https://doi.org/10.1109/ISCC.2006.74
16. Liu, Y.: An optimistic fair protocol for aggregate exchange. In: 2nd International Conference on Future Information Technology and Management Engineering. IEEE (2009). https://doi.org/10.1109/FITME.2009.145
17. Liu, Z., Pang, J., Zhang, C.: Verification of a key chain based TTP transparent CEM protocol. Electron. Notes Theoret. Comput. Sci. **274**, 51–65 (2011). https://doi.org/10.1016/j.entcs.2011.07.006
18. Mukhamedov, A., Ryan, M.D.: Fair multi-party contract signing using private contract signatures. Inf. Comput. **206**(2–4), 272–290 (2008). https://doi.org/10.1016/j.ic.2007.07.007
19. Onieva, J.A., Lopez, J., Zhou, J.: Secure Multi-Party Non-Repudiation Protocols and Applications. Springer, Heidelberg (2009). https://doi.org/10.1007/978-0-387-75630-1
20. Turuani, M.: The CL-Atse protocol analyser. In: Pfenning, F. (ed.) RTA 2006. LNCS, vol. 4098, pp. 277–286. Springer, Heidelberg (2006). https://doi.org/10.1007/11805618_21

21. Vigano, L.: Automated security protocol analysis with the AVISPA tool. Electron. Notes Theoret. Comput. Sci. **155**, 61–86 (2006). https://doi.org/10.1016/j.entcs.2005.11.052
22. Yanping, L., Liaojun, P.: Multi-party non-repudiation protocol with different message exchanged. In: 5th International Conference on Information Assurance and Security. IEEE (2009). https://doi.org/10.1109/IAS.2009.329
23. Zhang, Q., Markantonakis, K., Mayes, K.: A practical fair exchange e-payment protocol for anonymous purchase and physical delivery. In: 4th ACS/IEEE International Conference on Computer Systems and Applications. IEEE (2006). https://doi.org/10.1109/AICCSA.2006.205188
24. Zhou, J., Onieva, J.A., Lopez, J.: Optimised multi-party certified email protocols. Inf. Manag. Comput. Secur. J. **13**(5), 350–366 (2005). https://doi.org/10.1108/09685220510627250

Security for Distributed Machine Learning Based Software

Laurent Gomez[1(✉)], Alberto Ibarrondo[2], Marcus Wilhelm[3], José Márquez[4], and Patrick Duverger[5]

[1] SAP Global Security, SAP Security Research, Mougins, France
laurent.gomez@sap.com
[2] Eurecom, Sophia Antipolis, France
alberto.ibarrondo@eurecom.com
[3] Hasso Plattner Institute, University Potsdam, Potsdam, Germany
marcus.wilhelm@student.hpi.com
[4] Portfolio Strategy and Technology Adoption, SAP SE, Walldorf, Germany
jose.marquez@sap.com
[5] City of Antibes - Juan les Pins, France
patrick.duverger@ville-antibes.fr

Abstract. Current developments in Enterprise Systems observe a paradigm shift, moving the needle from the backend to the edge sectors of those; by distributing data, decentralizing applications and integrating novel components seamlessly to the central systems. Distributively deployed AI capabilities will thrust this transition.

Several non-functional requirements arise along with these developments, security being at the center of the discussions. Bearing those requirements in mind, hereby we propose an approach to holistically protect distributed Deep Neural Network (DNN) based/enhanced software assets, i.e. confidentiality of their input & output data streams as well as safeguarding their Intellectual Property.

Making use of Fully Homomorphic Encryption (FHE), our approach enables the protection of Distributed Neural Networks, while processing encrypted data. On that respect we evaluate the feasibility of this solution on a Convolutional Neuronal Network (CNN) for image classification deployed on distributed infrastructures.

Keywords: Intellectual property protection · Fully homomorphic encryption neural networks · Distributed landscapes · Smart cities

1 Introduction

1.1 Motivation

Until now, the backend (on-prem & cloud) deployments were considered as the single source of truth & unique point of access in regards of Enterprise Systems (ES). Nevertheless, a paradigm shift has been recently observed, by the deployment of ES assets towards the Edge sectors of the landscapes; by distributing

M. S. Obaidat (Ed.): ICETE 2018, CCIS 1118, pp. 111–134, 2019.
https://doi.org/10.1007/978-3-030-34866-3_6

data, decentralizing applications, de-abstracting technology and integrating edge components seamlessly to the central backend systems.

Capitalizing on recent advances on High Performance Computing along with the rising amounts of publicly available labeled data, Deep Neural Networks (DNN), as an implementation of AI, have and will revolutionize virtually every current application domain as well as enable novel ones like those on autonomous, predictive, resilient, self-managed, adaptive, and evolving applications.

Distributively deployed AI capabilities will thrust the above mentioned transition. As reported by Deloitte, "*... companies are incorporating artificial intelligence in particular, machine learning into their 'Internet of Things applications' and seeing capabilities grow, including improving operational efficiency and helping avoid unplanned downtime*" [28].

1.2 Problem Statement

The deployment of data processing capabilities throughout Distributed Enterprise Systems rises several security challenges related to the protection of input & output data [26] as well as of DNN-based/enhanced software assets.

In the specific context of distributed intelligence, DNN-based/enhanced software assets will represent key investments in infrastructure, skills and governance, as well as in the acquisition of data and talents. The software industry is therefore in the direct need to safeguard these strategic investments by enforcing the protection of this new form of Intellectual Property.

Furthermore, on the wake of Data Protection (DP) regulations such as the EU-GDPR [26], Independant Software Vendors (ISVs) have the non-transferable requirement to comply with those.

Therefore, ISVs aim to protect both: data and the Intellectual Property of their DNN-based/enhanced software assets, deployed on potentially unsecure edge hardware & platforms [15].

1.3 State-of-the-Art

Security of Deep Neural Networks is a current research topic taking advantage of two major cryptographic approaches: variants of Fully Homomorphic Encryption/FHE [12] and Secure Multi-Party Computation/SMC [8]. While FHE techniques allow addition and multiplication on encrypted data, SMC enables arithmetic operations on data shared across multi-parties.

Several approaches can be found in the literature, at different phases of the development and deployment of DNNs.

Secure Training. Secure DNN training has been addressed using FHE [16] and SMC [30], disregarding protection once the trained model is to be productively deployed. Other Machine Learning models such as linear and logistic regressions have also been trained in a secure way in [24]. In those approaches, confidentiality of training data is guaranteed, while runtime protection (i.e. input, model, output) is out of scope.

Processing on Encrypted Data. At processing phase, SMC has led to cooperative solutions where several devices work together to obtain federated inferences [21], not supporting deployment of the trained DNN to trusted decentralized systems. DNN processing on FHE encrypted data is covered in CryptoNets [13], improved in [4,18]. More recently, in [2], the authors proposed a privacy-preserving framework for deep learning, making use of the SEAL [29] FHE library. While disclosure of data at runtime is prevented in these solutions, protection of DNN models remains out of the scope.

Intellectual Property Protection of DNN Model. In [31], the authors tackles IP protection of DNN models through model watermarking. While infringement can be detected with this method, it can not be prevented. Furthermore, runtime protection of input, model and output are out of scope.

To the best of our knowledge, no other publication has holistically tackled the protection of both trained DNN models and data, targeting distributed untrusted systems.

1.4 Data and Intellectual Property Protection for Deep Neural Networks

In this paper we propose a novel approach for the Intellectual Property Protection of DNN-based/enhanced software assets while enabling data protection at processing time, making use of concepts such as Fully Homomorphic Encryption (FHE).

Once trained, DNN model parameters (i.e. weights, biases) are encrypted homomorphically. The resulting (encrypted) DNN can be distributed across untrusted landscapes, preserving its IP while mitigating the risk of reverse engineering. At runtime, FHE-encrypted insights from encrypted input data are produced by the homomorphically encrypted DNN. Confidentiality of both trained DNN, input and output data will be therefore guaranteed.

Despite of recent improvements of FHE schemes [3,5] and implementations [17,25,29], homomorphic encryption remains computationally expensive. Hence it could represent a bottleneck having a negative impact on overall performance, and on the accuracy of encrypted DNNs outputs, handling encrypted inputs. In this paper, we therefore evaluate as well the overall performance (e.g. CPU, memory, disk usage) along with the accuracy of encrypted DNNs.

This paper is organized as follows: Sect. 2 details the fundamentals of our approach. Section 3 provides an overview of our solution. In Sects. 4 and 5, we present the architecture and evaluation, concluding with an outlook in Sect. 6.

2 Fundamentals

2.1 Deep Neural Network

Figure 1 depicts a DNN with multiple layers. It is composed of L layers:

1. An **input layer**, the tensor of input data $\mathbf{X}$.
2. $L - 1$ **hidden layers**, mathematical computations transforming $\mathbf{X}$ sequentially.
3. An **output layer**, the tensor of output data $\mathbf{Y}$.

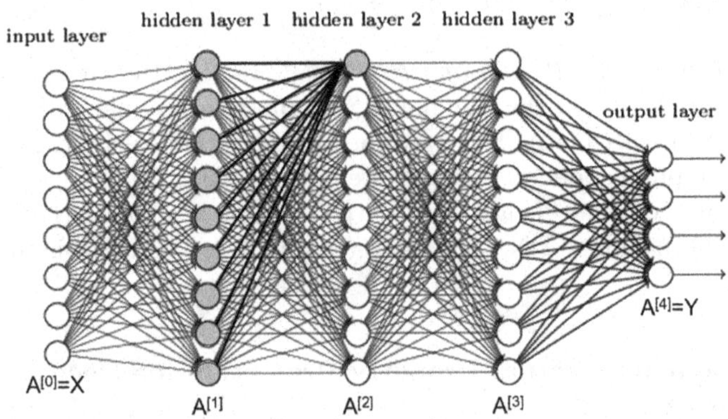

Fig. 1. Deep neural network [14].

We denote the output of layer i as a tensor $\mathbf{A}^{[\mathbf{i}]}$, with $\mathbf{A}^{[\mathbf{0}]} = X$, and $\mathbf{A}^{[\mathbf{L}]} = Y$. Tensors can have different sizes and number of dimensions.

Each layer $\mathbf{A}^{[\mathbf{i}]}$ depends on the mathematical computations performed at the previous layer $\mathbf{A}^{[\mathbf{i-1}]}$. At each layer $\mathbf{A}^{[\mathbf{i}]}$, two types of function can be computed:

- *Linear*: involving polynomial operations.
- *Non-linear*, involving non-linear operations, so called activation function, such as *max*, *exp*, *division*, ReLU, or Sigmoid.

Linear Computation Layer. For the sake of clarity, we exemplify the inner linear computation with a Fully Connected (FC) layer, as depicted in Fig. 2.

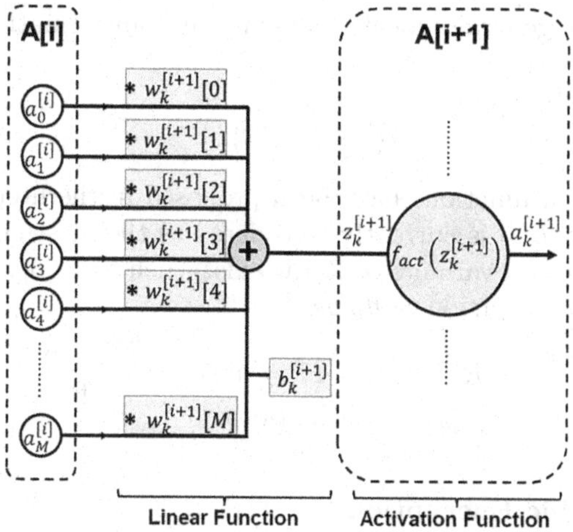

Fig. 2. Fully Connected layer with activation function [14].

A Fully Connected layer, noted $\mathbf{A}^{[i]}$, is composed of n parallel *neurons*, performing a $\mathbb{R}^n \rightarrow \mathbb{R}^n$ transformation (see Fig. 2). We define:

$\mathbf{a}^{[\mathbf{i}]} = \left[a_0^{[i]} \ldots a_k^{[i]} \ldots a_N^{[i]}\right]^T$ as the output of layer $\mathrm{A}^{[i]}$;

$\mathbf{z}^{[\mathbf{i}]} = \left[z_0^{[i]} \ldots z_k^{[i]} \ldots z_N^{[i]}\right]^T$ as the linear output of layer $\mathrm{A}^{[i]}$; ($\mathbf{z}^{[\mathbf{i}]} = \mathbf{a}^{[\mathbf{i}]}$ if there is no activation function)

$\mathbf{b}^{[\mathbf{i}]} = \left[b_0^{[i]} \ldots b_k^{[i]} \ldots b_N^{[i]}\right]^T$ as the bias for layer $\mathrm{A}^{[i]}$;

$\mathbf{W}^{[\mathbf{i}]} = \left[\mathbf{w}_\mathbf{0}^{[\mathbf{i}]} \ldots \mathbf{w}_\mathbf{k}^{[\mathbf{i}]} \ldots \mathbf{w}_\mathbf{N}^{[\mathbf{i}]}\right]^T$ as the weights for layer $\mathrm{A}^{[i]}$.

Neuron k performs a linear combination of the output of the previous layer $\mathbf{a}^{[\mathbf{i-1}]}$ multiplied by the weight vector $\mathbf{w}_\mathbf{k}^{[\mathbf{i}]}$ and shifted with a bias scalar $b_k^{[i]}$, obtaining the linear combination $z_k^{[i]}$:

$$z_k^{[i]} = \left(\sum_{l=0}^{M} w_k^{[i]}[l] * a_l^{[i-1]}\right) + b_k^{[i]} = \mathbf{w}_\mathbf{k}^{[\mathbf{i}]} * \mathbf{a}^{[\mathbf{i-1}]} + b_k^{[i]} \text{ [14]} \tag{1}$$

Vectorizing the operations for all the neurons in layer $A^{[i]}$ we obtain the dense layer transformation:

$$\mathbf{z}^{[\mathbf{i}]} = \mathbf{W}^{[\mathbf{i}]} * \mathbf{a}^{[\mathbf{i-1}]} + \mathbf{b}^{[\mathbf{i}]} \text{ [14]} \tag{2}$$

where $\mathbf{W}$ and $\mathbf{b}$ are the parameters for layer $A^{[i]}$.

Activation Functions. Activation functions are the major source of non-linearity in DNNs. They are performed element-wise ($\mathbb{R}^0 \rightarrow \mathbb{R}^0$, thus easily vectorized), and are generally located after linear transformations such as Fully Connected layers.

$$a_k^{[i]} = f_{act}\left(z_k^{[i]}\right) \tag{3}$$

Several activation functions have been proposed in the literature but *Rectified Linear Unit (ReLU)* is currently considered as the most efficient activation function for DL. Several variants of ReLU exist, such as Leaky ReLU [23], ELU [7] or its differentiable version *Softplus*.

$$\begin{aligned} ReLU(z) &= z^{+} = max(0, z) \\ Softplus(z) &= log(e^{z} + 1) \end{aligned} \quad [14] \tag{4}$$

2.2 Homomorphic Encryption

While preserving data privacy, Homomorphic Encryption (HE) schemes allow certain computations on ciphertext without revealing neither its inputs nor its internal states. Gentry [12] first proposed a Fully Homomorphic Encryption (FHE) scheme, which theoretically could compute any kind of arithmetic circuit, but is computationally intractable in practice. FHE evolved into more efficient schemes preserving addition and multiplication over encrypted data, such as BGV [3], FV [11] or CKKS [5], allowing approximations of multiplicative inverse, exponential and logistic function, or discrete Fourier transformation. Similar to asymmetric encryption, a public-private key pair (*pub*, *priv*) is generated.

Definition 1. *An encryption scheme is called homomorphic over an operation* $\odot$ *if it supports the following*

$$Enc_{\mathbf{pub}}(m) = \langle m \rangle_{pub}, \forall m \in \mathcal{M}$$
$$\langle m_1 \odot m_2 \rangle_{pub} = \langle m_1 \rangle_{pub} \odot \langle m_2 \rangle_{pub}, \forall m_1, m_2 \in \mathcal{M}$$

where $Enc_{\mathbf{pub}}$ *is the encryption algorithm and* $\mathcal{M}$ *is the set of all possible messages.*

Definition 2. *Decryption is performed as follows*

$$Enc_{\mathbf{pub}}(m) = \langle m \rangle_{pub}, \forall m \in \mathcal{M}$$
$$Dec_{\mathbf{priv}}(\langle m \rangle_{pub}) = m$$

where $Dec_{\mathbf{priv}}$ *is the decryption algorithm and* $\mathcal{M}$ *is the set of all possible messages.*

2.3 Challenges

Even though HE schemes seem theoretically promising, their usage comes with several drawbacks, particularly when applied to Deep Learning.

Noise Budget. In Gentry's lattice-based HE schemes [12] and subsequent variants of it, ciphertexts contain a small term of random noise drawn from some probability distribution. While every operation performed on a ciphertext increases the noise of the resulting ciphertext, it is important to keep the noise below a certain threshold, because once the noise reaches that threshold, it is no longer possible to decrypt the ciphertext. To estimate the current magnitude of noise, a **noise budget** can be calculated, that starts as a positive integer, decreases with subsequent operations and reaches 0 exactly when the ciphertext becomes indecipherable. The noise budget is more strongly affected by multiplications as by additions.

In order to cope with that challenge, encryption parameters can be adjusted accordingly to the required computation depth of an arithmetic circuit. In addition, Gentry introduced the so called bootstrapping procedure, which resets the noise budget of a ciphertext, but requires significant additional computational costs. Recently in [5], the authors proposed a optimized bootstrapping approach with improved performance.

FHE Libraries and APIs. As summarized in Table 1, multiple FHE libraries are available. Depending on the supported HE schemes, those libraries show noticeable difference on performance (e.g. computational, memory consumption), on supported operations type (e.g. addition, multiplication, negative, square, division), datatype (e.g. floating point, integer), and chipset infrastructure (e.g. CPU, GPU).

In addition, and regardless on their level of maturity and performance, HE libraries can be configured through several encryption parameters such as:

- Polynomial degree or modulus: which determines the available noise budget and strongly affects the performance.
- Plaintext modulus: which is mostly associated to the size of input data.
- Security parameter: which sets the reached level of security in bits of the cryptosystem (e.g. 128, 192, 256-bit security level).

Fine-tuning of those encryption parameters enables developers to optimize the performance of encryption and encrypted operations. The selection of the right encryption parameters depends on the size of the plaintext data, targeted accuracy loss or level of security.

Table 1. FHE implementation libraries [14].

Library	Language	Dependencies	License	Description
HElib [17]	C++ 11	NTL, GMP	Apache 2.0	Mature. Low level implementation, hard to use but complete. Ciphertext packing, integers, bootstrapping, multi-threading
PALISADE [25]	C++ 11	None	Copyrighted	Many functionalities & multiple schemes. Well documented but fairly new. Ciphertext packing, integers, fractionals, bootstrapping, multi-threading
SEAL [29]	C++ 17	None	Microsoft	Well documented and easy to use. Ciphertext packing, fractionals, automatic parameter selection and multi-threading. Latest version SEAL 3.0 - Oct'18
FHEW [10]	C++ 11	FFTW	GNU-GPLv2	NAND gate with ciphertext packing, works over bits
TFHE [6]	C++ 11	FFTW	Apache 2.0	Binary gates at 20 ms per gate. Works over bits. Bootstrapping is included in all operations
cuFHE [9]	CUDA C++ 11	NVIDIA CUDA $arch >= 6.0$	MIT	Binary gates at 0.1 ms per gate. Works over bits. Bootstrapping included in operations

Linear Function Support Only. By construction, linear functions, composed of addition and multiplication operations, are seamlessly protected by FHE. But, non-linear activation functions such as ReLU or Sigmoid require approximation to be computed with FHE schemes.

The challenge lies on the transformation of activation functions into polynomial approximations supported by HE schemes. We elaborate more on approximation of activation functions in Sect. 3.2.

Supported Plaintext Type. The vast majority of HE schemes allow operations on integers [17,29], while others use booleans [6] or floating point numbers [5,29]. In the case of integer supporting HE schemes, rational numbers can be approximated using fixed-point arithmetic by scaling with a scaling factor and rounding.

Performance. FHE schemes are computationally expensive and memory consuming. In addition, ciphertexts are often significantly bigger than plaintexts and thus use more memory and disk space.

Even if in the past years the performance of FHE made it impractical, recent FHE schemes show promising throughput. New FHE libraries take also advantage of GPU acceleration.

In addition, modern implementations of HE schemes such as **HELib** [17], **SEAL** [29], or **PALISADE** [25] benefit from Single Instruction Multiple Data

(SIMD), allowing multiple integers to be stored in a single ciphertext and vectorizing operations, which can accelerate certain applications significantly.

3 Approach

As introduced in Sect. 1.2, the delivery of DNN-enriched insights come at a cost. ISVs aim to guarantee data security, together with the IP protection of their DNN-based/enhanced software assets, deployed on potentially unsecure edge hardware & platforms. In order to achieve those security objectives on DNN, we utilize FHE schemes to operate on ciphertext at runtime.

Consequently, secure training of DNN is out of scope of our approach as we focus on runtime execution. We assume that DNN training already preserves both data privacy & confidentiality, and the resulting trained model. Once a model is trained, as discussed in Sect. 2.1, we obtain a set of parameters for each DNN layer; i.e weights $\mathbf{W}^{[i]}$ and biases $\mathbf{b}^{[i]}$ for Fully Connected layers DNN are not solely made of FC layers, and in [14], we identified different type of linear operations parameters within DNN such as Batch Normalization [19] or Convolutional Layer [20]. Those parameters constitute the IP to be protected when deploying a DNN to distributed systems.

3.1 Linear Computation Layer Protection

Our approach is agnostic from the type of layer. In [14], we detail the encryption of layers such as Convolutional Layer or Batch Normalization. For sake of simplicity, we exemplify the encryption of DNN layers parameters on FC layers. Since FC are simply a linear transformation on the previous layer's outputs, encryption is achieved straightforwardly as follows

$$\begin{aligned}\left\langle \mathbf{z}^{[i]} \right\rangle_{\mathbf{pub}} &= \left\langle \mathbf{W}^{[i]} * \mathbf{a}^{[i-1]} + \mathbf{b}^{[i]} \right\rangle_{\mathbf{pub}} \\ &= \left\langle \mathbf{W}^{[i]} \right\rangle_{\mathbf{pub}} * \left\langle \mathbf{a}^{[i-1]} \right\rangle_{\mathbf{pub}} + \left\langle \mathbf{b}^{[i]} \right\rangle_{\mathbf{pub}} \quad [14]\end{aligned} \tag{5}$$

Fully Connected Layer (FC). Also known as Dense Layer, it is composed of N parallel *neurons*, performing a $\mathbb{R}^1 \rightarrow \mathbb{R}^1$ transformation (Fig. 1). We will define:

$\mathbf{a}^{[i]} = \left[a_0^{[i]} \dots a_k^{[i]} \dots a_N^{[i]}\right]^T$ as the output of layer i;

$\mathbf{z}^{[i]} = \left[z_0^{[i]} \dots z_k^{[i]} \dots z_N^{[i]}\right]^T$ as the linear output of layer i; ($\mathbf{z}^{[i]} = \mathbf{a}^{[i]}$ if there is no activation function)

$\mathbf{b}^{[i]} = \left[b_0^{[i]} \dots b_k^{[i]} \dots b_N^{[i]}\right]^T$ as the bias of layer i;

$\mathbf{W}^{[i]} = \left[\mathbf{w}_0^{[i]} \dots \mathbf{w}_k^{[i]} \dots \mathbf{w}_N^{[i]}\right]^T$ as the weights of layer i.

Neuron k performs a linear combination of the output of the previous layer $\mathbf{a}^{[i-1]}$ multiplied by the weight vector $\mathbf{w}_\mathbf{k}^{[i]}$ and shifted with a bias scalar $b_k^{[i]}$, obtaining the linear combination $z_k^{[i]}$:

$$z_k^{[i]} = \left(\sum_{l=0}^{M} w_k^{[i]}[l] * a_l^{[i-1]} \right) + b_k^{[i]} = \mathbf{w}_\mathbf{k}^{[i]} * \mathbf{a}^{[i-1]} + b_k^{[i]} \text{ [14]} \tag{6}$$

Vectorizing the operations for all the neurons in layer i we obtain the dense layer transformation:

$$\mathbf{z}^{[i]} = \mathbf{W}^{[i]} * \mathbf{a}^{[i-1]} + \mathbf{b}^{[i]} \text{ [14]} \tag{7}$$

Protecting FC Layer. Since FC is a linear layer, it can be directly computed in the encrypted domain using additions and multiplications. Vectorization is achieved straightforwardly:

$$\begin{aligned} \left\langle \mathbf{z}^{[i]} \right\rangle_{\mathbf{pub}} &\equiv \left\langle \mathbf{W}^{[i]} * \mathbf{a}^{[i-1]} + \mathbf{b}^{[i]} \right\rangle_{\mathbf{pub}} \\ &= \left\langle \mathbf{W}^{[i]} \right\rangle_{\mathbf{pub}} * \left\langle \mathbf{a}^{[i-1]} \right\rangle_{\mathbf{pub}} + \left\langle \mathbf{b}^{[i]} \right\rangle_{\mathbf{pub}} \end{aligned} \text{ [14]} \tag{8}$$

$$\begin{aligned} \left\langle \mathbf{z}^{[i]} \right\rangle_{\mathbf{pub}} &\equiv \left\langle \mathbf{W}^{[i]} * \mathbf{a}^{[i-1]} + \mathbf{b}^{[i]} \right\rangle_{\mathbf{pub}} \\ &= \left\langle \mathbf{W}^{[i]} \right\rangle_{\mathbf{pub}} * \left\langle \mathbf{a}^{[i-1]} \right\rangle_{\mathbf{pub}} + \left\langle \mathbf{b}^{[i]} \right\rangle_{\mathbf{pub}} \end{aligned} \text{ [14]} \tag{9}$$

$$\left\langle \mathbf{a}_\mathbf{k}^{[i]} \right\rangle_{\mathbf{pub}} \equiv \left\langle \mathbf{f}_{\mathbf{approxact}} \left(\mathbf{z}_\mathbf{k}^{[i]} \right) \right\rangle_{\mathbf{pub}} \text{ [14]} \tag{10}$$

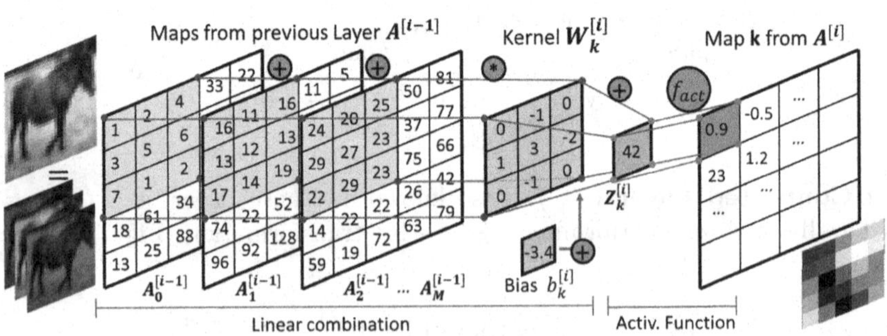

Fig. 3. Conv layer with activation for map k [14].

Convolutional Layer (Conv). Conv layers constitute a key improvement for image recognition and classification using NNs. The $\mathbb{R}^{2|3} \rightarrow \mathbb{R}^{2|3}$ linear transformation involved is **spatial convolution**, where a 2D $s * s$ filter (a.k.a. *kernel*) is multiplied to the 2D input image in subsets (*patches*) with size $s * s$

and in defined steps (**strides**), then added up and then shifted by a bias (see Fig. 3). For input data with several channels or *maps* (e.g.: RGB counts as 3 channels), the filter is applied to the same patch of each map and then added up into a single value of the output image (cumulative sum across maps). A map in Conv layers is the equivalent of a neuron in FC layers. We define:

$\mathbf{A_k^{[i]}}$ as the map k of layer i;
$\mathbf{Z_k^{[i]}}$ as the linear output of map k of layer i;
($\mathbf{Z_k^{[i]}} = \mathbf{A_k^{[i]}}$ in absence of activation function)
$b_k^{[i]}$ as the bias value for map k in layer i
$\mathbf{W_k^{[i]}}$ as the $s * s$ filter/kernel for map k.

This operation can be vectorized by smartly replicating data [27]. The linear transformation can be expressed as:

$$\mathbf{Z_k^{[i]}} = \left(\sum_{m=0}^{M\ maps} \mathbf{A_m^{[i-1]}} \oplus \mathbf{W^{[i]}}_k \right) + b_k^{[i]} \ [14] \tag{11}$$

Protecting Convolutional Layers. Convolution operation can be decomposed in a series of vectorized sums and multiplications over patches of size $s * s$:

$$\begin{aligned} \left\langle \mathbf{Z_k^{[i]}} \right\rangle_{\mathbf{pub}} &= \left\langle \left(\sum_{m=0}^{M\ maps} \mathbf{A_m^{[i-1]}} \oplus \mathbf{W_k^{[i]}} \right) + b_k^{[i]} \right\rangle_{\mathbf{pub}} = \\ \sum_{m=0}^{M\ maps} &\left\langle \mathbf{A_m^{[i-1]}} \oplus \mathbf{W_k^{[i]}} \right\rangle_{\mathbf{pub}} + \left\langle b_k^{[i]} \right\rangle_{\mathbf{pub}} = \qquad [14] \\ &\left\{ \sum_{m=0}^{M} \left\langle \mathbf{A_m^{[i-1]}}[j] \right\rangle_{\mathbf{pub}} * \left\langle \mathbf{W^{[i]}}_k \right\rangle_{\mathbf{pub}} \right\}_{[s*s]} + \left\langle b_k^{[i]} \right\rangle_{\mathbf{pub}} \end{aligned} \tag{12}$$

Pooling Layer. This layer reduces the input size by using a packing function. Most commonly used functions are **max** and **mean**. Similarly to convolutional layers, pooling layers apply their packing function to patches (subsets) of the image with size $s * s$ at strides(steps) of a defined number of pixels, as depicted in Fig. 4.

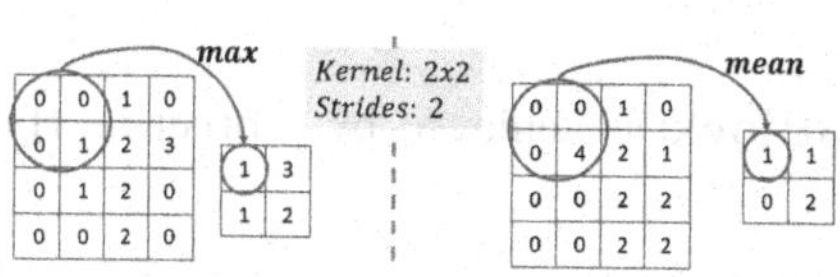

Fig. 4. Max and mean packing for pooling layers [14].

Protecting Pooling Layer. Max can be approximated by the sum of all the values in each patch of size $s * s$, which is equivalent to scaled *mean* pooling. $Mean$ pooling can be scaled (sum of values) or standard (multiplying by $1/N$). By employing a flattened input, pooling becomes easily vectorized.

Other Techniques

- **Batch Normalization (BN):** reduces of the range of input values by 'normalizing' across data batches: subtracting mean and dividing by standard deviation. BN also allows finer tuning using trained parameters β and γ (ϵ is a small constant used for numerical stability).

$$a_k^{[i+1]} = BN_{\gamma,\beta}(a_k^{[i]}) = \gamma * \frac{a_k^{[i]} - E[a_k^{[i]}]}{\sqrt{Var[a_k^{[i]}] + \epsilon}} + \beta \; [14] \tag{13}$$

Protection of BN: is achieved by treating division as the inverse of a multiplication.

$$\begin{aligned}\left\langle a_k^{[i+1]} \right\rangle_{\mathbf{pub}} &= \langle\gamma\rangle_{\mathbf{pub}} * \left(\left\langle a_k^{[i]} \right\rangle_{\mathbf{pub}} - \left\langle E[a_k^{[i]}] \right\rangle_{\mathbf{pub}} \right) \\ &* \left\langle \frac{1}{\sqrt{Var[a_k^{[i]}] + \epsilon}} \right\rangle_{\mathbf{pub}} + \langle\beta\rangle_{\mathbf{pub}} \end{aligned} \; [14] \tag{14}$$

- **Dropout and Data Augmentation:** only affect training procedure. They don't require protection.
- **Residual Block:** is an aggregation of layers where the input is added unaltered at the end of the block, thus allowing the layers to learn incremental ('residual') modifications (Fig. 5).

$$\mathbf{A}^{[\mathbf{i}]} = \mathbf{A}^{[\mathbf{i-1}]} + ResBlock\left(\mathbf{A}^{[\mathbf{i-1}]}\right) \tag{15}$$

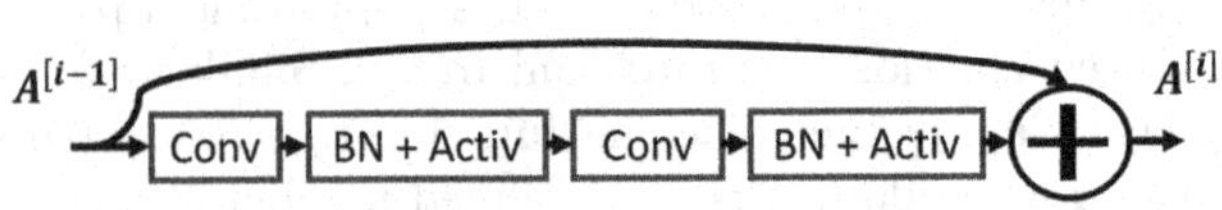

Fig. 5. Example of a possible residual block [14].

Protection of ResBlock: is achieved by protecting the sum and the layers inside ResBlock:

$$\left\langle \mathbf{A}^{[\mathbf{i}]} \right\rangle_{\mathbf{pub}} = \left\langle \mathbf{A}^{[\mathbf{i-1}]} \right\rangle_{\mathbf{pub}} + \left\langle ResBlock\left(\mathbf{A}^{[\mathbf{i-1}]}\right) \right\rangle_{\mathbf{pub}} \; [14] \tag{16}$$

3.2 Activation Function Protection

Due to their innate non-linearity, activation functions need to be approximated with polynomials to be encrypted with FHE. Several approaches have been elaborated in the literature. In [13,22], the authors proposed to use a square function as activation function. The last layer, a sigmoid activation function, is only applied during training. Chabanne et al. used Taylor polynomials around $x = 0$, studying performance based on the polynomial degree [4]. In [18], Hesamifard et al. approximate instead the derivative of the function and then integrate to obtain their approximation.

Regardless on the approximation technique, we denote activation function $f_{act}()$ approximation as

$$\mathbf{f_{act}}() \approx \mathbf{f_{approxact}}() \text{ [14]} \tag{17}$$

By construction, we have

$$\begin{aligned} \left\langle \mathbf{a_k^{[i]}} \right\rangle_{\mathbf{pub}} &= \left\langle \mathbf{f_{act}} \left(\mathbf{z_k^{[i]}} \right) \right\rangle_{\mathbf{pub}} \\ &\equiv \left\langle \mathbf{f_{approxact}} \left(\mathbf{z_k^{[i]}} \right) \right\rangle_{\mathbf{pub}} \end{aligned} \text{ [14]} \tag{18}$$

- *Rectifier Linear Unit (ReLU):* is currently considered as the most efficient activation function for DL. Several variants have been proposed, such as Leaky ReLU [23], ELU [7] or its differentiable version *Softplus.*

$$\begin{aligned} ReLU(z) &= z^+ = max(0, z) \\ Softplus(z) &= log(e^z + 1) \end{aligned} \text{ [14]} \tag{19}$$

- *Sigmoid* σ. The classical activation function. Its efficiency has been debated in the DL community.

$$Sigmoid(z) = \sigma(z) = \frac{1}{1 + e^{-z}} \text{ [14]} \tag{20}$$

- *Hyperbolic Tangent (tanh):* is currently being used in the industry because it is easier to train than ReLU: it avoids having any inactive neurons and it keeps the sign of the input.

$$tanh(z) = \frac{e^z - e^{-z}}{e^z + e^{-z}} \text{ [14]} \tag{21}$$

Protecting Activation Functions. Due to its innate non-linearity, they need to be approximated with polynomials. [13] proposed using only $\sigma(z)$ approximating it with a square function. [4] used Taylor polynomials around $x = 0$, studying performance based on the polynomial degree. [18] approximate instead the derivative of the function and then integrate to obtain their approximation. One alternative would be to use Chebyshev polynomials.

4 Architecture

In this section we outline the architecture of our IP protection system, as depicted in Fig. 6.

4.1 Encryption of Trained DNN

At backend-level, a DNN is trained by the *DNN Training Agent*, ①. Training outcome (NN architecture and parameters) is pushed to the *Trained DNN Protection Agent*, ③. Alternatively, an already trained DNN can be imported directly into the *Protection Agent.* The *DNN Protection Agent* generates a Fully Homomorphic key pair from the *Key Generator* component, ②. The DNN is then encrypted and stored together with its homomorphic key pair in the *Trained and Protected DNN Database*, ④.

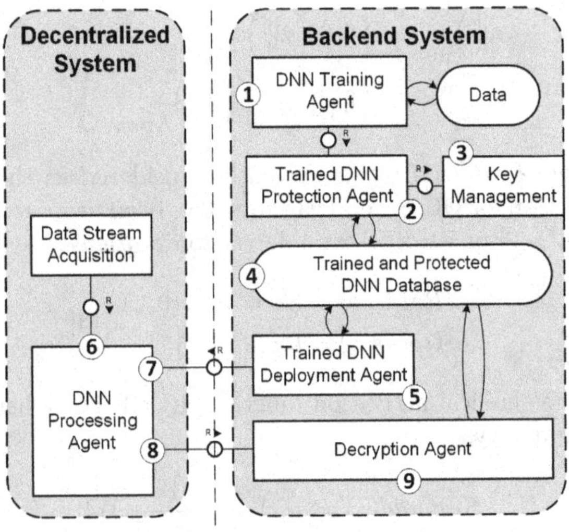

Fig. 6. Activity diagram in our solution [14].

4.2 Deployment of Trained and Protected DNN

At the deployment phase, the *Trained DNN Deployment Agent* deploys the DNN on distributed systems, together with its public key, ⑤.

4.3 DNN Processing

On the distributed system, data is collected by a *Data Stream Acquisition* component, ⑦, and forwarded to the *DNN Processing Agent*, ⑥. Input layer does not involve any computation, and therefore can be seamlessly FHE encrypted as follows

$$\mathbf{X} \xrightarrow{encryption} Enc_{\mathbf{pub}}(X) = \langle X \rangle_{\mathbf{pub}} \text{ [14]} \tag{22}$$

Encrypted inferences are sent to the *Decryption Agent*, ⑧, for their decryption using the private key associated to the DNN, ⑨. FHE encryption propagates across the DNN layers, from input to output layer. By construction, output layer is encrypted homomorphically.

IP of the DNN, together with the computed inferences, is protected from any disclosure on the distributed system throughout the entire process.

The decryption of the last layer's output **Y** is done with the private encryption key *priv*, as in standard asymmetric encryption schemes:

$$\left\langle \mathbf{A}^{[\mathbf{L}]} \right\rangle_{\mathbf{pub}} \xrightarrow{decryption} Dec_{\mathbf{priv}}\left(\left\langle \mathbf{A}^{[\mathbf{L}]} \right\rangle_{\mathbf{pub}} \right) = \mathbf{Y} \text{ [14]} \tag{23}$$

4.4 Sequential Processes

Encryption of Trained NN. Once a Neural Network is trained or imported, we encrypt all its parameters, using the Protected NN DataBase to store it and handle Homomorphic Keys (Fig. 7).

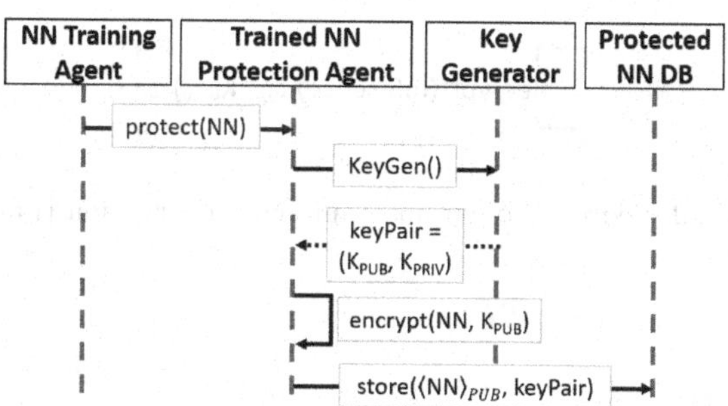

Fig. 7. Sequence diagram of trained NN Encryption [14].

Deploy Trained and Protected NN. The newly trained and protected deep neural network is deployed on the decentralized systems, including:

1. Network architecture;
2. Network model: Encrypted parameters;
3. Public encryption key.

Encrypted Inference. On the decentralized system, data is collected and injected into the deployed NN. We must encrypt $\mathbf{A}^{[0]} = \mathbf{X}$ with the public encryption key associated to the deployed NN (Fig. 8).

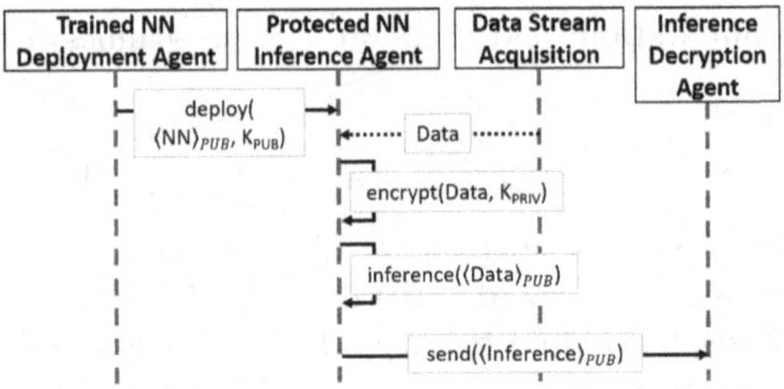

Fig. 8. Sequence diagram of inference processing [14].

Inference Decryption. Encrypted inferences are sent to backend, together with an identifier of the NN used for the inference. The inference is homomorphically decrypted using the mapping private decryption key (Fig. 9).

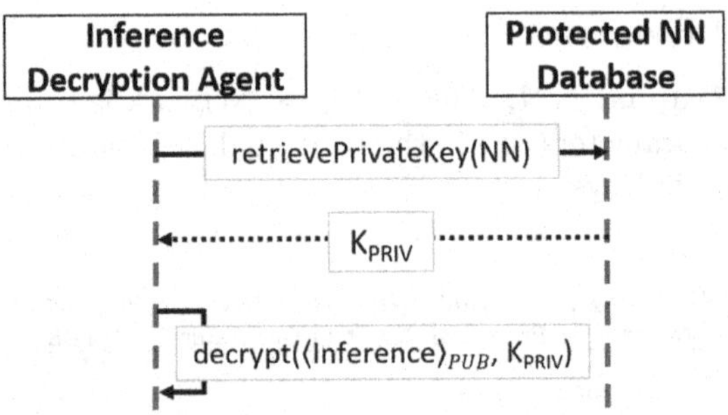

Fig. 9. Sequence diagram of inference decryption [14]

5 Evaluation

As detailed in Sect. 2.3, FHE introduces additional computational costs at each step of the DNN life-cycle. In this section, we evaluate performance overhead from computation time, memory load and disk usage perspectives at DNN model and processing encryption and output decryption.

5.1 Hardware Setup

As *backend*, we use a NVIDIA DGX-1[1] server, empowered with 8 Tesla V100 GPUs. This machine is theoretically not resource-constrained (computation & memory). We reasonably neglect the impact of the performance overhead introduced by FHE on DNN trained model encryption and output decryption.

[1] https://www.nvidia.com/en-us/data-center/dgx-1/.

We deploy and execute our encrypted DNN on a NVIDIA Jetson-TX2[2]. Powered by NVIDIA Pascal architecture, this platform embeds 256 CUDA cores, CPU HMP Dual Denver 22 MB L2 + Quad ARM® A572 MB L2, and 8 GB of memory. This platform gets closer to the hardware configuration of a Distributed Enterprise System.

5.2 Software Setup

DNN Model. As demonstrated in Sect. 3, our approach is fully agnostic from NN topology, or implementation. For the sake of our evaluation, involving several modifications to the NN model, we choose a simple CNN classifier[3], implemented with the Keras library[4]. Two datasets have been used in our experiment: CIFAR10[5], for image classification, and MNIST[6] for handwritten digits classification.

As depicted in Fig. 10, we distinguish two main parts in this CNN: a *feature extractor* and a *classifier*. The feature extractor reduces the amount of information from the input image, into a set of high level and more manageable features. This step facilitates the subsequent classification of the input data.

Composed of four layers, $[FC \rightarrow ReLU \rightarrow FC \rightarrow Softmax]$, the classifier categorizes the input data according to the extracted features, and outputs discrete probability distribution over 10 classes of objects.

As reference point, we evaluate key performance figures at model training and processing time without encryption. Once trained, the size of the CNN plaintext model is 9.6 Mb. On Jetson TX2, single unencrypted image classification is computed on average in 89.1 ms.

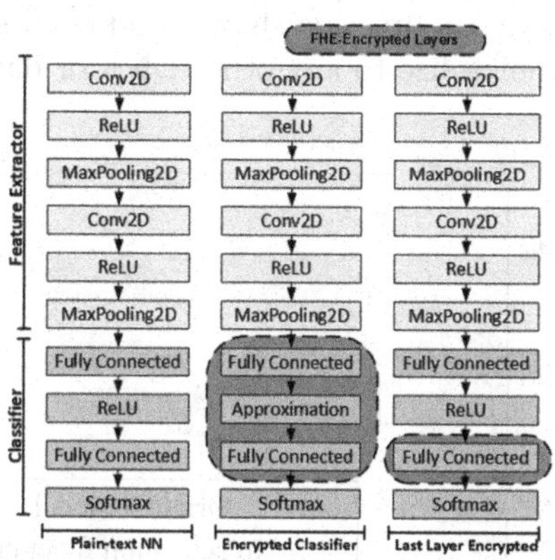

Fig. 10. Keras convolutional neural network.

[2] https://www.nvidia.com/en-us/autonomous-machines/embedded-systems-dev-kits-modules/.
[3] https://github.com/keras-team/keras/blob/master/examples/cifar10_cnn.py.
[4] https://keras.io.
[5] https://www.cs.toronto.edu/~kriz/cifar.html.
[6] http://yann.lecun.com/exdb/mnist/.

FHE Library. As introduced in Sect. 2.3, several libraries are available for FHE. We use SEAL [29] C library from Microsoft Research running on CPU. This choice is motivated by the library's performance, support of multiple schemes such as BGV [3], stability, and documentation. The use of SEAL, implemented in C++, with the Keras Python library requires some engineering efforts. To enable both fast performance of the native C++ library and rapid prototyping using Python, we use Cython[7].

We conduct our evaluation with the BGV scheme [3], utilizing the integer encoding with SIMD support. To handle the floating-point DNN parameters, we use fixed-point arithmetic with a fixed scaling factor, similarly to CryptoNets [13]. This has no noticeable impact on the classification accuracy, if a suitable scaling factor is applied. The SIMD operations allow for optimized performance through vectorization.

5.3 Linearization

We tackle the problem of linearization of the ReLU functions following approaches: we approximate it with a modified square function, and we skip activation function. The modified square function $x^2 + 2x$ (see Fig. 13) is derived from the ReLU approximation proposed in [4]. In order to optimize the computation of that function on ciphertexts, we used simpler coefficients.

In order evaluate the impact of these approaches, we trained the CNN on the CIFAR10 and MNIST datasets, replacing the last ReLU activation. Depicted in Figs. 11 and 12, we report the accuracy loss. Both approximations have merely a minor impact on the output classification accuracy.

Skipping the last activation function shows good results on this simple CNN, but we do not want to generalize to any other DNN or dataset.

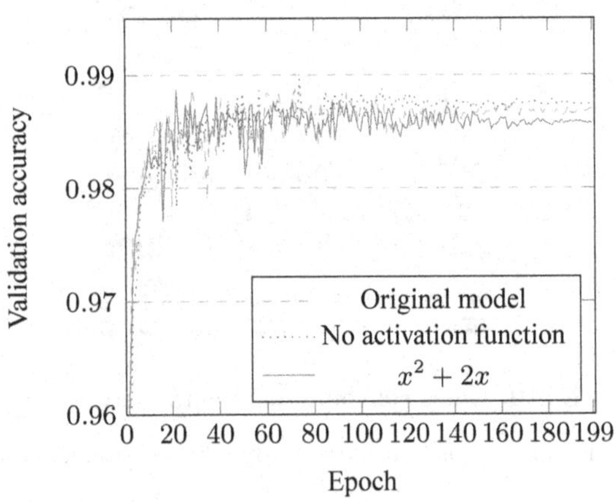

Fig. 11. Classification accuracy with ReLU approximation - MNIST dataset.

[7] https://cython.org/.

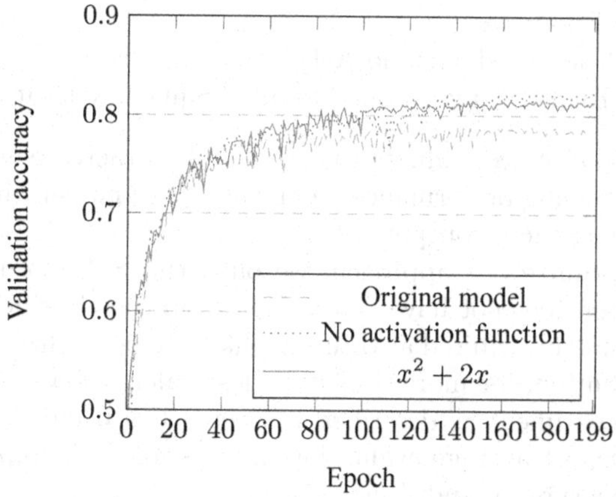

Fig. 12. Classification accuracy with ReLU approximation - CIFAR10 dataset.

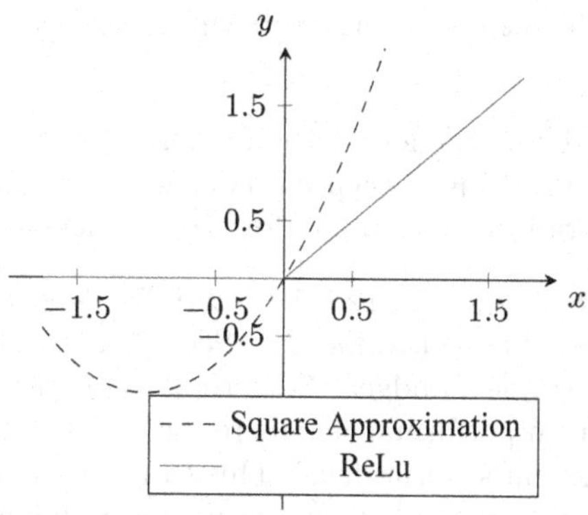

Fig. 13. ReLU approximation as square function.

5.4 Experimentation Results

Model & Data Protection. Intellectual Property-wise, we consider the feature extractor as of minor importance, as CNNs generally use state of the art feature extractor. The IP of the model rather lies in the parameters, weights and bias, of the trained classifier. For that reason, we encrypt the classifier only, as a first step towards full model encryption, as depicted in Fig. 10. To better understand the impact of computation depth, we also complete our evaluation with the encryption of the last FC layer only.

Confidentiality-wise, we evaluate the impact of extracted features encryption by comparing processing performance on an encrypted model with plaintext and encrypted feature extractor outputs.

As depicted in Fig. 10, we evaluate our approach on three modified versions of the model:

- Last FC Layer Encrypted
- Full Classifier Encrypted with no Activation Function
- Full Classified Encrypted with our Modified Square Activation Function

Confidentiality-wise, we evaluate the impact of extracted features encryption by comparing processing performance on an encrypted model with plaintext and encrypted feature extractor outputs.

In order to optimize our approach, we omit the *Softmax* layer within the classifier. This layer does not have any influence on the classification results, as *Softmax* layer is mostly required at training phase, to normalize network outputs probability distribution, for more consistent loss calculations.

The overall experiment as described in Sect. 4 has been applied 5 times on each model. We report average evaluation metrics for each step: model encryption, processing encryption and decryption.

DNN Model Encryption. Each trained CNN model is encrypted on DGX-1's CPU. In Table 2, we depict the resource consumption average on the following metrics:

- Time to Compute: Time to encrypt the model.
- Model Size: Size of resulting encrypted model.
- Memory Load: Overall memory usage for model encryption.

We target three security levels: 128, 192, and 256-bits. For each of those, we optimize SEAL parameters as introduced in Sect. 2.3, maximizing performance, and minimizing leftover noise budget. Note that the security levels can have a counter-intuitive effect on performance, where for instance 192-bit security level might be faster that 128-bit security level. This can be explained by the fact that 128-bit security level offers more (unnecessary) noise budget, depending on the choice of FHE scheme parameters (e.g. plaintext modulus, polynomial degree). Therefore, we target a remaining noise budget as close as possible to zero.

Compared to the plaintext model size (9.6 Mb), encrypted model size increases by a factor of 8,22 in the best case, up to 1173,33.

Table 2. Model encryption

	Achieved Security Level (bits)								
	128	*192*	*256*	*128*	*192*	*256*	*128*	*192*	*256*
	Full Classifier - $x^2 + 2x$			*Full Classifier - No Act.*			*Last Layer*		
Time to Compute (s)	256.7	191.5	212.6	86.9	78.0	96.0	3.4	3.4	7.3
Model Size	11G	6.4G	11G	2.5G	4.4G	2.5G	79Mb	79Mb	158Mb
Memory (Mb)	2257.9	1112.4	2389.5	557.9	459.2	566.1	300.6	301.4	324.2

DNN Processing Encryption. The three encrypted CNN models deployed on Jetson-TX2 for CPU based encrypted processing. At this stage, we evaluate the following metrics

- Time to compute: Processing time for an encrypted classification.
- Memory: Memory usage for encrypted classification.
- Remaining Noise Budget: At the end of processing encryption, we evaluate the remaining noise budget, which determines if additional encryption operations could be performed on the output vector.

In Tables 3 and 4, we depict the performance of encrypted processing with plaintext and encrypted previous layer outputs. We study the impact of confidentality preservation of the preceding layer outputs. SEAL library supports secure computation over plaintext and ciphertext producing ciphertext. As a consequence, output of the last MaxPooling2D layer can be processed in FHE-encrypted Fully Connected layer. Secure computation between plaintext and ciphertext has a lower impact on performance.

We observe a slight performance improvement on time to compute and memory between 128 and 192-bit security level. This is due to the FHE parameters optimization as described in Sect. 5.4, where initial noise budget is oversized for 128-bit security level, which has a direct impact to performance.

Experiment results show that, depending on the level of achieved security, and targeted scenario, we can achieve at best encrypted classification in 2.1 s (for 128 level security and only one layer encrypted). In the worst case, with encrypted input, full classifier encrypted with a modified square function as activation layer, 5627 s (93 mins) is required for a single classification.

Decryption. Following our approach, encrypted output are decrypted by the backend, on DGX-1. We therefore consider decryption as not computationally expensive, compared to encryption. Results are available in Table 5.

Table 3. Runtime encryption with plaintext input.

	Achieved Security Level (bits)								
	128	*192*	*256*	*128*	*192*	*256*	*128*	*192*	*256*
	Full Classifier - $x^2 + 2x$			*Full Classifier - No Act.*			*Last Layer*		
Time to Compute (s)	287.2	174.6	1221.3	43.7	32.9	90.2	2.1	2.1	4.5
Memory Load (Mb)	4683.1	2924.3	4899.2	1162.5	869.2	2342.3	53.9	54.0	117.7
Remaining Noise Budget	221.6	80.2	88.8	91.4	23.8	16.2	58.8	20.2	60.2

Table 4. Runtime encryption with encrypted input.

	Achieved Security Level (bits)								
	128	*192*	*256*	*128*	*192*	*256*	*128*	*192*	*256*
	Full Classifier - $x^2 + 2x$			*Full Classifier - No Act.*			*Last Layer*		
Time to Compute (s)	2902.6	1048.6	5627	367.1	272.2	835.9	19.2	19.2	40.2
Memory Load (Mb)	5047.8	5809	4906	2314.8	1733.7	4644.5	119.5	118.5	253
Remaining Noise Budget	206.0	65.0	76.0	79.0	11.0	3.0	45.0	10.0	52.0

Table 5. Decryption - performance.

	Achieved Security Level (bits)								
	128	*192*	*256*	*128*	*192*	*256*	*128*	*192*	*256*
	Full Classifier - $x^2 + 2x$			*Full Classifier - No Act.*			*Last Layer*		
Time to Compute (s)	2.9	1.7	3.2	0.6	0.6	1.0	0.2	0.1	0.2
Memory Load (Mb)	963.8	397.4	2062.5	123.4	73.4	267.1	17.8	17.8	38.7

6 Conclusion

In this paper, we discuss and evaluate a holistic approach for the protection of distributed DNN-based/enhanced software assets, i.e. confidentiality of their input & output data streams as well as safeguarding their Intellectual Property. On that matter, we take advantage of Fully Homomorphic Encryption (FHE). We evaluate the feasibility of this solution on a Convolutional Neural Network (CNN) for image classification.

Our evaluation on NVIDIA DGX-1 and Jetson-TX2 shows promising results on the CNN image classifier. Firstly, the impact of activation function approximation is negligible, with almost no accuracy loss on output classification probability. Most of the overhead is introduced at processing time, affecting computation time & memory consumption. Performances vary from 2.1 s for an encrypted classification, with only 53.9 Mb consumed memory, up to 1 h 33 min with almost 5 Gb of consumed memory. This requires a balancing between expected classification throughput, targeted security level and encryption depth of the model. Currently this approach would be unrealistic for the protection of DNN-based/enhanced software assets real-time analytics. Still, the Industry calls for numerous scenarios – such as predictive maintenance – matching the current performance of our approach.

As future work, we aim to improve the performance of our approach by different means: following the constant evolution of FHE, such as with the recent CKKS scheme [5], acceleration of FHE libraries on GPU based infrastructure or optimized vectorized operations on FHE encrypted data [1]. In addition, we foresee a deployment of our solution into a Smart City scenario for risk prevention in public spaces; while expanding our approach to different types of DNNs, and complete encryption of CNNs, including the feature extraction layers.

References

1. Badawi, A.A., et al.: The AlexNet moment for homomorphic encryption: HCNN, the first homomorphic CNN on encrypted data with GPUs. CoRR abs/1811.00778 (2018)
2. Boemer, F., Ratner, E., Lendasse, A.: Parameter-free image segmentation with SLIC. Neurocomputing **277**, 228–236 (2018). https://doi.org/10.1016/j.neucom.2017.05.096
3. Brakerski, Z., Gentry, C., Vaikuntanathan, V.: Fully homomorphic encryption without bootstrapping. Cryptology ePrint Archive, Report 2011/277 (2011). https://eprint.iacr.org/2011/277

4. Chabanne, H., de Wargny, A., Milgram, J., Morel, C., Prouff, E.: Privacy-preserving classification on deep neural network. IACR Cryptology ePrint Archive 2017, 35 (2017)
5. Cheon, J.H., Han, K., Kim, A., Kim, M., Song, Y.: Bootstrapping for approximate homomorphic encryption. IACR Cryptology ePrint Archive 2018, 153 (2018). http://eprint.iacr.org/2018/153
6. Chillotti, I., Gama, N., Georgieva, M., Izabachène, M.: TFHE: fast fully homomorphic encryption over the torus. Cryptology ePrint Archive, Report 2018/421 (2018). https://eprint.iacr.org/2018/421
7. Clevert, D.A., Unterthiner, T., Hochreiter, S.: Fast and accurate deep network learning by exponential linear units (ELUs). arXiv preprint arXiv:1511.07289 (2015)
8. Cramer, R., Damgård, I.B., et al.: Secure Multiparty Computation. Cambridge University Press, Cambridge (2015)
9. Dai, W., Sunar, B.: cuHE: a homomorphic encryption accelerator library. In: Pasalic, E., Knudsen, L.R. (eds.) BalkanCryptSec 2015. LNCS, vol. 9540, pp. 169–186. Springer, Cham (2016). https://doi.org/10.1007/978-3-319-29172-7_11
10. Ducas, L., Micciancio, D.: FHEW: bootstrapping homomorphic encryption in less than a second. In: Oswald, E., Fischlin, M. (eds.) EUROCRYPT 2015. LNCS, vol. 9056, pp. 617–640. Springer, Heidelberg (2015). https://doi.org/10.1007/978-3-662-46800-5_24
11. Fan, J., Vercauteren, F.: Somewhat practical fully homomorphic encryption. Cryptology ePrint Archive, Report 2012/144 (2012). https://eprint.iacr.org/2012/144
12. Gentry, C.: A fully homomorphic encryption scheme. Ph.D. thesis, Stanford University, Stanford, CA, USA (2009). aAI3382729
13. Gilad-Bachrach, R., Dowlin, N., Laine, K., Lauter, K., Naehrig, M., Wernsing, J.: Cryptonets: applying neural networks to encrypted data with high throughput and accuracy, pp. 201–210 (2016)
14. Gomez, L., Ibarrondo, A., Márquez, J., Duverger, P.: Intellectual property protection for distributed neural networks - towards confidentiality of data, model, and inference. In: Samarati, P., Obaidat, M.S. (eds.) Proceedings of the 15th International Joint Conference on e-Business and Telecommunications, ICETE 2018. SECRYPT, Porto, Portugal, 26–28 July 2018, vol. 2, pp. 313–320. SciTePress (2018). https://doi.org/10.5220/0006854703130320
15. Goodfellow, I.: Security and privacy of machine learning. RSA Conference (2018). https://www.rsaconference.com/speakers/ian-goodfellow
16. Graepel, T., Lauter, K., Naehrig, M.: ML confidential: machine learning on encrypted data. In: Kwon, T., Lee, M.-K., Kwon, D. (eds.) ICISC 2012. LNCS, vol. 7839, pp. 1–21. Springer, Heidelberg (2013). https://doi.org/10.1007/978-3-642-37682-5_1
17. Halevi, S., Shoup, V.: Algorithms in HElib. In: Garay, J.A., Gennaro, R. (eds.) CRYPTO 2014. LNCS, vol. 8616, pp. 554–571. Springer, Heidelberg (2014). https://doi.org/10.1007/978-3-662-44371-2_31
18. Hesamifard, E., Takabi, H., Ghasemi, M.: CryptoDL: deep neural networks over encrypted data. CoRR (2017)
19. Ioffe, S., Szegedy, C.: Batch normalization: accelerating deep network training by reducing internal covariate shift. In: International Conference on Machine Learning, pp. 448–456 (2015)
20. Krizhevsky, A., Sutskever, I., Hinton, G.E.: Imagenet classification with deep convolutional neural networks. In: Advances in Neural Information Processing Systems, pp. 1097–1105 (2012)

21. Liu, J., Juuti, M., Lu, Y., Asokan, N.: Oblivious neural network predictions via minionn transformations. In: Proceedings of the 2017 ACM SIGSAC Conference on Computer and Communications Security, pp. 619–631. ACM (2017)
22. Livni, R., Shalev-Shwartz, S., Shamir, O.: On the computational efficiency of training neural networks. In: Ghahramani, Z., Welling, M., Cortes, C., Lawrence, N.D., Weinberger, K.Q. (eds.) Advances in Neural Information Processing Systems, vol. 27, pp. 855–863. Curran Associates, Inc. (2014). http://papers.nips.cc/paper/5267-on-the-computational-efficiency-of-training-neural-networks.pdf
23. Maas, A.L., Hannun, A.Y., Ng, A.Y.: Rectifier nonlinearities improve neural network acoustic models. In: Proceedings of the ICML, vol. 30, p. 3 (2013)
24. Mohassel, P., Zhang, Y.: SecureML: a system for scalable privacy-preserving machine learning. In: 2017 IEEE Symposium on Security and Privacy (SP), pp. 19–38. IEEE (2017)
25. PALISADE: The palisade lattice cryptography library (2018). https://git.njit.edu/palisade/PALISADE
26. European Parliament and of the Council: General data protection regulation (2016). https://eur-lex.europa.eu/eli/reg/2016/679/oj
27. Ren, J.S., Xu, L.: On vectorization of deep convolutional neural networks for vision tasks. In: AAAI, pp. 1840–1846 (2015)
28. Schatsky, D., Kumar, N., Bumb, S.: Intelligent IoT. Bringing the power of AI to the Internet of Things, Deloitte Insights (2017). https://www2.deloitte.com/insights/us/en/focus/signals-for-strategists/intelligent-iot-internet-of-things-artificial-intelligence.html
29. Simple Encrypted Arithmetic Library (release 3.1.0), Microsoft Research, Redmond, WA, December 2018. https://github.com/Microsoft/SEAL
30. Shokri, R., Shmatikov, V.: Privacy-preserving deep learning. In: Proceedings of the 22nd ACM SIGSAC Conference on Computer and Communications Security, pp. 1310–1321. ACM (2015)
31. Uchida, Y., Nagai, Y., Sakazawa, S., Satoh, S.: Embedding watermarks into deep neural networks. In: Proceedings of the 2017 ACM on International Conference on Multimedia Retrieval, pp. 269–277. ACM (2017)

Predicting CEO Misbehavior from Observables: Comparative Evaluation of Two Major Personality Models

Adam Szekeres(✉) and Einar Arthur Snekkenes

Department of Information Security and Communication Technology, Norwegian University of Science and Technology, Gjøvik, Norway
{adam.szekeres,einar.snekkenes}@ntnu.no

Abstract. The primary purpose of this study is to demonstrate how publicly observable pieces of information can be used to build various psychological profiles that can be utilized for the prediction of behavior within a risk analysis framework. In order to evaluate the feasibility of the proposed method, publicly available interview data is processed from a sample of chief executive officers (CEOs) using the IBM Watson Personality Insights service. The hypothesis-that group membership gives rise to a specific selection bias-is investigated by analyzing the IBM Watson-derived personality profiles at the aggregate level. The profiles are represented by two major theories of motivation and personality: the Basic Human Values and the Big Five models. Both theories are evaluated in terms of their utility for predicting adverse behavioral outcomes. The results show that both models are useful for identifying group-level differences between (1) the sample of CEOs and the general population, and (2) between two groups of CEOs, when a history of rule-breaking behavior is considered. The predictive performance evaluation conducted on the current sample shows that the binary logistic regression model built from the Basic Human Values outperforms the Big Five model, and that it provides a practically more useful measurement of individual differences. These results contribute to the development of a risk analysis method within the domain of information security, which addresses human-related risks.

Keywords: CEO · Psychological profiling · Unobtrusive measures · Basic Human Values · Big Five · Behavior prediction

1 Introduction

Strategic decisions are long-term plans produced by a small number of senior managers aimed at achieving well-defined organizational objectives, with significant impact (positive or negative) on the safety and security of organizations and information systems spanning across the entire range of the corporate hierarchy.

M. S. Obaidat (Ed.): ICETE 2018, CCIS 1118, pp. 135–158, 2019.
https://doi.org/10.1007/978-3-030-34866-3_7

Such decisions affect a wide range of stakeholders, thus a certain level of friction is unavoidable [4,32,37]. The principal-agent problem within the economics and management literature addresses the tension between management interests and governance objectives. The principal-agent problem arises in agency theory and describes a situation in which one party (principal) delegates work to another party (agent) who is responsible for performing that work on behalf of the principal. The theory is concerned with resolving two problems that may arise in any agency relationship [8]. The first problem relates to the possibility that the agent's and the principal's desires or goals are in conflict, and it is difficult or expensive for the principal to verify what the agent is actually doing (i.e. hidden actions). The second problem arises from the difference between the parties' attitude towards risk, where the principal and the agent might prefer different actions due to different risk preferences and due to information asymmetry (i.e. hidden information).

Information security is a domain where negative externalities (e.g. principal-agent problem) may be present at various levels of abstraction. The highly complex threat landscape is characterized by misaligned stakeholder incentives (e.g. cost of developing sufficiently secure hardware and software vs. being first on the market, etc.), asymmetric knowledge about vulnerabilities (hidden information) and various other factors [1]. Internet of Things (IoT)-enabled critical infrastructures are becoming more and more prevalent due to their economic benefits. While they offer increased levels of automation, crucial strategic decisions are still the responsibility of people in leading positions. This may lead to situations in which the safety, security and stability of societies is increasingly dependent on the motivation of fewer and fewer key decision-makers [9].

Most information security risk analysis frameworks focus on the technological aspects and neglect the strategic decision-making perspective. The Conflicting Incentives Risk Analysis (CIRA) method developed by Rajbandhari and Snekkenes aims to bridge this gap by focusing on human motivation when addressing information security risks [24]. The method's applicability to real-world cases is limited by the lack of psychological theories that would enable the prediction of stakeholder behavior. Therefore, this study aims at evaluating two major psychological models of personality in terms of their performance for predicting undesirable stakeholder actions without direct access to subjects. The necessity for using unobtrusive profiling methods arises from the assumption that real-world stakeholders would be reluctant to explicitly reveal their motivations and they would be inclined to provide socially desirable answers when traditional assessment methods (i.e. questionnaire, interview, etc.) are utilized, which would confound the validity of the whole risk analysis process. While this study focuses on the misconduct of CEOs, the analysis is applicable to any other class of stakeholders.

1.1 Problem Statement

The CIRA method focuses on the misalignment between stakeholder motivations for risk identification [25]. To improve the method, it is necessary to incorporate psychological theories that enable the characterization of individual stakeholders and the prediction of their future behavior without requiring direct interaction between the analyst and the subjects. Based on these requirements, the objectives of this study are as follows:

- compare two personality models that can be used to characterize individual stakeholders,
- assess an unobtrusive profiling method's suitability for the purpose of risk analysis,
- analyze how a specific group membership gives rise to a selection bias, manifested in the psychological profiles,
- compare the predictive performance of the personality models with regard to undesirable behavioral outcomes.

1.2 Research Questions

Based on the aforementioned requirements and goals, the primary research question is as follows: *can publicly observable variables reflecting individual choice be used to construct psychological profiles suitable for predicting behavior in the context of risk analysis* [35]*?*

The following sub-questions were constructed in order to answer the main research question:

- **RQ 1:** To what extent is it feasible to use an unobtrusive profiling method to derive stakeholder characteristics?
- **RQ 2:** Is it feasible to detect a potential selection bias by analyzing personality profiles at the group-level?
- **RQ 3:** How does the *Basic Human Values* model compare to the *Big Five* model in terms of predicting stakeholder misbehavior?

This work contributes to the literature of information security risk analysis by presenting how publicly observable stakeholder data (i.e. recorded interviews) can be utilized for the purpose of risk analysis. The method relies on an existing application (IBM Watson Personality Insights), while the purpose of the analysis differs significantly from its established use cases. To assess the method's feasibility this study focuses on organizational leaders due to the fact that other classes of stakeholders might not be allowed to interact officially with the public, however the approach can be applicable to any other classes of stakeholders (e.g. CFO, COO, CIO, CISO). This study extends on previous work [35], by including an additional psychological model, and by comparatively evaluating the two personality models in terms of their capabilities for predicting real-world behavior. The paper is structured as follows: Sect. 2 introduces relevant theories and the IBM Watson application, Sect. 3 provides an overview about the methods used in the study. Results of the conducted analyses are presented in Sect. 4. Section 5 provides an overview about the results and their relevance, including limitations and plans for further work. Section 6 summarizes and concludes the present study.

2 Related Work

This section provides an overview about the psychological theories, constructs and the application that served as the foundations of this study.

2.1 Sources of Bias

There are several research perspectives that aim to provide an explanation about the processes that guide people with certain traits or characteristics into various work positions. Extensive research investigates how different characteristics are desirable on one hand, and how they might have a negative impact on organizational or societal objectives. Several disastrous outcomes have been linked to the decision-maker's psychological attributes, which explains the increased research interest into the ethical aspects of high-impact decision-making [34,38]. This section introduces two main mechanisms that contribute to a selection bias in executive roles (i.e. personal attraction to a specific role and selection of candidates by the board of directors).

Selection Bias by Personal Motivations. Need for power, prestige and money are assumed to be key motivators that draw individuals to the highly competitive corporate world. Various decisions which contribute to undesirable social outcomes (e.g. exploiting sweatshop labor, environmental pollution, etc.) have been attributed to key decision-maker's psychological features. Furthermore, several organizational risks (e.g. embezzlement, bribery, etc.) can be enumerated which represent a conflict between the self-interested individual and the overall organizational objectives. One explanation for such incidents is proposed by Boddy, who discusses the over-representation of corporate psychopaths in key decision-maker positions. According to his definition corporate psychopaths are "people working in corporations who are self-serving, opportunistic, ego-centric, ruthless and shameless who can be charming, manipulative and ambitious" who are drawn to corporations since they can provide individuals with highly valued resources [3]. Corporate psychopaths are outwardly charming, and engaging, skillful at manipulating others to their own advantage, with a lack of concern for the consequences of their actions, and give a high priority for their own goals and ambitions. Their ability to demonstrate desirable traits that the organization values for a certain position is easily exploited by such individuals when presenting a charming facade, which distinguishes them from the commonly held perception of the insane psychopath.

The authors of [2] set out to investigate the prevalence and consequences of psychopathic tendencies in a sample of 203 corporate professionals taking part in a management development program. The study was motivated by the "growing public and media interest in learning more about the types of person who violate their positions of influence and trust, defraud customers, investors, friends, and family, successfully elude regulators, and appear indifferent to the financial chaos and personal suffering they create" [2]. The findings revealed the complex association between situation-congruent self-presentation and how psychopathic traits (although not classified as Antisocial Personality Disorder) can be beneficial in corporate environments. The results showed that the highest psychopathy scores were obtained from high-potential candidates in senior management positions. A noteworthy finding of the study is how the corporation evaluated individuals with several psychopathic traits. High psychopathy scores were associated with perceptions of good communication skills, strategic thinking, and creative/innovative abilities and simultaneously, with poor management style, failure to act as a team player, and poor performance appraisals (as rated by immediate bosses).

Another empirical study investigated the association between the Dark Triad personality traits and the basic human values structure [13]. The Dark Triad (Machiavellianism, Narcissism, and Psychopathy) is a popular grouping of individual differences that represent antisocial personality traits below clinical threshold. The antisocial aspect of the triad comes from the shared underlying attitudes and modes of behavior that characterize these traits. Entitlement, superiority, dominance, manipulativeness, lack of remorse, impulsivity are the common features of the Triad [13]. The study found in two different cultures (i.e. Swedish and American) that Hedonism, Stimulation, Achievement and Power values were the highest ranking values for individuals high on Dark Triad traits. The authors claim that those characterized by high scores on the Dark Triad traits, hold values that promote Self-enhancement at the expense of others, thus treating other people as means toward their gains. The association between Self-enhancement values and the Dark Triad traits is referred to as dark value system which has further moral implications.

Selection Bias by Role Requirements. The match between certain personality features and various organizational settings is investigated by the Person-Organization (P-O) fit theories. Morley [20] discusses a shift in recent recruitment practices in which the traditional focus on knowledge, skills and abilities (KSAs), has moved toward seeking an optimal fit between the candidate's personality, beliefs and values and the organization's espoused culture, norms and values. In a similar vein, the Attraction-Selection-Attrition (ASA) framework seeks a fit at the personal level between the candidate and the organization's work values. According to the ASA model, candidates are attracted to organizations that exhibit characteristics similar to their own, and organizations tend to select employees who are similar to the organization in key aspects [28]. Value congruence has become a widely accepted operationalization of P-O fit [16].

Role requirements vary a lot even within the same organization (e.g. managerial role requirements are different from the requirements of a production line worker). A large-sample study aimed at identifying a distinctive managerial profile in terms of the Big Five model of personality. Managers reached significantly higher scores on the following nine personality traits and facet when compared to members of other occupations: Extraversion, Assertiveness, Conscientiousness, Emotional Stability, Agreeableness, Optimism, Work Drive, Customer Service

Orientation, Openness. The results can be practically useful during the personnel selection process to increase the P-O fit required for specific job types [18].

Another investigation was conducted to test the hypothesis that different work environments can be differentiated by analyzing the value structures of the workers [14]. The enterprising environment (e.g. manager, banker, financial advisor) is characterized by material and concrete goals, and requires one to lead, convince or manipulate others in order to achieve desired organizational and financial goals. According to the hypothesis Power and Achievement values are most compatible with these requirements, while the enterprising environment would inhibit the expression of Benevolence and Universalism values. The results revealed a strong positive correlation between the enterprising occupations and Power and Achievement values, while a negative correlation was observed in relation to Universalism values. This study successfully differentiated occupations based on the dominant human values that are present in each particular field, providing further evidence about a selection bias in action.

The surveyed research results highlight some of the ways through which selection bias is introduced to different work roles and occupations. First, individuals with certain traits or characteristics are attracted to specific jobs, then the active selection process by the recruiters produces the final set of employees. Analyzing the risks to an organization largely depends on understanding the nature of these biases.

2.2 Conflicting Incentives Risk Analysis

The relevance of focusing on the stakeholder motivation is recognized in the Conflicting Incentives Risk Analysis (CIRA) method [25]. It identifies stakeholders (i.e. individuals), the actions that can be taken by these stakeholders and the consequences of the actions. A stakeholder is an individual who has interest in taking a certain action within the scope of the analysis. The procedure distinguishes between two types of stakeholders: *Strategy owner* (the person who is capable of executing an action) and the *Risk owner* (whose perspective is taken - the person at risk). At the core of the method is the economic concept of utility, which captures the benefit of implementing a strategy for each stakeholder. The cumulative utility encompasses several utility factors, each representing valuable aspects for the corresponding stakeholders, thus modelling an individual's motivation. Two types of risks are identified in the method: *Threat risk* relates to the perceived decrease in the total utility for the risk owner, and *Opportunity risk* relates to missed utility gains due to the strategy owner's lack of motivation (i.e. costs associated with a beneficial action). Thus, risk is conceptualized as a misalignment of incentives between these two classes of stakeholders, and risk identification focuses on uncovering activities that would be beneficial for the Strategy owner while potentially harmful for the Risk owner [31]. Threat risk closely resembles the concept of moral hazard as it captures a wide range of behaviors that are beneficial for one party and detrimental for the other who has to suffer the consequences [6]. This study focuses on Threat risks that can be attributed to the motivation of organizational leaders.

2.3 Theory of Basic Human Values

The theory of *Basic Human Values* by Schwartz [29] identifies 10 distinct values that are universally recognized across various cultures and provides a unified and comprehensive view on the motivation of individuals. Values both represent desirable end goals and prescribe desirable ways of acting. Six key features characterize all values:

- "Values are beliefs linked to affect.
- Values refer to desirable goals that motivate action.
- Values transcend specific actions and situations.
- Values serve as standards or criteria.
- Values are ordered by importance.
- The relative importance of multiple values guide action." [29]

Furthermore, all 10 values capture one of the three key motivational aspects that are grounded in universal requirements of human existence: needs of individuals as biological organisms, requisites of coordinated social interaction, and survival and welfare needs of groups. Values guide behavior, given that the context or situation activates the relevant values. The values form a circular structure which represents a motivational continuum, where adjacent values are compatible with each other and opposing values are in conflict. The ten values are grouped under 4 higher dimensions as represented by Fig. 1. The theory acknowledges that most actions are expressive of more than one value, and that a person's specific value-hierarchy modifies his/her perceptions about the relevant aspects of a situation. This may give rise to different interpretations of the same situation across individuals.

Fig. 1. Circular value structure, with 4 higher dimensions. Source: [29].

2.4 Big Five Personality Traits

The five factor model of personality or the *Big Five* defines five broad, distinct dimensions, that capture individual differences in terms of emotional, interpersonal experiences, recurring ways of behavior, and motivational styles [19]. The model is the result of several decades of extensive research in the domain of personality psychology, and represents one of the most widely accepted and utilized conceptualizations of personality. The five factors emerged from lexicographic investigations and are regarded as fundamental and stable dimensions of human personality, recognized across cultures. The large-scale acceptance of the model, and the consensus in relation to the utility of the Big Five provided researchers with a common framework from different traditions, which enabled productive investigations in a wide range of domains. It's practical applicability has been demonstrated extensively in industrial/organizational, educational, clinical and other (e.g. [11]) settings. According to trait theory, individuals can be placed on a continuum along the five main dimensions, which comprise of six facets (narrower, more specific aspects of personality [19]) as shown in Table 1.

Table 1. The Big Five dimensions and narrow facets of personality, based on [19].

Openness to experience	Conscientiousness	Extraversion	Agreeableness	Neuroticism
Fantasy	Competence	Warmth	Trust	Anxiety
Aesthetics	Order	Gregariousness	Straightforwardness	Hostility
Feelings	Dutifulness	Assertiveness	Altruism	Depression
Actions	Achievement striving	Activity	Compliance	Self-consciousness
Ideas	Self-discipline	Excitement-seeking	Modesty	Impulsiveness
Values	Deliberation	Positive emotions	Tender-mindedness	Vulnerability

2.5 IBM Watson Personality Insights

Personality Insights (PI) is part of IBM's artificial intelligence platform called Watson. Previously known for defeating the top human players in Jeopardy, the service these days is a comprehensive set of artificial intelligence solutions available for the consumer market. The service is utilized in a wide range of fields including health care, weather forecast, electric load optimization, etc. The PI utilizes machine learning solutions to uncover an individual's psychological characteristics based on texts produced by the person. The PI service's main use cases involve targeted marketing, customer care services, automated personalized interactions, among several others. The service produces profiles based on four different models of individual differences [35]:

1. Big Five personality model - these characteristics describe relatively stable behavioral tendencies and modes of experiences.
2. Needs - based on the earliest investigations into human motivation capturing an individual's high-level desires.
3. Basic Human Values - values capture both desirable goals that people pursue and standards of acting, thus providing a summary about the underlying motivations behind one's actions.

4. Consumption preferences - optimized for predicting the user's likelihood for buying a certain product or engaging in different activities.

In terms of the Basic Human Values, the service calculates scores for five high-level dimensions: Conservation, Openness to change, Self-enhancement, Self-transcendence and Hedonism separately, whereas the original formulation identifies only four dimensions, and places Hedonism in either Openness to change or Self-enhancement. The service provides scores on all the Big Five dimensions as well as scores for each facet. For each personality model the PI computes two scores: percentile scores and raw scores. "To compute the percentile scores, IBM collected a very large data set of Twitter users (one million users for English, ...) and computed their personality portraits. IBM then compared the raw scores of each computed profile to the distribution of profiles from those data sets to determine the percentiles. The service computes normalized scores by comparing the raw score for the author's text with results from a sample population" [12]. While the percentile scores can provide insights about an individual's position on a trait compared to PI's original sample, it is not well-suited to characterize an individual's profile for the purpose of choice predictions, since the value structure relative to a sample population does not necessarily correspond to the individual's own value priorities. To allow comparison between different populations and scenarios the service also provides raw scores which resemble scores the person would get when completing a corresponding personality inventory. Thus raw scores are more useful for making comparisons to results derived from other studies.

3 Methods

3.1 Participants

The convenience sampling method produced a sample which consisted of 116 CEOs (105 male, 11 female), aged between 34–95 years (M = 59.41, SD = 9.23) with sufficient amount of texts for running accurate analysis by the IBM Watson service. The amount of text available for the individuals ranged between 264–11384 words (M = 3830.98, SD = 1672.28). The majority of the subjects were born in the USA (N = 52.6%), followed by India (N = 12.9%), United Kingdom (N = 6.9%) and 21 other countries (N = 27.6%). 84.4% of the sample had at least bachelor or equivalent level degrees. The total compensation for the CEOs in year 2016 ranged between $45,936 – $46,968,924 (M = $15,988,276.78, SD = $10,600,982.56) according to publicly available sources [27].

3.2 Data Collection

The data collection and production activities (i.e. interview source identification, preprocessing, Watson analysis) are identical to those explained in [35]. In order to answer the Research Questions it was necessary to run an initial pilot study to assess the feasibility of the data collection activity. During the pilot study the first step involved the identification of relevant sources of data. To this end the Wikipedia article on the List of chief executive officers of notable companies was used that contains CEOs with diverse national and industrial backgrounds [39]. At the time of the start of the data collection the list consisted of 174 subjects. The second step involved the identification of suitable sources of information that could be linked to the individual and provided sufficient input to the Watson service for achieving it's maximum precision (3000 words/subject is recommended by the service description). In this phase we relied on video interviews, interviews published in online newspapers, news articles, company communications and social media profiles. Although it was possible to collect the necessary amount of data from the individuals, the procedure was not feasible due to high diversity of contexts, the uncertainty related to the actual author of the texts and the time needed to collect the data, so in the final data collection phase this procedure was modified in the following way:

- The search was restricted to videos published on YouTube that (a) were in English, (b) the subject could be clearly identified while providing his thoughts, and (c) were supplemented with captions.
- The search then was executed by using the subject's name with the following additional terms (in the same order): - interview, talk, presentation. In case the first search term did not provide sufficient amount of text the next one was used.
- In order to achieve as high validity as possible for the analysis we aimed at collecting mainly interviews and discussions that are more spontaneous and reflective in content (thus we aimed at minimizing the reliance on well-rehearsed communications or texts written by other parties for presentation purposes).
- Each video was carefully observed in real time to check the accuracy of the captions and to ensure that only the subject's utterances are extracted for analysis, while omitting any noise (interviewer/audience questions, false transcriptions, etc.)
- A fresh install of Google Chrome was utilized in incognito mode, to keep personalized search results to a minimum and to maximize the reproducibility of the search results.

After a sufficient amount of text was collected from the subjects, the texts were submitted to the Watson PI service producing the psychological profiles for each individual [35].

For the purpose of a more fine grained analysis, CEOs that have been associated with various forms of rule breaking behavior leading to moral hazard have been identified in the current sample. To this end extensive web searches were conducted with the name of the individual and the additional search term (e.g. fraud, scandal, corruption). The first 20 search results were screened for each subject in order to identify possible associations with moral hazard. Using a broad sense of the moral hazard concept, any behavior was eligible for inclusion which had a negative effect on the reputation of the organization by drawing public attention to the underlying misconduct (irrespective of the nature of the misconduct) and the actions were conducted under the administration of the CEO in focus. The activities included: bribery of public officials, tax evasion, accounting fraud, insider deals, ethical misconduct, etc. The procedure resulted in the identification of 31 CEOs (26.7% of the sample) associated with undesirable behavior, and enabled profile comparisons between the two CEO groups [35].

3.3 The Concept of Difference

To characterize group differences several approaches were considered. In the first approach the percentile scores derived from the Watson PI service were used, that inherently contain a comparison between the subject's results and the original sample's distribution, on which the service was validated (N $\sim$ 1 million users) [12]. This approach provides an understanding about the CEO sample's overall position across each personality dimension. Since the parameters are not publicly available for the original sample, a reference distribution was used to test differences between the current and the hypothesized original sample.

The second approach utilizes the raw scores derived from the PI service, which are equivalent to the scores one would get when completing an actual psychometric test (as suggested by the Watson manual [12]). These scores can be compared to results obtained from different populations, therefore are more suitable for validation. The second procedure followed this line of reasoning, and aimed at identifying differences between the profiles of CEOs and the general population.

However, rank orders in isolation do not provide all the necessary information about and individual's trade-off decisions, since a preference reversal (i.e. choosing different strategies with the same value orders among individuals) is possible. Considering this fact and in accordance with the theory's formulation, the relative importance of values should be analyzed when certain strategies are evaluated. Furthermore, since several studies use different instruments and methodologies for assessing the personality models or use different levels of analysis, it was necessary to enhance the compatibility and comparability of research findings [17]. To this end, in the third procedure the raw scores were summed across all dimensions, and each score was multiplied by the Sum^{-1}, to quantify each value's contribution to the overall utility (=1). The same procedure was carried out for research results that served as reference for the comparisons. This approach provides an assessment of an individual's personality profile independent of the instrument used for conducting the profiling. All analyses were conducted with SPSS 25 by IBM.

4 Results

4.1 Percentile Score Comparisons with Watson PI Sample

The first procedure aimed at detecting the existence of a selection bias using the percentile scores of each personality model. Percentile scores from the Basic

Human Values and the Big Five scores were transformed by mapping them to a standard normal distribution, then for each dimension One-Sample t-tests were conducted with a reference standard normal distribution (M = 0) to assess whether the scores were drawn from the specific hypothesized distribution.

Basic Human Values. The results indicate that the group means for Conservation (M = −1.57), t(115) = −29.30, Hedonism (M = −1.95), t(115) = −81.24, Self-enhancement (M = −1.24), t(115) = −30.06, and Self-transcendence (M = −0.84), t(115) = −21.19, were significantly different from the reference distribution's mean scores, $p \leq 0.001$ for each. The group mean score of Openness to change (M = 0.06), t(115) = 1.14, p = 0.25 was not significantly different from the hypothesized population mean. Figure 2 shows the distribution of all the values based on the transformed percentile scores.

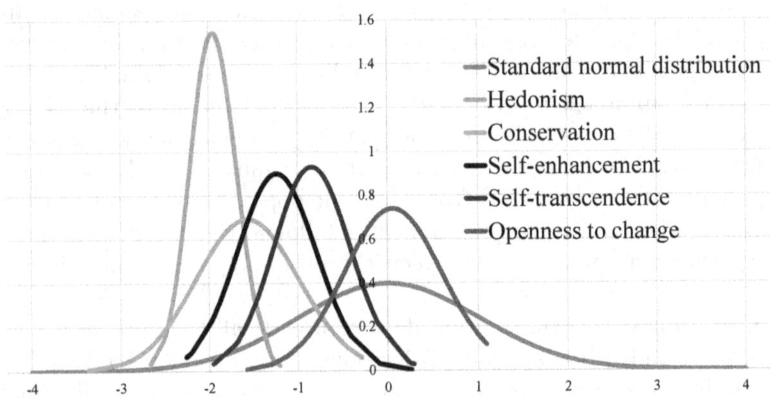

Fig. 2. Basic Human Values percentile score distributions [35].

Big Five. The same procedure was conducted for the Big Five dimensions and the results indicate that mean scores for the Big Five dimensions Openness to experience (M = 1.94), t(115) = 51.80, Conscientiousness (M = 0.62), t(115) = 14.58, Agreeableness (M = −0.79), t(115) = −11.33, and Neuroticism (M = 0.79), t(115) = 23.90 were significantly different from the reference distribution's mean scores, $p \leq 0.001$ for each. The mean score for Extraversion (M = −0.03), t(115) = −0.62, p = 0.54 was not significantly different from the hypothesized population mean. Figure 3 shows the distribution of scores on all the dimensions of the Big Five personality model using the transformed percentile scores.

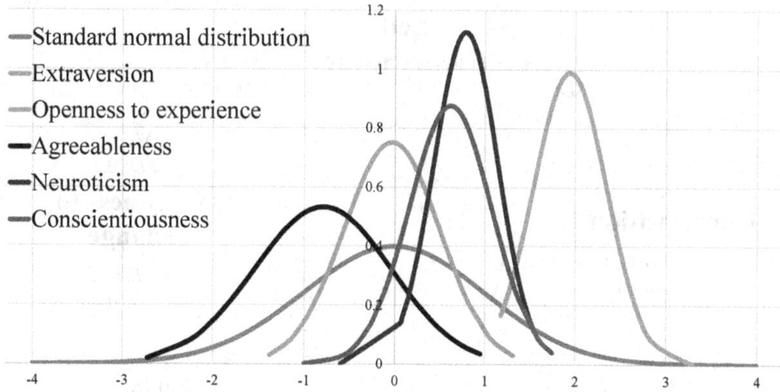

Fig. 3. Big Five percentile score distributions.

4.2 Raw Score Comparison with Samples from Other Studies

Raw scores provide information on how an individual would be scored when providing answers on the related personality inventory. Therefore, raw scores are more suitable for performing comparisons with results obtained from other published research studies.

Basic Human Values. In the following procedure the raw scores have been transformed to match with the original scale's scoring system used in the study by Schwartz and Bardi [30]. The representative or near-representative samples provide the necessary comparison that allows for a more detailed description of the value profiles. Figure 4a shows the general population's value priorities compared with the CEO value priorities based on the raw scores.

Big Five. The Big Five profile scores were compared to a large-scale study, which gathered personality profiles from a sample of 132,515 American and Canadian internet users aged between 21–60 years [33]. The scores are reported using the percentage of maximum possible (POMP) scoring method, which is a metric constructed by a linear transformation of raw metric scores into a 0 to 100 scale, where 0 represents the minimum possible score and 100 represents the maximum possible score [5]. Therefore these scores are directly comparable to the raw scores derived from the IBM PI service (range 0–1). Figure 4b shows the mean score comparison between the large scale sample and the current CEO sample.

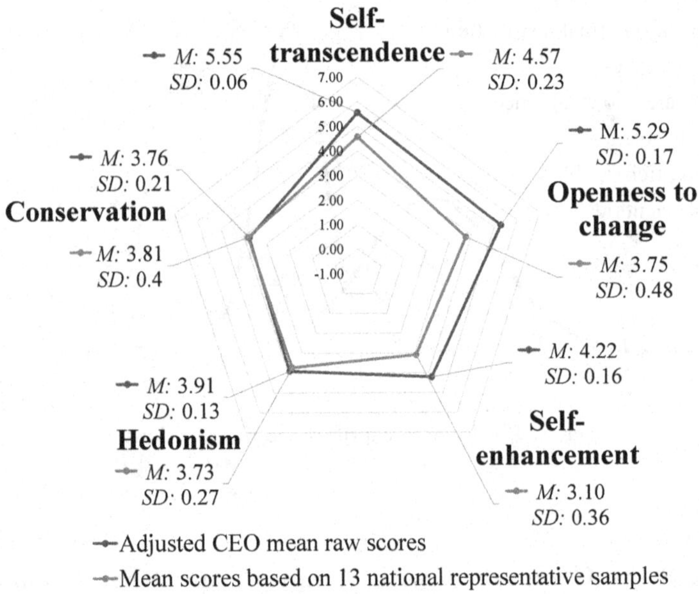

(a) Basic Human Values profile.

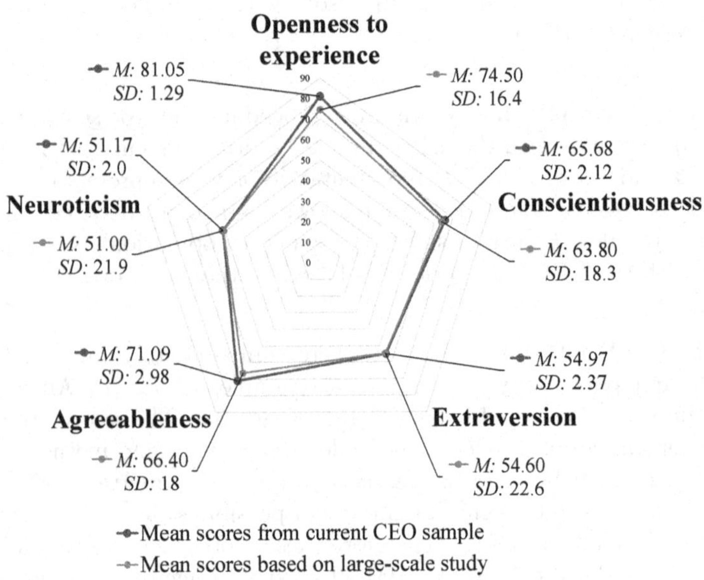

(b) Big Five personality dimensions.

Fig. 4. Comparison of CEO raw profile scores from the IBM Watson PI service to research results obtained from representative samples.

4.3 Comparison Between CEO Sub-groups

The following procedures aimed at analyzing differences among the two groups in the present CEO sample, based on a classification that identified a track record of rule-breaking behavior.

Basic Human Values. For the purpose of individual level choice prediction, the relative importance among the values has to be considered according to the original formulation of the theory. To this end, the profiles from the two CEO groups were converted to reflect relative importance among the Basic Human Values as described in Sect. 3.3, and five independent samples t-tests were performed on the raw scores to compare each value's importance across the two classes of CEOs to detect differences in the value profiles. Figure 5 illustrates the relative importance of values among the two CEO groups and the general population. Rank order of the values is marked above the bars where the CEO sample's ranking is followed by the general population's rank on each value. Table 2 shows the results of the performed t-tests.

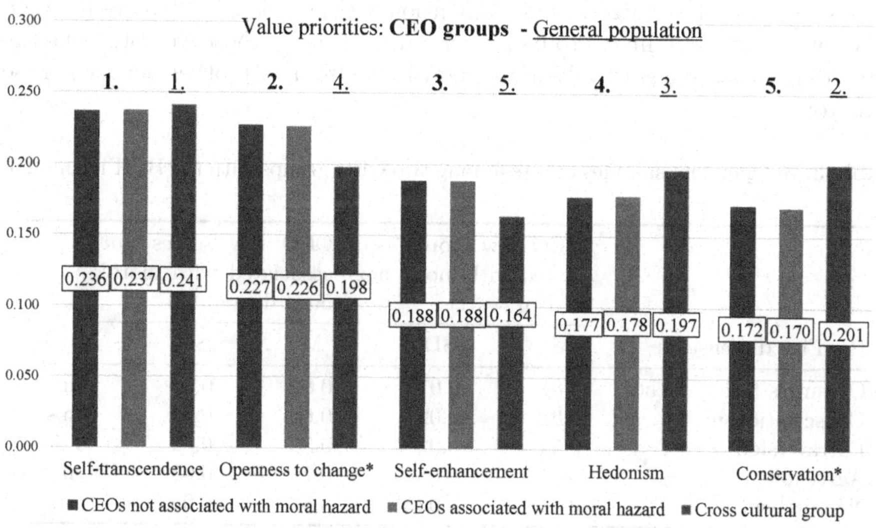

Fig. 5. Comparison between the relative importance of the Basic Human Values among two groups of CEOs and general population. *marks a significant difference between the two CEO groups in terms of the importance of corresponding values [35].

Table 2. Results of the independent samples t-tests among two CEO groups using the Basic Human Values model [35].

	CEO raw scores associated with moral hazard (n = 31)		CEO raw scores not associated with moral hazard (n = 85)		
Values	M	SD	M	SD	t-test
Self-transcendence	0.82	0.01	0.82	0.01	n.s.
Openness to change	0.78	0.02	0.79	0.02	2.20*
Self-enhancement	0.65	0.02	0.65	0.02	n.s.
Hedonism	0.61	0.01	0.61	0.02	n.s.
Conservation	0.59	0.02	0.60	0.03	2.07*

Note. *$p < .05$; two-tailed.
M = Mean. SD = Standard Deviation

Big Five. The same grouping was used when running five independent samples t-tests to analyze which dimensions of the Big Five personality model indicate group-level differences among the two classes of CEOs. Table 3 presents results of the tests. Extraversion was the only dimension with significant difference between CEOs who have been linked to moral hazard, and those who have not, while the other dimensions are statically indistinguishable from each other between these sub-groups.

Table 3. Independent samples t-tests among two CEO groups with the Big Five model.

	CEO raw scores associated with moral hazard (n = 31)		CEO raw scores not associated with moral hazard (n = 85)		
Big Five dimensions	M	SD	M	SD	t-test
Openness to experience	0.81	0.01	0.82	0.01	n.s.
Conscientiousness	0.65	0.02	0.66	0.02	n.s.
Extraversion	0.54	0.02	0.55	0.02	1.98*
Agreeableness	0.71	0.03	0.71	0.03	n.s.
Neuroticism	0.51	0.02	0.51	0.02	n.s

Note. *$p = .05$; two-tailed.
M = Mean. SD = Standard Deviation

4.4 Predictive Performance Comparison of the Basic Human Values and Big Five Models

The final set of analyses focused on comparing the predictive capabilities of the two different personality models. Raw scores were transformed to z-scores and the guidelines provided by [23] were followed when conducting the analyses and presenting the results. Binary logistic regression models were built separately and the variables were entered in a single step in order to assess the overall predictive performance of the two theories. The dependent variable had two levels (i.e. clean track record vs evidence of rule-breaking, coded as 0 and 1). In case of the Basic Human Values model, the overall model evaluation proved that the model provided a significant improvement over the intercept only model, and the inferential goodness-of-fit test (Hosmer–Lemeshow) was insignificant ($p > .05$), suggesting that the model was fit to the data well. In case of the Big Five model, the overall model evaluation was not significantly better than the null-model.

Table 4 presents the overall model using the Basic Human values as predictors and Table 5 shows the details of the predictive performance evaluation of the model. For the Big Five personality dimensions, Table 6 shows the overall model and Table 7 shows the performance metrics related to this conceptualization of personality. Sensitivity and specificity were computed according to the guidelines provided by [10].

A final model was built, to test whether a combination of predictors from the two different theories could yield improved predictive performance. Predictors were entered by using the conditional forward stepwise selection method with entry testing based on the significance of the score statistic, and removal testing based on the probability of a likelihood-ratio statistic based on conditional parameter estimates. The first block contained all Basic Human Values as predictors, and the next block contained all the Big Five dimensions. The resulting final model is shown in Table 8.

Table 4. Logistic regression model using the Basic Human Values profiles.

Predictor	β	*SE* β	Wald's χ^2	*df*	*p*	Odds ratio
Constant	−1.15	0.24	23.68	1	0.00*	0.32
Conservation	−0.50	0.27	3.47	1	0.06	0.61
Openness to change	−0.74	0.29	6.38	1	0.01*	0.48
Hedonism	−0.05	0.29	0.03	1	0.87	0.87
Self-enhancement	0.22	0.32	0.47	1	0.49	1.24
Self-transcendence	−0.24	0.28	0.78	1	0.38	0.78
Test			χ^2	*df*	*p*	
Overall model evaluation			**12.82**	**5**	**0.02***	
Goodness-of-fit-test:						
Hosmer & Lemeshow			12.34	8	0.14	

Note. $^*p < 0.05$. Cox and Snell $R^2 = .105$. Nagelkerke $R^2 = .152$.

Table 5. Predictive performance evaluation of the Basic Human Values model.

	Predicted		
Observed	Yes	No	% Correct
Yes	7	24	22.6
No	4	81	95.3
Overall %			75.9

Note. TP: True Positive, TN: True Negative, FP: False Positive, FN: False Negative, Sensitivity = TP / (TP + FN) = 22.6%. Specificity = TN / (TN + FP) = 95.3%.

Table 6. Logistic regression model using the Big Five profiles.

Predictor	β	*SE* β	Wald's χ^2	*df*	*p*	Odds ratio
Constant	−1.11	0.23	23.66	1	0.00*	0.33
Openness to experience	−0.09	0.25	0.13	1	0.71	0.91
Conscientiousness	−0.40	0.30	1.75	1	0.19	0.67
Extraversion	−0.61	0.27	5.12	1	0.02*	0.54
Agreeableness	−0.08	0.26	0.09	1	0.77	0.93
Neuroticism	0.70	0.31	4.97	1	0.03*	2.01
Test			χ^2	*df*	*p*	
Overall model evaluation			**10.76**	**5**	**0.06**	
Goodness-of-fit-test:						
Hosmer & Lemeshow			13.65	8	0.09	

Note. *p < 0.05 Cox and Snell R^2 = .089. Nagelkerke R^2 = .129.

Table 7. Predictive performance evaluation of the Big Five Model.

	Predicted		
Observed	Yes	No	% Correct
Yes	4	27	12.9
No	2	83	97.6
Overall %			75

Note. TP: True Positive, TN: True Negative, FP: False Positive, FN: False Negative Sensitivity = TP / (TP + FN) = 12.9%. Specificity = TN / (TN + FP) = 97.6%.

Table 8. Results of the logistic regression model by combining predictors from both theories.

Predictor	β	$SE\ \beta$	Wald's χ^2	df	p	Odds ratio
Constant	−1.13	0.23	23.73	1	0.00**	0.32
Openness to change	−0.61	0.23	6.93	1	0.01**	0.54
Conservation	−0.59	0.23	6.34	1	0.01**	0.56
Test			χ^2	df	p	
Overall model evaluation			**11.57**	**2**	**0.00****	
Goodness-of-fit-test:						
Hosmer & Lemeshow			9.36	8	0.31	

Note. **$p \leq 0.01$ Cox and Snell $R^2 = .095$. Nagelkerke $R^2 = .138$.

5 Discussion

This study aimed at analyzing two different models of personality to detect a selection bias among chief executive officers by using text-based personality inferences provided by the IBM Watson PI service. Our results suggest that a selection bias can be detected by the Basic Human Values and the Big Five models as well. According to the results there are clearly identifiable differences among the universally established value structures in the general population and the sample of CEOs. Furthermore, differences can be identified in the Big Five profiles between these groups. This marked difference is interpreted as an evidence of a selection bias among organizational leaders. The importance of these differences in the motivational and personality structures is discussed in this section with directions for further work.

The analyses based on percentile scores revealed that both the Basic Human Value structure and the Big Five profile of the current sample of CEOs shows significant differences from the Watson Personality Insight service's hypothesized sample. With the exception of Openness to change (Basic Human Values) and Extraversion (Big Five), all other dimensions of the corresponding models showed differences from the original sample's hypothesized distributions. Due to the large sample size used during the validation of the service, it can be regarded as an indicator of valid differences between these samples, however due to the lack of detailed information about the original sample it is not possible to draw further conclusions based on percentile scores.

The second set of analyses focused on the utility of raw scores and the comparisons relied on established results from other large-scale studies. In terms of the Basic Human Values, the investigations revealed that there are important differences between the rank order of values among CEOs and the general population. While Self-transcendence values (i.e. care for the welfare of closely related others, as well as care for all the people and for nature) are most important for both groups the similarities between CEOs and non-CEOs end at this point. Openness to change (i.e. self-direction, independence, creating, stimulation and seeking out challenges) ranks as the second most important value in case of corporate leaders, while it is the second least important motivational factor for the general population. Openness to change and Conservation values can be found at opposing sides of the motivational circumplex, which reflects that decisions that promote the obtaining of a particular goal inhibit the simultaneous fulfillment of the competing need. Therefore a high priority given to Openness to change values would result in choices increasing novelty and chances for expressions of independent action at the expense of maintaining stability and stability. Self-enhancement values (i.e. expression of competence, achievement of status and control over others) rank at the third position for CEOs, while it is the least important motivational value in the general population. Although one might expect that leaders of world-leading organizations (expressing power and achievement values) would be mainly motivated by Self-enhancement values at the expense of Self-transcendence values, these results contradict this expectation. The rank order difference of Self-enhancement values between non-CEOs (5.) and CEOs (3.) however clearly expresses their preference for high social status and prestige. While for non-CEOs, the second most important motivational tendencies relate to Conservation values (i.e. security, safety of self and of society, restraint of actions likely to harm others, respect for customs), these goals are less important to leaders, as it ranks the lowest on the their motivational hierarchy, indicating that actions promoting Conservation values have a much lower intrinsic motivational effect (e.g. in order to make an action appear at least as rewarding as an action expressing Openness to change values it has to be incentivized much more externally). The relative importance of values matches closely with the various Enterprising value profiles as discussed in [14], placing CEOs close to other occupations characterized by material and concrete goals.

In terms of the Big Five model, raw scores are more closely matched with those of the general population. A higher mean score on Openness to experience indicates elevated preference for adventure, novel experiences, curiosity and intellectual challenges, which can be seen as a desirable attribute for organizational leaders promoting growth, and motivating employees. On the other hand, it is also related to risk-taking behavior. Higher scores on Agreeableness is surprising, since lower scores are associated with competitiveness and self-direction, which are considered important leader characteristics. A more detailed analysis of the facet scores on this dimension could reveal which aspects contribute to the elevated score.

The third set of analyses aimed at identifying between-group differences within the current CEO sample, when previous history of misbehavior is taken into account. Based on the Basic Human Values model a slight, but significantly lower relative importance attributed to Openness to change and Conservation values was associated with various undesirable behaviors that can be detrimental to the reputation of the organization lead by the particular CEOs. Out of the Big Five dimensions only Extraversion showed a significant difference between groups, where lower Extraversion scores were associated with undesirable actions. This finding is similar to the results obtained by [26] which showed that self-reported computer criminal behavior was associated with higher levels of Introversion (i.e. lower levels on Extraversion) and similarly, no other significant differences were found between the two student groups in terms of the Big Five profiles.

The final evaluations were conducted to test the utility of the two major theories for the prediction of behavioral outcomes. Since both theories aim at providing a comprehensive view on the organization of the human psyche by identifying basic and necessary structures that are pervasive and relatively stable within individuals [19], they were used in two separate logistic regression models as a single unit. A third model was built to investigate whether a combination of the two theories could achieve improvements over any of the models in isolation. The model built from the Basic Human Values represented a significant improvement from the null-model, and achieved the highest score on the R^2 metric ($R^2 = 0.152$) out of the three models. The logistic regression analysis including all the Big Five dimensions resulted in a model that was not significantly better than a null-model, which purely guesses the majority class. This finding is surprising considering that the Big Five is the most widely accepted and utilized model of personality, and several studies claim that it has substantial predictive utility in a wide range of domains [21,22]. The final combined model contained no predictors from the Big Five (none of them reached the inclusion criteria), thus all variance explained by the model is attributed to Basic Human Values. The overall model reached a higher significance level (i.e. lower p value) at the expense of some explained variance (change from the model with all Basic Human Values in terms of R^2 is: -0.014). This results suggests that the two models are to a great extent overlapping, but the Basic Human Values model might be more comprehensive.

A limitation of the present study is the relatively small sample size, which can be extended in future studies, since the method of analyzing personality profiles by using the Watson PI service is a feasible method for gathering information about the motivation of decision makers for the purpose of risk analysis. Sample size limitations may potentially hamper the performance of the binary logistic regression models, therefore it would be necessary to increase the number of observations for events and non-events for improved models. It would potentially lead to better sensitivity and specificity scores, and in order to compute positive and negative predictive values, the prevalence rates of offending behavior could be investigated in future work [10]. Furthermore, a more detailed description and classification of the various forms of rule-breaking behavior could clarify the connection between the particular strategy owner's profile and the nature of negative impact inflicted upon the organization, to achieve a better assessment of the risks relating to individuals.

In a risk analysis setting direct access to subjects is a major limitation. Since previous work has established the extent to which the most easily available pieces of information (i.e. demographic features) are useful for constructing stakeholder profiles [36], future work will focus on other classes of observable features (e.g.

ownership of items [7], or various forms of online behavior with digital traces [15], etc.) for the construction of psychological profiles.

6 Conclusion

This exploratory study aimed at analyzing how publicly observable pieces of information (i.e. spoken texts, group membership) associated with individuals can be utilized to detect a selection bias among groups of people working in similar roles. A set of chief executive officers were selected for the purpose of testing the methods' usefulness, for two main reasons: the availability of relevant and necessary data, and due to the significance of the role they play in organizations. However, the principles presented in this study are applicable to other classes of stakeholders as well, and are not limited to the CEO role. The selection bias is revealed by patterns of specific psychological characteristics that distinguish CEOs from the general population. Furthermore, within the analyzed CEO sample, additional differences could be detected among two groups that were generated by considering available evidence about rule-breaking behavior (i.e. association with moral hazard).

The specific psychological differences were investigated through two major theories that account for stable individual differences among people. The Big Five personality model is evaluated against the Basic Human Values model in terms of group-level differences, and in terms of predictive capabilities. The results show that both models are useful in detecting a hypothesized selection bias, but the Basic Human Values model performs better in terms of predictive utility as a comprehensive model of individual differences and motivation. The unobtrusive nature of the text analysis combined with the procedures described in this study enables risk analysts to study human-related risks in various environments where adversarial stakeholder behavior is assumed and it is crucial to be prepared against undesirable consequences of those actions (e.g. information security).

Acknowledgements. This work was partially supported by the project IoTSec – Security in IoT for Smart Grids, with number 248113/O70 part of the IKTPLUSS program funded by the Norwegian Research Council.

References

1. Anderson, R., Moore, T.: Information security: where computer science, economics and psychology meet. Philos. Trans. R. Soc. London A: Math. Phys. Eng. Sci. **367**, 2717–2727 (2009)
2. Babiak, P., Neumann, C.S., Hare, R.D.: Corporate psychopathy: talking the walk. Behav. Sci. Law **28**(2), 174–193 (2010)
3. Boddy, C.R.: The implications of corporate psychopaths for business and society: an initial examination and a call to arms. Australas. J. Bus. Behav. Sci. **1**(2), 30–40 (2005)

4. Cohan, J.A.: "I didn't know" and "i was only doing my job": Has corporate governance careened out of control? A case study of enron's information myopia. J. Bus. Ethics **40**(3), 275–299 (2002)
5. Cohen, P., Cohen, J., Aiken, L.S., West, S.G.: The problem of units and the circumstance for pomp. Multivar. Behav. Res. **34**(3), 315–346 (1999)
6. Dembe, A.E., Boden, L.I.: Moral hazard: a question of morality? New Solutions: J. Environ. Occup. Health Policy **10**(3), 257–279 (2000)
7. Dohmen, T., Falk, A., Huffman, D., Sunde, U., Schupp, J., Wagner, G.G.: Individual risk attitudes: measurement, determinants, and behavioral consequences. J. Eur. Econ. Assoc. **9**(3), 522–550 (2011)
8. Eisenhardt, K.M.: Agency theory: an assessment and review. Acad. Manag. Rev. **14**(1), 57–74 (1989)
9. Fosso, O.B., Molinas, M., Sand, K., Coldevin, G.H.: Moving towards the smart grid: the Norwegian case. In: 2014 International Power Electronics Conference (IPEC-Hiroshima 2014-ECCE-ASIA), pp. 1861–1867. IEEE (2014)
10. Kajonius, P.J., Persson, B.N., Jonason, P.K.: Hedonism, achievement, and power: universal values that characterize the dark triad. Pers. Individ. Differences **77**, 173–178 (2015)
11. Grassegger, H., Krogerus, M.: The data that turned the world upside down, January 2017. https://motherboard.vice.com/en_us/article/mg9vvn/how-our-likes-helped-trump-win
12. IBM: The science behind the service (2017). https://console.bluemix.net/docs/services/personality-insights/science.html#science. Accessed 14 February 2018
13. Kajonius, P.J., Persson, B.N., Jonason, P.K.: Hedonism, achievement, and power: universal values that characterize the dark triad. Pers. Individ. Differ. **77**, 173–178 (2015)
14. Knafo, A., Sagiv, L.: Values and work environment: mapping 32 occupations. Eur. J. Psychol. Educ. **19**(3), 255–273 (2004)
15. Kosinski, M., Stillwell, D., Graepel, T.: Private traits and attributes are predictable from digital records of human behavior. Proc. Nat. Acad. Sci. **110**(15), 5802–5805 (2013)
16. Kristof-Brown, A.L., Zimmerman, R.D., Johnson, E.C.: Consequences of individuals' fit at work: a meta-analysis of person-job, person-organization, person-group, and person-supervisor fit. Pers. Psychol. **58**(2), 281–342 (2005)
17. Lindeman, M., Verkasalo, M.: Measuring values with the short schwartz's value survey. J. Pers. Assess. **85**(2), 170–178 (2005)
18. Lounsbury, J.W., Sundstrom, E.D., Gibson, L.W., Loveland, J.M., Drost, A.W.: Core personality traits of managers. J. Manag. Psychol. **31**(2), 434–450 (2016)
19. McCrae, R.R., John, O.P.: An introduction to the five-factor model and its applications. J. Pers. **60**(2), 175–215 (1992)
20. Morley, M.J.: Person-organization fit. J. Manag. Psychol. **22**(2), 109–117 (2007)
21. Paunonen, S.V.: Big five factors of personality and replicated predictions of behavior. J. Pers. Soc. Psychol. **84**(2), 411 (2003)
22. Paunonen, S.V., Ashton, M.C.: Big five factors and facets and the prediction of behavior. J. Pers. Soc. Psychol. **81**(3), 524 (2001)
23. Peng, C.Y.J., Lee, K.L., Ingersoll, G.M.: An introduction to logistic regression analysis and reporting. J. Educ. Res. **96**(1), 3–14 (2002)
24. Rajbhandari, L., Snekkenes, E.: Intended actions: risk is conflicting incentives. In: Gollmann, D., Freiling, F.C. (eds.) ISC 2012. LNCS, vol. 7483, pp. 370–386. Springer, Heidelberg (2012). https://doi.org/10.1007/978-3-642-33383-5_23

25. Rajbhandari, L., Snekkenes, E.: Using the conflicting incentives risk analysis method. In: Janczewski, L.J., Wolfe, H.B., Shenoi, S. (eds.) SEC 2013. IAICT, vol. 405, pp. 315–329. Springer, Heidelberg (2013). https://doi.org/10.1007/978-3-642-39218-4_24
26. Rogers, M.K., Seigfried, K., Tidke, K.: Self-reported computer criminal behavior: a psychological analysis. Digit. Invest. **3**, 116–120 (2006)
27. Salary.com: Executive compensation it starts with the CEO (2004). https://www.salary.com/executive-compensation-it-starts-with-the-ceo/. Accessed 14 Feb 2018
28. Schneider, B., Goldstein, H.W., Smith, D.B.: The ASA framework: an update. Pers. Psychol. **48**(4), 747–773 (1995)
29. Schwartz, S.H.: An overview of the schwartz theory of basic values. Online Readings Psychol. Cult. **2**(1), 11 (2012)
30. Schwartz, S.H., Bardi, A.: Value hierarchies across cultures: taking a similarities perspective. J. Cross Cult. Psychol. **32**(3), 268–290 (2001)
31. Snekkenes, E.: Position paper: privacy risk analysis is about understanding conflicting incentives. In: Fischer-Hübner, S., de Leeuw, E., Mitchell, C. (eds.) IDMAN 2013. IAICT, vol. 396, pp. 100–103. Springer, Heidelberg (2013). https://doi.org/10.1007/978-3-642-37282-7_9
32. Soltani, B.: The anatomy of corporate fraud: a comparative analysis of high profile american and European corporate scandals. J. Bus. Ethics **120**(2), 251–274 (2014)
33. Srivastava, S., John, O.P., Gosling, S.D., Potter, J.: Development of personality in early and middle adulthood: set like plaster or persistent change? J. Pers. Soc. Psychol. **84**(5), 1041 (2003)
34. Stenmark, C.K., Mumford, M.D.: Situational impacts on leader ethical decision-making. Leadersh. Quart. **22**(5), 942–955 (2011)
35. Szekeres, A., Snekkenes, E.A.: Unobtrusive psychological profiling for risk analysis. In: Proceedings of the 15th International Joint Conference on e-Business and Telecommunications - Volume 1: SECRYPT, pp. 210–220. SciTePress (2018)
36. Szekeres, A., Wasnik, P.S., Snekkenes, E.A.: Using demographic features for the prediction of basic human values underlying stakeholder motivation. In: Proceedings of the 21st International Conference on Enterprise Information Systems - Volume 2: ICEIS, pp. 377–389. INSTICC, SciTePress (2019)
37. Van Peursem, K.A., Zhou, M., Flood, T., Buttimore, J.: Three cases of corporate fraud: an audit perspective (2007)
38. Whyte, G.: Decision failures: why they occur and how to prevent them. Acad. Manage. Perspect. **5**(3), 23–31 (1991)
39. Wikipedia: List of chief executive officers Wikipedia, the free encyclopedia (2004). https://en.wikipedia.org/wiki/List_of_chief_executive_officers. Accessed 06 Dec 2017

Compile-Time Security Certification of Imperative Programming Languages

Sandip Ghosal[1(✉)], R. K. Shyamasundar[1], and N. V. Narendra Kumar[2]

[1] Department of Computer Science and Engineering, Indian Institute of Technology Bombay, Mumbai 400076, India
sandipsmit@gmail.com

[2] Institute for Development and Research in Banking Technology, Hyderabad, India

Abstract. With the ever increase in the demand of building secure systems, recent years are witnessing a plethora of research on information flow control (IFC) techniques in programming languages to enforce a finer-grained restriction on the propagation of information among untrusted objects. In this paper, we introduce a *dynamic labelling* (DL) algorithm (This paper is an extended version of the article [1] presented in SECRYPT'18.) for security certification of imperative programming languages that follows a combination of mutable and immutable labelling referred to as *hybrid* labelling approach. First, we study the possible methods of binding security labels with the subjects and objects of the program which include *program counter* that represent implicit flow within a program and compare the precision achieved by the applications of methods on benchmark programs. Next, we describe our labelling algorithm that generates labels for intermediate subjects/objects of a program from the given set of initial labels (some of which could be immutable throughout the computation) adhering to the constraints defined in [2] for a program to be *information-flow secure*. Apart from the usual control statements found in the imperative languages, we also present the labelling approach for a procedure call highlighting subtleties of different parameter passing mechanisms adopted in modern languages. Further, we discuss a variant of the algorithm for concurrent programs. It is shown that our algorithm always terminates after a finite number of iterations, also establish the soundness concerning non-interference as given by [3]. We compare the labelling precision realizable by our approach with the existing approaches in the literature.

1 Introduction

The seminal work of Denning [4] on security certification of programs built on *information-flow security* led to a firm foundation for language-based security. The extension of such a theory through the proposal of the Decentralized Label Model (DLM) [5] provided a momentum for language-based security. Since then there has been an enormous amount of literature on language-based security [6–9]. Various well articulate assessments of the status of language-based security

M. S. Obaidat (Ed.): ICETE 2018, CCIS 1118, pp. 159–182, 2019.
https://doi.org/10.1007/978-3-030-34866-3_8

have been discussed in [10–12]. With the need for security everywhere including IoT, language-based security is becoming prominent as it deals with security at various levels, and also brings out various points of leaks and attacks.

Non-interference was developed after Denning's security certification as a more semantic characterization of security [13], followed by many extensions. Informally the non-interference property says the impact on the program due to changes in *high* inputs should not be observable by the *low* outputs. [3] have used a purely value-based interpretation of non-interference as a semantic characterization of information-flow, and derived sound typing rules to capture Denning's certification semantics effectively. Volpano *et al.*'s notion of non-interference, and its extensions have become the de-facto standard for the semantics of information-flow in the literature on language-based security. Usually, the objective of IFC is to enforce non-interference property to ensure end-to-end flow security.

A broad spectrum of information-flow security mechanisms varies from fully dynamic ones, e.g., in the form of execution-monitors [14,15] to static ones, e.g., in the form of type systems [3]. While one would prefer static labels as that leads to certification of programs at compile-time, it has the problem of classifying programs that would not leak any information under the information-flow policy at execution time due to the underlying inputs that arrive at run-time. Real-world web applications often require to interact with the external environment that cannot be predicted during compile-time which motivates researchers to enforce security at run-time. For instance, security settings of files and database records are updated frequently, and these changes might affect the information flow control which cannot be handled by static mechanisms. Dynamic labels are essential to capture the changes in security label and accordingly labels are changed at run-time. However, unlike static or immutable labelling implementation, a dynamic mechanism has a cost that user has to pay in the form of significant run-time overhead, and also *implicit flows* introduced due to uncovered flow paths not considered at run-time. Hence, an ideal label-checking mechanism should have a *hybrid labelling* that would have an excellent trade-off for mutable and immutable labels to realize acceptable precision and performance.

In this paper, we first discuss various labelling approaches that use a combination of attributes like mutable, immutable, static, compile-time, run-time, etc., for the security certification along with the corresponding realizable precision of security. Having assessed the shortcomings [1], we propose a new hybrid (mutable and immutable) labelling approach for certifying programs for information-flow security using the standard certification of constraints as elaborated by Denning. Our dynamic labelling algorithm is sound with respect to non-interference, and we further prove the termination of the labelling algorithm. Our proposed labelling algorithm leads to certification that is more security precise than other labelling approaches in the literature [7,8,16–20]. It may be pointed out that the labels are generated succinctly without unnecessarily blowing up the label space. As the method is not tied to any particular security model, it provides a sound basis for the security certification of programs for information-flow security. We further compare the precision realizable by our approach with those in the literature. The comparison of our approach also brings to light, an intrinsic property of our labelling algorithm that could be effectively used for non-deterministic or concurrent programs illustrated in Sect. 4.

Structure of the Paper. Section 2 presents different labelling schemes, and assess the limitations of them. Section 3 describes the proposed dynamic labelling algorithm along with illustrative examples, and proofs of characteristic properties as well as soundness with respect to *non-interference*. Section 4 presents an extended version of the labelling algorithm for concurrent programs. Section 5 provides a comparison with earlier approaches. Finally, Sect. 6 summarizes the contributions along with the ongoing work.

2 Certification of Programs

According to Denning's Information Flow Model (DFM) the necessary and sufficient condition for the flow security of a program P is: if there is an information flow from object x to object y, denoted by $x \to y$, the flow is secured by P only if $\lambda(x) \leqslant \lambda(y)$. '$\lambda$' is a labelling function, responsible for binding subject/object of the program to a security class (either statically or dynamically depending on the application) from the lattice of security classes as described in Denning's lattice model [4]. '$\leqslant$' is a binary relation on security classes that specifies permissible information flows. '$\oplus$' is a binary class-combining operator evaluates least upper bound (LUB) of two security classes in the lattice. The above condition is usually referred to as the *Information-flow policy* (IFP). A program is certified for IFP if there are no violations of the policy during program execution. The *Information Flow Secure* policy forms a basis for certifying programs for security. The crux of certification lies in assuring that all the information flows over legitimate channels or storage channels follow the specified flow-policy. The outcome of approaches could be measured in terms of *precision* defined below.

Let us suppose that F is the set of possible flows in an information flow system, and let A be the subset of F authorized by a given flow policy, and let E be the subset of F "executable" given the flow control mechanisms in operation. The system is said to be **secure** if $E \subseteq A$; that is all executable flows are authorized. A secure system is **precise** if $E = A$.

The method of binding security classes/labels to objects play an essential role in the analysis of programs. Each of the static certification and runtime enforcement algorithms proposed in the literature chooses an object labelling method, some of which may also use the label of the implicit variable, usually referred to as *Program Counter* (PC) which may be reset after every statement or keeps updating monotonically. First, let us consider the following three broad object labelling schemes:

Scheme 1: fixed labels for all the variables,
Scheme 2: labels of all the variables can be modified; for example, based on the information contained in them at any given program point, and

Table 1. There is implicit flow from x to y while there is no direct flow (Cf. [1]).

```
void test(int x){
  int y=0;
  int z=0;
  if(x==0)
     z=1;
  if(z==0)
     y=1;
}
```

Table 2. Need to label local variables dynamically (Cf. [1]).

```
void test(){
  int a;
  a=x;
  y=a;
  a=z;
}
```

Scheme 3: labels of some variables are fixed while the labels of the other variables could be modified.

In this section, we argue that from the perspective of capturing the notion of security,
(i) Scheme 1 is inappropriate as it is too stringent, and results in secure programs being incorrectly rejected as insecure,
(ii) Scheme 2 is also inappropriate as it allows all programs as secure programs, and
(iii) Scheme 3 is the ideal candidate, if the variables whose labels can be allowed to be modified are carefully chosen.

A majority of literature on language-based security follows Scheme 1, as it has advantages in certifying tricky programs such as the one given in Table 1.

As the program in Table 1 executes, the following information flow is observed: if the value of x is 0, the value of z becomes 1, and the second *if* block will not execute, thus the value of y remains 0. On the other hand, if the value of x is 1, the second *if* block executes, and y is initialized to 1. In either case, the value of y is the same as the value of x although there is no such explicit assignment, e.g., $x = y$. If we consider the security labels of x and y are $\underline{x}$ and $\underline{y}$ and $\underline{x} \nleqslant \underline{y}$ then this is an example of the insecure program as there is an implicit flow from x to y even though they belong to different security classes where an explicit flow is not allowed. Table 3 analyzes two different labelling approaches, i.e., Scheme 1 and Scheme 2 in respect of the program in Table 1.

However, purely static labelling is too restrictive and rejects secure programs as insecure. This is illustrated by considering the program fragment shown in Table 2, where x, y, and z are global variables, and a is a local variable (we do not consider pointer variables).

If the program in Table 2 is analyzed under Scheme 1, it generates the following set of flow-constraints to be satisfied for the program to be secure: $\underline{x} \leqslant \underline{a}$, $\underline{a} \leqslant \underline{y}$, and $\underline{z} \leqslant \underline{a}$. These constraints will be satisfied only if $\underline{z} \leqslant \underline{y}$, which implies that there is an information-flow from z to y. However, from an intuitive perspective, the program never causes an information flow from z to y and must be

Table 3. Analyzing information flow at each line from example in Table 1 according to static and dynamic labelling (Cf. [1]).

Line No.	Static labelling (Scheme 1)	Dynamic labelling (Scheme 2)
3	Label of z would be inferred in such a way that all the flows to and from z should be secured. If z is assigned to $\underline{x}$, the flow from $z \rightarrow y$ is not permitted. There is no way to label z so that all the flows are safe. For this reason the program is insecure	Label of z is initialized to least confidential security class e.g. public ($\perp$)
4		As there is a flow from $x \rightarrow z$ z is updated to $\underline{x}$ such that $\underline{x} \leqslant \underline{z}$
5		
6		There is a flow from $z \rightarrow y$. But $\underline{x}$ cannot flow into $\underline{y}$. Hence the program is insecure
7		

considered secure if $\underline{x} \leqslant \underline{y}$. Table 4 analyzes two different labelling approaches, i.e., Scheme 1 and Scheme 2 in respect of the program in Table 2.

Table 4. Analyzing information flow at each line of example shown in Table 2 according to static and dynamic labelling (Cf. [1]).

Line No	Flow direction	Static labelling (Scheme 1)	Dynamic labelling (Scheme 2)
5		Label of a is automatically inferred in such a way that all the flows to and from a is secure. If a is labelled as $\underline{x} \oplus \underline{z}$ due to explicit flows from x and y to a, the constraint $\underline{x} \oplus \underline{z} \leqslant \underline{y}$ will not be satisfied because $\underline{z} \nleqslant \underline{y}$ As static labelling fails to label the local variable a, the program is insecure	Label of a is initialized to least confidential security class e.g. public $\perp$
6	$x \rightarrow a$		Label of a is updated to label of x i.e. $\underline{x}$ so that x can flow to a
7	$a \rightarrow y$		Flow is allowed as the constraint $\underline{x} \leqslant \underline{y}$ is satisfied.
8	$z \rightarrow a$		Label of a is updated to $\underline{x} \oplus \underline{z}$ so that flow is allowed as $\underline{z} \leqslant \underline{x} \oplus \underline{z}$. Hence the program is flow-safe

From the above examples, it follows that the use of purely static labelling is too conservative, and misses several secure programs.

2.1 Refinement via PC Labels

Information flow is quite tricky to capture and can happen even if a statement does not get executed. Such flows are called "implicit" [21], and are possible due to conditional and iteration statements. To keep track of such impact, the notion of the program counter (*pc*) label is introduced that denotes the sensitivity of the current context. Traditionally, once the control exits the conditional or iteration statements, the pc label is reset to its previous value, thus denoting that the variables in the condition expression no longer impact the current context. Subsequently, a sequential composition $S_1; S_2$ is deemed secure if both S_1 and S_2 are individually secure.

Examples copy3 and copy4 in [21] have highlighted that certain subtle flows cannot be captured unless the pc label is updated monotonically, and tracks the influence of all the information the program has accessed. It was noted that this might lead to a phenomenon called "label creep" [11] wherein the pc label rises too high resulting in rejecting any further flows. To avoid label creeping, the current literature on language-based security takes the route of resetting pc label after exiting from a control structure.

Tracking PC Labels [18]**.** The method described for Haskell envisaged in [18] uses a label for current control without reinitializing every time the control exits a statement. A labeled IO Haskell library unit `LIO` is built to track a single mutable *current label* (similar to *pc*) at run-time and allows access to IO operations. The unit is responsible for ensuring that the current label keeps track of all the observed data and regulates label modifications. At each computation, `LIO` keeps tracks of the *current label* and allows access to IO functionality, e.g., labeled file systems. The current label is evaluated as an *upper bound* of all the labels observed during program execution.

2.2 Labelling Schemes: A Summary

Table 5 summarizes possible ways of binding labels with objects.

Table 5. Binding labels with objects for certification (Cf. [1]).

pc Label→	Reset	Monotonic
Labelling↓		
Static	P_1	P_2
Hybrid	P_3	P_4

Some programs where ignoring the label of program point leads to incorrect certification are given in Tables 6 and 7. Table 6 shows an example with information leaks due to abnormal termination of a program. The value of x can be calculated from the value of *sum* (maximum possible integer value) and y on terminating the program due to integer overflow. There is an implicit flow from x to y although the assignment to y is conditioned on the *sum*.

A non-terminating flow insecure program is shown in Table 7. Let us consider the given label of the global variables x and y are given as $\underline{x}$ and $\underline{y}$ such that $\underline{x} \not\leq \underline{y}$. It can be observed that the variable y holds the value equal to x depending on the termination of the program.

Although `LIO` follows the label binding P_2 that keeps track of program point, the run-time monitor fails to stop an adversary from obtaining the *high* values by observing the termination of programs. Later in Sect. 3, we illustrate examples that manifest P_4 also covers P_2. Considering all the limitations discussed above, a compile-time monitor based on the labelling Scheme 3 and binding mechanism P_4

Table 6. Information-flow through abnormal termination (cf. Copy6 from [21]).

Program	Label constraints	
y=0;	$\underline{y} = high$	
int sum=0;	$\underline{x} = high$	
while(true){		
sum=sum+x;	$\underline{sum} \oplus \underline{x} \leqslant \underline{sum}$	$\underline{sum} = \underline{x}$
y=y+1;	$\underline{y} \oplus Low \leqslant \underline{y}$	
}		

Table 7. Information-flow through non-termination (Cf. Copy5 from [21]).

Program	Label constraints
y=0;	$\underline{y} = high$
while(x==0)	$\underline{x} = high$
skip;	
y=1;	$\underline{y} \oplus Low \leqslant \underline{y}$

would be a better candidate for secure certification of programs. A comparative study is given in Sect. 5 where we categorize the existing prominent IFC tools and platforms based on the labelling mechanisms.

From the above studies, we can infer:

1. While static labelling has advantages for the security certification of programs, over-approximately annotated static labels of local variables may lead to imprecision, and adversely impacts the soundness of these approaches.
2. For certifying iterative programs (terminating, non-terminating, abnormally terminating including exceptions), annotating local variables with improper static labels, and following the scheme that resets the label of the program counter, often miss to capture both the forward label propagation, and impact on static labels due to repeated backward information flow and leads to a loss of precision and soundness.
3. While the certification approach of Denning generates the relevant constraints, it fails to assert the existence of possible labelling for local variables/objects that satisfy the initial labels of global variables/objects.

If we can compute labels (or policies) for local variables such that the flow security is satisfied at all the program points, then we could consider such programs to be secure. Thus the question will be: is there a dynamic labelling procedure that realizes the same? A sound dynamic labelling approach that overcomes the limitations of the current techniques listed above shall be presented in Sect. 3.

3 Our Approach to Certification

Our approach of certification is based on a hybrid labelling of objects in the program, that could be unrolled a finite number of times. Possibility (or otherwise) of labelling the objects of the program leads to certification (or otherwise) of the program; the same could be used in the execution monitor for checking flow security at run-time.

In the following, we describe our Dynamic Labelling (DL) algorithm. The algorithm finds its basis in Denning's certification semantics.

3.1 Dynamic Labelling (DL) Algorithm for Sequential Programs

Notation: Let G be the set of global variables/objects, L the set of local variables of a program, $(var)(e)$ the set of variables appearing in expression e, pc the program counter, and $\lambda, \lambda_0, \lambda_1, \cdots$ the labelling functions that give the security label/sensitivity-level of variables and pc.

SV is a function that takes a statement/command as input, and returns the set of source variables appearing in it as output. TV is a function that takes a statement/command as input and returns the set of target variables appearing in it as output. DL is a dynamic labelling procedure/function that takes a command, clearance level of the subject executing the program, and a labelling function, as inputs, and returns either a labelling or UNABLE TO LABEL as output.

λ_{init} denotes the initial labelling. $\forall x \in G : \lambda_{\text{init}}(x)$ is given, $\forall x \in L : \lambda_{\text{init}}(x) = \perp$, and $\lambda_{\text{init}}(\text{pc}) = \perp$, where '$\perp$' is the least restrictive security class or *public*. Let P be a given program together with initial labelling for the global objects. Let s denote the subject trying to execute the program, and cl denote his clearance. If $\text{DL}(P, \text{cl}, \lambda_{\text{init}})$ returns a valid labelling, then the program preserves information-flow security when executed by the subject s. If $\text{DL}(P, \text{cl}, \lambda_{\text{init}})$ returns 'UNABLE TO LABEL', then information-flow security will be violated if the program is executed by the subject s, and the algorithm exits at that point without proceeding further.

Algorithm DL is described in Table 8. It is illustrated through examples followed by its' soundness in the sequel.

Illustrative Examples

We illustrate the advantages of our dynamic labelling procedure by analyzing the example programs from Sect. 2. Examples clearly highlight the advantages of the dynamic labelling procedure in capturing subtle information-flows through control flow path, non-termination/abnormal termination channels, etc. For each example, initial labels of the global variables are provided. We assume that the subject executing the program has the highest security label, and thus ignore the clearance field; dynamic labelling is shown in a tabular form.

We apply the proposed algorithm to the example shown in Table 2. It can be observed that the algorithm successfully labels the intermediate variable a as shown in Table 9.

Example 1. *Initial labels for global variables:* $\lambda(x) = \lambda(y) = \underline{x}$, $\lambda(z) = \underline{z}$.

Table 8. Description of algorithm DL for sequential programs (Cf. [1]).

<table>
<tr><td colspan="2">1. S : skip:: SV(S)={∅}; TV(S)={∅}; DL(S, cl, λ) : return λ</td></tr>
<tr><td>2. $S : x := e$:: SV(S)=$var(e)$; TV(S)={x};
DL(S, cl, λ):
  tmp = $\bigoplus_{v\in \text{var}(e)\cap G} \lambda(v)$
  if (tmp $\nleqslant$ cl) then
    exit 'UNABLE TO LABEL'
  $\lambda_1 = \lambda$
  $\lambda_1(\text{pc}) = \lambda(\text{pc}) \oplus \text{tmp}$
  if $x \in L$:
    $\lambda_1(x) = \lambda(x) \oplus \lambda(\text{pc}) \oplus \text{tmp}$
    return λ_1
  if $x \in G$:
    if $\left(\left[\lambda(\text{pc}) \oplus \text{tmp} \oplus \text{cl}\right] \leqslant \lambda(x)\right)$ then
      return λ_1
    else exit 'UNABLE TO LABEL'</td><td>3. S : <code>if</code> e <code>then</code> S_1[<code>else</code> S_2]::
SV(S)=SV(S_1) ∪ SV(S_2) ∪ var(e);
TV(S)=TV(S_1) ∪ TV(S_2)
DL(S, cl, λ):
  tmp = $\bigoplus_{v\in \text{var}(e)\cap G} \lambda(v)$
  if (tmp $\nleqslant$ cl) then
    exit 'UNABLE TO LABEL'
  $\lambda' = \lambda$
  $\lambda'(\text{pc}) = \lambda(\text{pc}) \oplus \text{tmp}$
  $\lambda_1 = \text{DL}(S_1, \text{cl}, \lambda')$
  $\lambda_2 = \text{DL}(S_2, \text{cl}, \lambda')$
  $\lambda_3(\text{pc}) = \lambda_1(\text{pc}) \oplus \lambda_2(\text{pc})$
  $\forall x \in L : \lambda_3(x) = \lambda_1(x) \oplus \lambda_2(x)$
  return λ_3</td></tr>
<tr><td>4. S : <code>while</code> e <code>then</code> S_1::
SV(S)=SV(S_1) ∪ var(e);
TV(S)=TV(S_1);
DL(S, cl, λ):
  tmp = $\bigoplus_{v\in \text{var}(e)\cap G} \lambda(v)$
  if (tmp $\nleqslant$ cl) then
    exit 'UNABLE TO LABEL'
  $\lambda_1 = \lambda$
  $\lambda_1(\text{pc}) = \lambda(\text{pc}) \oplus \text{tmp}$
  $\lambda_2 = \text{DL}(S_1, \text{cl}, \lambda_1)$
  if ($\lambda_2 \neq \lambda_1$)
    $\lambda_1 = \lambda_2$
    λ_2 = DL(<code>while</code> e <code>do</code> S_1,
        cl, λ_1)
  return λ_2</td><td>5. $S : S_1; S_2$;::
SV(S)=SV(S_1) ∪ SV(S_2);
TV(S)=TV(S_1) ∪ TV(S_2);
DL(S, cl, λ):
  return DL(S_2, cl, DL(S_1, cl, λ));

Here, problem of "insecurity" will be indicated by one of the recusive calls.</td></tr>
<tr><td colspan="2">Note that "UNABLE TO LABEL" yields the control point where a certain object fails to satisfy the information flow policy.</td></tr>
</table>

Consider the example shown in Table 6 where x and y are global variables having labels $\underline{x}$ and $\underline{y}$ respectively. At the point `y=y+1` the program fails to satisfy the constraint $\underline{y} \oplus \underline{pc} \leqslant \underline{y}$ because the label of pc is updated to $\underline{x}$ and $\underline{x} \nleqslant \underline{x}$. Therefore the algorithm declares the program as flow-insecure.

The algorithm if applied to the program in Table 7 identifies the flow violation as shown in Table 10: the label of pc is updated to $\underline{x}$ while testing the predicate; detects the flow violation at the statement `y=1` because the constraint $\underline{pc} \leqslant \underline{y}$ does not satisfy. Hence the algorithm fails to proceed further and declares the program as flow-insecure, thus detects the control point where a particular object can leak information.

Table 9. DL successfully labels that was not possible by static labelling (Cf. [1]).

Statement	pc Label	Label of local variable(a)
	$\bot$	$\bot$
int a=x;	$\underline{x}$	$\underline{x}$
y=a;	$\underline{x}$	$\underline{x}$
a=z;	$\underline{x} \oplus \underline{z}$	$\underline{x} \oplus \underline{z}$

Table 10. DL detects "insecurity" by failing to label a non-terminating flow (Cf. [1]).

Statement	pc Label
	$\bot$
y=0;	$\bot$
while x==0 skip;	$\underline{x}$
y=1;	UNABLE TO LABEL

Example 2. *Global variable(s): x, y; No local variables.*
Initial labels for global variables: $\lambda(x) = \underline{x}$, $\lambda(y) = \underline{y}$.

3.2 DL Algorithm for Procedure Call

A procedure declaration in an imperative language contains: procedure identifier and name of the formal parameters along with the respective mode of binding with the actual arguments like `in`, `out`, `in out` etc., declaration of variables local to the procedure and a body of the procedure. Let us consider a call to a procedure, say $p(a_1, \ldots, a_m; b_1, \ldots, b_n)$, where $a_1, \ldots, a_m$ are the actual input arguments and $b_1, \ldots, b_n$ are the actual input/output arguments corresponding to formal input parameters $x_1, \ldots, x_m$ and input/output parameters $y_1, \ldots, y_n$. According to Denning's security certification [21], execution of a procedure call $p(a_1, \ldots, a_m; b_1, \ldots, b_n)$ is secure iff

1. Body of the procedure p is flow secure,
2. $\underline{a_i} \leqslant \underline{b_j}$ if $\underline{x_i} \leqslant \underline{y_j}$ $(1 \leqslant i \leqslant m, 1 \leqslant j \leqslant n)$, and
   $\underline{b_i} \leqslant \underline{b_j}$ if $\underline{y_i} \leqslant \underline{y_j}$ $(1 \leqslant i \leqslant n, 1 \leqslant j \leqslant n)$.

Note that, the specification of input/output arguments and corresponding parameters in a procedure call and definition respectively, are often deprecated in modern programming languages and implicitly identified by the information passing mechanisms between arguments and parameters. Therefore, these languages are more lenient on the rigid specifications compared to their legacy counterparts, and often distinguish a *function* from a *procedure* by the mere presence of a `return` construct. We consider the classic definition of the procedure as found in legacy languages and present the dynamic labelling algorithm for a procedure call adhering the security constraints as given by Denning. The dynamic labelling algorithm for a procedure call is presented in Table 11. Our algorithm evaluates the procedure as soon as it encounters a procedure call and returns the control at the point of invocation once it completes the evaluation.

Table 11. DL algorithm for a procedure call.

6. $S : p(a_1, \ldots, a_m; b_1, \ldots, b_n)$ ::
DL=(S, cl, λ):
//Initialize the label of the parameters
$\lambda' = \lambda_{\text{init}}$
forall $i \in 1 \ldots m$, $\lambda'(x_i) = \lambda(a_i)$
// Evaluate the body of the procedure
λ_1 =DL($p - body, cl, \lambda'$)
return λ_1

The dynamic labelling algorithm performs the following operations at the time of entry & exit from the procedure: it initializes the labels of the formal input parameters with the corresponding labels of the actual input arguments as per the order they appear in the list of the arguments; then, the label of the program counter (*pc*) is initialized with $\perp$; next, the algorithm evaluates the procedure body and finally, resets the *pc* to its initial label on exiting the procedure and returns the final labels to the caller. Note that, the algorithm adhere to the parameters transmission mechanisms during transferring the control from caller to the callee procedure and vice-versa. This will be clear from the subsequent example.

Consider the procedure `Add` written in Ada (shown in Fig. 1) that receives two actual input arguments by the formal input parameters X and Y, add them and store the result into formal output parameter Z. Then for a procedure call `Add`(A, B, C), the dynamic labelling algorithm shall transfer the label of actual input arguments A and B to formal input parameters X and Y respectively. The algorithm then evaluates the statement $Z := X + Y$ and generates the label of Z as LUB of the labels of X and Y. Finally, the algorithm returns the labelling function containing the mapping from Z to its new label to the caller. Note that, the DL algorithm by itself enforce the constraints given by Denning thus certify the procedure as flow secure.

We discuss the possible variants of our labelling algorithm for programming languages that have different information passing mechanisms for subprograms such as pass-by-value (e.g., Java,C,C++), pass-by-reference (e.g., C,C++) and pass-by-object reference (e.g., Python).

```
procedure Add(X, Y: in Integer; Z: out Integer) is
begin
  Z := X + Y;
end
```

Fig. 1. A procedure Add written in Ada.

Case 1: Consider a language where the actual input parameters act as local variables to the subprogram (like in parameters in Ada). Then, the labels of these local variables are initialized with the labels of the corresponding input arguments. Since the parameters are purely local variables, therefore, any changes in the labels during the evaluation process do not affect the corresponding arguments. However, it is necessary to have the construct return at the end of the subprogram to transfer the changes to the caller. Such subprograms are referred to as *function* and invoked within an expression. In such a case, we could refine the dynamic labelling algorithm which might treat the function return parameters as the output parameters.

Case 2: In case of a language that follows pass-by-reference (like C, C++) for passing the information to a subprogram, any reference to the label of the parameter is considered to be a reference to the label of the argument. Therefore, changes in the labels of the parameters are *direct* changes in the labels of corresponding arguments as they appear in the list of the arguments. Therefore, the dynamic labelling algorithm could be modified to consider the input parameters that are passed by reference, as the output parameters also and treat accordingly. Note that, in presence of global variables in the list of input arguments the corresponding formal parameters shall be considered as global within the scope of the procedure.

Case 3: A programming languages Python follows a complex pass-by-object reference mechanism – a combination of pass-by-value and pass-by-reference depending on the data type of the argument, i.e., *immutable* or *mutable* respectively. The original references of the immutable objects, e.g., integers, string, tuples etc. that are passed to subprogram cannot be changed in-place, therefore treated as local to the subprogram. Whereas, object references for mutable objects such as list might be changed in-place in the subprogram depending on the operation performed on it. E.g., a compound assignment, i.e., '+=' performs an in-place assignment for a list argument. Therefore, in the presence of such operations we might consider to refine the dynamic labelling algorithm and treat the mutable object references in the parameter's list as the formal output parameters and follow the approach similar to Case 2.

3.3 Soundness of Algorithm DL

We shall establish the termination of our dynamic labelling algorithm, and its soundness w.r.t. non-interference.

Clearly, the procedure in Table 8 always terminates and is efficient. In fact, it is linear in the size of the program. This fact is formally established through the propositions below.

Proposition 1. *$DL(S, cl, \lambda)$ always terminates for any program S not containing iteration, any label cl, and any labelling λ.*

Proof. The proof is by structural induction. For the base case, it is trivial to observe that the proposition holds for `skip`, and $x := e$.

For the inductive step, it is easy to prove that if the proposition holds for S_1 and S_2, then it also holds for `if` e `then` S_1 `else` S_2, and for $S_1; S_2$.

Proposition 2. *For any program S not containing iteration, any label cl, and any labelling λ, if $DL(S, cl, \lambda)$ returns a valid labelling λ_1, then $\lambda_1(pc) = \lambda(pc) \bigoplus_{v \in SV(S) \cap G} \lambda(v)$.*

The proof of this proposition is by structural induction and is omitted for brevity.

Proposition 3. *$DL($`while` e `do` $S, cl, \lambda)$ always terminates for any program S not containing iteration, any label cl, and any labelling λ.*

Proof. From the definition of DL, we note that the only case in which the evaluation of $DL($`while` e `do` $S, cl, \lambda)$ does not terminate is when either the evaluation of $DL(S, cl, \lambda_1)$ does not terminate, or $DL($`while` e `do` $S, cl, \bullet)$ goes into an infinite recursion.
The former is impossible due to Proposition 1. Impossibility of the latter is shown by considering the evaluation of $DL($`while` e `do` $S, cl, \lambda)$:

1. $\lambda_1 = \lambda$, $\lambda_1(\mathrm{pc}) = \lambda(\mathrm{pc}) \bigoplus_{v \in \mathrm{var}(e) \cap G} \lambda(v)$
2. $\lambda_2 = \mathrm{DL}(S, \mathrm{cl}, \lambda_1)$
3. If $\lambda_2 == \lambda_1$ the evaluation terminates and there is nothing to prove. So we assume that $\lambda_2 \neq \lambda_1$. In this case $DL($`while` e `do` $S, cl, \lambda_2)$ is invoked which proceeds as follows.
4. $\lambda_3 = \lambda_2$, $\lambda_3(\mathrm{pc}) = \lambda_2(\mathrm{pc}) \bigoplus_{v \in \mathrm{var}(e) \cap G} \lambda_2(v)$
5. $\lambda_4 = \mathrm{DL}(S, \mathrm{cl}, \lambda_3)$
6. If $\lambda_4 == \lambda_3$ the evaluation terminates and there is nothing to prove. So we assume that $\lambda_4 \neq \lambda_3$. In this case $DL($`while` e `do` $S, cl, \lambda_4)$ is invoked which proceeds as follows.
7. $\lambda_5 = \lambda_4$, $\lambda_5(\mathrm{pc}) = \lambda_4(\mathrm{pc}) \bigoplus_{v \in \mathrm{var}(e) \cap G} \lambda_4(v)$
8. $\lambda_6 = \mathrm{DL}(S, \mathrm{cl}, \lambda_5)$

We claim that $\lambda_6 == \lambda_5$. The proof is given below.

1. First iteration:
   $\lambda_1(pc) = \lambda(pc) \oplus_{v \in var(e) \cap G} \lambda(v)$

$$\begin{aligned}
\lambda_2(pc) &= \lambda_1(pc) \oplus_{v \in SV(S) \cap G} \lambda(v) \\
&= \lambda(pc) \oplus_{v \in var(e) \cap G} \lambda(v) \oplus_{v \in SV(S) \cap G} \lambda(v) \\
&= \lambda(pc) \oplus_{v \in (var(e) \cup SV(S)) \cap G} \lambda(v)
\end{aligned} \tag{1}$$

2. Second iteration:

$$\begin{aligned}\lambda_3(pc) &= \lambda_2(pc) \oplus_{v \in var(e) \cap G} \lambda(v) \\ &= \lambda(pc) \oplus_{v \in (var(e) \cup SV(S)) \cap G} \lambda(v) \\ &\oplus_{v \in var(e) \cap G} \lambda(v) \\ &= \lambda(pc) \oplus_{v \in (var(e) \cup SV(S)) \cap G} \lambda(v)\end{aligned} \tag{2}$$

$$\begin{aligned}\lambda_4(pc) &= \lambda_3(pc) \oplus_{v \in SV(S) \cap G} \lambda(v) \\ &= \lambda(pc) \oplus_{v \in (var(e) \cup SV(S)) \cap G} \lambda(v) \\ \lambda_4(x) &= \lambda_3(x) \oplus \lambda_3(pc) \oplus_{v \in SV(S) \cap G} \lambda(v) \\ &= \lambda_3(x) \oplus \lambda_3(pc) \\ &\text{This is because the label of PC is already} \\ &\text{influenced by all the global variables in } S. \\ &= \lambda_2(x) \oplus \lambda(pc) \oplus_{v \in (var(e) \cup SV(S)) \cap G} \lambda(v)\end{aligned} \tag{3}$$

3. Third iteration:

$$\begin{aligned}\lambda_5(pc) &= \lambda_4(pc) \oplus_{v \in var(e) \cap G} \lambda(v) \\ &= \lambda(pc) \oplus_{v \in (var(e) \cup SV(S)) \cap G} \oplus_{v \in var(e) \cap G} \lambda(v) \\ &= \lambda(pc) \oplus_{v \in (var(e) \cup SV(S)) \cap G} \lambda(v) \\ \lambda_5(x) &= \lambda_4(x) \\ &= \lambda_2(x) \oplus \lambda(pc) \oplus_{v \in (var(e) \cup SV(S)) \cap G} \lambda(v)\end{aligned} \tag{4}$$

$$\begin{aligned}\lambda_6(pc) &= \lambda_5(pc) \oplus_{v \in SV(S) \cap G} \lambda(v) \\ &= \lambda(pc) \oplus_{v \in (var(e) \cup SV(S)) \cap G} \lambda(v) \\ \lambda_6(x) &= \lambda_5(x) \oplus \lambda_5(pc) \oplus_{v \in SV(S) \cap G} \lambda(v) \\ &= \lambda_2(x) \oplus \lambda(pc) \oplus_{v \in (var(e) \cup SV(S)) \cap G} \lambda(v)\end{aligned} \tag{5}$$

It can be observed that $\lambda_6 = \lambda_5$. Thus, we can conclude that, for the iteration statement, the dynamic labelling procedure terminates after a maximum of three iterations.

Combining Propositions 1 and 3 leads to the following proposition.

Proposition 4. *$DL($`while` e `do` $S, cl, \lambda)$ always terminates for any program S, any label cl, and any labelling λ.*

Proposition 4 immediately establishes termination of DL as formalized below.

Proposition 5. *$DL(S, cl, \lambda)$ always terminates for any sequential program S, any label cl, and any labelling λ.*

Next, we prove some results that highlight the important characteristics of our dynamic labelling procedure.

Proposition 6. *During the dynamic labelling of any program S with any clearance cl, i.e. during the evaluation of $DL(S, cl, \lambda_{init})$, $\lambda(pc) \leqslant cl$ always holds.*

Proof. In the initial state $\lambda_{init}(pc) = \bot \leqslant cl$. From the definition of DL, we note that the label of pc gets updated by taking its LUB with tmp only when $tmp \leqslant cl$. Therefore $\lambda(pc) \leqslant cl$ always holds due to simple lattice properties.

Proposition 7. *An assignment to a global variable x is deemed safe by the dynamic labelling algorithm for a program executing with clearance cl if and only if $cl \leqslant \lambda(x)$.*

Proof. (Necessity of $cl \leqslant \lambda(x)$) From the definition of DL for an assignment statement, it is immediately clear that if the operation is deemed safe then it must be the case that $cl \leqslant \lambda(x)$.

(Sufficiency of $cl \leqslant \lambda(x)$) Note that we have $\lambda(pc) \leqslant cl$ from Proposition 6, and for the control to reach the point, we need $tmp \leqslant cl$, thus reducing the check $(\lambda(pc) \oplus tmp \oplus cl) \leqslant \lambda(x)$ to $cl \leqslant \lambda(x)$.

Proposition 8. *During the dynamic labelling of any program S, $\lambda(pc)$ is monotonically non-decreasing.*

The proof of the above is trivially obtained by structural induction and is omitted for brevity.

Next, we prove a generalization of the result in Proposition 2.

Proposition 9. *For any program S, any label cl, and any labelling λ, if $DL(S, cl, \lambda)$ returns a valid labelling λ_1, then $\lambda_1(pc) = \lambda(pc) \bigoplus_{v \in SV(S) \cap G} \lambda(v)$.*

The proof of this proposition is by structural induction and is omitted for brevity.

Proposition 10. *During the dynamic labelling of any program S, for all $x \in L$, $\lambda(x)$ is monotonically non-decreasing.*

Proof. For $x \in L$, the label of x is updated by the dynamic labelling procedure only in the case of explicit assignment. In this case the label of x changes to $\lambda(x) \oplus \lambda(pc) \oplus tmp$. Monotonicity of $\lambda(pc)$ immediately gives us that $\lambda(x)$ is also monotonically non-decreasing.

Proposition 11. *During the dynamic labelling of any program S i.e. $DL(S, cl, \lambda_{init})$, $\forall x \in L$ $\lambda(x) \leqslant \lambda(pc)$ always holds.*

Proof. In the initial state we have $\lambda_{init}(x) = \lambda_{init}(pc) = \bot$. We will show that every time the label of x is updated, the property holds in the new state also.

- $S :: x := e$

$$\begin{aligned}
&\lambda_1(x) \leqslant \lambda(x) \oplus \lambda(pc) \oplus tmp \\
&\lambda_1(x) \leqslant \lambda(pc) \oplus tmp \text{ [by hypothesis } \lambda(x) \leqslant \lambda(pc)] \\
&\lambda_1(x) \leqslant \lambda_1(pc)
\end{aligned} \tag{6}$$

– $S :: \text{if } e \text{ then } S_1 \text{ else } S_2$

$$\begin{aligned} &\lambda_3(x) \leqslant \lambda_1(x) \oplus \lambda_2(x) \\ &\lambda_3(x) \leqslant \lambda_1(pc) \oplus \lambda_2(pc) \text{ [by hypothesis]} \\ &\lambda_3(x) \leqslant \lambda_3(pc) \end{aligned} \tag{7}$$

Relation with Non-interference

In this section, we establish that the dynamic labelling algorithm is sound w.r.t. non-interference [3].

A simple example illustrates the relation with non-interference. Consider the program $P_1 : x := y;$ - where x, y are global objects, and the labelling $\lambda(y) = l_2$, $\lambda(x) = l_3$, where l_2 and l_3 come from a total order $l_1 \leqslant l_2 \leqslant l_3 \leqslant l_4$. Consider four subjects s_1, s_2, s_3, and s_4, with clearances l_1, l_2, l_3, and l_4 respectively.

P_1 is non-interfering. Dynamic labelling of P_1 succeeds only for subjects s_2 and s_3. Dynamic labelling fails for s_1 because his clearance is below y, and therefore should not be allowed to access y. Similarly, dynamic labelling fails for s_4 because his clearance is above x and therefore should not be allowed to update x.

In the following, we shall formally establish the soundness of the dynamic labelling procedure w.r.t. non-interference. Note that globals are the only observables in this setting.

Theorem 1 (Soundness). *If there exists a subject for which a program is declared secure by the dynamic labelling procedure in Table 8, then the program is non-interfering.*

Proof. For reasoning about value based non-interference, it suffices to work with the last update to a low labelled variable. From the definition of DL, we observe that the only place where a global variable is potentially updated is guarded by the condition $\lambda(pc) \oplus tmp \oplus cl \leqslant \lambda(x)$. In particular, since we are dealing with $\lambda(x) = \text{low}$, and the program is declared secure by the dynamic labelling procedure, we can immediately infer that $\lambda(pc) = tmp = cl = \text{low}$. This guarantees that no high labelled variable could have been accessed by this time in the execution.

Traditional methods for the security certification of programs do not consider the subject labels. Let $DL_1(S, \lambda)$ be a modified dynamic labelling algorithm obtained by ignoring *cl* from the algorithm given in Table 8. We now prove that even this algorithm is sound w.r.t non-interference.

Theorem 2. *If a program S is declared secure by procedure DL_1 i.e., $DL_1(S, \lambda)$ returns a valid labelling, then the program is non-interfering.*

Proof of this theorem is exactly the same as the proof of the previous theorem, and is omitted.

Finally, the set of programs declared secure by traditional certification methods that reset PC and use static labels for variables (Jif is a prominent representative of this class) is incomparable to the set of programs declared secure by our dynamical labelling algorithm as shown below.

Proposition 12. *There are programs declared secure by static labelling that cannot be dynamically labelled (insecure by our definition), and there are programs declared secure by our approach that static labelling rejects as insecure.*

Proof: Programs in Tables 6 and 7 provide an example for the former, while the program in Table 2 provides an example for the latter.

4 DL Algorithm for Concurrent Programs

The dynamic labelling algorithm we propose for a sequential imperative programming language can be easily extended for concurrent programs, where shared variables among the concurrent threads are potential threats for leaking information. In our approach apart from the set of global variables, the dynamic labelling algorithm shall be given a set of variables that are shared among the threads during the execution. The labels of the shared variables might be defined globally and immutable or local to the system and mutable. In case of a shared variable with an immutable label, the label shall not be changed throughout the computation of the algorithm, whereas, the shared variables with mutable labels are changed to accommodate the flows between threads.

Table 12. DL algorithm for concurrent programs.

7. $S : T_1 \| \ldots \| T_n$ ::
DL=(S, cl, λ):
$\lambda_{final} = \lambda$
do
$\lambda_{start} = \lambda_{final}$
for each $i \in 1 \ldots n$
$\lambda_i(v) = \lambda_{final}(v), \forall v \in H$
$\lambda_i = \mathrm{DL}(T_i, cl, \lambda_i)$
$\lambda_{final}(v) = \lambda_i(v), \forall v \in H$
while $\exists v \in H(\lambda_{start}(v) \neq \lambda_{final}(v))$
return λ_{final}

Let us consider n number of threads $T_1, \ldots T_n$ that are executing simultaneously, where each thread is considered as a sequential program comprise of the statements discussed in Sect. 3. Further, assume that a set of shared variables H is provided to the algorithm. The dynamic labelling algorithm for concurrent programs is shown in Table 12. The algorithm, first computes the label of shared variables by executing each thread independently. Then, it compares the final labels of shared variables with their initial labels. The algorithm repeats the process again if there exist a single shared variable with unequal label. The process is iterated until the label of all the shared variables converge in the lattice.

Proposition 13. *$DL(T_1 \| T_2 \| \ldots \| T_n, cl, \lambda)$ always terminates for any n number of concurrent threads given a priori, and any cl & λ.*

Proof. The algorithm DL for the concurrent programs might not terminate only for the cases in which either evaluation of any thread T_i, i.e., $\text{DL}(T_i, cl, \lambda_i)$ does not terminate, or $\text{DL}(T_1||T_2||\dots||T_n, cl, \bullet)$ goes into an infinite recursion. The former case is not possible since each thread is a sequential program and Proposition 5 holds good for the sequential programs. The latter case is impossible due to the reason shown below by considering the evaluation of $\text{DL}(T_1||T_2||\dots||T_n, cl, \lambda)$:

1. $\lambda_1 = \lambda$
2. For all $v \in H$, $\lambda_2(v) = \lambda_1(v) \oplus \lambda^1(v) \oplus \dots \oplus \lambda^n(v)$, where λ^i denotes the labelling function received after evaluating the thread T_i, i.e., $\lambda^i = \text{DL}(T_i, cl, \bullet)$, $1 \le i \le n$
3. If $\lambda_1(v) == \lambda_2(v)$ for all $v \in H$ then the evaluation terminates. Therefore, let us assume there exist at least a v for which $\lambda_1(v) \neq \lambda_2(v)$
4. $\lambda_3 = \lambda_2$
5. For all $v \in H$, $\lambda_4(v) = \lambda_3(v) \oplus \lambda^1(v) \oplus \dots \oplus \lambda^n(v)$
6. If $\lambda_3(v) == \lambda_4(v)$ for all $v \in H$ then the evaluation terminates. Therefore, let us assume there exist at least a v for which $\lambda_1(v) \neq \lambda_2(v)$
7. $\lambda_5 = \lambda_4$
8. For all $v \in H$, $\lambda_6(v) = \lambda_5(v) \oplus \lambda^1(v) \oplus \dots \oplus \lambda^n(v)$

We claim that $\forall v \in H$, $\lambda_6(v) == \lambda_5(v)$. The proof is similar to the proof for the Proposition 3 as likewise *pc*, the algorithm performs LUB for each shared variable while evaluating the threads individually to accommodate the changes. Therefore, we can conclude that, for the concurrent threads, the dynamic labelling algorithm terminates after maximum of three iterations.

The proof for the Propositions 5 and 13 for the concurrent context shows that the procedure requires a finite number of unrolling rather than a full termination to converge the labels.

Illustrative Example
An example of information leakage due to concurrent access is presented by [22]. The order of the assignments to x and y variables in VIP program depends on the secret value of h. The program in Newsmonger runs simultaneously and prints the values of x and y inside an infinite loop that are shared variables having no explicit label. If Newsmonger runs in between any of the assignments that exist in line 3 and 5 of VIP, it could reveal the value of h. In our approach the DL procedure would evaluate the labels for the threads VIP and Newsmonger separately along with the shared variables x and y until the label of the variables converge in the lattice. Therefore, it would compute the labels for x and y as equivalent to h and identify the possible flow security risk while executing the statement "`output y`" in Newsmonger as label of h cannot flow to public.

5 Comparison with Related Work

In this section, we first briefly describe tools and platforms that enforce rich information flow policies and then compare our approach with the existing

Table 13. (a) VIP (left) and (b) Newsmonger (right) (Cf. [1]).

```
x:=0; y:=0
if h then
  x:=1; y:=1;
else
  y:=1; x:=1;
end;
```

```
while true do
  output x;
  output y;
done;
```

approaches. Further, we discuss the applicability and limitations for certifying different classes of programs like (i) *termination-sensitive* programs, (ii) concurrent/non-deterministic programs, etc.

Information Flow Tools

In the last decade a large number of information flow secure tools have been developed to enforce rigorous flow security policies through prevailing programming languages. For example, Jif [7], JOANA [17], Paragon [19] for Java, FlowFox [23], JSFlow [24], IFC4BC [25] for JavaScript, FlowCaml [8] for Caml, λ_{DSec} [16] for lambda calculus, LIO [18], HLIO [20] for Haskell and SPARK flow analysis [26] for SPARK. Also flow secure platforms for instance, Jif/split [27], Asbestos [28], HiStar [29], Flume [30], Aeolus [31] and flow checking systems that implements *sparse information labeling* [15], permissive-upgrade strategy [32] and identifies public labels and delayed exception [33] incorporate different label mechanisms shown in Table 14. While we have omitted some similar prominent platforms for lack of space, it may be noted that DL realizes the needed characteristics required for IFC.

Table 14. Comparison of IFC tools and platforms (Cf. [1]).

Tools and Platforms	Labelling mechanism	Flow-sensitive	Termination-sensitive
Jif	P_1	✗	✗
Paragon	P_1	✗	✗
FlowCaml	P_1	✗	✗
λ_{DSec}	P_3	✓	✗
LIO	P_2	✗	✗
$\lambda_l^{\texttt{LIO}}$	P_4	✓	✓
Aeolus	P_1	✗	✗
DL	P_4	✓	✓

The earliest attempt to capture flow-sensitive labels at run-time was observed in work on λ_{DSec}. This was the first to propose general dynamic labels whose type system was proved to enforce non-interference. The core language λ_{DSec} is a security-typed lambda calculus that supports first-class dynamic labels where labels can be checked and manipulated at run-time. Also, labels can be used as statically analyzed type annotations. The type system of λ_{DSec} prevents illegal information flows and guarantees that any well-typed program satisfies the non-interference property. In this language, the label of the *pc* is a lower bound on the memory effects of the function, and an upper bound on the *pc* label of the caller, but unlike DL, *pc* is not updated dynamically after executing each statement hence the language falls in the category P_3. The non-interference property discussed in λ_{DSec} is termination-insensitive, and also does not deal with timing channels. In the following, we provide a detail discussion on `LIO` that shares a common paradigm and also subsumes the results of λ_{Dsec}.

Comparison with [18]
Here, the authors have built a labelled `IO` Haskell library, called `LIO`, for certifying Haskell programs. `LIO` tracks a single mutable *current label* (like program-counter) at run-time and allows access to IO operations. The unit is responsible for ensuring that the current label keeps track of all the observed data and regulate label modification. A type constructor `Labeled` is used to hold the restriction only value and is mutable during run-time. At each computation, `LIO` keeps tracks of the *current label* and allow access to IO functionality, e.g., labeled file systems. Current label is evaluated as the *upper bound* of all the label observed during the program execution.

Consider reading a secret reference: `a` ← `readLIORef secret`, where the value "secret" is labeled as L_S. Now to satisfy the information flow check i.e., (L_S `canFlowTo` L_C) the *current label* shall rise to (L_C `join` L_S) to read the secret value. Note that the value *a* is not labeled explicitly. Now let us take an example that wish to write the value of an object (*a*) to an output channel: `writeLIORef output a`, where the output channel is labeled as L_O (set dynamically according to the user executing the command). It is only permissible to modify or write data into the output channel when (L_C `canFlowTo` L_O) is satisfied. A second label *current clearance* (L_{cl}) provides an upper bound to *current label*. Hence, the computation cannot create, read or write to objects labeled L if L `canFlowTo` L_{cl} == `False`.

Although our approach overlaps with that of `LIO`, there are subtle differences that are briefed below:

- Unlike statically evaluating the labels in our DL algorithm, the approach in `LIO` is based on run-time *floating-label* system.
- Compared to DL algorithm, the `LIO` library provides IO actions that perform *termination-insensitive* flow analysis.
- Due to *flow-insensitive* labelling `LIO` does not provide sensitivity level of each intermediate object precisely.

We illustrate each of these points in the following.

Comparison of Labelling Mechanism
The characterization of security labels, when associated with objects, is an essential aspect of IFC analysis [34]. Security labels of subjects/objects can be muta-

ble or immutable. *Flow-sensitive* IFC monitors allow changing the security labels throughout the computation thus increase the permissiveness, and also alleviate the burden of explicit label annotations. Note that these monitors perform the flow analysis during execution-time or compile-time. Mutable label flow analysis during execution-time helps to determine the flow-sensitivity of objects at run-time precisely, but compile-time analysis reduces the incident of *false-alarms* and allows more programs as secure.

`LIO` keeps track of a single mutable *current* floating-label that is elevated (e.g., from *low* to *high*) at run-time to accommodate sensitive reading; hence, `LIO` is *flow-sensitive* in the *current label.* However, `LIO` is *flow-insensitive* in intermediate object labels. To allow more programs by the run-time monitor, an extension of `LIO` presented by [35] that safely manipulates a label on the reference label. A *label on the label* describes the confidentiality of the `LIO` reference label itself. The run-time monitor upgrades a label of a reference only if that *label on the label can flow to floating-label.* Note that `LIO` follows the labelling mechanism P_2 whereas the proposed extension incorporates P_4. Another extension of `LIO` monad, i.e., HLIO that provides programmers the flexibility to defer flow check of part of the program to run-time (like `LIO`) or static-time (unlike `LIO`), boosts permissiveness of the monitor.

Algorithm DL, is *flow-sensitive* in the absence of method-calls and a compile-time monitor built upon it would satisfy P_4, and hence it is more permissive than the other approaches highlighted above. DL follows a hybrid labelling approach where the labels of global variables are assumed to be fixed, and label of each intermediate object is allowed to vary, thus, *flow-sensitive* dynamic labels are obtained.

Termination-insensitive Flow Analysis
Information leak depending on the termination of the program may remain undetected by the run-time monitor that extends the `LIO` library unit. A program that exploits `toLabeled` function as shown by [36] may lead to information leak through the termination channel. `toLabeled` l m executes the `LIO` operation m and encapsulates the returned value with label l. However, the function does not increase the *current label.* Hence one can write an iterative program that executes a `toLabeled` function depending on a secret value or diverges otherwise. Assuming the initial *current label* as *low*, and as it remains unchanged even after executing `toLabeled`, an adversary can determine the secret value by observing termination of the program through standard output.

The DL algorithm keeps track of the sensitive labels observed by the *pc* at compile-time. Therefore, a program that tries to pass termination information to standard output shall abide by the information flow policy. Hence the proposed labelling approach performs an exemplary *termination-sensitive* flow analysis.

Applicability of `LIO` in Concurrent Context
As initially `LIO` was not considered for dynamic flow-sensitive concurrent settings, an extension is proposed in [36] that mitigates and eliminates termination and timing channels in concurrent programs. In that article, a separate *current label* for each thread is mentioned that keeps track of the sensitivity of the

data it has observed, and restrict the locations to which the thread can write. Hence, while termination and timing of these threads that may expose the secret values, the thread requires to raise its *current label.* This prevents lower security threads from observing confidential information written in shared locations. Another extension of `LIO` proposed by [35] provides the primitive of automatic upgrade that safely updates *flow-sensitive* label references. Both the extensions are shown to be equally applicable for concurrent context. However, the extensions may not stop the concurrent programs from revealing the secret value. Let us assume the assignments in the program shown in Table 13 are `LIO` operations and the labels of the *current label* and h are L_C and L_h respectively. Then, the label of y is evaluated as L_C `join` L_h when h is false. Now, before labelling of x is done by LIO, Newsmonger might disclose the value in x which in turn would reveal the secret value h.

Determining the Label of Intermediate Variables
As early as 1975, Dorothy Denning proposed in her thesis [37] a run-time source-to-source transformation to guarantee flow security of programs having the selection or iteration statements. The method introduces additional code for checking possible flow violations at run-time. In a sense, her method, simulates possible information flows for each variable that has to lie between possible highest and lowest levels. As against this, our method succinctly captures security labels of variables explicitly without introducing additional code in the program.

6 Conclusions

We have presented a dynamic labelling algorithm, i.e., DL for flow security certification of imperative programs. Our labelling algorithm is appropriate for not only classic actual-formal parameter passing mechanism but also for mechanisms like pass-by-object reference used in Python as illustrated in this paper. Another characteristic of our approach allows us to capture the labels for termination-,progress-sensitive programs and has shown to be more security precise compared to existing approaches. Also, we have established the soundness of our approach with respect to non-interference. We have extended the DL algorithm to evaluate a concurrent context consisting of a finite number of sequential programs referred to as threads, sharing a given set of variables and executing concurrently. The algorithm DL is shown to be always terminating after a finite number of iterations. So far, we have built a platform for certifying sequential Python programs. The platform is enriched with the novel features such as *declassification* that helps to build a multi-level secure system that follows a decentralized labelling model. We have illustrated the efficacy of DL to concurrent programs and currently extending our platform for certification of concurrent programs as well.

Acknowledgements. The authors thank the Ministry of Electronics and Information Technology (MeitY), Govt. of India, for the generous support to the Information Security Research & Development Center (ISRDC) at IIT Bombay.

References

1. Ghosal, S., Shyamasundar, R.K., Kumar, N.V.N.: Static security certification of programs via dynamic labelling. In: Proceedings of the 15th International Joint Conference on e-Business and Telecommunications, ICETE 2018 - Volume 2: SECRYPT, Porto, Portugal, 26–28 July 2018, pp. 400–411 (2018)
2. Denning, D.E., Denning, P.J.: Certification of programs for secure information flow. CACM **20**(7), 504–513 (1977)
3. Volpano, D.M., Irvine, C.E., Smith, G.: A sound type system for secure flow analysis. J. Comput. Secur. **4**(2/3), 167–188 (1996)
4. Denning, D.E.: A lattice model of secure information flow. CACM **19**(5), 236–243 (1976)
5. Myers, A.C., Liskov, B.: Protecting privacy using the decentralized label model. ACM TOSEM **9**(4), 410–442 (2000)
6. Myers, A.C.: JFlow: practical mostly-static information flow control. In: Proceedings of 26th ACM Symposium on POPL, pp. 228–241 (1999)
7. Myers, A.C., Zheng, L., Zdancewic, S., Chong, S., Nystrom, N.: Jif: Java information flow (2001). http://www.cs.cornell.edu/jif
8. Simonet, V., Rocquencourt, I.: Flow Caml in a nutshell. In: Proceedings of 1st APPSEM-II Workshop, pp. 152–165 (2003)
9. Stefan, D., Russo, A., Mitchell, J.C., Mazières, D.: Flexible dynamic information flow control in the presence of exceptions. CoRR abs/1207.1457 (2012)
10. Ryan, P., McLean, J., Millen, J., Gligor, V.: Non-interference, who needs it? In: Proceedings of 14th IEEE CSF Workshop, pp. 237–238 (2001)
11. Sabelfeld, A., Myers, A.C.: Language-based information-flow security. IEEE J. Sel. Areas Commun. **21**(1), 5–19 (2003)
12. Hicks, B., King, D., McDaniel, P.: Jifclipse: development tools for security-typed languages. In: Proceedings of Workshop on PLAS, pp. 1–10 (2007)
13. Goguen, J.A., Meseguer, J.: Security policies and security models. In: IEEE Symposium on SP, p. 11 (1982)
14. Askarov, A., Sabelfeld, A.: Tight enforcement of information-release policies for dynamic languages. In: Proceedings of 22nd IEEE CSF Symposium, pp. 43–59 (2009)
15. Austin, T.H., Flanagan, C.: Efficient purely-dynamic information flow analysis. In: Proceedings of the ACM SIGPLAN 4th Workshop on PLAS, pp. 113–124 (2009)
16. Zheng, L., Myers, A.C.: Dynamic security labels and static information flow control. Int. J. Inf. Secur. **6**(2–3), 67–84 (2007)
17. Hammer, C., Snelting, G.: Flow-sensitive, context-sensitive, and object-sensitive information flow control based on program dependence graphs. Int. J. Inf. Secur. **8**(6), 399–422 (2009)
18. Stefan, D., Russo, A., Mitchell, J.C., Mazières, D.: Flexible dynamic information flow control in haskell. ACM SIGPLAN Not. **46**, 95–106 (2011)
19. Broberg, N., van Delft, B., Sands, D.: Paragon for practical programming with information-flow control. In: Shan, C. (ed.) APLAS 2013. LNCS, vol. 8301, pp. 217–232. Springer, Cham (2013). https://doi.org/10.1007/978-3-319-03542-0_16
20. Buiras, P., Vytiniotis, D., Russo, A.: HLIO: mixing static and dynamic typing for information-flow control in Haskell. In: ACM SIGPLAN Notices, vol. 50, pp. 289–301. ACM (2015)
21. Robling Denning, D.E.: Cryptography and Data Security. Addison-Wesley Longman Publishing Co., Boston (1982)

22. Le Guernic, G.: Automaton-based confidentiality monitoring of concurrent programs. In: Proceedings of 20th IEEE CSF Symposium, pp. 218–232 (2007)
23. De Groef, W., Devriese, D., Nikiforakis, N., Piessens, F.: FlowFox: a web browser with flexible and precise information flow control. In: Proceedings of ACM CCS, pp. 748–759 (2012)
24. Hedin, D., Birgisson, A., Bello, L., Sabelfeld, A.: JSFlow: tracking information flow in Javascript and its APIs. In: Proceedings of 29th Annual ACM SAC, pp. 1663–1671 (2014)
25. Bichhawat, A., Rajani, V., Garg, D., Hammer, C.: Information flow control in WebKit's JavaScript bytecode. In: Abadi, M., Kremer, S. (eds.) POST 2014. LNCS, vol. 8414, pp. 159–178. Springer, Heidelberg (2014). https://doi.org/10.1007/978-3-642-54792-8_9
26. Barnes, J.G.P.: High Integrity Software: The Spark Approach to Safety and Security. Pearson Education, London (2003)
27. Zdancewic, S., Zheng, L., Nystrom, N., Myers, A.C.: Secure program partitioning. ACM Trans. Comput. Syst. (TOCS) **20**(3), 283–328 (2002)
28. Efstathopoulos, P., et al.: Labels and event processes in the asbestos operating system. In: Proceedings of 20th ACM SOSP, vol. 39, pp. 17–30 (2005)
29. Zeldovich, N., Boyd-Wickizer, S., Kohler, E., Mazières, D.: Making information flow explicit in HiStar. In: Proceedings of 7th Symposium on OSDI, pp. 263–278 (2006)
30. Krohn, M.N., et al.: Information flow control for standard OS abstractions. In: Proceedings of 21st ACM SOSP, pp. 321–334 (2007)
31. Cheng, W., et al.: Abstractions for usable information flow control in Aeolus. In: USENIX Annual Technical Conference, pp. 139–151 (2012)
32. Austin, T.H., Flanagan, C.: Permissive dynamic information flow analysis. In: Proceedings of the 5th ACM SIGPLAN Workshop on PLAS, p. 3 (2010)
33. Hritcu, C., Greenberg, M., Karel, B., Pierce, B.C., Morrisett, G.: All your IFCException are belong to us. In: IEEE Symposium on SP, pp. 3–17 (2013)
34. Hunt, S., Sands, D.: On flow-sensitive security types. ACM SIGPLAN Not. **41**, 79–90 (2006)
35. Buiras, P., Stefan, D., Russo, A.: On dynamic flow-sensitive floating-label systems. In: Proceedings of IEEE 27th CSF Symposium, pp. 65–79 (2014)
36. Stefan, D., Russo, A., Buiras, P., Levy, A., Mitchell, J.C., Maziéres, D.: Addressing covert termination and timing channels in concurrent information flow systems. ACM SIGPLAN Not. **47**, 201–214 (2012)
37. Denning, D.E.R.: Secure information flow in computer systems (1975)

Real-Time Noise Reduction Algorithm for Video with Non-linear FIR Filter

Seiichi Gohshi(✉) and Chinatsu Mori

Kogakuin University, 1-24-2 Nishi-Shinjuku, Shinjuku-ku, Tokyo 163-8677, Japan
gohshi@icc.kogakuin.ac.jp, ed15002@ns.kogakuin.ac.jp

Abstract. Noise is an essential issue for images and videos. Recently, a range of high-sensitivity imaging devices have become available. Cameras are often used under poor lighting conditions for security purposes or night time news gathering. Videos shot under poor lighting conditions are afflicted by significant noise which degrades the image quality. The process of noise removal from videos is called noise reduction (NR). Although many NR methods are proposed, they are complex and are proposed as computer simulations. In practical applications, NR processing of videos occurs in real-time. The practical real-time methods are limited and the complex NR methods cannot cope with real-time processing. Video has three dimensions: horizontal, vertical and temporal. Since the temporal relation is stronger than that of horizontal and vertical, the conventional real-time NR methods use the temporal infinite impulse response (IIR) filter to reduce noise. This approach is known as the inter-frame relation, and the noise reducer comprises a temporal recursive filter. Temporal recursive filters are widely used in digital TV sets to reduce the noise affecting images. Although the temporal recursive filter is a simple algorithm, moving objects leave trails when it reduces the high-level noise. In this paper, a novel NR algorithm is introduced. The proposed method uses finite impulse response (FIR) filter. The FIR filter does not suffer from this trail issue and shows better performance than NR using temporal recursive filters is proposed.

Keywords: Video noise reducer · 4KTV · 8KTV · Real time
Non-linear signal processing · Image quality

1 Introduction

Imaging technology advanced in the 21st century and HDTV (1920×1080) resolution cameras have become a reasonably priced commodity. Recently, high-sensitivity imaging devices have also become widely available and video cameras can work under poor lighting conditions. This high-sensitivity imaging technology makes 4K/8K ultra-high-resolution video systems possible. The size of one 4K imaging pixel is 1/4 that of an HDTV pixel and the size of one 8K pixel is 1/16 that of an HDTV pixel. The light energy collected by one pixel is proportional to the size of the imaging cell; therefore, the light energy collected

M. S. Obaidat (Ed.): ICETE 2018, CCIS 1118, pp. 183–198, 2019.
https://doi.org/10.1007/978-3-030-34866-3_9

by one 4K or 8K pixel is 1/4 or 1/16 that of an HDTV pixel. Since imaging cells generate a voltage that is proportional to the collected light energy, 4K/8K imaging cells generate a lower voltage than those of HDTV imaging cells. The light intensity is often insufficient when 4K/8K imaging, which causes noise to appear in videos, degrading the image quality.

Aside from 4K/8K videos, noise is also a crucial issue in security cameras. Crimes are often committed after sunset. In the night time, the lighting conditions are worse and the recorded videos usually contain a lot of noise. When using recorded videos to investigate a crime, noise is often a problem when trying to identify the person of interest. Low noise and high resolution, such as 4K/8K, are important factors for high-quality videos. There are many signal processing methods for reducing the noise and improving the resolution of recorded videos to achieve high-quality videos.

Noise reduction (NR) is a signal processing method for reducing noise in recorded videos, and super-resolution (SR) is a signal processing method for improving the video resolution. Unfortunately, these two technologies are trade-offs. Noise occurs as small dots that have high-frequency elements. The high resolution is also created by high-frequency elements. If we try to reduce the noise in a video, the high-frequency elements are reduced and the video becomes blurry; this is the first issue with NR. The second issue is real-time signal processing, which is essential for all video systems. Although there are many NR approaches, most of them are proposed for still images. There are no real-time requirements for still-image NR. The frame rates of video systems are 50/60 (analogue TV/HD/4K) or 120 Hz (8K). This means that the NR processing for a frame has to be finished within 25/16 ms for current practical video systems (analogue TV/HD/4K). Due to these time constraints, it is impossible to adopt as complex NR algorithms for videos as used for still images. In this paper, a novel real-time NR algorithm for videos is proposed [16]. It exploits video characteristics that are different from those of still images and reduces noise without blurring, unlike conventional NR algorithms for videos.

2 Previous Works

Still images have horizontal and vertical (spatial) axes, but videos have spatial and temporal axes. Many two- (2D) and three-dimensional (3D) NR systems have been proposed by researchers.

In [10,15,18,19,23], and [20], the authors proposed the use of spatial (two-dimensional) and spatiotemporal (three-dimensional) filters to remove video noise. However, spatial filters only consider spatial information; therefore, these filters can cause spatial blurring at high noise levels. Using a combination of temporal and spatial information can reduce this blurring effect. This approach can also be used to improve the filtering performance at low noise levels. In [15], a wavelet domain spatial filter in which the coefficients are manipulated using a Markov random field image model has been proposed. A Wiener filter was utilized in the wavelet domain to remove the image noise in [10]. Noise reduction using the wavelet transform was proposed in previous studies [5,8,13,14,18–20,23], which provides a high performance and results in images of a high quality. However, currently, these approaches are only feasible at the computer simulation level, and they do not work in real time. The wavelet transform is a complex algorithm; therefore, it is difficult to apply it to NR, and it is not cost-effective. Currently, there are no practical real-time NR systems employing the wavelet transform method. The authors in [19] proposed a fuzzy logic-based image noise filter that considers directional deviations.

In addition, a recursive estimator structure has been proposed to differentiate a clean image from a film-grain noisy image where the noise is considered to be related to the exposure time in the form of a non-Gaussian and multiplicative structure [18]. In addition, a pixel-based spatiotemporal adaptive filter that calculates new pixel values adaptively using the weighted mean of pixels over motion compensated frames has been proposed in [23]. An edge preserving spatiotemporal video noise filter that combines 2D Wiener and Kalman filters has been presented in [20]. The authors of [5] proposed a nonlinear video noise filter that calculates new pixel values using a 3D window. In this method, the pixels are arranged with respect to the related pixel values in the form of a 3D window according to their difference and the average of the pixels in the window after weighting them with respect to their sorting order, which gives good results in the case of no or slow local motion, but it deforms image regions in the case of abrupt local motion. For local motion, the 3D filtering performance of this method is low. To improve the 3D filtering performance of the method proposed in [18], video de-noising uses 2D and 3D dual-tree complex wavelet transforms. The authors of (9) proposed 2D wavelet-based filtering and temporal mean filtering that uses pixel-based motion detection. The authors in [14] proposed 2D wavelet-based filtering and temporal mean filtering that uses pixel-based motion detection. The authors in reference [8] proposed a wavelet transform-based video filtering technique that uses spatial and temporal redundancy. A content adaptive video de-noising filter was also proposed recently [13]. This method filters both impulsive and non-impulsive noises, but the filtering performance is low in cases with Gaussian noise with high variance. In this work, a new pixel-based spatiotemporal video noise filter that incorporates motion changes and spatial standard deviations into the de-noising algorithm is proposed.

Bilateral filtering has also been proposed for NR [26]. Although it is a simple algorithm, in principle, it could cause spatial blurring in stationary areas. Our eyes are sensitive to blurring in stationary areas than in moving areas. Stopping the video signal, we perceive a large blur in the moving areas. However, when playing the same video again, you cannot find the same blur. The reason for this is that our dynamic eyesight is inferior to the static eyesight. Since NRs employing recursive temporal filters do not cause spatial blurring but cause blurring in moving areas, they give the perception of a better image quality. Many other proposals have been made to reduce noise in images and videos [2,4,9,12,21,22]. However, none of them are sufficiently fast for their use with real-time videos.

Videos have a strong correlation along the temporal axis compared to the horizontal and vertical axes. This characteristic has been used to reduce noise in videos. Conventional real-time NR algorithms use temporal correlation to reduce noise [1, 11, 25]. Frame memory is required to exploit temporal correlation. This is called inter-frame signal processing. Although the memory cost has been reduced, the overall cost is still high if we use it for many frames. Traditionally, a recursive temporal filter with one frame memory was used in this configuration. It is a temporal direction infinite impulse response (IIR) filter. Most of digital TV sets are equipped with the recursive temporal type noise reducers. However, there is an issue in the motion areas which have blur trails because the recursive filters have infinite responses. This issue is discussed in the next section.

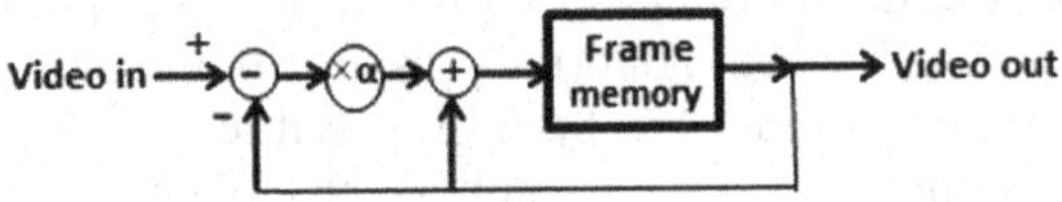

Fig. 1. A conventional real-time video noise reducer [16].

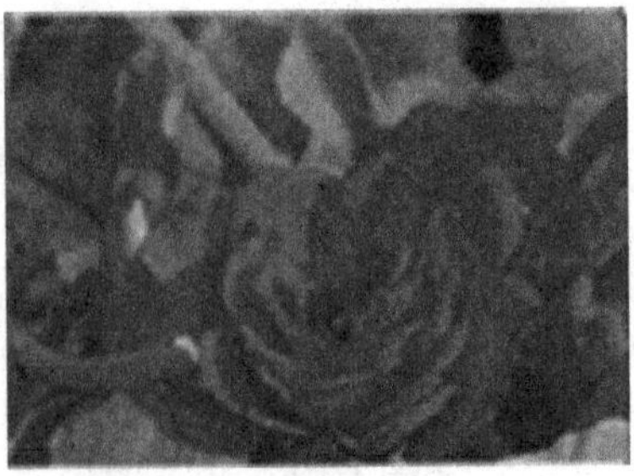

Fig. 2. A noisy video frame [16].

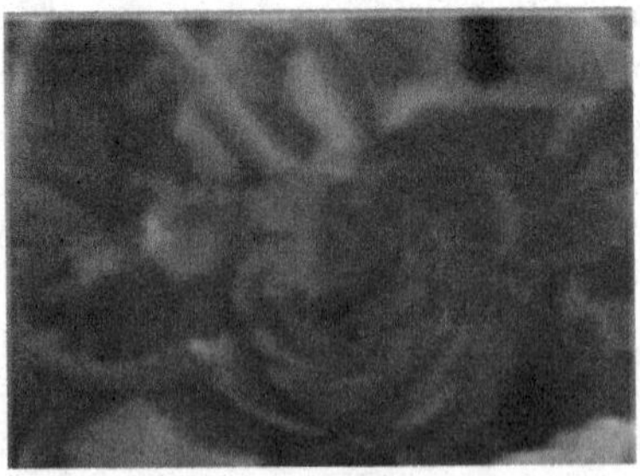

Fig. 3. The processed result of Fig. 2 using the conventional method (Fig. 1) [16].

3 Issues with the Conventional Method

A block diagram of a real-time noise reducer is shown in Fig. 1. The parameter, α, is set based on a range 0:1 (low level noise) to 0:3 (high level noise). It reduces the pixel value changes using a temporal recursive low pass filter at every pixel. Currently, only this type of noise reducer is practical since it is cost-effective. It can work in real time and is commonly used in TV systems [24]. As mentioned earlier in this section, the stationary areas have the same pixel values. However, the pixels in the moving areas change their values in every frame. Although conventional noise reducers successfully reduce noise in stationary areas by averaging the values of each pixel, they create a motion trail blur behind the moving objects.

Figure 2 shows a frame from a noisy video. In this video, the camera is panning from left to right. Figure 3 shows the processed result using NR shown in Fig. 1. Although the noise is reduced in Fig. 3, there is a trail from left to right in accordance with the camera panning direction. If the noise is high and visible, the recursive filter in the noise reducer has to work more heavily, i.e. with a larger recursive coefficient (α in Fig. 1). The larger recursive coefficient reduces the noise. However, as shown in Fig. 3, it also causes blur in the moving areas. This type of NR involves a trade-off between the strength of NR and the extent of blurry trails.

A video signal can be written as $f(x, y, t)$. Here, x is the horizontal axis, y is the vertical axis and t is the temporal axis. We assume noise as $n(t)$, and the video with noise can be expressed as follows:

$$f_n(x, y, t) = f(x, y, t) + n(t) \tag{1}$$

The noise reduction process of the conventional method shown in Fig. 1 can be expressed as follows:

$$Fn(x, y, t) = (1 - \alpha)f_n(x, y, t - 1) + \alpha f_n(x, y, t) \tag{2}$$

The spatial position (x,y) is the same in all frames and only the temporal parameter t changes. Therefore, Eq. 2 can be written as follows:

$$Fn(t) = (1 - \alpha)f_n(t - 1) + \alpha f_n(t) \tag{3}$$

Equation 3 is a recursive filter that has an infinite impulse response (IIR). Theoretically, IIR leads to infinite trails in movement areas. In the real video, the trails continue until the output of the IIR filter becomes smaller than the least significant bit (LSB) level. A temporal finite impulse filter (FIR) does not cause the long trails associated with IIR. However, a couple of frames of temporal relation cannot reduce noise to the practically required level. If we increase the number of frames in memory, blur/trail occurs. The spatial processing (intra-frame) NR does not cause trails or blur. It does not work well because the spatial correlation is not strong compared with the temporal relation in images/videos. The spatial NR causes a spatial blur instead of the temporal blur that is caused by temporal recursive NR. The conventional NR is a kind of low pass filter (LPF). Noise in videos looks like it comprises high-frequency elements. However, noise comprises a wide range of frequencies, including low-frequency elements and DC. NR works as an LPF against noise which eliminates the high-frequency elements while retaining the low-frequency elements. Although the peak level of noise decreases, the noise changes its shape and becomes low-level widespread spots. Since human eyes are sensitive to the low-frequency elements, the frequency shifted low-level noise becomes more visible. This means that conventional NR changes the noise shape and makes it more visible.

4 Proposed Method

Figure 4 shows an image comparison of the conventional and the proposed NR. In Fig. 4, the horizontal axis is the horizontal/vertical line of the video and the vertical axis is the level of the video. Figure 4(a) is the input of the NR filter, which is a video with noise. Figure 4(b) is the conventional NR processed result of Fig. 4(a). As discussed in the previous section, the levels of noise are reduced but become widespread, as shown in Fig. 4(b). In Fig. 4(b), the levels of noise are lower than those in Fig. 4(a) after the application of the LPF. However, the noise spreads over wider areas than that in Fig. 4(a). Noise becomes more visible with LPF especially for high-noise videos that are shot under poor lighting conditions. When these kinds of videos are processed by the conventional NR equipped with LPF, the low-level widespread noise appears everywhere. The conventional noise reducer changes the noise frequency from high to low, which makes the noise more visible. If the noise is converted to the high-frequency areas, it becomes less visible. Figure 4(c) shows the processed result obtained by using the proposed method. In Fig. 4(c), the levels of noise become lower but the noise does not spread. The ends of the noise become sharp edges that contain high-frequency elements. Therefore, the noise is successfully converted to the high-frequency areas.

We propose a novel nonlinear FIR for NR [17]. Here, we assume $f(x, y, t-1)$, $f(x, y, t)$, and $f(x, y, t+1)$ are three sequential frames. The target frame for processing is $f(x, y, t)$. $f(x, y, t-1)$ and $f(x, y, t+1)$ are the reference frames. We also assume the noise in the video is Gaussian noise with deviation δ because it is the most common noise for images created under poor lighting conditions. Noise is the undesired signal. If $f(x, y, t)$ contains noise, the level of $f(x, y, t)$ is higher or lower compared with the true value. However, although the video contains noise, $f(x, y, t)$ may be the true value. The proposed method changes the value of $f(x, y, t)$ according to the following three cases, which occur depending on their probability.

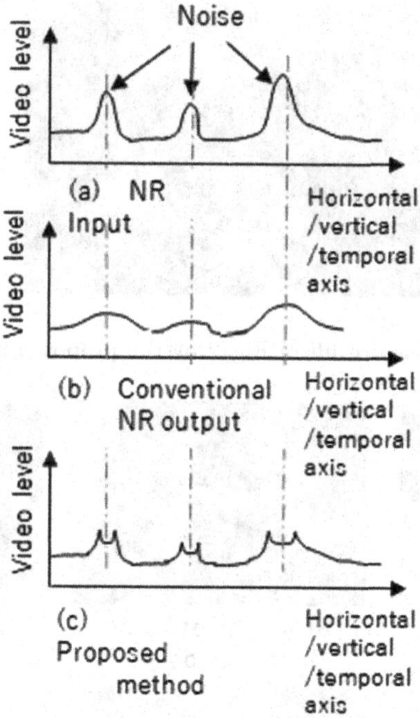

Fig. 4. Proposed NR signal processing [16].

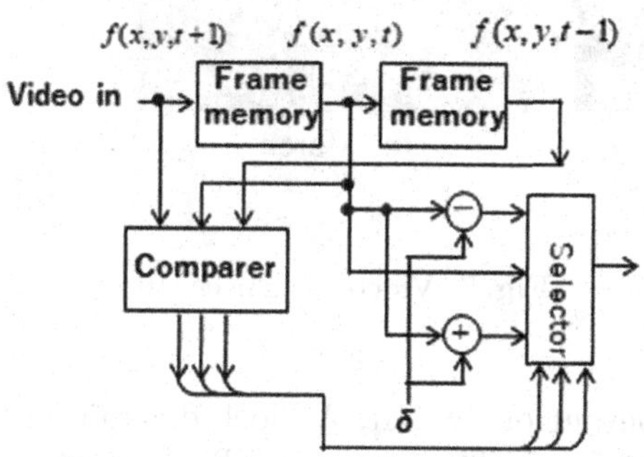

Fig. 5. Block diagram of proposed NR signal processing [16].

- $f(x, y, t-1) \leq f(x, y, t) \leq f(x, y, t+1)$ or $f(x, y, t+1) \leq f(x, y, t) \leq f(x, y, t-1) \Longrightarrow$ the output of the NR is $f(x, y, t)$
- $f(x, y, t)$ is the highest$\Longrightarrow$ the output of the NR is $f(x, y, t) - \delta$
- $f(x, y, t)$ is the lowest$\Longrightarrow$ the output of the NR is $f(x, y, t) + \delta$

Condition 1.: if f(x, y, t) is in the middle, f(x, y, t) does not contain noise and no signal processing is necessary for f(x, y, t). The output of the NR is f(x, y, t). Condition 2.: if f(x, y, t) is the highest of the three signals, f(x, y, t)-δ is the output of the NR. Condition 3.: if f(x, y, t) is the lowest of the three signals,

Fig. 6. Processed result of Fig. 2 by the proposed method [16].

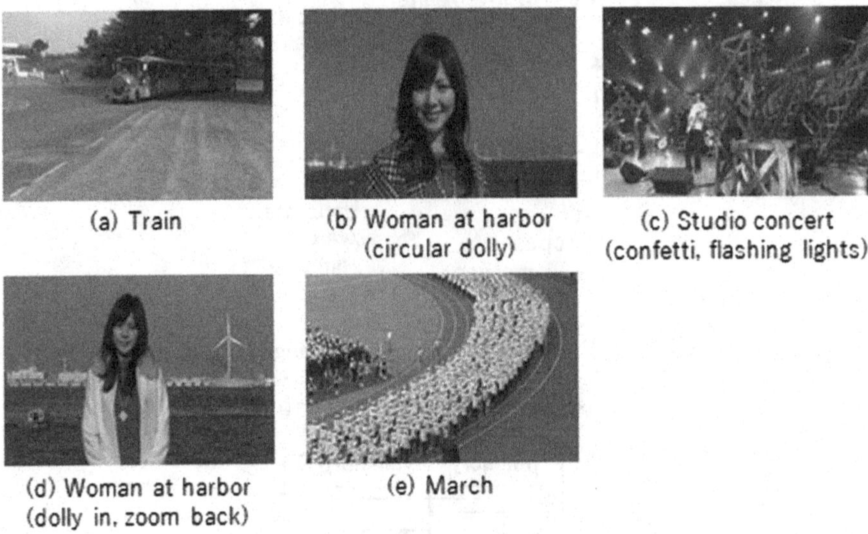

Fig. 7. Video sequences [16].

f(x, y, t) + δ is the output of the NR. A block diagram of the proposed signal processing is shown in Fig. 5. The proposed NR comprises two frame memories, one comparer, one adder, one subtracter, and one selector. The comparer has three inputs. It compares f(x, y, t) with the other two signals, f(x, y, t−1) and f(x, y, t + 1). The output of the comparer is three bits, which represent three conditions: f(x, y, t) is the highest, f(x, y, t) is in the middle, and f(x, y, t) is the lowest of the three values . These three bits are introduced to the selector. This approach is sufficiently simple to embody as a real-time noise reducer.

In Fig. 5, the top left is the video input of the NR filter and the bottom right is the output of NR filter. f(x, y, t−1), f(x, y, t), and f(x, y, t + 1) are obtained with the two frame memories. By comparing f(x, y, t) with the other two values, the order of f(x, y, t) is obtained. If the value of f(x, y, t) is in the middle (case 1), f(x, y, t) is the output of the NR. If f(x, y, t) is the highest, f(x, y, t)-δ is the output of NR (case 2). If f(x, y, t) is the lowest, f(x, y, t)+δ is the output of NR. f(x, y, t)-δ and f(x,y,t)+δ are created by the adder and the subtracter. The three paths, f(x, y, t), f(x, y, t)-δ, and f(x, y, t)+δ, are the inputs of the selector, and one of them is selected as the output of the comparer. The block diagram shown in Fig. 5 indicates practical hardware that could implement the proposed algorithm. Since it is a three taps transversal filter and a finite impulse response (FIR) filter, it does not cause the trails in motion areas. It is a simple and compact design for the development of real-time NR hardware.

5 Experiment

5.1 Simulation Results

Computer simulations were conducted to compare the peak signal-to-noise ratios (PSNRs) of the proposed and conventional NR methods. Figure 7 shows stills from five video sequences. In Fig. 7(a) and (e), the train and marching people are moving and the camera is panning slowly. In Fig. 1(b), the camera was moved using a circular dolly, whereas in Fig. 7(d), it was dollied in and then zoomed back. The woman stood at the same place in both sequences and did not move significantly. Figure 7(c) shows a music concert with flashing lights and confetti.

We prepared test video sequences by adding Gaussian noise ($\sigma = 7$) to Fig. 7(a)–(e). We then compared the PSNRs of the proposed NR method with those of conventional NR using computer simulations. The simulation results of Fig. 7(a)–(e) are presented in Figs. 8, 9, 10, 11 and 12 respectively. Herein, the horizontal axis shows the frame number, and the vertical axis shows the PSNR. The blue lines show the PSNRs for the videos with added noise compared with the original videos. These stay constant because a constant level of noise ($\sigma = 7$) was added. The yellow green and purple lines show the results of processing the videos with conventional NR using parameters $\alpha = 0.2$ and 0.5, respectively, whereas the brown lines show the results of processing the videos using the proposed method.

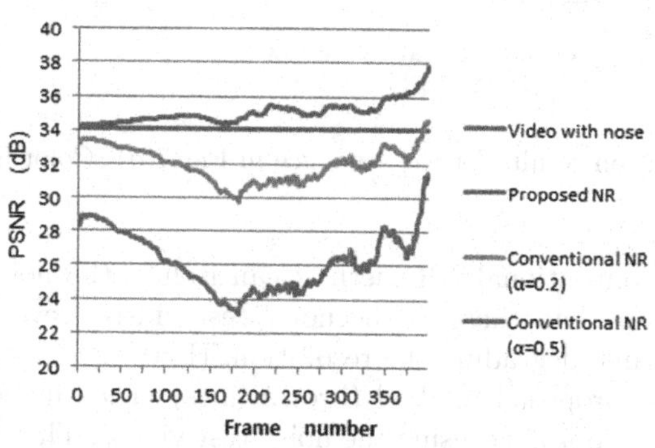

Fig. 8. Simulation results for the sequence in Fig. 7(a) [16] (Color figure online).

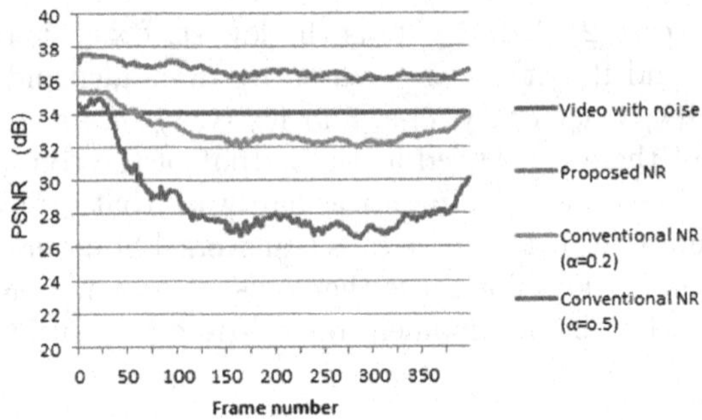

Fig. 9. Simulation results for the sequence in Fig. 7(b) [16] (Color figure online).

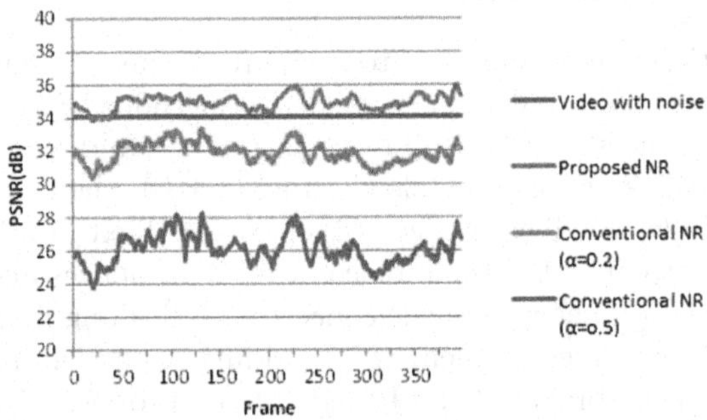

Fig. 10. Simulation results for the sequence in Fig. 7(c) (Color figure online).

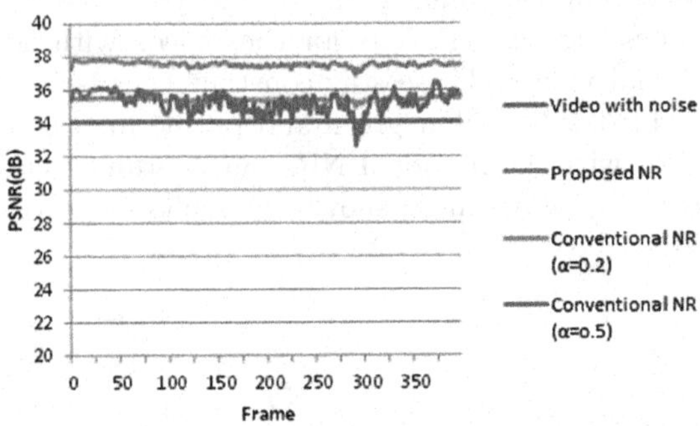

Fig. 11. Simulation results for the sequence in Fig. 7(d) (Color figure online).

Although the conventional NR method can reduce the noise in the videos, its PSNRs are lower than those of the noisy test videos, revealing that it can reduce the noise while degrading the resolution. However, Figs. 8, 9, 10, 11 and 12 denote that the proposed method (brown lines) yields higher PSNRs when compared with those obtained using the noisy test videos. These results indicate that the proposed NR method outperforms the conventional NR method. In

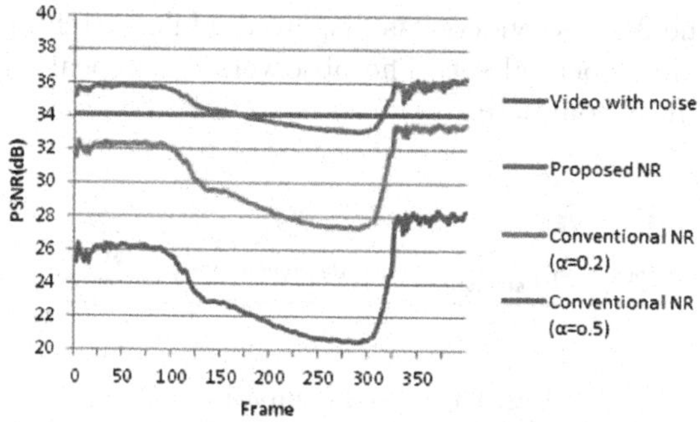

Fig. 12. Simulation results for the sequence in Fig. 7(e) (Color figure online).

Fig. 12, the brown line is lower between frames 160 and 320, and this tilts the camera vertically. Marching in the video creates a big frame difference on the right and left edges. Although each object in the video is small and random, every frame changes with differences in shape; further, noise is similar to the differences in the noise level ($\sigma = 7$). This indicates the existence of two different noise levels between the frames 160 and 320. In our future work, we plan to cope with videos containing randomly moving objects.

5.2 Subjective Assessments

Subjective assessments evaluate the video quality based on human perceptions; results are obtained despite significant barriers (e.g., observers and experimentation time) in a subjective assessment. In the proposed NR method, we selected subjective assessment because the subjective image quality is more important than the objective assessment while selecting a TV set from a shop. To obtain subjective assessment results with appropriate reproducibility, proper adjustment and unification of experimental conditions are crucial. ITU-R BT. 500 [6], which is the international criteria for assessing the quality of television broadcast, recommends a general video experimental method to obtain reproducible results.

Furthermore, ITU-T P.910 [7] specifies the evaluation methods with respect to several multimedia video contents; ITU-T P.910 recommends an absolute category rating and paired comparison assessment methods [3]. In this study, we perform an experiment using a paired comparison that requires a significant amount of time; this helps to detect the differences in terms of video quality with high accuracy.

Figure 13 denotes the paired comparison experimental procedure with respect to time on the horizontal x-axis.

Figure 13 denotes the order in which the videos are displayed. Thus, assessment pairs are created based on stimuli and are relatively compared. The first is a reference video, whereas the second is an assessment video. Figure 13 depicts that a 15-s reference video is initially displayed, followed by a 15-s assessment video. However, the 2-s gray video was displayed while switching videos by considering a single and repeated set. The observers can repeatedly watch videos until the assessment is complete.

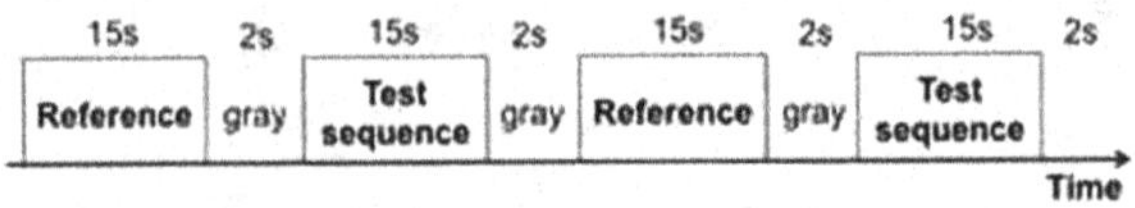

Fig. 13. Paired comparison.

Table 1. Assessment score.

Assessment score	Assessment word
2	Excellent
1	Good
0	Fair
−1	Poor
−2	Bad

In Table 1, the assessment video was evaluated using a 0-scale reference video based on a 5-grade scale (−2 to 2). Noise and resolution are the video quality evaluation criteria. The lower the noise, the higher will be the resolution and the better will be the video quality. The observers assess the three videos using NR processing in case of a noisy video; if the non-recursive NR video has higher resolution and less noise when compared with those of the noisy video, the assessment value is either 2 or 1. Contrarily, the assessment point is −2 or −1; further, the assessment value is 0 when the video quality is equal. The reference video changed during the assessment for all the combinations. During the training, the observers were instructed about the experimental procedure, resolution procedure, noise, and evaluation scale to facilitate understanding.

The viewing distance was thrice the height according to BT. 500. Hence, the observers considered the influence of the viewing angle and assess the videos from within 30^0 of the displayed center. Based on the BT. 500 assessments, at least 15 observers are required to perform statistical analysis with a recommendation of using non-video experts. A total of 18 observers with normal visual acuity and color vision participated in the experiment. To recognize the noise in the videos, all the observers were trained before performing the subjective assessments. An analysis of variance significance test was performed, and Fig. 14 showed the results in graphical form to determine the capability of the proposed method. The horizontal axis represents the scale values. The marks (rhombus, square, triangle, and x) indicate the scale values of each stimulus (noise image, proposed NR, conventional NR ($\alpha = 0.2$), and conventional NR ($\alpha = 0.5$), respectively). Higher scale values correspond to higher evaluations. The two asterisks (**) represent a significant difference of 1%. Figure 14 depicts a significant difference of 1% in the four proposed NR-processed images and the noise image, indicating the reproducibility of the results. Using the conventional method, one image was improved from among five images, whereas the remaining four images were degraded.

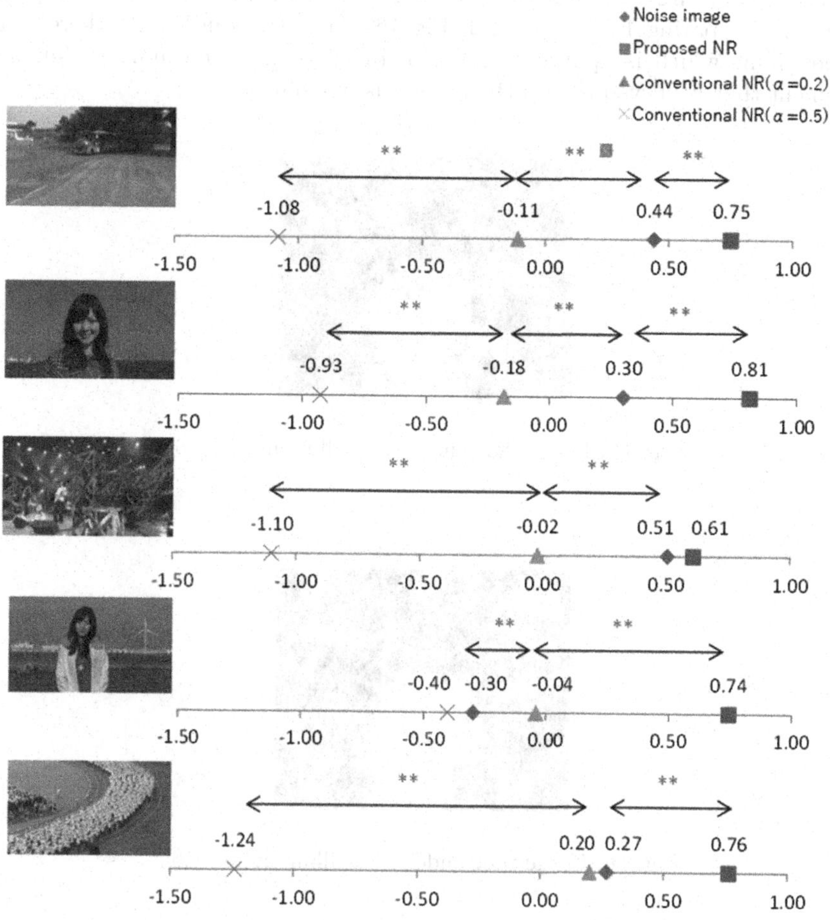

Fig. 14. Results of subjective assessment.

5.3 Low Luminace Video

Figure 6 shows the processed result of Fig. 2 using the proposed method three times sequentially. Comparing Fig. 3 with Fig. 6, the image quality of Fig. 6 is better than that of Fig. 3. Blur in Fig. 6 is less than that in Fig. 3 and noise is greatly reduced. Note that Figs. 2, 3, and 6 are just computer simulation results.

We apply the proposed method to an actual video. Figure 15 shows a video frame shot under 3.5 lx illumination by a high-sensitivity video camera. Although 3.5 lx illumination is not sufficient for imaging, noise is not visible. In the video, the doll is rotating and the hair ornament is curving due to centrifugal force. Figure 16 shows a video frame shot under 0.4 lx illumination taken by the same video camera. Even though a high-sensitivity camera is used, noise is visible everywhere. Figure 17 shows the processed result of Fig. 15 by the proposed method. Comparing Figure 17 with Fig. 16, noise is reduced and there is no motion blur, which is apparent in Fig. 3. In particular, the moving thin hair ornament that is curved due to the motion is not blurry.

Fig. 15. Image shot under 3.5 lx illumination [16].

Fig. 16. Image shot under 0.4 lx illumination [16].

It should be noted that the proposed method does not cause any blur in moving areas, unlike the conventional NR. As shown in Fig. 6, the proposed NR algorithm is simple, cost-effective, and can process videos in real time. However, the noise levels differ depending on the video. It is necessary to precisely detect the noise level to make the NR work in real time. Future work will focus on developing a method to detect the noise level automatically. Combining the proposed NR and an automatic noise level detector can reduce video noise effectively without human intervention.

Fig. 17. Processed result of Fig. 7 by the proposed method [16].

6 Conclusion

In this study, we propose a novel NR algorithm, which does not suffer from the artifacts that afflict conventional NR algorithms, including the trails behind moving objects, to process the videos in real time. Further, noisy-video computer simulations were conducted; the proposed NR algorithm exhibited better results with objective and subjective assessments when compared with those obtained using the conventional NR method. The proposed method can reduce the shot noise in a dark room. The proposed NR method can eliminate the video noise despite its simplicity. Therefore, the proposed method is effective for developing real-time hardware. In future work, we will attempt to automatically detect the noise level.

References

1. Brailean, J.C., Kleihorst, R.P., Efstratiadis, S., Katsaggelos, A.K., Lagenfdijk, R.L.: Noise reduction filter for dynamic image sequeces : review. Proc. IEEE **83**, 1272–1292 (1995)
2. Dabov, K., Foi, A., Katkovnik, V., Egiazarian, K.: Image denoising by sparse 3-D transform-domain collaborative filtering. IEEE Trans. Image Process. **16**(8), 2080–2095 (2007)
3. David, H.A.: Method of Paired Comparisons (Statistical Monograph). Virginia Polytechnic Institute, Blacksburg (1969)
4. Elad, M., Aharon, M.: Image denoising via sparse and redundant representations over learned dictionaries. IEEE Trans. Image Process. **15**(12), 3736–3745 (2006)
5. Gupta, N., Swamy, M.N., Plotkin, E.: Low-complexity video noise reduction in wavelet domain. In: IEEE 6th Workshop on Multimedia Signal Processing, pp. 239–242 (2004)
6. ITU-R-SG6 (2012). https://www.itu.int/rec/r-rec-bt.500/en
7. ITU-T (2008). https://www.itu.int/rec/t-rec-p.910/en
8. Jovanov, L., et al.: Combined wavelet domain and motion compensated video denoiding based on video codec motion estimation method. IEEE Trans. Circuits Syst. Video Technol. **19**(3), 417–421 (2009)
9. Kaur, L., Gupta, S., Chauhan, R.: Image denoising using wavelet thresholding. In: Indian Conference on Computer Vision. Graphics and Image Processing (2002)

10. Kazubek, M.: Wavelet domain image denoising by thresholding and wiener filtering. IEEE Sig. Process. **10**(11), 324–326 (2003)
11. Kondo, T., Fujimori, Y., Horishi, T., Nishikata, T.: Patent: noise reduction in image signals: Pct, ep0640908 a1, ep19940306328 (1994)
12. Lebrun, M., Buades, A., Morel, J.M.: A nonlocal Bayesian image denoising algorithm. SIAM J. Imaging Sci. **6**(3), 1665–1688 (2013)
13. Luisier, F., Blue, T., Unser, M.: Surelet for orthonormal wavelet domain video denoising. IEEE Trans. Circuits Syst. Video Technol. **20**(6), 913–919 (2010)
14. Mahmoud, R.O., Faheem, M.T.: Comparison between DWT and dual tree complex wavelet transform in video sequences using wavelet domain. In: INFOS (2008)
15. Malfait, M., Roose, D.: Wavelet based image denoising using a markov random field a priori model. IEEE Trans. Image Process. **6**(4), 549–565 (1997)
16. Mori, C., Gohshi, S.: Real-time non-linear noise reduction algorithm for video. In: SIGAMP 2013, pp. 321–327, August 2018
17. Mori, C., Gohshi, S.: Real-time non-linear noise reduction algorithm for video. In: SIGMAP, ICETE, pp. 321–327 (2018)
18. Lian, N.X., Zagorodnov, V., Tan, Y.P.: Video denoising using vector estimation of wavelet coefficients. In: ISPACS (2006)
19. Piurica, A., Zlokolica, V., Philips, W.: Noise reduction in video sequences using wavelet-domain and temporal filtering. In: Truchetet, F. (ed.) Wavelet Applications in Industrial Processing, Proceedings of the SPIE, vol. 5266, pp. 48–49 (2004)
20. Pizurica, A., Zlokolica, V., Philips, W.: Combined wavelet domain and temporal video denoising. In: IEEE Conference on Advanced Video and Signal Based Surveillance, AVSS 2003, pp. 334–341 (2003)
21. Portilla, J., Strela, V., Wainwright, M.J., Simoncelli, E.P.: Image denoising using scale mixtures of gaussians in the wavelet domain. IEEE Trans. Image Process. **12**(11), 1338–1351 (2003)
22. Rudin, L., Osher, S.: Nonlinear total variation based noise removal algorithms. Physica D **60**(1–4), 259–268 (1992)
23. Selesnick, I.W., Li, K.Y.: Video denoising using 2D and 3D dual-tree complex wavelet transforms. In: Wavelet Applications in Signal and Image Processing, SPIE 2003, vol. 5207, pp. 607–618 (2003)
24. TI: TVP5160 3D Noise Reduction Calibration Procedure Application Report: SLEA110 May, Texas Instrument Manual (2011)
25. Yagi, S., Inoue, S., Hayashi, M., Okui, S., Gohshi, S.: Practical Video Signal Processing, Ohmusha, pp. 143–145 (2004). (in Japanese). ISBN 4-274-94637-1
26. Yang, Q.X., Tan, K.I., Ahuja, N.: Real time O(1) bilateral filtering. In: Computer Vision and Pattern Recognition (CVPR) (2009)

Cloudless Friend-to-Friend Middleware for Smartphones

Jo Inge Arnes(✉) and Randi Karlsen

University of Tromsø - The Arctic University of Norway, Tromsø, Norway
{jo.i.arnes,randi.karlsen}@uit.no

Abstract. Using smartphones for peer-to-peer communication over the Internet is difficult without the aid of centralized services. These centralized services, which usually reside in the cloud, are necessary for brokering communication between peers, and all communication must pass through them. A reason for this is that smartphones lack publicly reachable IP addresses. Also, because people carry their smartphones with them, smartphones will often disconnect from one network and connect to another. Smartphones can also go offline. Additionally, a network of trusted peers (or friends) requires a directory of known peers, authentication mechanisms, and secure communication channels. In this paper, we propose a peer-to-peer middleware that provides these features without the need for centralized services.

Keywords: Mobile peer-to-peer middleware · Friend-to-friend networking · Unreachable IP addresses · Location transparency

1 Introduction

About 2.5 billion people in the world use smartphones [17]. They use smartphones for a wide range of online services that are important in their lives, such as news, banking, education, career, and health. Many use apps for social networking. They communicate with friends and share pictures and videos.

Most apps are backed by cloud services. The apps connect to a cloud, which consists of data centers, and transfer data to services there. The cloud services store and process the data. By using a centralized cloud service, it is easier to access data from multiple smartphones and share with others.

For example, when someone shares a picture with their friends via Snapchat (https://www.snapchat.com), the picture is uploaded to Snapchat's servers in the cloud. A cloud service sends a notification to the friends. The friends open

---

This paper is an updated and extended version of Cloudless Wide Area Friend-to-Friend Networking Middleware for Smartphones [2], which was presented at the ICETE 2018 conference. Note that the concept of reconnectable channels, introduced in Sect. 4.6, has not before been published.

M. S. Obaidat (Ed.): ICETE 2018, CCIS 1118, pp. 199–218, 2019.
https://doi.org/10.1007/978-3-030-34866-3_10

the picture in their Snapchat app, which downloads the picture from Snapchat's cloud service. The pattern is typical for how smartphone apps communicate and share data.

Sending data through a third-party service in the cloud can be a source of privacy concerns. In addition to storing data that the user uploads, other types of user data are collected. The app provider usually gathers metadata about user activities, such as whom they communicate with, when, where, how often, and about what.

The extensive use of cloud services also raises concerns about wasting computing resources. Smartphones today have as much processing power, memory, and storage capacity as a standard desktop PC a decade ago. With the increasing popularity of smartphones [12], it seems sensible to explore ways to harness more of these hardware resources.

An alternative to the cloud-based solutions is to enable smartphones to communicate directly in a peer-to-peer fashion over the Internet. However, this is not a trivial solution, since smartphones usually lack publicly reachable IP addresses and often change networks, which makes it challenging to keep track of the devices' addresses. Most smartphone apps of today, therefore, depend on clouds or application servers as middlemen to enable communication between devices.

In this work, we describe a novel approach to mobile peer-to-peer communication in wide area networks, which allows direct communication between devices that frequently change networks and lack public IP addresses. We introduce *Swirlware*, a middleware that enables wide area peer-to-peer communication for smartphones, without the need for clouds or application servers for storing, processing, or sharing data. Our approach also supports incorporating smartphones as nodes in a peer-to-peer or distributed system, so that storage and processing capacities of the smartphones can be utilized as a part of a bigger whole.

Experiments show that Swirlwave handles cloudless, mobile peer-to-peer communication well. It enables smartphones to be directly reached and supports continued communication when devices move between networks.

In the following, we first compare Swirlwave to related work. We then give an overview of the proposed system, describing the architecture and underlying communication. Section 4 describes the Swirlwave middleware. Experiments and results are presented in Sect. 5, while the last sections present discussions and conclusion.

2 Related Work

The Swirlwave middleware provides a novel solution to peer-to-peer mobile communication, where obstacles, such as unreachable IP addresses, disconnections and frequently changing network locations, are handled. We here describe how Swirlwave relates to previous work on mobile communication.

Popescu et al. [14] describe a friend-to-friend (F2F) architecture, called Turtle, for safe sharing of sensitive data. As Swirlwave, it builds an overlay network from pre-existing trust relationships. Turtle differs from Swirlwave by being a theoretical description of a file sharing network architecture, where search queries are flooded through the network. Swirlwave, on the other hand, is a middleware enabling friend-to-friend networking without being tied to specific applications.

A variety of apps for using smartphones as servers exist, for example, web servers for Android, but they only work as part of a local area network. To connect, clients must be on the same local area network as the server. This is a serious restriction when using mobile devices. Swirlwave enables smartphone server apps to be available outside local area networks and continue communicating with clients despite network changes.

Orbot (https://guardianproject.info/apps/orbot) allows smartphones to be reached outside local area networks, but it has no mechanism for changing addresses when the smartphone changes location. This problem is solved in Swirlwave, which handles address changes.

Thali (http://thaliproject.org) is a Microsoft sponsored experimental platform for building peer web. It is described as an open-source software platform for creating apps that exploit the power of personal devices and put people in control of their data. Thali planned to use the Tor Onion Service protocol [20], which at the time was called hidden services. This is the same protocol that Swirlwave builds on, but Thali abandoned the idea because onion services were designed for stationary services, not mobile ones. [19] It is clear from the project's homepage that Thali instead communicates over Bluetooth Low Energy (BLE), Bluetooth, and Wi-Fi direct, none of which are wide area communications. In contrast to Thali, Swirlwave provides functionality that enables the use of the Tor Onion Service protocol on mobile devices, can thus support wide area mobile communication.

3 Mobile Peer-to-Peer Communication Without Public IP Address

This section describes the architecture for Swirlwave and how it builds on Tor and the Tor Onion Service protocol (https://www.torproject.org). We also describe the problem of unreachable IP addresses.

3.1 Unreachable Addresses

Usually, when a personal computer is connected to the Internet, other computers cannot directly contact it. This is because of network address translation (NAT). The computer can initiate contact with a server, but it cannot act as a server itself. The same is true for smartphones. The reason is that computers are not directly connected to the Internet, but are part of a local area network (LAN) that communicates with the outside world through a router.

Devices on a LAN are assigned IP addresses that are only valid inside the LAN. In the most common configuration, IPs are assigned by a DHCP-server. A device is given an address when it connects to a LAN, but this address can be different the next time the device connects to the same network.

When a computer connects to a server on the Internet, the server will see the IP of the router. The server sends its replies to the router, which performs network address translation and routes the traffic to the correct computer [5]. IPs of computers inside the LAN are not reachable from the Internet. This is also the case for smartphones connected to the Internet via local Wi-Fi or cellular data such as 4G.

3.2 Architecture

A system based on Swirlwave has a shared-nothing architecture with independent and self-sufficient nodes that do not share memory or disk storage. The nodes will generally run on separate physical devices, most notably smartphones connected to the Internet through Wi-Fi or cellular data. It is a peer-to-peer system that does not rely on cloud computing or application server middleboxes.

Friend-to-Friend Network. Swirlwave is based on friend-to-friend (F2F) networking [3], a category of unstructured, private peer-to-peer networking where peers only connect directly to already known peers (friends) [16]. Friendships are commutative, but not automatically transitive.

In Fig. 1, peers A, B, and D are all friends and can connect to each other. Peer C is only friends with B, and cannot contact A and D directly. However, it is possible to reach unknown, faraway peers indirectly. Using a far-reaching query, A can ask B to relay the query to its friends, which again could query friends, and so on.

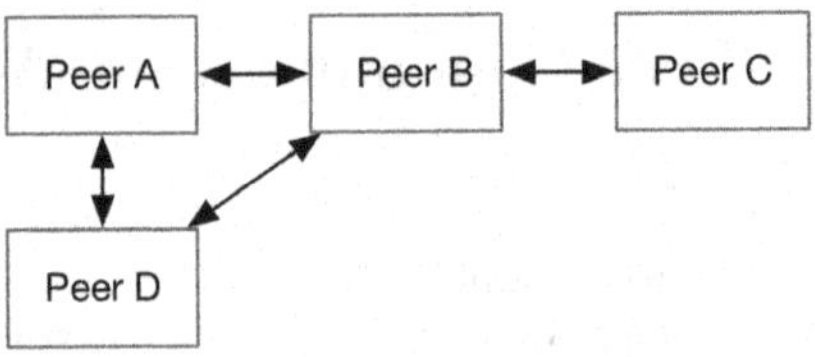

Fig. 1. Friend-to-friend network [2].

Friend-to-friend networks are useful for distributed systems with a predefined set of dedicated nodes that should not be available to everyone. It can, for example, be used for connecting a set of company-owned smartphones or for setting up a social network of friends to chat or share data.

Swirlwave Middleware. Swirlwave is designed as a middleware that facilitates communication between applications on mobile devices. It is located between the application and operating system (including transport layer services, such as TCP/IP). The devices are connected to the Internet, and traffic is routed through the Tor overlay network.

All peers can be clients and servers at the same time; they can expose several services for peers to consume, and they can be clients to services published by other peers. To contact a server, the client application need not know the address of the server peer. Neither does it need to know how to connect to the underlying communication service Tor.

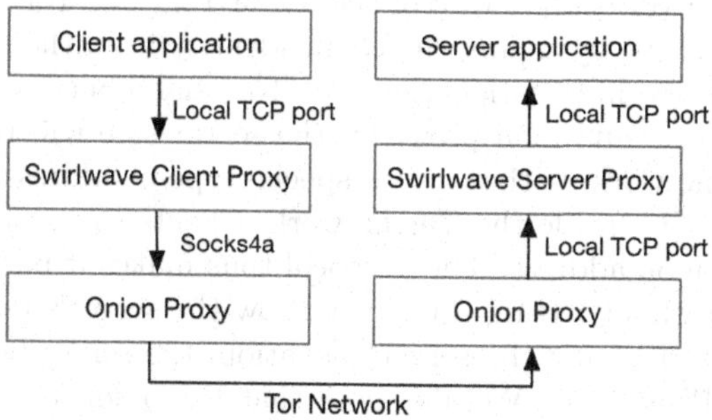

Fig. 2. Proxying from client to server [2].

Applications built on top of Swirlwave communicate over TCP and register as plug-ins with Swirlwave along with their capabilities, such as properties of the application. Swirlwave is designed so that existing applications and libraries easily can make use of it. This is achieved by creating two proxies, a client- and a server-side proxy.

Figure 2 shows two peers, one acting as client, the other as server. Any client application using TCP connections can connect to the locally running Swirlwave proxy, and the middleware will automatically route the traffic to the correct peer. The client proxy listens to connections from local clients on a range of ports. When a client application connects, the port number is used to find the correct peer and requested service. The Swirlwave client proxy connects to the locally running onion proxy through the SOCKS4a protocol [11], which sends the traffic through the Tor network.

On the other end, a Swirlwave server proxy receives data from the onion proxy and directs the traffic via ordinary TCP to the correct service running locally on the receiving peer.

3.3 Tor and Tor Onion Services

The main objective of Tor (https://www.torproject.org) is anonymity, not connectivity. It is designed to conceal online traffic from surveillance and monitoring by relaying through several nested proxies, compared to the layers of an onion. Per February 2018 the network consisted of over 6000 volunteer relays (https://metrics.torproject.org).

Tor is a public overlay network where encrypted traffic is routed through at least three onion routers before reaching its destination. On each end of the network, there are onion proxies. The client-side onion proxy has access to a directory of onion routers, and when choosing the preferred onion routers, a circuit is built. Each onion router in a circuit knows only its predecessor and successor.

At the destination end of the circuit, an onion proxy receives the traffic and sends it to the destination server, which is just an ordinary server reachable from the Internet. The server is not aware of the use of Tor. The Tor network protects the privacy of the client by hiding the client identity from the server.

If a server wants to hide its location, the Tor Onion Service protocol can be used. In this protocol, an onion proxy on the server side will register an onion service in the Tor network. It then gets a special type of address, called an onion address, which is valid inside the Tor network. Clients can reach the server via Tor by using the onion address. The protocol thus makes it possible for a client to reach a server without letting the client know the server's real location.

As a side effect of hiding the server's location, the server becomes available without a public IP-address. We also note that the onion proxy that registers the onion service, initiates a connection from the server side to the Tor overlay network. This means that the server can be behind a NAT, since NAT only prevents connections from the Internet to the server, not in the opposite direction [5]. An unintended consequence of the protocol is therefore that onion services can be used to reach servers behind NAT. This is useful for Swirlwave, and the reason for building the Swirlwave communication on Tor.

The use of the Tor Onion Service protocol makes it possible to reach smartphones outside local area networks. However, Tor does not include any means to announce new addresses to clients, so clients are not able to connect anymore when a smartphone changes location. Also, there is no protocol transparency, so a client connecting to the smartphone server app must understand the protocol used by Tor. The Swirlwave system is designed to solve these problems transparently as a middleware.

4 Swirlwave

Swirlwave builds on the Tor Onion Service protocol, not because of the anonymity provided by the protocol, but because of the onion addresses assigned to participating devices. Thus, Swirlwave uses onion addresses to reach devices that are lacking publicly visible IP addresses. However, since the Tor Onion Service protocol is not designed for mobile devices, but rather devices that never change location, Swirlwave adds functionality for locating devices and keeping peers up to date with correct addresses. As anonymity is not required in Swirlwave, as opposed to in Tor, authentication of peers is also added to Swirlwave.

4.1 Contacts

Keeping track of peer addresses is a central feature of Swirlwave. This is achieved without external directory services or single points of failure. Each peer in Swirlwave keeps its own, locally stored, contact list of the known peers. New contacts

Table 1. Information in a contact list record [2].

Field name	Description
Name	A human-readable name of the friend
Peer ID	An ID that is unique across all installations
Address	The friend's onion-address
Address version	Each time a peer changes its address, it will increment the address version number
Secondary address	The phone number used when sending SMS-messages to the peer
Public-key	The public-key from the friend's asymmetric keys
Online status	Offline if last attempt to reach the friend was unsuccessful, otherwise online
Last contact time	The last time contact was made with the peer
Known friends	A list of peer IDs for mutual friends
Capabilities	A list of capabilities supported by this friend. Such as available services and protocol UUIDs
Awaiting answer	A flag indicating if an answer from the SMS fallback protocol is pending

are added out-of-band, for example through near-field communication (NFC) when friends meet face-to-face.

An entry in the contact list contains data that is needed to communicate with that specific peer. It also contains information about services offered by the peer. An entry includes the peer ID, onion address, services offered by the peer, phone number (used as an alternative address in an SMS fallback protocol) and its public-key. See Table 1 for the complete contact list information.

To conduct meaningful communication, client and server must use the same protocol. Swirlwave allows applications to use whichever protocol that is suitable. This flexibility is possible by representing protocols as universally unique identifiers (UUID) [10]. More generally, they are identifiers of contracts or agreements that server and client must comply to in order to properly communicate. Swirlwave does not care about the details of this contract, but simply uses the identifier to match clients and servers.

For example, to send a message to a friend, a user selects the friend from the Swirlwave contact list. Based on protocol UUIDs registered for this friend, Swirlwave presents a list of available communication types. If the user has an application that can be used as client, Swirlwave detects it by matching the identifiers of the locally installed applications with the identifier of the friend's messaging service.

4.2 Authentication and Confidentiality

Each peer is equipped with its own key-pair for public-key encryption [8]. This is used for authentication purposes. It is also used for ensuring confidentiality, integrity, and non-repudiation of data when communicating over other channels. Tor Onion Service communication is end-to-end encrypted, which provides communication confidentiality.

The Tor protocol is designed for anonymity. Consequently, the onion proxy on the server side will not know the origin of incoming connections. In our approach, this anonymity hinders the identification of incoming requests from friends.

Swirlwave solves this by providing an authentication mechanism for validating the identity of incoming connections. This functionality is part of the Swirlwave client and server proxies and is based on public-key cryptography.

To establish a new connection, the client-side proxy sends a system message encrypted with the client's private key. To validate the identity of the sender, the server-side proxy decrypts the message with the client's public key. The connection request is refused if the claimed identity of the client cannot be authenticated.

Table 2. Connection message information [2].

Field name	Description
Sender ID	The peer ID of the client
Random number	A random number initially generated and sent by the server proxy
Message type	Whether this is a system message or an application-layer connection
Destination	An identifier of a capability representing a service that the client wishes to consume This will only be set for application-layer connections
System message	A system message that will be dispatched to a module that handles system messages This will only be set for system message types

4.3 Establishing Connections

To establish a connection, a request is sent from a Swirlwave client proxy through the onion proxy. The message header contains (among others) the friend's onion-address. If the onion proxy returns a positive response code (0x5A) telling that it successfully connected to the remote onion service, the client proxy also receives a four-byte number. This number is later returned to the server as part of the connection message. If the server proxy accepts the connection (after evaluating the connection message from the client) it responds with a success code (0x10).

The client proxy then starts reading and writing bytes between the incoming socket from the application-layer client and the outbound onion proxy socket. Figure 3 illustrates this communication.

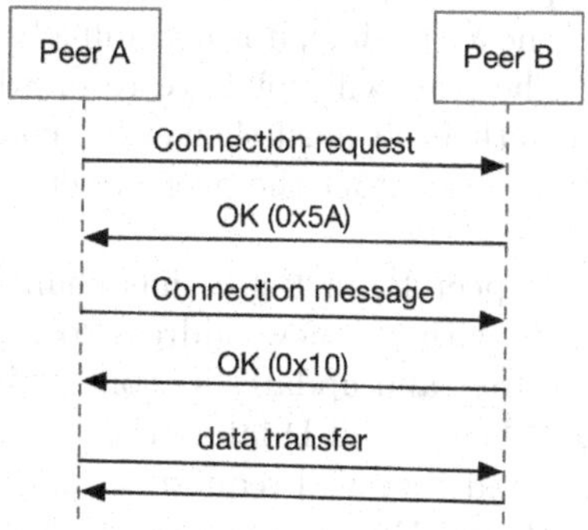

Fig. 3. Establishing connection [2].

In the connection message, everything except the client ID is encrypted with the client's private-key. The server proxy looks up the peer ID in the contact list and rejects the connection if the peer is unknown. If the ID is found in the contact list, the registered public-key is used to decrypt the message. If the message is successfully decrypted, and the returned number equals the one that was sent to the client, the client is authenticated and the connection is accepted.

The connection message also specifies if the connection is for transmitting system messages or application-layer data. For an application-layer connection, the server proxy will use the identifier in the destination field, to match a local service endpoint, and set up a connection from the client to the service. For a system message, the content of the message field will be dispatched to an internal module in the Swirlwave middleware that handles system messages. See Table 2 for a complete list of information included in the connection message.

If the onion proxy fails to connect to the remote onion service, the client proxy marks the peer as being offline. It then starts the process of obtaining an updated address to the peer, either by asking a mutual friend, or using an SMS fallback protocol that contacts the peer directly. The client proxy will not try to establish new connections to the friend until an updated address is obtained. The friend will then be marked as online again.

4.4 Address Changes

When a smartphone moves from one network to another, for instance from Wi-Fi to cellular data, its access point is not the same as before. The IP address will most likely be different, and the route to the device will most certainly be different.

Address changes must be announced to friends. A device that has been offline, or has changed its location, will contact its friends as soon as it is online again. The new address is passed with a version number. This version number is increased every time a peer changes its address, and is used to determine the newest address when comparing registered addresses across peers.

If the peer has been offline for a while, it is not unlikely that some of its friends have changed addresses. The peer will not have received the updated address, and will not be able to reach them. It must then either contact a mutual friend to obtain a peer's new address, or contact the peer directly using an SMS fallback protocol.

As an example, assume peer B, in Fig. 4, has changed address. It sends a system message (marked 1) with the new address to its three friends. Peer A successfully receives the address and updates its contact list, while the two other peers cannot be reached. When C and D later tries to contact B, they discover that it cannot be reached, and they will request an updated address. Peer A is a mutual friend of D and B, and D can therefore ask A for B's address (marked 2a). Peer C, on the other hand, does not have any other friends to ask. Instead, it uses an alternative channel to ask B directly for its address (marked 2b). As phone numbers represent stable addresses where peers can always be reached, Swirlwave uses SMS as the alternative channel.

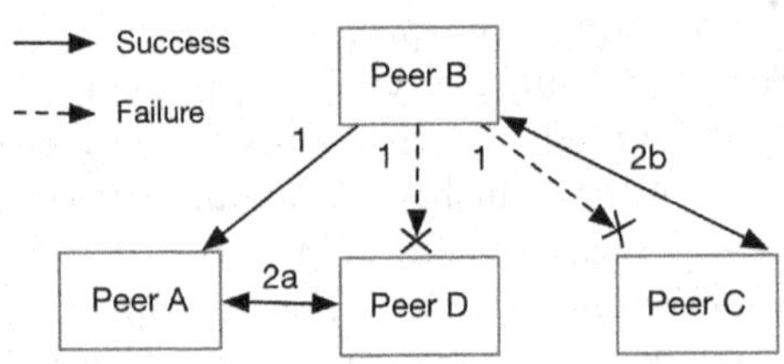

Fig. 4. Peer B changes address [2].

Swirlwave uses onion-addresses that make it possible to connect to peers, even if their IP addresses are unreachable from the Internet. Nevertheless, routing is dependent on IP addresses under the hood, just as everything else on the Internet. It is possible to reuse an onion-address so that it resolves to a new access point. However, there is no support in the Tor control protocol for letting the client refresh the route to an onion service.

The Swirlwave solution is to monitor network changes on the device and register a new onion service when the smartphone connects to a new network. If a network and access point address is recognized from earlier, the onion service and onion-address from last time is reused.

If a connection is broken while being used by an application, Swirlwave does not try to reconnect automatically. In the current implementation of Swirlwave, it is the responsibility of the application to reconnect and resume transfers. To support continuous communication when devices change network, the Swirlwave proxies can be improved so that the connection is kept open between application-layer and Swirlwave proxy-layer. This will allow peers to continue communication when the new address is available.

4.5 SMS Fallback Protocol

The SMS fallback protocol is used to request new addresses from unresponsive peers. When the client proxy of peer C discovers that it cannot connect to a friend, B, and there are no other friends to ask for the address, it will send a data SMS to B. In contrast to an ordinary text SMS, a data SMS will not be visible to the user. Instead it will be received directly by Swirlwave.

The fallback protocol starts by C sending B an SMS, including C's address and a secret one-time code. This is encrypted with C's private key. The one-time code has several purposes; it enables duplicate message detection, and it is a combined message-ID and anti-forgery token sent back to C.

On the receiving side, B looks up C's phone number in the contact list, to confirm that the SMS is from a friend. B decrypts the message and updates the contact list with C's address. If Swirlwave is running and connected, C is answered immediately over the Internet with B's current address. Otherwise C will receive the answer as soon as Swirlwave connects again.

In the response, B sends its new address together with the one-time code originally send by C. The message is encrypted with B's private key. When received, C updates the contact list with B's new address.

4.6 Reconnectable Channels

So far, we have described how peers automatically announce address changes and how they keep track of each other. However, when a peer disconnects from one network location to connect to another, it will necessarily break any open connections to its peers. The peer will not be available for others until it has finished the process of changing its network location. This frequent breaking of connections is undesirable from an application perspective, and it can affect the user experience negatively. The underlying middleware should instead hide the instabilities from the application, whenever possible.

In this section, we propose the concept of reconnectable channels. The aim is that if peers A and B are communicating over a connection, and peer A changes its network, then the applications on A and B can continue unaffected for a while. Within this time frame, A has the opportunity to reconnect to B and resume communication from where it got lost. If successful, the applications will be unaware of the temporary disconnect.

The enabling factor for implementing reconnectable channels is the use of client and server proxies, which already provide location and protocol transparency. When two peers communicate, all traffic passes through the local proxies on each side. On both sides, each proxy keeps two sockets: One socket connects the proxy to a locally running application, the other socket connects the proxy to the external network. The proxy sits in between the two sockets and transfers data back and forth, from one to the other.

When a peer disconnects from the network, the connections between the proxies and the external network inevitably become closed on both sides of the ongoing communication. However, the situation is very different for the sockets that connect the proxies and local applications. These connections are purely local and are unaffected by the status of the external network. Thus, they are still available to the applications. Figure 5 shows that the application connection is still open after the external connection has closed.

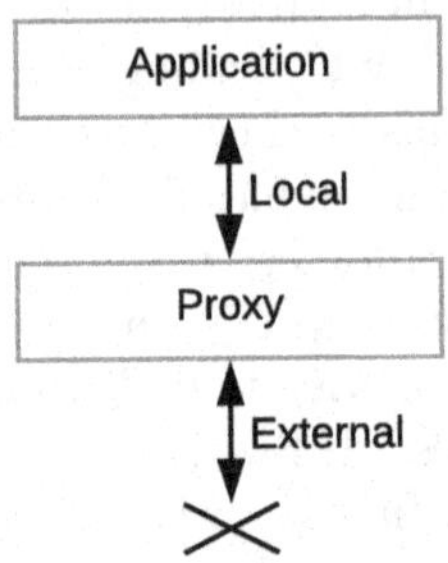

Fig. 5. The connection between the proxy and the external peer is closed, but the connection between the application and the proxy is still open.

For a limited time, a local proxy can hide that the connection to the external network has closed from an application. It does this by keeping the connection to the application open and simulate a low transfer rate. The proxy continues to read and write data at a rate just high enough to keep the connection alive by preventing a timeout. The application can receive and send data as before.

The proxy continues to receive data from the application, but it has nowhere to send the data because the intended recipient is temporarily disconnected. Instead, the proxy stores the data in a buffer. If the external recipient successfully reconnects within a reasonable time, it will send the buffered data to it. This is illustrated in Fig. 6.

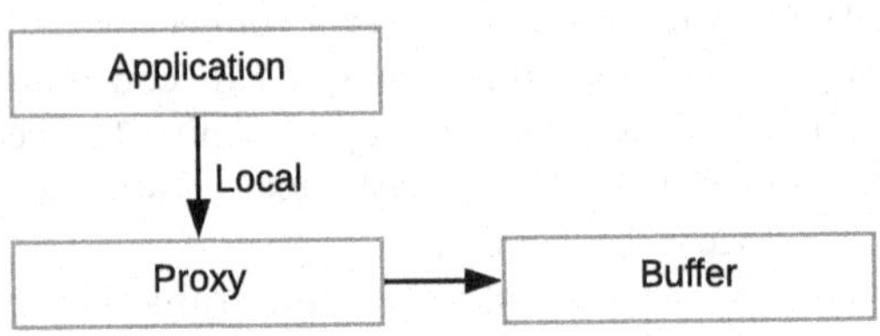

Fig. 6. The external connection is temporarily unavailable, and the proxy has started using buffers instead.

According to Cleary [4], broken TCP-connections are only detected when trying to send data, not during reading. The sender expects an acknowledgment from the other end of the connection that the data was received. Reading data from a connection in TCP is a passive act and does require an acknowledgment. An application will not detect a broken connection through reading operations. The phenomenon is known as a half-open connection. There is no need for the proxy to send data to the application to hide that the external connection is down.

After a device has finished changing its network location, it will attempt to restore the previously ongoing communication with its peers. The proxy will open sockets to the peers, and send reconnection messages requesting to reestablish and continue the communication. On success, the proxies on both sides of the communication will start sending their buffered data over the external network, now at high speed. The local proxy does not read at maximum speed from the application socket until it has finished sending the buffered data to the external peer.

Another challenge that arises is that data can become lost on its way from the source to the destination when a connection closes abruptly. There will be a discrepancy between what the source (A) has sent and what the destination (B) has received. After reestablishing the communication between A and B, the data transfer should continue from the last data that B received. It should not continue from the last data that A sent.

Consequently, B must tell A where to resume the data transfer. The sender (A) must always remember the most recent data that it has sent to B. The proxies achieve this through the use of buffers. A proxy will gradually fill a buffer with data as it has sent, and when the buffer is full, the proxy will begin filling it up from the beginning. The proxy does not clear the buffer before starting at the beginning again, so the buffer constitutes a sliding window over the data that A already has sent. On the other side, B will maintain a counter for how much data it has received, which B sends to A on a reconnect. The modulo of the buffer size can be used to calculate the index of the last received data and if the data is still available. In this way, it is possible to resume the communication between A and B without any loss of data due to a disconnect.

Lastly, each peer can have multiple connections to many other peers simultaneously. To properly reconnect, each connection has an associated identifier. If A wants to reconnect to B, it has to send a message including this identifier. B will then look up information locally to verify that A indeed was the other side of the communication before the connection broke.

In this section, we have introduced the concept of reconnectable channels, which seamlessly enables applications to continue communicating with peers even when connections break due to network location changes on either side.

5 Experiments

We have conducted several experiments using the Swirlwave middleware. Testing included both functionality of the system and the ability to support location transparent communication, and performance measurements, for startup time, connection establishment time, throughput, transmission time and latency. This section describes our results.

5.1 Peer-to-Peer Communication

We have tested peer-to-peer communication using Swirlwave for establishing connections to the network, connecting to peers and transferring data. In these experiments, we have in particular tested how the system handles network changes and the ability to stay connected despite location changes.

In one of the experiments, we use two smartphones, directly connected using Swirlwave. A web-cam app was installed on one phone, and the Swirlwave connection enabled the user of the other phone to receive live streaming from the web-cam in the phone's browser. Because of Swirlwave, this is possible while both phones are connected to 4G. We also demonstrated that the phones can change network between 4G and Wi-Fi during streaming. In that case, the phones will update each other's addresses and the streaming from the web-cam to the browser continues.

The address used by the browser, is a port on localhost. Thus, from the browser's point of view, the web-cam seems to be on the same phone. However, Swirlwave keeps the current address to the peer and routes the traffic to the correct smartphone. This means the browser can continue to use the localhost-address and can be kept unaware of network changes. This demonstrates location transparency and that we can stream from anywhere, without being connected to Wi-Fi.

5.2 Performance

When evaluating the performance of Swirlwave, we compared with two alternative configurations; one where Tor is used without Swirlwave, and another using a plain Internet connection.

We used two smartphones during the experiments; a Huawei P9 Lite, used as client and connected to cellular data (4G), and a Samsung Galaxy Note 4, used as server and connected to Wi-Fi. Experiments that collected measurements that are compared, were carried out within a short time-frame.

Orbot, which is the official version of the Tor onion routing service on Android, was used as to test communication with Tor without Swirlwave. Orbot enables smartphones to be reached outside local area networks, but has no mechanism for changing addresses when a smartphone changes location.

To enable direct Internet connection between smartphones, an Internet subscription with a static, public IP address was used in the experiments. For this environment, a wireless router was manually configured to forward from a specific port to one of the smartphones. This means that the server smartphone could be contacted directly from the Internet. The limitation of this approach, compared to Swirlwave, is that the server smartphone cannot be reached if it leaves the manually configured Wi-Fi. Also, the smartphone cannot have the role as server when connected to cellular data.

Starting Onion Proxy. This experiment measures how long it takes from the onion proxy is started to the onion service is registered and ready for use. The difference between starting a new onion service and reusing an existing one is compared.

Table 3. Onion proxy start-up times [2].

	Median	90th percentile	Num. trials
New onion service	18.080 s	43.941 s	10
Reused onion service	8.401 s	8.855 s	10

The implementation of Swirlwave reuses an already registered onion service when reconnecting to a previously seen network location. As seen in Table 3, there is a clear difference in onion proxy start-up times between registering a new onion service and reconnecting to one that is already registered (and the registration process is avoided). Registering a new onion service took about twice as long. Also, the start-up time varied much more when registering new onion services than for reusing. When comparing the 90th percentiles, the start-up time for registering a new onion service was approximately five times slower than reusing.

Establishing Connections. We here measure how long it takes to establish a connection between client and server in the three different cases:

- Connecting via Swirlwave. This includes the time it takes to authenticate the client.
- Both client and server use Orbot.
- Connecting directly over the Internet.

Table 4. Times for establishing connection [2].

	Median	95th percentile	Num. trials
Connecting via Swirlwave	1.829 s	3.557 s	100
Onion service w/Orbot	1.384 s	2.931 s	100
Directly over Internet	1.827 s	3.597 s	100

According to our experiments, the time it took to establish connections is nearly identical for connecting via Swirlwave and directly via Internet. This is a bit surprising, since the connections in case of Swirlwave must be made through the Tor overlay network. Additionally, the Swirlwave connection times include authenticating the client. Connecting via Tor using Orbot, which does not include any authentication, is faster than connecting directly via a plain Internet connection. This may suggest that the difference between connecting via Tor and via the Internet roughly equals the time Swirlwave uses to authenticate the client (Table 4).

Throughput. Throughput is the rate of successful data delivery over a communication channel [7]. Given that a connection is established and the client authenticated, we measure how long it takes from the client starts reading the first byte until 12.5 MB has been read. The rate is subsequently calculated (Table 5).

Table 5. Throughput [2].

	Median	95th percentile	Num. trials
Swirlwave	2.510 Mbps	1.380 Mbps	74
Onion service w/Orbot	1.950 Mbps	0.910 Mbps	100
Directly over Internet	18.58 Mbps	11.95 Mbps	100

The throughput was lower when routing via Tor than directly over the Internet. This was true for both Swirlwave and Orbot. The throughput for Swirlwave was in this case higher than Orbot. Transmitting directly over the Internet without Tor was 7.4 times faster than Swirlwave, and 9.5 times faster than Orbot.

Transmission Time. Transmission time is the time it takes from the first bit till the last bit of a message is sent from a node. Transmission time is depending on message size and bandwidth [7], as shown in 1.

$$Transmissiontime = MessageSize/Bandwidth \tag{1}$$

To estimate transmission time for our system, the median throughput is used in place of the bandwidth, and the message size is set to 8 bits.

Table 6. Transmission times [2].

	Transmission time 1 byte (8 bits)
Swirlwave	3.200×10^{-6}s (3.200 µs)
Onion Service w/Orbot	4.103×10^{-6}s (4.103 µs)
Directly over Internet	4.306×10^{-7}s (0.4306 µs)

The results show that transmission time for all three alternatives are very low, with the Internet-connection having the lowest result, followed by Swirlwave and Orbot.

Latency. Network latency specifies how long it takes for a bit of data to travel across the network from one node to another [7]. Latency depends on several components, as shown in 2.

$$Latency = PropagationTime + TransmissionTime + QueuingTime + ProcessingTime \quad (2)$$

We first measure round-trip time (RTT), which is the time it takes from the client sends a byte until it receives a response byte from the server. This has the advantage that start and end times can be measured at the same smartphone. RTT is described in 3

$$RTT = 2 \times Latency + ProcessingDelay \quad (3)$$

The extra processing delay represents the time from the byte is read by the server until it sends a response byte to the client (Table 7).

Table 7. Round-trip times [2].

	Median	95th percentile	Num. trials
Swirlwave	0.637 s	0.816 s	100
Onion service w/Orbot	0.639 s	1.554 s	100
Directly over Internet	0.106 s	1.039 s	100

We estimate latency based on the RTT measures, using the simplified calculation in 4.

$$Latency = RTT/2 \quad (4)$$

Table 8. Latency [2].

	RTT median	Latency
Swirlwave	0.637 s	0.3185 s
Onion service w/Orbot	0.639 s	0.3195 s
Directly over Internet	0.106 s	0.053 s

Latencies were almost similar for Swirlwave and Orbot, at about three tenths of a second, while latency when transmitting directly over the Internet were approximately six times less.

From Table 6 we have that transmission time is very low, and thus negligible when considering latency. Latency in Table 8 therefore depend on propagation time, and the time used for processing and queuing in the nodes.

6 Discussions

To establish connections from the Internet to hosts behind NAT, a technique, known as NAT Traversal [9], is needed for circumventing the problems associated with address translations and private IP addresses.

Before choosing Tor as a basis for Swirlwave, we considered other approaches to NAT traversal, including Virtual Private Network (VPN) [5], UDP hole punching [9] and SSH (https://www.ssh.com/ssh). These alternatives had several drawbacks that made them unsuitable for Swirlwave. Setting up VPN servers requires public IPs and an amount of manual work for configuration and management. Also, for clients to act as servents, they need reserved IP addresses or some other mechanism for locating peers. UDP hole punching only supports UDP communication, and needs a server middlebox to establish peer-to-peer communications, while SSH requires a server with a public IP address.

Another choice we made, was using SMS as fallback protocol. Gossiping, hand-offs, and other techniques [18] were considered, but they were all regarded more complicated, less secure, less reliable, and they require the involvement of more than two participants. We consider the SMS fallback protocol to have several advantages. SMS is available on all smartphones, the phone number is a stable address, it works when only two peers exist, and the protocol does not require extra hardware, servers or software.

The functionality and performance of Swirlwave has been tested in several experiments. We find that Swirlwave handles peer-to-peer communication between smartphones well. Phones can act as both client and servers, and Swirlwave enables continued communication also when phones move between networks.

From the experiments, the most prominent downside with Swirlwave communication is the lower throughput caused by the use of Tor. The extra round trips and processing involved in authenticating the client does not seem to affect the performance much. Neither does the processing done by the Swirlwave proxies. The experiments also show that establishing a connection between peers takes time. It will therefore be beneficial to keep connections open, instead of closing when a session is finished.

The use of *IP* here, refers to IPv4 [15], which is by far the most widespread IP version as of today. However, with the use of the more recent IPv6 [6], each device will be given an address that is public, and NAT will no longer be needed. An addition to this protocol, called mobile IPv6, is designed to let devices keep their address even when changing networks [13]. In this scenario, Swirlwave would not need Tor for connectivity, but would rather build on IPv6. However, the adoption of IPv6 is still low in most countries. Per June 2019, it is estimated to about 26.9% in the U.K., 15.1% in Norway and 46.5% in the U.S. [1] Also, even with a full adoption of IPv6, NAT may still be used for security reasons, since it shields devices from direct access from the Internet. We therefore believe that Swirlwave (or similar types of middleware) will continue to be useful in the future.

7 Conclusion

Wide area peer-to-peer for smartphones usually relies on cloud services as brokers of communication. These solutions thus have more in common with client-server architectures than peer-to-peer. We have presented a middleware that aims to remove the need for centralized services, which is not trivial. We have explained the many challenges regarding peer-to-peer for smartphones and provided solutions for them integrated into the middleware. The middleware hides the details from the application layer, which can remain unaware of aspects such as lack of publicly reachable IP addresses, location changes, authentication, and security. Through the concept of reconnectable channels, the applications can also continue to operate during disconnects in conjunction with network changes.

References

1. Akamai: Ipv6 adoption visualization. https://www.akamai.com/uk/en/resources/our-thinking/state-of-the-internet-report/state-of-the-internet-ipv6-adoption-visualization.jsp. Accessed 01 June 2019
2. Arnes, J., Karlsen, R.: Cloudless wide area friend-to-friend networking middleware for smartphones. In: Proceedings of the 15th International Joint Conference on e-Business and Telecommunications - Volume 2: ICETE, pp. 255–264. INSTICC, SciTePress (2018). https://doi.org/10.5220/0006830104210430
3. Bricklin, D.: Friend-to-friend networks (2000). http://www.bricklin.com/f2f.htm
4. Cleary, S.: Detection of half-open (dropped) connections (2009). https://blog.stephencleary.com/2009/05/detection-of-half-open-dropped.html
5. Comer, D.: Internetworking with TCP/IP, 6th edn. Pearson, London (2014)
6. Deering, S.E.: Internet protocol, version 6 (IPv6) specification (1998)
7. Forouzan, B.: Data Communications and Networking, 5th edn. McGraw-Hill, New York (2013)
8. Goodrich, M., Tamassia, R.: Introduction to computer security, 1st edn. Pearson, London (2014)
9. Hu, Z.: Nat traversal techniques and peer-to-peer applications (2005)
10. Leach, P.J., Mealling, M., Salz, R.: A universally unique identifier (UUID) URN namespace (2005)
11. Lee, Y.: Socks 4a: A simple extension to socks 4 protocol (2012). https://www.openssh.com/txt/socks4a.protocol
12. Myers, J.: World economic forum: 4 charts that explain the decline of the PC (2016). https://www.weforum.org/agenda/2016/04/4-charts-that-explain-the-decline-of-the-pc/

13. Perkins, C., Johnson, D., Arkko, J.: Mobility support in IPv6. Technical report (2011)
14. Popescu, B.C., Crispo, B., Tanenbaum, A.S.: Safe and private data sharing with turtle: friends team-up and beat the system. In: Christianson, B., Crispo, B., Malcolm, J.A., Roe, M. (eds.) Security Protocols. LNCS, vol. 3957, pp. 213–220. Springer, Heidelberg (2006). https://doi.org/10.1007/11861386_24
15. Postel, J., et al.: RFC 791: Internet protocol (1981)
16. Rogers, M., Bhatti, S.: How to disappear completely: a survey of private peer-to-peer networks. RN **7**(13), 1 (2007)
17. Statista: Number of smartphone users worldwide from 2014 to 2020 (in billions) (2019). https://www.statista.com/statistics/330695/number-of-smartphone-users-worldwide/
18. Tanenbaum, A., Steen, M.: Distributed Systems, Principles and Paradigms, 2nd edn. Pearson, London (2014)
19. Thali Project: Thali and tor hidden services. http://thaliproject.org/ThaliAndTorHiddenServices/. Accessed 01 June 2019
20. Tor Project: Onion service protocol. https://2019.www.torproject.org/docs/onion-services.html.en. Accessed 01 June 2019

A Mixed Traffic Sharing and Resource Allocation for V2X Communication

Ahlem Masmoudi(✉), Souhir Feki(✉), Kais Mnif(✉), and Faouzi Zarai(✉)

NTS'COM Research Unit, ENET'COM, University of Sfax, Sfax, Tunisia
ahlem.massmoudi@gmail.com, souhir.feki@gmail.com, faouzifbz@gmail.com, kais.mnif@enetcom.usf.tn

Abstract. Recently, Vehicle-to-Everything (V2X) communications has attracted much attentiveness due to its ubiquitous content sharing and massive data exchange among vehicular users (V-UEs) with the growth of the mobile communication technologies. Vehicular networks is one of the emerging applications for Long-Term Evolution (LTE) which is a capable technology to be useful by different applications due to its Quality-of-Service (QoS) support, high data rate, reliability and high penetration. As proposed by 3GPP the device-to-device (D2D) communication based on LTE network is also a good candidate to be applied for Vehicle-to-Vehicle (V2V) communications.

This paper investigates the resource block (RBs) allocation and RBs sharing in vehicular communication based cellular network where RBs are shared among Safety V-UEs, C-UEs, and non-Safety V-UEs. Moreover, we propose a Mixed traffic Sharing and Resource Allocation (MSRA) Algorithm to guarantee the low latency and the stringent reliability requirements of Safety V-UEs, and to maximize the sum rate capacity and respect the delay constraint of C-UEs and non Safety V-UEs, respectively, while respecting the signal-to-interference-plus-noise ratio (SINR) constraint of all users. Simulation results show that our proposed MSRA algorithm outperforms the other existing approaches in terms of network sum rate, Packet Reception Ratio (PRR) and RBs utilization.

Keywords: V2X services · Safety · Vehicular user · Radio resource management · Resource sharing/allocation · D2D communication

1 Introduction

Connecting Vehicles is a developed trend since the last decade. As mentioned in the literature cars will be one of the most important connected devices in the future. Connected vehicle has been suggested to connect all cars in roads together by exchanging messages on demand or periodically to improve the flow of traffic and avoid accidents. Furthermore, to avoid probable accidents, vehicles can connect to the pedestrians mobile devices such as tablets, mobile phones, etc. [1].

With Internet of vehicles (IoV), smart vehicles can exchange contents and information with the minimal human intervention. These communications are based on the mobile communication technology to gather the coordination among vehicle-to-everything (V2X) of the Intelligent Transportation Systems (ITS). V2X refers (and not

M. S. Obaidat (Ed.): ICETE 2018, CCIS 1118, pp. 219–233, 2019.
https://doi.org/10.1007/978-3-030-34866-3_11

limited) to vehicle-to-vehicle (V2V), vehicle-to-infrastructure (V2I), Vehicle-to-Network (V2N), and Vehicle-to-Pedestrian (V2P) communications as shown in Fig. 1 [2]. In IoV networks, infotainment messages sharing among vehicles require frequent access to the internet and to the servers, which involve the transmission data rate delivered by V2I links requiring high-capacity, and the safety-critical exchange messages supported by V2V links with the strict low latency and ultra-reliable requirements [3].

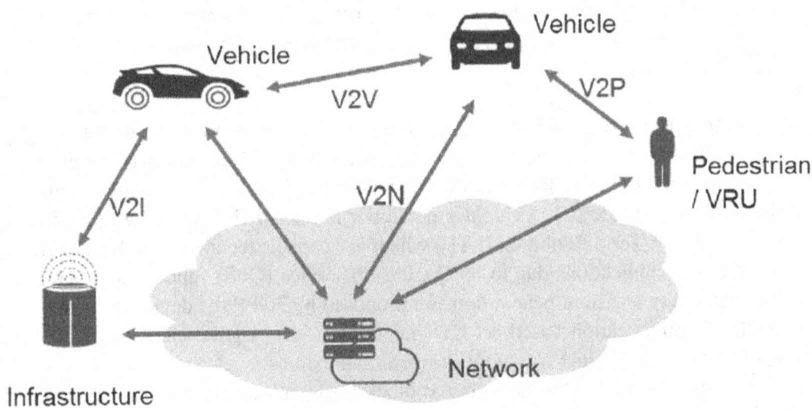

Fig. 1. V2X types of communications.

LTE-device-to-device (D2D) is described as a hopeful technology to offer QoS requirements of the V2V links [4]. For that reason, the radio resource management (RRM) is an influencing aspect in LTE-D2D performance, which designates the radio resources for each devices pair to communicate. Moreover, radio resource sharing between traditional (C-UEs) and D2D users is a significant challenge, which addressed in RRM algorithms. D2D resource allocation algorithms in LTE networks is not suitable for V2X services due to the strict safety service requirements and to the high mobility of vehicles. Therefore, the design of new resource allocation algorithms for V2X services based D2D communications is required.

We surveyed some existing RRM algorithms in this paper, which allocate radio resources in LTE-vehicular networks based D2D communications. In addition, a Mixed Sharing and Resource Allocation (MSRA) is proposed for resource sharing/allocation for Safety/non-Safety Vehicular User (V-UEs) and C-UEs in order to maximize the overall sum rate of the network while satisfying the QoS requirement of each users.

This paper is organized as follows: next section describes the RRM and resource allocation modes for V2X communication. Section 3 reviews the existing works related to resource allocation for V2X communication in LTE networks. Sections 4 and 5 introduce our system model and our proposed resource allocation and scheduling algorithm for vehicular and cellular communications, respectively. Section 6 concludes our paper.

2 RRM and Resource Allocation Modes for V2X Service

Thanks to the similarity between the V2V localized nature and the D2D communications, Release 14 declared that the D2D link could be useful in vehicular networks. Like D2D communication, the V2V links can allocate the cellular resources in non-orthogonal or orthogonal way [5].

Therefore, for V2V links there are two communication modes (as displayed in Fig. 2) the overlay mode (orthogonal) and the underlay mode (non-orthogonal).

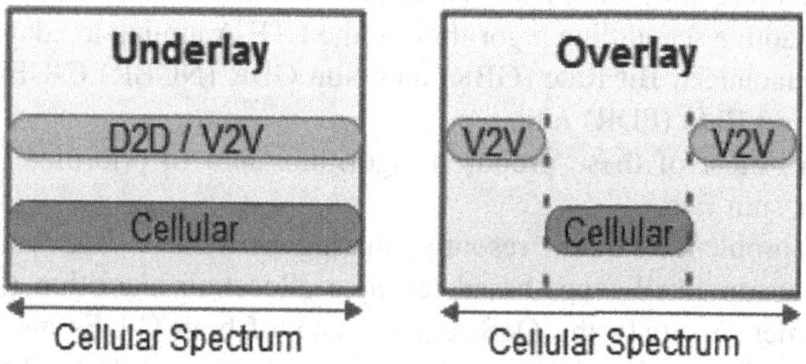

Fig. 2. Underlay vs overlay modes.

The Overlay resource allocation algorithm is easier to implement while underlay scheme leads to opportunistic and more efficient spectrum use. In the underlay mode, C-UEs and V2V-UEs share the same radio resources. This mode can enhance and improve the performance of many targets such as energy efficiency, spectrum efficiency, and cellular coverage by using a diversity of techniques including resource allocation and interference reduction.

The underlay mode leads to better spectral efficiency but an important interference among C-UEs and V-UEs should be managed. Otherwise, in the overlay mode, dedicated cellular resources are assigned to V-UEs. Thus, the problem of interference will be reduced but there is wastage at the level of radio resources consequently a poor spectral efficiency of the network system.

Currently, most of the literature contributions are opting for V2V communication underlying cellular network where V-UEs share the same radio resources with the C-UEs. Consequently significant degradation of system performance due to interference from the resources reutilization by the C-UEs and the V-UEs. Therefore, RRM plays an important role in the performance of V2X systems and faces these challenges (interference among users, wastage of resources …).

3 Related Works

In LTE, RRM including scheduling and resources allocation is an important paradigm to design the 5G mobile network.

The more openly discussed subjects in LTE based Vehicular network is the Resource allocation where several V2X resource allocation algorithms have been investigated in the literature. The main common objective is to efficiently share resources among users and to improve radio resources utilization.

For traditional C-UEs based LTE network, authors in [6] and [7] proposed novel packet scheduling and resource allocation algorithms based on reinforcement Learning for LTE and LTE-Advanced (LTE-A) networks, aiming to attain best trade-off between system throughput and fairness. Simulation results showed that these algorithms could attain better performance than traditional schedulers, but they did not consider the delay metric and therefore they could not be implemented for V2V services. In [8], we proposed an adaptive scheduling algorithm for the LTE-A aiming to adaptively allocate RBs among Guaranteed Bit Rate (GBR) and Non GBR (NGBR) C-UEs according to their Packet Drop Rate (PDR) ratio.

For LTE-V, most of these proposed algorithms aim to prioritize C-UEs and to maximize their sum rate.

In [9] the problem of radio resource sharing between C-UEs and V-UEs was discussed. A swarm intelligence-based resource allocation algorithm (ACORA) was proposed in order to satisfy the QoS requirements of both C-UEs and V-UEs while improving network sum rate. Radio resources are adaptively allocated to cellular and vehicular traffic-based on the PDR of C-UEs and the outage probability of V-UEs. The ant colony optimization algorithm was adopted in this approach to decrease the computational complexity while achieving performance satisfactory.

The proposed ACORA algorithm was improved in [10] by combining the resource allocation algorithm with a resource sharing algorithm between cellular and vehicular communications. The proposed ACO-based Resource Allocation and Resource Sharing (ACORA-Sh) algorithm consists in two main phases: resource allocation phase and resource sharing phase. In the first phase, the algorithm assigns RBs to C-UE based on user's outage probability and fairness index. In the second phase, it selects the suitable V-UE partner to each pair (C-UE, RB) to share the same resource, based on the interference link gain from the V-UE to the C-UE on this RB.

In [11], a dynamic neural Q-learning-based resource allocation and resource sharing algorithm is proposed for D2D-based V2V communication in the LTE-A cellular networks. The proposed algorithm aims to maximize the sum rate of C-UEs and V-UEs while satisfying the QoS requirements of safety V-UEs and minimizing the interference of V2V links to cellular links.

In our previous work [12], we investigated the radio resource management for vehicular environment where both V2I and V2V communication coexist. We proposed a resource allocation algorithm entitled ERAVC aiming at maximizing V2I-UEs sum rate and at guaranteeing the V2V-UEs reliability requirement. First, we separate V-UEs into two user types; the V2I-UEs and V2V-UEs. Each user type is sorted according to its corresponding metric in the TD scheduler. Then, in the FD scheduler, resources are allocated to V2I-UEs by maximizing their sum rate; whereas resources are allocated to

V2V-UEs by guaranteeing their SINR constraint where at most one user from each type can share the same RB. In [13], we add a power control mechanism to minimize the interference caused by the V2V-UEs when sharing RBs with V2I-UEs. Therefore, not only the SINR constraint are considered although the V2V-UEs power are controlled.

In [14], we proposed an Efficient Scheduling and Resources Allocation algorithm for Vehicular and Cellular Communications. This algorithm aims at maximizing the C-UEs sum rate under the constraint of taking into account the PDR and respecting the latency of V-UEs. In this proposed, users are classified in three classes, the first class for the GBR C-UEs the second class for the NGBR C-UEs and the third class for V-UEs. Firstly, packets are prioritized for each class according to their QoS requirement. Secondly, RBs are dynamically allocated for GBR and NGBR C-UEs based on their PDR ratio and then RBs already allocated by C-UEs are reused by the V-UEs.

In some other works, resource allocation was designed jointly with the power control/allocation to reach the entire potential of the V2V direct communications.

In [15] a heuristic two-stage resources allocation algorithm was proposed, available with only slow channel fading effects at the eNB and a long-term RRM method. Firstly, assuming equal power allocation, the eNB allocates RBs to both C-UEs and V-UEs in an optimal way. The C-UEs and V-UEs use orthogonal RBs to communicate with the eNB and among each other respectively. So, a RB can be used by both a V-UE and a C-UE, this will cause intra-cell interference to each other. This will be resolved by transforming the RB allocation problem into a maximum weight matching (MWM) problem for bipartite graphs. Secondly, based on the results from the first stage, the eNB adjusts the transmit power optimally for each C-UE and V-UE. Then, they extend it in [16] to maximize the sum rate of the C-UEs as much as possible and to minimize the transmit power for V-UEs.

Other works aims at maximizing the RBs utilization and minimizing the latency. In [17] authors designed two resource allocation for LTE-V based on V-UEs locations to better RBs utilization and to minimize the time delay. The first scheme is the centralized one, where RBs are allocated in orthogonal way to V-UEs in order to avoid the co-frequency interference and are reused in condition that the V-UEs distance is less than resource reuse distance. The second scheme is the distributed scheduler, where RBs are gathered into many groups and the highway is divided into many areas so, V-UEs select RBs from a specific group in each area. Simulation results demonstrate that the second scheduler performance is better than the first one.

In [18], a novel hybrid resource allocation based on C-V2X communication and 802.11p technology is proposed. This algorithm aims at minimizing the total latency and at improving the reliability for vehicular networks. A V-UE can transmit packets either using C-V2X or 802.11p interface. This will improve the reliability. V-UEs can transmit packets using C-V2X interface if the eNB requests a D2D link, otherwise they will use the 802.11p interface. The eNB periodically selects and assigns a set of RBs for V-UEs based D2D link in order to improve the latency performance.

4 System Model

We consider that the Safety V-UEs and the non-Safety V-UEs share the same radio resources with the C-UEs in a single V2X cell environment as shown in Fig. 3. Assume that there are K Safety V-UEs, M C-UEs, U non-Safety V-UEs and N RBs in each scheduling time unit. The C-UEs are allowed to use the cellular link (Uu interface) since they require high capacity for data transmission and the non-Safety and Safety V-UEs are allowed to use the direct links to communicate among each other.

For C-UEs, orthogonal RBs are allocated in the uplink subframe since this latter is less utilized compared with the downlink subframe. At most one Safety V-UE and one non-Safety V-UE share, simultaneously, the same RBs already assigned to C-UEs.

We assume that each user uses a single RB which means that no spectrum sharing among each users category. Therefore, interference occurs among safety V-UEs, C-UEs, and non-safety V-UEs due to the RBs sharing among users. In this model, the resource allocation among Safety V-UEs, C-UEs and non-Safety V-UEs is coordinated by the eNodeB because the interference is more manageable at the eNodeB.

Figure 3 displays the interference scenario, whereas the non-Safety V-UE pair and the safety V-UE pair are reusing the same RB with the C-UE. In order to allocate resources efficiently among C-UEs and V-UEs, reduce the complexity and manage the interference among users, a resource allocation algorithm is proposed and detailed in the next section.

To this end, the SINR received of the mth C-UEs $(\delta_{m,f})$, the SINR received of the kth Safety V-UEs $(\delta_{k,f})$ and the SINR received of the non-Safety V-UEs $(\delta_{u,f})$ u^{th} on the fth RB are respectively expected in (1), (2), (3) as follows:

$$\delta_{m,f} = \frac{p_{m,f}g_m}{\sigma^2 + p_{k,f}g_{k,m} + p_{u,f}g_{u,m}} \forall f \in F, m \in M \tag{1}$$

$$\delta_{k,f} = \frac{p_{k,f}g_k}{\sigma^2 + p_{m,f}g_{m,k} + p_{u,f}g_{u,k}} \forall f \in F, k \in K \tag{2}$$

$$\delta_{u,f} = \frac{p_{u,f}g_u}{\sigma^2 + p_{m,f}g_{k,u} + p_{k,f}g_{k,u}} \forall f \in F, u \in U \tag{3}$$

Where $p_{m,f}$, $p_{k,f}$ and $p_{u,f}$ are the transmit power of the C-UEs m, the Safety V-UEs k and the non-Safety V-UEs u on the RB f. $g_m, g_k, and\ g_u$ are the desired channel power gain of the mth C-UE, the kth Safety V-UEs and the uth non-safety V-UE, respectively. $g_{m,k}, g_{k,u}, g_{u,m}$ are respectively the interfering channel from the mth C-UE to the kth Safety V-UEs, from the kth Safety V-UEs to the uth non-safety V-UE and from the uth non-safety V-UE to the mth C-UE, respectively.

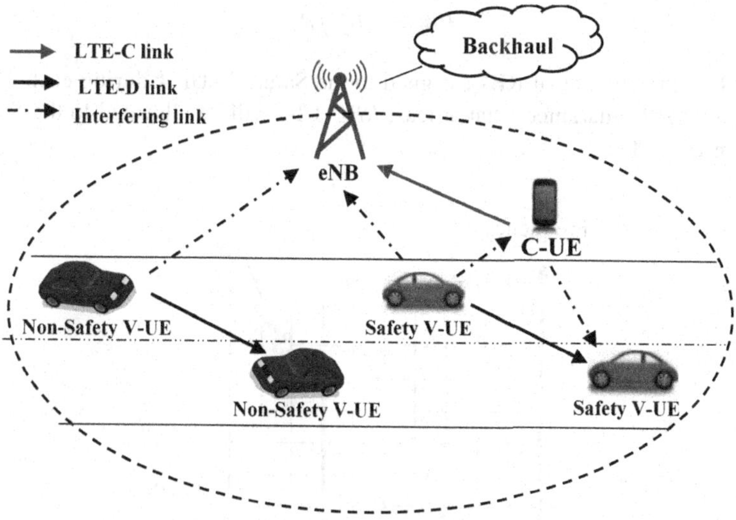

Fig. 3. System model.

5 Proposed Resource Allocation Algorithm

Our proposed algorithm's main is to satisfy the QoS requirement for Safety V-UEs in terms of Latency and reliability and to maximize the sum rate and respect the delay constraint of the C-UEs and the non Safety V-UEs, respectively, while respecting the SINR constraint in order to minimize the interference among users who share the same RBs.

5.1 QoS Requirements

Safety V-UEs Requirements
Safety V-UEs usually have severe latency and reliability requirements however are less concerned in high data rate. Owing to the constraints of latency of Safety V-UEs communication, the RBs assigned to each Safety V-UE should be contained in a restricted time interval.
We consider the latency requirement for the Safety V-UEs as a latency constraint. After defining the required RBs that should be allocated to each Safety V-UEs. The latency constraint permits each V-UEs to allocate their required RBs before the maximum tolerable latency in terms of the number of scheduling time units. Therefore, RB_k^{tot} should be assigned for V-UEs k within the region R_k as demonstrated in Fig. 4 where the R_k is the maximum latency of the Safety V-UEs.

Therefore, the latency requirement of each Safety V-UEs is interpreted as follows:

$$RB_k = RB_k^{tot}/R_k \quad (4)$$

where RB_k is the number of RBs assigned to the Safety V-UE k during each TTI. The calculation of RB_k guarantees that at least RB_k^{tot} RBs will be allocated to the Safety V-UE within R_k TTI.

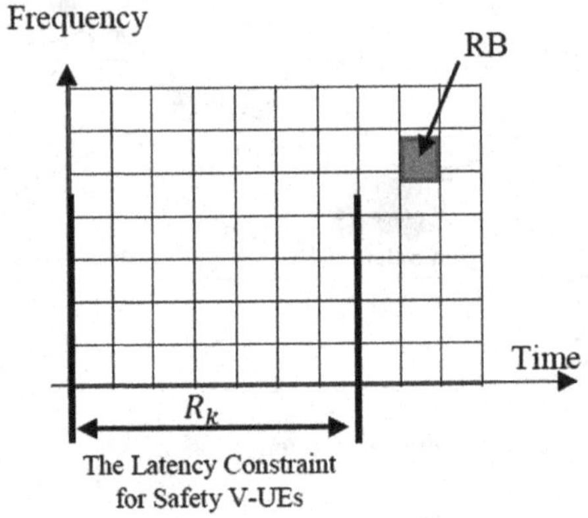

Fig. 4. Latency constraint for safety V-UEs with two dimensional RBs.

The reliability requirement is interpreted from the packet reception ratio (PRR). As defined in [19], the PRR is calculated for each Safety V-UEs by the ratio of the number of packets with successful reception and the total number packets.

Non-safety V-UEs Requirements

We are considering the situation where the non-Safety V-UEs and the C-UEs should be guaranteed a certain QoS requirement. Compared to C-UEs, the non-Safety V-UEs have a delay constraint. Therefore, we consider that the non-Safety V-UEs requirement is satisfied if the SINR constraint and the PDOR are respected. It means that the uth non-Safety V-UEs can allocate the fth RB if its SINR is higher than the SINR threshold ($\delta_{u,f} > \delta_u^{th}$) and its PDOR is above a certain Threshold ($PDOR_k < PDOR_k^{th}$).

The PDOR is defined as the ratio of the number of near_timeout packets and the total number of packets generated by the non-Safety V-UEs. A near_timeout packet is a packet that not fully transmitted before a threshold delay. The PDOR is a very appropriate metric for QoS, aims to allowing a better resources utilization. So the PDOR of the uth non-Safety V-UE is calculated as follows [20]:

$$PDOR_k = \frac{N_k^{out}}{N_k} \quad (5)$$

where N_k^{out} is the number of near_timeout packets of the uth non-Safety V-UE and N_k is the number of packets generated by this user.

C-UEs Requirements

The QoS for the C-UEs is satisfied if the SINR constraint is fulfilled, i.e. if the SINR of the mth C-UE is higher than the SINR threshold ($\delta_{m,f} > \delta_m^{th}$) then this C-UE can allocate the fth RB. In addition, since the C-UEs require particular throughput for data transmission C-UEs are prioritized to incorporate a certain degree of fairness and throughput maximization according the follows equation [12]:

$$\mathrm{TF} = \frac{r_k(t)}{R_k(t-1)} \times \frac{1}{QCI} \tag{6}$$

where $r_k(t)$ represents the throughput of the mth C-UEs and is calculated in [12] using the Shannon theorem, $R_k(t-1)$ is the average throughput for the mth C-UEs at time (t − 1) and $\frac{1}{QCI}$ aims to encourage GBR C-UEs.

5.2 The MSRA Resource Allocation Algorithm

Our proposed MSRA algorithm may classify users into three classes the C-UEs class, the safety V-UEs and the non-Safety V-UEs as shown in Table 1. Users in different classes are differentiated according to the above QoS requirements i.e. each class has its own metric. For C-UEs the overall mechanism to support QoS is the QoS class identifier (QCI) as demonstrated in [14, 21].

Table 1. V2X traffic classification.

V2X services		Message size	Maximum latency	Services examples
Safety V-UEs	V2I-UEs	400 bytes	50 ms	Emergency stop use cases
	V2V-UEs	50–300 bytes	20 ms	Emergency vehicle warning, Pre-crash Sensing warning
Non-Safety V-UEs	V2I-UEs	50–400 bytes	100 ms	Queue warning
	V2V-UEs	50–300 bytes	100 ms	Forward collision warning

After users prioritizing, RBs are assigned to each UE according to their QoS requirements as described above. We consider RBs allocation based on the cellular links for the C-UEs and D2D links for the non-Safety and Safety V-UEs whereas one RBs can be shared by at most one C-UEs, one Safety V-UEs and One non-Safety V-UEs, simultaneously. Firstly, RBs are allocated to C-UEs by maximizing their sum rate using Shannon capacity according to the following equation [12]:

$$max \sum_{m=1}^{M} \sum_{f=1}^{F} \log_2(1 + \delta_m^f) \tag{7}$$

where δ_m^f: is the SINR of the mth C-UEsover the fth RB.

After C-UEs resource allocation, the safety and the non-Safety V-UEs are allowed to share the same RBs already allocated to C-UEs in order to achieve their QoS requirements and to minimize the interference among them.

Therefore, the kth Safety V-UE and the uth non-Safety V-UE can share the fth RB with the corresponding m^{th} C-UE if the SINR of each UEs is higher than the SINR constraint according to the following constraints:

- For the Safety V-UEs: $\left(\delta_{k,f} > \delta_k^{th}\right)$ && $(RB_k = RB_k^{tot}/R_k)$.
- For the non-Safety V-UEs: $\left(\delta_{u,f} > \delta_u^{th}\right)$ && $(PDOR_k < PDOR_k^{th})$.
- For the C-UEs: $\left(\delta_{m,f} > \delta_m^{th}\right)$

6 Simulation Parameters and Results

This section describes the simulation results to show the effectiveness of our proposed resource allocation MSRA scheme. Simulation are composed of a single cell with 1.5 km of radius, one eNB and a bandwidth of 5 MHz with 25 RBs in each slot. The number of Safety/non-Safety V-UEs and the C-UEs varied between 50 and 500. We consider the freeway simulation where the V-UEs move in freeway scenario whereas the C-UEs are randomly dispersed within the cell. Each TTI, the allocation decision is performed. For every 100 ms during the simulation, the users' locations is updated.

Table 2 demonstrates the simulation and configuration parameters. The path loss model for V-UEs links is computed according to WINNER model [22]. Whereas the C-UEs path loss links is calculated as follows:

$$PL(d) = 128.1 + 37.6 \log_{10}(d) \tag{8}$$

To evaluate the effectiveness of our proposed MSRA algorithm, we compare it with the:

- Swarm intelligence-based resource allocation algorithm (ACORA) algorithm in [9], and
- Efficient Scheduling and Resource Allocation algorithm (ESRA) algorithm in [14].

Table 2. Simulation parameters [12].

Parameter	Value
Number of eNB	1
Cell radius	1.5 km
Bandwidth	5 MHz
Number of RBs	25 RBs
OFDM symbols per slot	7
Carrier frequency	2 GHz
Maximum C-UEs transmit power	23 dBm
Maximum V-UEs transmit power	23 dBm
SINR threshold of users	5 dB
C-UEs and V-UEs speed	Random (5, 150) km/h
TTI	1 ms
Number of C-UEs/V-UEs	100–500
Simulation length	5000 slot
Resource allocation	slot
Noise power σ^2	−114 dbm
Path loss model	LOS in Winner + B1

We can see that our proposed MSRA algorithm offers the best performance in terms of RBs utilization, Packet Reception Ratio (PRR) and the network sum rate compared to the ACORA and the ESRA algorithms.

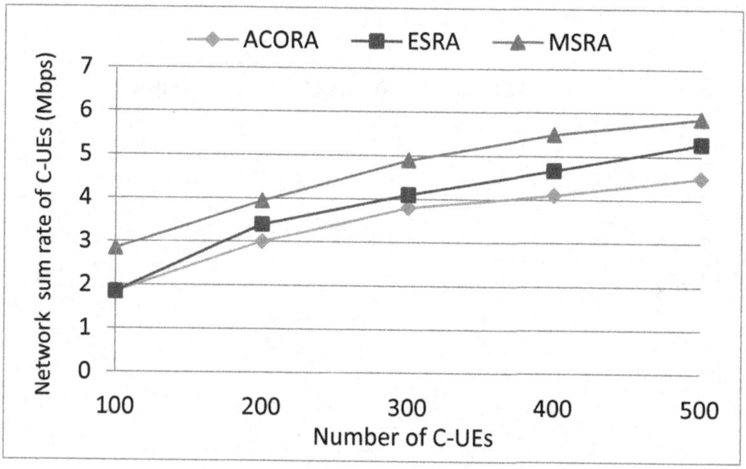

Fig. 5. Network sum rate of the C-UEs.

Figures 5 and 6 depicts the network sum rate of C-UEs and V-UEs as a function of the total number of users, respectively. The proposed algorithm provides better results and uses efficiently the radio resources. Firstly, our proposed MSRA algorithm allocates RBs for the C-UEs while maximizing the sum rate to improve the network sum rate. Secondly, in our algorithm, RBs are shared between three users: the C-UEs, the Safety V-UEs, and the non-Safety V-UEs. However, the ACORA algorithm is the worst because it is designed for the overlay mode where the resource allocation is done in an orthogonal manner. Thus, we improve the number of RBs allocated to UEs in our algorithm and especially for V-UEs.

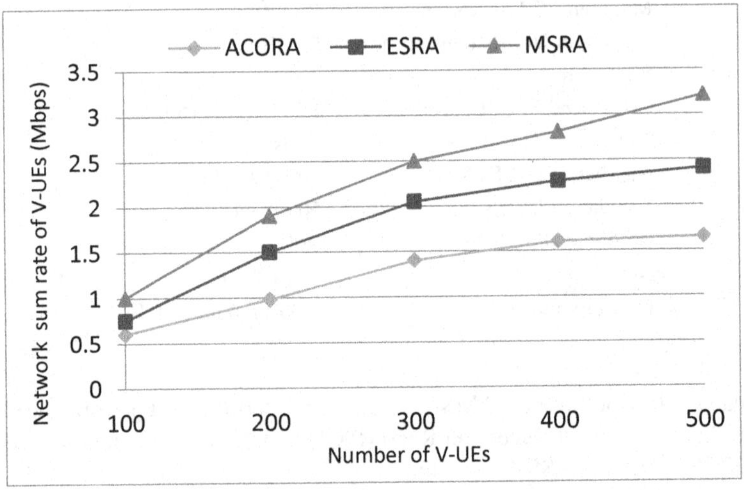

Fig. 6. Network sum rate of the V-UEs.

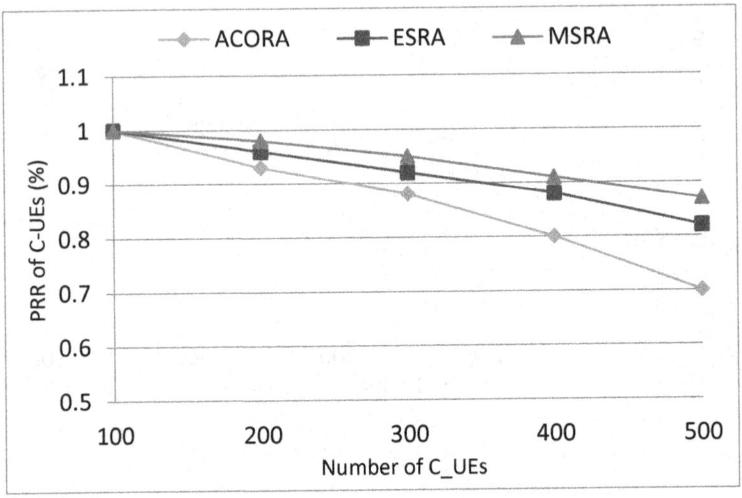

Fig. 7. Packet reception ratio of the C-UEs.

Figures 7 and 8 show the Packet Reception Ratio as a function of the C-UEs and V-UEs, respectively. Our Proposed MSRA algorithm achieve the best rate compared to the ESRA and the ACORA algorithm. Our proposed MSRA allows at most one C-UE, one Safety V-UE and one non-Safety V-UEs to share simultaneously the same RB as a result the PRR is improved mostly for V-UEs.

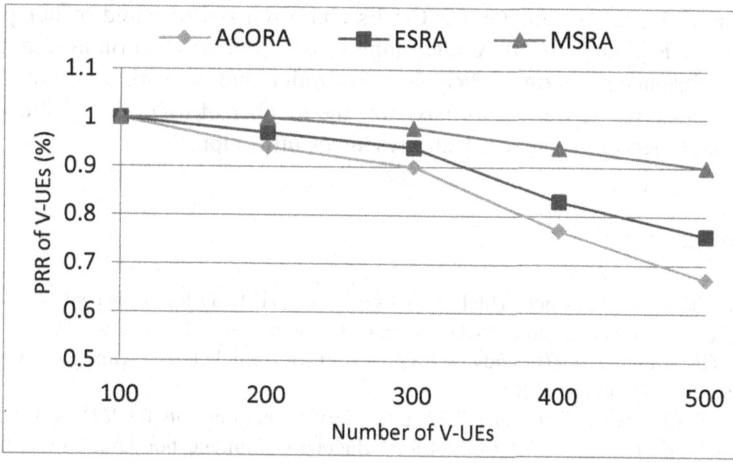

Fig. 8. Packet reception ratio of the V-UEs.

Figure 9 displays the percentage of RBs utilization as a function of the user's number. The RBs utilization performance of our proposed MSRA algorithm is the best compared to the ESRA and ACORA algorithms. As shown in Fig. 9, the percentage of RBs utilization of MSRA and ESRA algorithms exceed 100%, which is performed by RBs sharing among users. In addition, MSRA can perform a RBs utilization percentage by more than 20% compared to the ESRA algorithm because one RB may be shared by three different UEs (The safety V-UEs, the C-UEs and the non-Safety V-UEs).

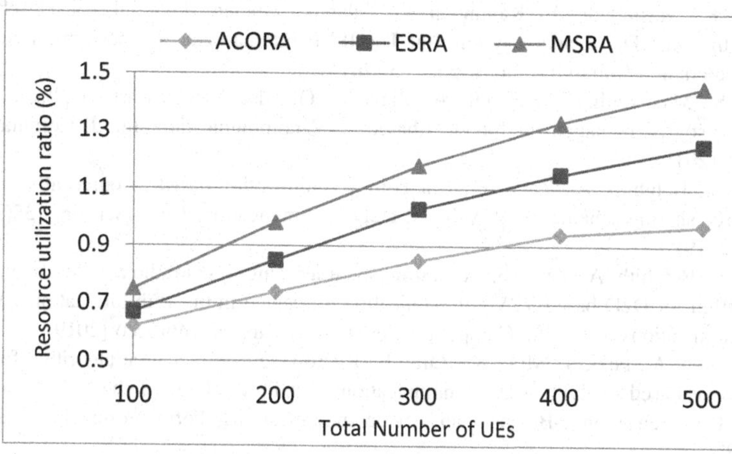

Fig. 9. RBs utilization ratio of all the network users.

7 Conclusion

In this paper, we investigates the RBs sharing and the RBs allocation where RBs are shared between the Safety V-UEs, the traditional C-UEs, and non-Safety V-UEs. Therefore, a Mixed traffic Sharing and Resource Allocation (MSRA) Algorithm is described to improve the resource utilization by RBs shared among users while satisfying the QoS requirement for the C-UEs and V-UEs. Compared to our previous algorithms ESRA and ACORA algorithms, our proposed algorithm can achieve greatest performance in term of PRR, RBs utilization and network sum rate.

In our future work, we aim to maximize the number of users that simultaneously share the same RBs to achieve a better resources utilization.

References

1. Harounabadi, M., Mitschele-Thiel, A., Akkasi, A.: LTE-D2D for connected cars: a survey on radio resource management schemes. Iran J. Comput. Sci. **1**, 187–197 (2018)
2. 3GPP TR 22.885, v14.0.0. Study on LTE support for Vehicle to Everything (V2X) services (Release 14), December 2015
3. 3GPP TS 22.185, v14.3.0, Release 14. LTE; Service requirements for V2X services (2017)
4. Sun, W.: On Medium Access Control for Vehicular Communication Over Device-to-device Links: Radio Resource Management and Network Synchronization. Chalmers University of Technology (2016)
5. Mach, P., Becvar, Z., Vanek, T.: In-band device-to-device communication in OFDMA cellular networks: a survey and challenges. IEEE Commun. Surv. Tutor. **17**(4), 1885–1922 (2015)
6. Feki, S., Belghith, A., Zarai, F.: A Q-learning-based scheduler technique for LTE and LTE-advanced network. In: Proceedings of the International Conference on Wireless Networks and Mobile Systems, pp. 27–35 (2017)
7. Feki, S., Zarai, F.: Cell performance-optimization scheduling algorithm using reinforcement learning for LTE-advanced network. In: Proceedings of the International Conference on Computer Systems and Applications, pp. 1075–1081 (2017)
8. Mnif, K., Masmoudi, A., Kammoun, L.: Adaptive efficient downlink packet scheduling algorithm in LTE-advanced system. In: The IEEE International Symposium on Networks, Computers and Communications, pp. 1–5 (2014)
9. Feki, S., Masmoudi, A., Belghith, A., Zarai, F., Obaidat, M.S.: Swarm intelligence-based radio resource management for D2D-based V2V communication. Int. J. Commun. Syst. e3817 (2018)
10. Feki, S., Belghith, A., Zarai, F.: Ant colony optimization-based resource allocation and resource sharing scheme for V2V-based D2D communication. J. Inf. Sci. Eng. **35**(3), 507–519 (2019)
11. Feki, S., Belghith, A., Zarai, F.: A reinforcement learning-based radio resource management algorithm for D2D-based V2V communication. Accepted in the 15th International Wireless Communications & Mobile Computing Conference, Tangier, Morocco (2019)
12. Masmoudi, A., Feki, S., Mnif, K., Zarai, F.: Radio resource allocation algorithm for device to device based on LTE-V2X communications. In: Proceedings of the 15th International Joint Conference on e-Business and Telecommunications, Porto, Portugal, pp. 265–271 (2018)

13. Masmoudi, A., Feki, S., Mnif, K., Zarai, F.: Efficient radio resource management for D2D-based LTE-V2X communications. In: IEEE/ACS 15th International Conference on Computer Systems and Applications (AICCSA), Aqaba, Jordan, pp. 1–6 (2018)
14. Masmoudi, A., Feki, S., Mnif, K., Zarai, F.: Efficient scheduling and resource allocation for D2D-based LTE-V2X communications. Accepted in the 15th International Wireless Communications & Mobile Computing Conference, Tangier, Morocco (2019)
15. Sun, W., Strom, E.G., Brannstrom, F., Sui, Y., Sou, K.C.: D2D-based V2V communications with latency and reliability constraints. In: 2014 IEEE Globecom Workshops (GC Wkshps), Austin, TX, USA, pp. 1414–1419 (2014)
16. Sun, W., Strom, E.G., Brannstrom, F., Sou, K.C., Sui, Y.: Radio resource management for D2D-based V2V communication. IEEE Trans. Veh. Technol. **65**(8), 6636–6650 (2016)
17. Zhang, X., Shang, Y., Li, X., Fang, J.: Research on overlay D2D resource scheduling algorithms for V2V broadcast service. In: 2016 IEEE 84th Vehicular Technology Conference (VTC-Fall), Montreal, QC, Canada, pp. 1–5 (2016)
18. Abbas, F., Fan, P.: A hybrid low-latency D2D resource allocation scheme based on cellular V2X networks. In: 2018 IEEE International Conference on Communications Workshops (ICC Workshops), Kansas City, MO, USA, pp. 1–6 (2018)
19. 3GPP. Study on LTE-based V2X services. Technical report, TR 36.885 (2016)
20. Ragaleux, A., Baey, S., Karaca, M.: Standard-compliant LTE-A uplink scheduling scheme with quality of service. IEEE Trans. Veh. Technol. **66**(8), 7207–7222 (2017)
21. 3GPP TS 23.203 V14.5.0. Policy and charging control architecture (Release 14), September 2017
22. WINNER II Channel Models, IST-4-027756 WINNER II D1.1.2 V1.2, September 2007. http://projects.celtic-initiative.org/winner+/WINNER2Deliverables/D1.1.2v1.1.pdf

Author Index

Printed in the United States
By Bookmasters